CHALLENGE AND RESPONSE

Anticipating US Military Security Concerns

Dr Karl P. Magyar
Editor in Chief

Associate Editors

Lt Col Maris McCrabb
Lt Col Albert U. Mitchum, Jr.
Dr Lewis B. Ware

Air University Press
Maxwell Air Force Base, Alabama 36112-6610

August 1994

Library of Congress Cataloging-In-Publication Data

Challenge and response : anticipating US military security concerns / Karl P. Magyar, editor-in-chief; associate editors, Maris McCrabb, Albert Mitchum, Lewis B. Ware.
443 p.
Includes bibliographical references.
1. Military planning—United States. 2. National Security—United States. 3. World politics–1989–. I. Magyar, K. P. (Karl P.)
U153.C49 1994
355'.033073—dc20 94-18448
CIP

ISBN 1-58566-053-1

First Printing August 1994
Second Printing April 1999
Third Printing March 2001
Fourth Printing April 2003
Fifth Printing May 2004
Sixth Printing March 2006

DISCLAIMER

This publication was produced in the Department of Defense school environment in the interest of academic freedom and the advancement of national defense-related concepts. The views expressed in this publication are those of the authors and do not reflect the official policy or position of the Department of Defense or the United States government.

This publication has been reviewed by security and policy review authorities and is cleared for public release.

Air University Press
131 West Shumacher Avenue
Maxwell AFB AL 36112-6615
http://aupress.maxwell.af.mil

The editors wish to dedicate this volume to

Col John A. Warden III

whose vision, energy, and leadership

make it all happen.

Contents

PART II

The Response

Preface

The formal dissolution of the Soviet Union and the Warsaw Pact and the coalition war to oust Iraq from Kuwait occurred within months of each other. These events were of great significance to Western statesmen and strategic planners who recognized that a fundamental transformation of the international system was taking place.

The decline of the Soviet Union and the Warsaw Pact as a cohesive unit raises the most fundamental question for the military planner: Who will be the likely enemies in the future for which they must prepare? This was not a dilemma during the cold war as all conflicts in the world were evaluated within the prevailing East-West context. Having assessed the challenges posed by the enemy's capabilities, military planners worked on the assumption of the existence of a hierarchy of responses that could be used as required, with a massive strategic nuclear attack being reserved for the belligerent members of the Warsaw Pact—if necessary. Such a response is not envisioned for any conceivable enemy today.

The 1991 Gulf War, however, affirmed very early the prevalence of war outside the cold war context and that military responses to future conflicts will have to be formulated in a wide subnuclear range. The United States–led coalition's response to Iraq's initiatives did just that. New weapon systems, supporting equipment, strategies, and tactics were implemented in the defeat of Iraq's armed forces. Influencing the prosecution and management of that war was the absence of the Soviet Union as a balancing variable. The lessons learned from that encounter will certainly influence future engagements—but against whom is not clear.

The authors of this volume agree on one point: That conflicts will continue in the future and that the US will perhaps find it in its interest to become an active participant in some wars. This volume attempts to bring together thoughts about the environmental context in which sucn wars will take place and about possible US military reactions.

The Introduction and Overview offers a broad review of the major determinants of international change. Part I follows with a current review of two regions, the Middle East and the area covered by the former Warsaw Pact, whose conflicts have the greater potential of expansion and negative consequence to the US and to our traditional allies than those conflicts in any other region. No attempt is made to systematically review other regions where conflict is not as globally threatening. This section also offers insight into other factors that portray the global conflict environment, war, changing US military concerns, and US security perceptions. Together, these essays address what we perceive as the "Challenge."

Part II ranges over some specific security situations, the changing nature of warfare, and some anticipated avenues of responding to the emerging challenges. Conflicts and wars may be resolved by more than only violent means, and these are considered within the context of diplomatic or collective efforts. Responses to nonpolitical conflicts—those in which the defeat of a regime or an insurgent force is not an objective—are examined. Peacekeeping operations, which have recently placed great demands on the US, are investigated. The new technological capabilities are reviewed. Air power, parallel warfare, and war termination theory are presented. And the utility of nuclear forces as well as space assets are updated. These topics and others address the "Response."

The authors of this volume are all affiliated with the US Air Force Air Command and Staff College at Air University, Maxwell Air Force Base, Alabama. The book is to comprise one of the texts for our students, but it is expected that it will generate a wider interest among military and civilian audiences. The editors have not imposed methodological restrictions, and indeed, we have encouraged a diversity of opinions but within an academic context. Our own immediate challenge was to produce this wide-ranging review under great time constraints in order to make a very up-to-date volume available to those contemplating future US military security concerns. It is important to stress that we all write in our personal capacities and that no portion of this volume necessarily reflects the official view of the US Air Force or any US government agency.

We, the editors, wish to thank the authors for their timely response to our request for quality work under severe time constraints. At the Air University Press, we wish to thank Dr Elizabeth Bradley, director; Ms Debbie Banker; Ms Joan Hickey; Ms Linda Colson; Mr Steve Garst; and our editors, Mr Hugh Richardson and Dr Glenn Morton, for responding to the challenge of producing this volume on such short notice.

Karl P. Magyar, PhD

INTRODUCTION AND OVERVIEW

The Emerging Post–Cold-War International Order and Changing Conflict Environment

Dr Karl P. Magyar

We have recently experienced the rather sudden end of the cold war, an event that ranks among not only the top public events of this century, but in view of the projected consequences had a nuclear war occurred, may be judged as a seminal point in the history of our civilization. Mankind's highest level of technology had been impressed into the service of military security as two sizable alliances faced each other nervously as they contemplated the horrendous costs of implementing their war-making capabilities. For the great powers, a big war didn't make sense. But for many states, smaller wars may well remain attractive.

This was made amply evident by Iraq's attempted absorption of Kuwait and refusal to back down in the face of poignant warnings by the US to do so. The ensuing war in 1991 ranked as a major engagement, yet not long thereafter it did not deter the loosely organized forces of Somalia's warlord Gen Mohamed Farah Aidid from shooting up UN peacekeeping forces and from inflicting heavy casualties on America's highly trained Ranger Force. And while US attention focused on Iraq and Somalia, Yugoslavia was undergoing a very bloody breakup; many countries, including parts of what had been the Soviet Union, experienced violent civil wars; and numerous prolonged conflicts raged throughout Africa, scarcely affected by the demise of the cold war. We may deduce that civilization has been spared, but history's relentless onslaught on numerous societies and their warriors continues unabated.

We are inundated by analyses that portray as revolutionary the changes taking place in the post–cold-war era, yet we must qualify such dramatic assessments to keep a sober view.[1] A broad sweep of recorded history since Thucydides wrote *The Peloponnesian War* reveals the pervasiveness of the use of force as the final arbiter of unresolved disputes, and this method and tendency have not been stilled. What does change over history is the nature of war-making tools and the methods of their implementation. The cold war demonstrated history's pervasive penchant for the use of force, but nuclear weapons had been created whose potential use made peaceful resolution of conflicts more advantageous. However, while that rationally derived decision not to employ these weapons should properly be celebrated, the resort to lesser levels of force remains as attractive as ever.[2] It may indeed be argued that the use of force may increase in light of the global proliferation of information that has sensitized the masses about their relative deprivations and hence diminished respect for their traditional political structures.[3]

Anticipating future challenges, then, concerns the identification of several factors:

Who will do the fighting?

What will be their objectives?

Which war-making tools will be implemented?

How can we contain the wars and keep external intervenors at bay?

How can we reduce their frequency as well as intensity?

Which of those conflicts and battles will concern US security interests?

Preparing responses to these conflicts entails, above all, sophisticated sociocultural analysis and the ability to constantly adjust the war machinery in terms of its tools as well as their methods of implementation. Changes have occurred and will continue to be experienced regarding which means are employed in addressing conflict and, to a lesser extent, what the objects of forcible acquisition will be. But a fundamental transformation in human nature, as depicted so well by Thucydides, is not to be anticipated, and hence the attraction for the use of force will most likely continue the prevalence of war. Security will be ensured for those who most concisely anticipate the challenges—and prepare appropriate responses.

The Changing Structure of the International Order

The end of the cold war marked an acceleration of change in the international order. This section examines changes in and the evolution of the international order, the transition to a two-worlds system, the proliferation of nonviable states, regional identification, and ideological developments.

Change and Evolution

History has experienced numerous eras of distinct international systems—which may be viewed as established patterns of relationships between states. The cold-war system, with its overarching characteristic of two predominant powers, the US and the Soviet Union, each leading its respective military alliances—NATO and the Warsaw Pact—has recently disintegrated as the Soviet Union fragmented along largely ethnic and historical lines. As with the disintegration of all such systems, the transition to a new order is fraught with uncertainty as a system in transition is not formulated by anyone's grand design.[4] Indeed, no one power needs to predominate at all times although an international hierarchy inevitably emerges since power abhors a vacuum. The US is certainly poised to continue exercising its established global role, but we are uncertain of emerging military competitors. Whoever they will be, they will have to attain history's necessary mix: ambition matched by resources. An imbalance in these two variables leads to certain defeat—as was experienced by the Germans and Japanese in World War II, by the Soviets in the cold war, and by the Iraqis in the 1991 Gulf War.

Change and transformation, then, are to be expected as they express the historical tendency of societies to predominate over others and to advance their interests. Even those without ambitions for acquisition must take cognizance of those who embark on the path of aggrandizement, lest they be absorbed. Change offers fortuitous opportunity to some; others suffer its wrath.

An examination of history also reveals a pervasive hierarchic order among states with virtually all states embarked on a course of evolution from weak, dependent quasi-states or colonies, to eventually great powers or imperial nations.[5] After new states are formed, they enter what is, for most, a long period of internal consolidation in search of legitimate sociopolitical institutions. Thereafter, a state is prepared to export its influence or military controls into usually weak or vulnerable neighboring states or its subregion, often resulting in the enlargement of the state. Such states then may undertake imperial or global ventures to exercise direct controls for purposes of exploitation or the strategic pacification of territories far removed from the home base. However, at that level, when expanding ambitions are not matched by developed resources, and the domestic base becomes delegitimized, the compulsive phase sets in as the state declines, usually precipitously, losing its great power ranking. This is precisely what happened to the Soviet Union recently.

This evolutionary model suggests that the historically pervasive competition among states will soon see new challengers to the US as the only truly global power, while for the US, the challenge remains to match our global interests with resources. The model also identifies fundamentally different types of wars that states fight at different stages of their evolutionary cycle. The bulk of the world's nations are presently in their consolidative stage with roughly half of them experiencing serious civil strife. Every region in the world contains expansionists; however, only the US may be properly characterized as a global power.

Today, there are few remaining colonial dependencies fighting liberation wars for independence. The Western Sahara is one such example. Others in the formative stage are the breakaway territories from the Soviet Union and Yugoslavia. Bosnia is an excellent example of a new state undergoing a formative war. Most of the conflicts in the world, however, are civil wars which typically occur in the early consolidative period of a nation's evolution. These proliferate largely in the states that have recently received their independence. America's own civil war was a classic example of a consolidative war. Civil wars traditionally tended not to attract significant direct foreign military intervention, but during the cold-war days, such civil wars often incorporated the contest between the two superpowers.

It is the expansive phase in the evolution of a nation that experiences the most disruptive wars as such conflicts are internationalized, and they may upset the regional power balances. If the wars are not quickly halted or contained, they could expand to global proportions. Germany and the Soviet Union engaged in such an expansive-stage conflict when they carved up contiguous Poland on the eve of World War II. More recently, Iraq's attempted absorption of contiguous Kuwait demonstrated the tendency today of such a war of expansion to attract distant external involvement. Finally, global powers tend to be busy military interventionists—but rarely as blatant initiators of conflicts. Rather, they intervene in existing conflicts around the globe to redress a deteriorating balance or, during the cold-war days, to neutralize the perceived gains by the adversary. The popular image of such global powers depicts them as perennial aggressors, but more precisely, their frequent involvements in conflicts tend to be limited and geared towards halting conflicts before they develop into major confrontations. Great powers are interested in maintaining a balance of power rather than risk having a minor distant regional conflict escalate to the point where the home base may be threatened. The Soviets confronted such a prospect during the 1962 Cuban missile crisis.

States may be hierarchically organized according to their evolutionary phase, but another traditional classification system must also be addressed as it, too, reflects the waning cold-war structures. For several years we had referred to the "first world," meaning the democratic, free market, economically developed states. The "second world" included the authoritarian, command economy states of the Soviet Union and its Warsaw Pact allies. The "third world" included everyone else, assumed to be the economically less developed. However, this latter group may be further delineated by further subgroups to acknowledge the great differences among this mixed collection of states.

The Warsaw Pact has now been dissolved and the Soviet Union has fragmented, and therefore the second world is now but an historical expression. In effect we now have only two worlds—the first and third worlds. However, this two-worlds context may also express not only the division of the world between the "haves" and the "have nots," but also within most states the division between the privileged minorities and the impoverished masses—which implies that all states reflect this two-worlds division. This is especially the case in traditional third world countries where such divisions are becoming evermore significant. Poverty does not drive a poor state to make war on a rich nation, but the acute class differences within states may engender civil wars, especially when evident, significant socioeconomic differences are also delineated along ethnic lines. Such civil wars in turn may often spill into neighboring states or invite external participants. A prime example of a civil conflict stemming from extreme social disparities is the vortex of conflict in Liberia since 1989, which spilled into neighboring countries within two years. Such factional discontent has been in great evidence during the last few years, and much of it may be ascribed to the impact of modern communications as they portray the possibilities of better lifestyles to restive populations around the globe. The enemy in such cases is seen by the masses to be not other countries but their own inept and corrupt governments.

The Transition to a Two-Worlds System

The world is steadily polarizing into two socioeconomic camps and the gulf between them is widening despite the programs of structural reforms introduced by international agencies to rectify this situation. Vast parts of the third world are becoming marginalized. The ultimate characteristic that distinguishes the two camps is their economic competitiveness. Again, this criterion is as valid among states as within them. What fuels this competitive ability is of secondary consideration as it may be based on technological abilities, productive workers, access to financial resources, or commercially attractive geographic or natural resources. But what matters is the capability to convert such advantages into a competitive edge. The new global economic network increasingly connects the economies of the first world and the small developed sectors of the states in the third world—which has the effect of isolating further the world's noncompetitive people from the first world and from their own privileged elites in the third world. Today, the members of the third world number about three-fourths of the global population, and their plight as well as their numbers are increasing.

Another problem with the two-worlds division is the placement of the members of the dissolved Warsaw Pact. Some of those states such as Hungary, Czechoslovak Republic, Poland, the Baltic states, and Russia may realistically expect to join the first world, but their competitive abilities must for the most part first undergo a major transition.[6] Should they succeed, some may aspire to join the European Union. Russia may strive to attain a renewed global role—possibly more powerful than when she led the Soviet Union—now that Russia is socially somewhat more cohesive than before, while not having to be responsible for the poorer southern region. And the former southern republics of the Soviet Union such as Tajikistan, Kyrgyzstan, and Turkmenistan, as well as Eastern Europe's Bulgaria and Rumania, will most likely qualify as third world states. This may also be the fate of certain areas of the former Yugoslavia. The key is competitiveness, the imbalance of which in the Soviet Union, Yugoslavia, and Czechoslovakia contributed to their breakup and much of the subsequent violence. The result is that the frontiers of the third world have now shifted considerably northwards, directly into Europe, and expanded the numbers of the Middle Eastern region's third world countries with the addition of the Soviet Union's southern republics. This may imply greater instability, as the Middle East has already been a volatile area, to which are now added numerous conflicts in contiguous states.

The Proliferation of Nonviable States

The world has always known poor states but they had existed in isolation, removed from the mainstream of international affairs, or they were colonial territories of European empires whose traditional character was maintained as if by virtuous design. In fact, only their rare commercial advantages were developed and then only to suit the requirements of the colonial power and not the subjects. As these colonies became independent, it was feared that most lacked the essential prerequisites for a meaningful independent existence. They would not be capable competitors. Analysts identified the "small state" problem with its focus on small size and population bases. Soon there were numerous "micro" and "mini" states in the United Nations whose populations were often less than those of modest-sized cities in the developed world.[7] Would these states be "viable"?

Today there are two dimensions to this problem. First, what constitutes viability? Neither size nor population can be the sole criterion as small political entities such as Switzerland, Luxembourg, the Gulf Emirates, Singapore, and Hong Kong are doing well. By contrast, huge countries such as Mauritania, Niger, Sudan, Mongolia, or Afghanistan are barely able to function. Viability, then, has a qualitative aspect which means that more than only quantifiable criteria must be considered. We may suggest that to be considered viable, a state should be able to convert its resources into socioeconomic progress for its inhabitants in accordance with the more advanced standards of the international community. We may also ask, if only a restricted elite profits from the little economic progress that is made, ought the state to be considered to be viable? This debate is heavily informed by the character and successes of the first world. As the gulf widens between the two worlds, more states become nonviable and thus potential sources of instability.[8]

The second dimension of the viability problem concerns the consequences of the proliferation of many such small states as well as large, but noncompetitive, nonviable states in the international system. It was feared, as in the case of Grenada, that small states would barter their scarce resources such as strategic location to the superpowers or to other regionally ambitious states. As a small state, Cuba had managed to be the most dangerous confrontation point of the cold war. Kuwait, with its population of less than 1 million, became the object of a major war due ultimately to its own nonviable defensive capability. Despite its size and population of some 8 million, Somalia's descent to anarchy may portend a possible flood of other third world states that will demonstrate the problems of nonviability. Yet another related problem surfaced in 1993 when the elected president of Haiti, the newly elected civilian president of Nigeria, and the elected government of Burundi were ousted by their militaries. They all called on the international community to help install them in power.[9] If done, would their rule be truly legitimate if it had relied on external force or influence? The end of the cold war will ensure that not all conflicts stemming from nonviable conditions will be the object of global interests; however, they may still be exploited by regional expansionists with far-reaching consequences.

Regional Identification

During the cold war the superpowers in effect developed the world community into an integrated global system. Conflicts anywhere in the world attracted the attention of one, then of the other, superpower; hence, even distant developments were examined for strategic advantage. However, the end of the cold war has influenced the regionalization of global affairs again as vast areas are now turning inward while some regions are becoming marginalized in relation to the major global players. While certain positive developments may emerge from this tendency in terms of conflicts that will not engulf the globe, such regionalization may have adverse effects on certain members of the regions who possess only limited resources for their own defense and who may not be able to prevent becoming involved in local conflicts. And another problem concerns the consequences of marginalization of certain states and entire regions with its adverse economic implications that may engender civil strife.

Prominent areas subject to such regionalist tendencies include Eastern Europe, the territories of the former Soviet Union and of Yugoslavia, the Middle East, Southeast Asia, North America, North and Northeast Africa, and Sub-Saharan Africa.[10] A review of these regions will quickly reveal the missing cold-war context as was amply illustrated by the absence of the Soviet Union as a factor in the Gulf War. Eastern Europe has largely been abandoned by the Soviet Union, and its countries are seeking their own separate links with the European Union, NATO, or with the external world community. The former republics of the Soviet Union are seeking their own new ties and redefining relations with Russia. Yugoslavia's breakup would scarcely have been tolerated by the Soviet Union during the cold-war days, but today, beyond the United Nations' peacekeeping role, Western Europe has been reluctant to intervene militarily, which in turn discouraged a greater role by the US. That conflict may yet spill into the rest of the Balkan region, but despite dire predictions, the war and atrocities of Yugoslavia have not spread beyond its borders.

The Gulf War was the first major confrontation of the post–cold-war days, the prosecution of which was enabled to a large extent by the nonavailability of the Soviet Union on Iraq's side. The allied coalition, which included several regional states, and the peace initiatives among Israel, the Palestine Liberation Organization (PLO), and neighboring states in 1993 also bear the imprint of the new regionalization. However, as previously noted, the Middle Eastern region is not necessarily becoming more pacific as new forces are emerging and volatile new territories are being appended to this region. More positive prospects for regionalization may be found in Southeast Asia. With the absence of the Soviet Union and the recent initiatives by Vietnam to invite foreign economic ties, regionalization is becoming identified with intensified economic interaction which, if successful, should imply the stabilization of this previously volatile region, which had played such a major role in the cold war. Regionalization was also evident in the 1993 debate in the US regarding the signing of the North American Free Trade Agreement (NAFTA). And the US is recognizing the economic interest shift from its traditional European orientation to that of the Pacific rim region and to its own hemisphere. The US acknowledged the effectiveness of Europe's economic regionalization by participating in the formation of our own competitive trade structures.

It is in Africa where the negative dimensions of regionalization are most in evidence. With the absence of the Soviet Union as an adversary on that continent, Africa has ceased to be an area of strategic global competition, while its generally declining economic performance has rendered Africa of marginal utility value as a global partner. North and Northeast Africa have become the objects of Islamist designs which may aspire to incorporate both areas into a coherent Islamic fundamentalist (Islamist) region with the goal of eliminating all secular governments. Closer ties to the Middle East may be expected, and should Islamism there engulf Saudi Arabia and other states, a new Islamic bloc could emerge as a very formidable strategic region which would redefine traditional Western security interests stretching from Portugal to Pakistan.[11]

Sub-Saharan Africa is undergoing another regionalist episode since its initial attempts to establish a meaningful united identity following independence. Much of the continent was divided along ideological lines with excolonial, Soviet, Cuban, Chinese, and US interests vying for strategic advantage and surrogate battlegrounds. Africa is presently forced to turn inward as it has quickly lost its attraction to external powers. The peacekeeping effort in Somalia started off as an enthusiastic international operation, but the ensuing frustration soon demonstrated the limited interests in that anarchic conflict which, despite a substantial investment in manpower and money, would not be resolved without a prolonged commitment. Recommendations for direct participation by the Organization for African Unity (OAU) or for the formation of a regional peacekeeping force to be constituted by neighboring countries were soon made. These proposals followed on the heels of the questionable effort by the Economic Community of West African States (ECOWAS) to bring peace in Liberia's civil war with the insertion of a well-armed, multinational military force from the region. After more than three years of massive efforts which included much aerial bombing, the fighting had not stopped; and it may be questioned if this regional effort did not in fact prolong the war and suffering. Certainly, much of the region became destabilized in the process.

Regionalism bears close scrutiny as it may offer positive steps to resolve local problems, but regionalism may also contribute to tensions due to insufficient local resources. In such regions, we may expect the emergence of dominant actors whose hegemonial aspirations will naturally be resisted by potential victims. Regionalism may also lead to intensified cooperation in economic fora such as integrated communities. This would be a welcome development as it has been amply ascertained that such integration subsequently dissuades hostile relations. However, we need to guard that regionalization does not become a euphemism for marginalization as in the case of Africa.

Ideological Developments

Has history ended, and has Western-style liberal democracy won and will it sweep across the globe? This is a question asked by Francis Fukuyama.[12] Previously, Daniel Bell had asked if ideology had ended.[13] We may ask: is ideology dead or are global ideologies undergoing transformation—as they have done throughout history? Two major developments this century have contributed to the skepticism regarding doctrinaire ideologies, those which express not only an historical mission and ethic of a society but also a dynamic action plan for the future. First, Adolf Hitler's extreme national socialist ideology led Germany on its path of unprecedented destruction. Second, the collapse of the Soviet Union and the Warsaw Pact, as well as the fundamental changes taking place in China and other socialist states, has discredited communism as another extreme ideology. The result is that whether right or left, in their extreme forms, there has emerged widespread distrust about ideologies as they inevitably introduce authoritarianism and atrocities. Ideologies which are to be tolerated are those that are in the political center and demonstrate a social ethic but retain a good degree of flexibility, pragmatism, and vagueness. They also do not proselytize aggressively.

In this sense, ideologies have gotten a bad reputation, but they have not been eliminated. It is not conceivable that mankind's sociopolitical development can advance in an ideological vacuum. Values and collective aspirations are universal cultural characteristics; what changes over time are only the specific contents. "Pragmatism" in the sense of "whatever works" may sound very nonideological, but identifying what works to attain a specific goal reveals an ideological orientation.

Liberal democracy, the well-established ideology of the West, concerns near universal participation in determining the composition and direction of governments, protecting certain rights, and maintaining essentially private ownership and decentralized market economies. This is the prevailing ideology of the first world whose members exhibit mostly subtle differences on the issue of government intervention in socioeconomic policy. Because of the attainment of the advanced economic welfare levels of the members of the first world, liberal democracy is held in high esteem by that sector and is gaining adherents in other parts of the world. Interestingly, while it is widely assumed that the socio-economic success of the first world derives directly from its moderate ideology, this cause and effect relationship is subject to debate. China's economy has grown at an astounding rate for well over a decade while maintaining largely centralized controls—although there is no question that recent liberalization measures over certain sectors have contributed to these rapid advances. In a similar vein, Asia's newly industrializing countries (NIC) advanced impressively under less-than-democratic conditions and with the governments playing a heavy interventionist role. In essence, we must guard against making unwarranted assumptions about liberal democracy as a universal political ideal and as an economic panacea.

Opposition to liberal democracy stems from two sources. Some argue that the inherent socioeconomic inequality, as is evident in many liberal democracies, is a necessary feature in order for it to work. Those who are noncompetitive fall by the wayside and are either exploited or neglected. The result is crime, slums, drugs, unemployment, and poverty—in essence, the prevailing third world component within first world societies. The other source of opposition stems from a variety of other ideological foundations that allude to the inappropriateness of liberal democracy for their societies, or they posit the superior ethic of their own ideologies. In the former case, militant national socialists (fascists) saw liberal democracy as weak and unlikely to survive in a competitive and hostile world. A nation's human resources had to be melded into a militant productive machine to advance that nation's security. Communism, on the other hand, promised an egalitarian utopia to all, but it invariably stumbled into variations of Stalin's gulags. Liberal democracy won the contest for survival with the leading proponents of both national socialism and communism, although there is in evidence an occasional revival of interest in fascist-leaning sentiment as in Russia's 1993 election, and there exists considerable residual support for communism among its previous adherents and those who never abandoned all Marxist orthodoxy. The latter still comprise a quarter of the world's population.

Others reject liberal democracy on the grounds of its inappropriateness to their conditions or because of the existence of long-standing culturally based opposition. In the former case, many third world states may pay lip service to the tenets of liberal democracy, but the reality depicts oligarchic authoritarianism whose leaders defend their position by arguing that the standard features of liberal democracy are premature for their societies as they lack the essential institutional prerequisites. Their critics reply that this explanation conveniently assures the perpetuation of the oligarchies in power—whether military or civilian. These arguments need to be reconciled, especially for those states judged to be nonviable as even with the best of efforts, it is unrealistic to expect that liberal democracy will flourish long in a failing socioeconomic environment.

Those who base their opposition on cultural considerations present more formidable challenges. Many argue that their cultural traditions ascribe a different context for human rights or for universal political participation. The Chinese ask if the US, with a mere 200-year political tradition, can teach a country with a tradition dating 4,000 years. Here, we should guard lest we underestimate the influence of the cultural environment that shapes the interpretation of ideologies. In other words, liberal democracy, socialism, capitalism, human rights, and so on, have gained wide respect as ideological concepts, but they will be manifested in different ways. This was demonstrated by Mao Tse Tung whose Communist Party adopted a Marxist ideology, which had been conceived within the context of Europe's industrial revolution, but which was steadily modified in China to suit the needs of a peasant movement striving to lift China from the feudal age into the twentieth century. Many of Marx's philosophical premises deriving from Europe's intellectual history were discarded as Mao gradually altered the imported ideology to suit the traditional Chinese context. Towards the end of Mao's rule, many age-old Confucian tenets were validated again—though they had been actively suppressed during his first decade in power. Certainly he used Marxist ideology as an operational doctrine to justify his assumption of power within China, but he did not accept the assumptions of his Eastern European and Soviet counterparts whose claims to universalistic truths had been well-grounded in Europe's philosophical traditions and periodic demonstrations of messianic proselytization. The consequence of this cultural difference was the Sino-Soviet split, which fueled the failures of Marxism in the West. China's more parochial cultural tradition enabled that country to survive—as it has for four millennia—while the more orthodox Soviet-style Marxist regimes all collapsed, as did Hitler's projected 1,000-year Reich, and in a previous age, Europe's globe-spanning empires—all after comparatively short life spans.

There are several indicators pointing toward new ideological developments. The foremost force that is enjoying a resurgence is religion—which throughout history has rarely been far removed from political concerns.[14] The current episode was inspired by the 1979 ouster of the Shah of Iran by the Islamic fundamentalists, led by Ayatollah Khomeini. Soon, several other such Islamist movements swept the Middle East and North and Northeast Africa, gaining, if not outright power, much respect among the secular governments who were their targets. The enemies are not only the non-Muslim infidel, but also the degenerate and secular governments in Muslim societies that hold any governing doctrine other than those derived from the *Koran*. Western-style liberal democracy certainly cannot be compromised with such tenets. Should this political movement succeed in ousting all non-Islamic governments in the huge Muslim world stretching from Mauritania to Pakistan, by uniting, it could aspire to become a new superpower, fueled by the substantial resources of the Arabian peninsula—an area identified as a prime target. Other religious sources of political influence include a new wave of Hindu fundamentalism in India, while Christian fundamentalists have become a potent political force in the US. And the Russian Orthodox Church may emerge as another such political force as was evidenced by its mediative role in the turbulent days in Moscow in 1993.

In the third world, variations of socialism will survive but not for long in their militant or doctrinaire forms. Ideological flexibility will be conditioned by hard socioeconomic realities. Yesterday's liberation heroes have failed to produce, but unless the economic fortunes of their countries are reversed, the emergence of new controversial leaders is to be expected. Their doctrines will certainly call for a redefinition of relations with the first world, reparations to be paid by the first world to compensate for historical injustices, and a call for greater unity among themselves to maximize their bargaining power. Variations of democracy will be in evidence, but they will enjoy only a short life span in the absence of dramatic socio-economic progress. Ultimately, the solutions to the third world's problems will probably be addressed more effectively by evolving ideological developments in the first world as they are modified for the third world context, than by the third world's own formulations. As economically marginalized territories, their own ideologies will also remain marginalized.

Redefining the United Nations's Global Mission

Like its predecessor the League of Nations, the United Nations (UN) was established to prevent the outbreak of another world war by implementing collective security measures. The emphasis in both cases was the prevention of wars between states, but today most conflicts are within states. Certainly many of these civil wars have the potential of spilling into their regions, and indeed, many have done so. However, as in the case of Somalia, emerging international humanitarian sentiment is demonstrating concern for lives lost regardless of the nature of the conflict. This new global vision is being developed rapidly as the United Nations is expanding its traditional concern with only international wars to include wars at the domestic level as well. A clear distinction between the two levels is becoming difficult to make as civil wars increasingly tend to become internationalized.

During the cold war, the United Nations was the scene of the spirited diplomatic struggle between East and West for allegiance of the "South"—the third world.[15] When united, the South's voting strength in the General Assembly would invariably determine whose views would prevail. After the massive armed intervention by the United Nations in the Korean conflict in the early 1950s, the United Nations was subsequently excluded from participating militarily in most major cold war conflicts such as the war in Vietnam. Instead, the United Nations focused its attention on the vast social and humanitarian concerns of especially the numerous nations that had recently received their independence. It was reasoned that addressing the source of problems should reduce the likelihood of war's breaking out. In the security realm, the United Nations turned its attention to peaceful intervention in third world conflicts in the form of peacekeeping operations as a replacement for the much more ambitious designs of collective security.

In that endeavor, the results are mixed. Lucia Mouat expressed the reason for the peacekeeping trend, "Often more by default than by design, UN peacekeepers have been taking on the role of world cop."[16] In theory, the United Nations ought to be the ideal institution for addressing these regional conflicts, but the organizational structure of the United Nations has not been developed sufficiently to take on such a huge responsibility. In a speech to the United Nations in September 1993, President Clinton warned that the United Nations cannot become engaged in every one of the world's conflicts and that the United Nations must know when to say no.[17] As of the date of that speech, the United Nations had 17 peacekeeping missions under way at an annual cost of $3.5 billion and with results far from universally positive. One hundred thousand United Nations–sponsored peacekeeping troops were deployed, one-fourth of them in the former Yugoslavia alone—yet the atrocities there had not ceased and peace remained elusive. The United Nations's operation in

Somalia consumed over a third of its peacekeeping budget and, likewise, peace remained elusive. Addressing the evolving problem posed by renegade general Mohamed Farah Aidid in Somalia, the *New York Times* noted, "Arresting and trying criminals is completely uncharted territory for the United Nations."[18] Other controversial involvements include Cambodia, where despite the expenditure of $2 billion, that country has not been pacified and could erupt in war again. In Angola, the United Nations's efforts came to naught as the insurgency against the government resumed after election results were rejected by the government's opponents. And in Cyprus, the internal standoff persists with the United Nations's peacekeeping mission in place 29 years. By contrast, the UN's operation in Sinai is judged to be a success.

Besides the peacekeeping controversies, another notable debate concerns the work of the United Nations World Conference on Human Rights which convened in Vienna in mid-1993. A major ideological debate emerged as delegates debated and disagreed on certain aspects of human rights. Are human rights universal or culturally relative, it was asked.[19] Beyond agreeing on the morality of the broad concept of human rights, can there be universal agreement on the specific contents? Not surprisingly, the Muslim world posited the necessarily superior position of *sharia*—Islamic law. China and other oriental countries insisted that the human rights issue cannot disregard economic factors. Indonesia argued that national development must take priority over human rights. Also, it was argued that the collective rights of society must supersede those of individuals who may threaten society's stability. And going beyond mere abstract rhetoric of human rights, 52 Islamic states demanded the condemnation of Serbian aggression against Muslim Bosnia.

The US led the arguments for the universalistic view and for the rights of the individual. In this the US reflected the standard Western tendency towards exporting aggressively its universalistic ideological views—which others see as arrogant and intrusive. The debate has not been stilled, but the conference may indicate that the United Nations is becoming perhaps the major forum for ideological debate and that there may be emerging a United Nations–based global value system.

Where ideology had traditionally developed in isolation and often spilled out of its borders, the United Nations may provide an invaluable venue to sharpen such debates at the intellectual level and not on the battlefield.

In these post–cold-war days, the United Nations may experience a renaissance, but its fortune lies not in its own hands. Rather, it will be the leaders of the global community who will define that organization's role as a security, social, humanitarian, or intellectual force. The US pays one-fourth of the UN's upkeep and hence will shape much of its agenda. The desire to provide the United Nations with a permanent crisis-response instrument has been expressed, but opposition may be expected from US sources harking back to similar opposition during the League of Nations's days. Now that global tensions at the superpower level have been reduced, is there a need for such an ambitious and costly undertaking, it is asked.

Global Challenges

US Perspectives

This section examines and discusses US understanding of and interaction with global challenges. Taken up in turn are US perspectives of global affairs; changing interests; emerging security interests; identifying the challenges; levels of response to them; managing those responses; and a discussion of history, leadership, and power.

US Perceptions of Global Affairs

The US is justified in viewing its future global role with some trepidation. We won the cold war contest for survival against the menacing Soviet adversary and have gained a reprieve from major threats of other credible enemies for awhile. However, we are not certain of the future in terms of emerging challenges. History has not ended and, while it is not a comfortable prospect, history's own logic suggests that we are the next great power to decline. This is not necessarily imminent; in the meantime, much work remains to be undertaken to improve the welfare of the land and to extend that welfare to the greater commonwealth of humanity. The demand for America's positive intervention is ever increasing, but as noted at the outset, the ultimate challenge is to match ambition with resources. This seems to be an evident formula, but in view of history's vicissitudes, managing successfully its implementation has proven to be mostly elusive.

The US views a world in transition, characterized by two significant developments. First, despite data which depicts declining political rights and civil liberties, the Western notion of liberal democracy is becoming a widely accepted ideological framework governing the relations between rulers and the ruled.[20] However, there are powerful exceptions, and we cannot rule out the emergence of new ideological extremists. Also, the operational forms of democracy are not always encouraging. The US also sees as positive the greater global acceptance of market-based economies—which the US believes is inherently tied to democracy and necessary for the real advancement of nations.[21] However, concerning free market ideology, we may expect more opposition as, indeed, the US economy is itself taking some new directions. The US has also taken the leadership in spreading the seeds of human rights—but the manifestation of this is far from uniform. These are the forces which support the stabilization of the world, and the US is widely credited with leadership in spreading these principles.

The second development has been the tendency towards national fragmentation and ethnic polarization.[22] The US generally attempts to discourage such fragmentation, fearing the likelihood of spreading violence that may accompany the process, the weakening of the economies, and the prospect for some of the resultant units to be nonviable. The international community is called upon with ever-increasing frequency to intervene in such conflicts which can become expensive and can get bogged down. This fragmentationist tendency could proliferate widely and sweep Sub-Saharan Africa, Russia, and parts of the Orient—possibly even China. Its origins may usually be traced to the failure to develop nationally or to uneven development of ethnically delineated subnational units. Occasionally sociocultural reasons may be the source of dissent, and these too may become prevalent in the future. These fragmentationist states encounter violence as they disintegrate and subsequently as they enter new formative and consolidative stages. Numerous wars over minority populations and new borders such as those in the former Yugoslavia will proliferate. For the US, merely discouraging this development will not suffice; the problem will have to be addressed at the economic and strategic levels. If tractors don't bring the desired results, tanks will inevitably have to be called in.

Other developments which contribute to America's current global outlook include a more regionalist view of international affairs. By signing NAFTA, the US hedged its bet that its own region may be developed in competition with the European Union. Similarly, the notable inroads made at the US-hosted Asia-Pacific Economic Cooperation (APEC) forum in 1993 signaled once again America's shift away from its historic Eurocentric view of the world, while also acknowledging the primacy of economic over strategic concerns—the latter which had been the case during the cold war. Geographically and commercially, the US is well poised to intensify relations with the Pacific rim.[23] Russia remains of commercial interest to the US private sector while the rest of the old Soviet Union's territories remain primarily of strategic concern due to the numerous wars in that region and the unsettled problem of the dispersal of nuclear weapons in several of the new states. Western Europe remains the most stable political partner with whom our long-standing commercial differences are addressed peacefully, primarily in General Agreement on Tariffs and Trade (GATT) negotiations. As for the third world in general, its huge sector of marginalized states are advised by the US to adopt democratic structures and market economies, but their success or failure with them will hardly impact on the US except if certain ensuing conflicts become internationalized.

Changing Interests

A nation's external interests may be classified as core, intermediate, and peripheral. Core interests concern strategic matters as they ensure the security of the state; intermediate interests are those that seek to maximize welfare; and peripheral interests are those that advance more abstract socioideological values. During the height of the cold-war days, the pursuit of core interests predominated in US foreign policy as all global events were scrutinized for their prospects of altering the tense power equation. Presently, this practice has been somewhat relaxed because the conflicts that do erupt will not wreak imminent global catastrophe nor will all conflicts, if isolated, affect US strategic interests adversely.

There has now occurred a perceptible shift towards the pursuit of intermediate interest-level economic objectives. This direction has been inspired by widespread public awareness of structural economic problems—especially the long-term damage potential of the growing deficit. The international marketplace is where some solutions to economic growth are to be found. Accordingly, the US may be expected to increasingly engage in spirited debate and bargaining at international economic fora and to re-examine its competitive posture.[24] In this regard, Europe and Japan have been good teachers but the widespread domestic resistance to signing the NAFTA accord identified significant vestiges of traditional US isolationism. Having just disengaged from the global security stage, many are reluctant to transfer the battle to the world's economic arena. The US did well in the strategic competition with the Soviets, but the new competition is against capable adversaries who have long concentrated their energies in that arena out of opportunity as well as necessity. Except for occasional responses to moderate-size security threats to our core interests, most of our innovative international activities in the near future should be at this intermediate level.

At the peripheral level, little overt hostility is to be expected. Radical variations of socialism have rapidly lost influence, and the US State Department has been emphatic not to portray Islamism as a threatening ideology. Nor is there much opposition to America's basic ideological tenets. National Security Adviser Anthony Lake noted that "democracy and market economics, are more broadly accepted than ever before. We have arrived at neither the end of history nor a clash of civilizations, but a moment of immense democratic and entrepreneurial opportunity, and we must not waste it."[25] The first world's ideological cohesiveness and advanced socioeconomic status is a very powerful challenge to those who would decry the virtues of Western liberal democracy. More significant at the peripheral level are the humanitarian interventions undertaken in conflicts—such as those in Somalia and Bosnia—which do not pose direct or immediate threats to US core interests. Of the 6,000-some US troops engaged in peacekeeping operations as of October 1993, 5,000 were on the ground in Somalia alone.[26] There exists substantial opposition within the US to such ventures, illustrating well the limited energies to be engaged in such peripheral pursuits. This is corroborated in US relations with China, whose human rights record has been identified as requiring much improvement, while at the same time the US is avidly seeking to expand the already-large trade ties.[27] At a time of reduced great power tensions, it might be expected that concern with peripheral issues may intensify, but countervailing isolationist sentiment may depress any enthusiasm for such involvements.

As is evident, US perceptions of global affairs certainly accept that a fundamental transition is taking place. Anthony Lake summarized its main features: the broad acceptance of democracy; the US is this new era's dominant power; there exists an explosion of ethnic conflicts; and the pulse of the planet, and the pace of change in human events, have changed dramatically.[28] As a response, he counsels a "strategy of enlargement"—of the world's free community of market democracies. At the official level, there is an upbeat tone about the new era and its promising prospects for market democracies, but the evidence suggests also a greater degree of pragmatism. This is illustrated by tolerance of regimes which either do not fully conform to such structures, providing they offer advantage to our intermediate-level economic interests, or, as in the case of Boris Yeltsin's Russia, such tolerance advances in the long run the desirable end product.[29]

Emerging US Security Interests

Traditionally, "security interests" have implied narrow military concerns, but this concept has now been broadened to include other areas as well. The 1993 White House *National*

Security Strategy of the United States notes, "Today's challenges are more complex, ambiguous, and diffuse than ever before. They are political, economic, and military; unilateral and multilateral; short- and long-term."[30] Victory over the Soviets in the cold war is attributed to, among other factors, America's political, economic, and military strength. These all constitute part of the total security equation.[31] Firm democracies ensure stability, and the document states the need to eliminate any perception that the US will turn inward and "renounce our mandate for global leadership."[32] In the economic realm, the US faces the "continuing challenge of protecting and broadening open markets and of formidable economic competitors such as Japan and Germany."[33]

Militarily, the *National Security Strategy of the United States* observes: "While we no longer face the single defining threat which dominated our policy, budgets, force structures . . . multiple threats to our security still remain."[34] Threats to global security emanate from regional instabilities, proliferation of advanced conventional arms, ballistic missiles, weapons of mass destruction, terrorism, and the international drug trade. A concise statement of US security perceptions is offered:

> Our experience in the Gulf War demonstrated that we cannot be sure when or where the next conflict will arise; that regions critical to our interests must be defended; that the world must respond to straightforward aggression; that international coalitions can be forged . . . that the proliferation of advanced weaponry represents a clear, present, and widespread danger; and that the United States remains the nation whose strength and leadership are essential to a stable and democratic world order.[35]

This official statement of US security perceptions expresses the acceptance of the changing strategic environment, it acknowledges the cessation of the cold war, and it cautions us not to assume a reduced conflict environment. Aggression in the world will continue; it may even intensify. However, the warriors, their objectives, and their weapons and methods of implementing them will change. The challenge is now more nebulous—and multifarious—than during the cold war, and while we may have more time to engineer responses to threatening situations, in view of the proliferation of advanced weaponry and the frequent eruption of new conflicts, military vigilance will remain the order of the day.

The *National Security Strategy of the United States* envisages an ambitious global leadership role for the US, but in view of the enormous burden that may have to be borne as in the projected response to "straightforward aggression," the American public has offered early indications that there might be limits to such ventures. Responding to Iraq's aggression in Kuwait was palatable as there were severe implications for the first world's industrial viability. But the failure to respond to the commission of atrocities in Liberia, Rwanda, or Angola at the same time suggests a more selective degree of engagement. Indeed, our involvement in Somalia, whose damage in terms of human misery is not greater than that in Angola, suggests that more than only humanitarian concerns may be at stake. Core geopolitical considerations, rather than peripheral-level concerns, may still be the driving force in determining which conflicts shall receive our attention. In this regard, the US maintains its established realist proclivity and, despite frequent official-level pronouncements, the new era will not likely be shaped by idealist actions.

Having turned away from the Soviet Union and the Warsaw Pact as the focal point of military threats, the US now faces the third world as the source of conflicts and regional destabilization. This global sector has been enlarged with the addition of sizable territories from the old Soviet Union. Most conflicts in the third world will be primarily domestic affairs as they reflect the characteristics of states in the formative and early consolidative stages—in which civil wars are fought in the process of state formation and legitimation. Usually, such wars pose no global threats unless they spill into the region or they attract external support and intervention. However, some of the former Soviet territories may retain the nuclear weapons emplaced on their territories during the cold war. Also, their proximity to established Middle Eastern hot spots increases the likelihood of these civil wars having an adverse regional impact. The US may be expected to offer mediative and diplomatic services to those with nonthreatening civil wars but to offer financial inducements to those with a more menacing capability such as Ukraine or North Korea. Working through multilateral organizations such as NATO or the United Nations may also receive renewed impetus.

However, the third world also contains states in their expansive phase and these, like Iraq, will pose the most likely challenges with potentially grave consequences. As they aspire to great-power status, their regional ambitions may be seen as a first step. Accumulating new resources will help in the realization of their goals in turn. As such, regional hegemons require special attention and only a global power can monitor and, if need be, contain such emerging powers. Most conceivable threats to global stability will emanate from these third world expansionists.

In this regard, the US has not had a consistent policy with respect to expansionist states, as some had served useful purposes during the cold war. Certain expansionists such as Israel, South Africa, Morocco, Iran under the Shah, and India provided valuable regional balancing roles to offset Soviet, Chinese, or other locally generated designs. Some expansionists such as Cuba or North Vietnam were seen as serving Soviet purposes; others, such as Iraq, threatened long-term global economic stability; while regionally active states such as Nicaragua or Libya pursued their own third world leadership agendas. Now, with the decline of the Soviet Union from the world power stage, there will be less reason for the US to respond to all such attempts at regional hegemony, and we may witness a host of second rank powers attempting to reorder their respective regions. Unless they threaten vital US interests, the US will not interfere with their efforts.

The previous bipolar global system is giving way to a regional-based multihegemonial system out of which should emerge the next great powers. The US shows little evidence of wishing to remain the only active superpower, but much apprehension is expressed about the uncertainty of the new candidates. Although the US would be most comfortable with the Europeans or the Japanese, as they are well-known quantities, neither harbors such ambitions. Global responsibilities are costly and entail risk. Russia could conceivably be favored for such a role due to that country's proximity to the volatile southern territories of the old Soviet Union, the Middle East, and China, and its traditional interests in the Balkans—an area which West Europeans are reluctant to sort out.[36] However, Russia's own internal problems must first be resolved, which will most likely be a lengthy process. Barring these candidates, others will emerge from the third world. The foremost prospect is China—which has been history's grand master of regional hegemony but has previously avoided major global roles. The US was unsuccessful at dissuading China from testing a nuclear device in October 1993.[37] For the US, monitoring the hegemonial intentions of such emerging regional powers will rank, alongside tracking nuclear capabilities, as our most important strategic planning responsibilities.

Identifying the Challenges

In times of war, identifying developments that will require responses is a relatively easy task because of the comparative immediacy and clarity of the confrontational situation. In peacetime identifying challenges that require responses becomes a supreme challenge in itself. We have argued that, in the future, conflicts as well as deteriorating environments that may lead to conflicts are to be expected. If not identified in time, wars may quickly ensue and spread beyond the borders of the combatants and engulf entire regions. As a global power, the US must monitor all such developments if we are to exercise control over international order. Not all wars can be stopped nor can they all be ignored. Certain wars will bear more serious consequences than others and distinguishing in a timely manner between them will challenge the global statesmen.[38] However, correctly anticipating those developments that will shape future conflicts will constitute a more vital service. Deciding which wars to enter requires the calculation of one's own interest and risk, but anticipating which deteriorating situations will lead to conflict requires sophisticated sociopolitical analysis and an appreciation of the subtleties of foreign cultures. It is to be expected that some will argue that the end of the cold war allows the US an opportunity to turn inward and focus on long-standing domestic issues. But the historical facts of international competition do not allow a global power the luxury of ignoring certain events before they have been properly assessed.

Response Options

Appropriate responses to global challenges require careful selection from the options available. This section lists and discusses some of those options.

Levels of Response

The framework for anticipating such challenges and formulating responses is offered by the security interest model which depicts core, intermediate, and peripheral interests. At the peripheral level, responses may be expected to be less certain, ad hoc, and reflective of changing political perceptions and ideologies of new administrations in charge of the decision-making apparatus. Those traditionally identified as idealists in foreign affairs will promote activist agendas aimed at ameliorating the antagonisms and disparities among global cultures. Peace, they argue, can be attained by addressing mankind's fundamental needs for dignity and welfare. This globalist view calls for positive programs for the advancement of human rights and democratic freedoms and is flexible on the question of economic structures. And global institutions and the rule of law are to be actively supported as they enhance the emergence of a global community of man. It is an admittedly long-term view requiring a substantial investment of resources in a moral venture which, however, is not supported by the evidence of man's continuing proclivity towards war. It is not only the poor who fight—as both world wars have shown.

Those who insist on concentrating the nation's external energies almost exclusively on core issues tend to be identified traditionally as realists. They argue that the Soviets were offered ample opportunity to integrate themselves and the Warsaw Pact members into a peaceful world community. What kept the peace, however, was not morality or the cooperative formulation of a global community but America's superior economic and military power which, by the mid-1980s, the Soviets could not hope to challenge. This realist position holds that all nations seek power and preponderance over others and that this condition cannot be ignored. The correct assessment of the military strength of potential protagonists can contribute to peace—as it did between the US and the Soviet Union during the cold war. Realists are reluctant to make assumptions about global values and hence they disdain grandiose international institutional designs. Pursuing peripheral interests aggressively is an exercise in frustration as it requires more resources than anyone possesses while it also imposes cultural universalism on hesitant nations. What can be understood is immediate power and self-interest, which need to be unambiguously portrayed to reduce the likelihood of war breaking out. The Soviets understood what constituted our core interests, but the range of our interests was not adequately portrayed to Saddam Hussein in advance of the Gulf War.

Identifying problems according to this framework does not simply assume that idealists focus only on peripheral concerns and realists on core interests.[39] Far from it. Both recognize the preeminent need for physical security as a core value. But realists are not comfortable at pursuing peripheral interests while idealists are uncomfortable if they ignore them. However, the gap between these perspectives may be narrowed by the focus on intermediate interests—those that involve a nation externally in the pursuit of welfare maximization. Certainly, the unprincipled pursuit of exploitative economic advantage may easily be disdained, but the peacefully negotiated intensification of international economic relations may be mutually advantageous to all involved in accordance with the classic theories of international trade. And in view of the peace that prevails, among members of the first world who enjoy very complex economic ties, it is postulated that extending this net to a wider array of nations should add to global stability.

In this regard, with major and immediate threats to America's core security interests having receded, but with the overextension of scarce resources being a likely consequence of pursuing avidly peripheral objectives, the US may find that its prime diplomatic interest and method will lie in this intermediate-level economic realm. For the US such a response to global affairs is logical in view of ours being comfortably the world's largest economy, but it will not be without problems as we face formidable competitors for whom economic survival forms part of their core interests and because the US finds it difficult to shirk isolationist sentiments. Responding at this level will require rapid adjustment, away from our military means with which we are more familiar. As greater success accrues in economic diplomacy, it may be expected that the calls for military intervention will decline—but also, that when military means are implemented, it will probably be in substantial confrontations on the order of the Gulf War.

Managing Responses

Identifying correctly the challenges will test our statesmen but formulating appropriate responses will, of course, be equally important. Once the decision has been made to intervene in a deteriorating situation, and the level of required response has been assessed, another option will have to be considered: should the response be unilateral, multilateral, or through global organizations.

Responding to Soviet-centered threats during the cold war required, for the most part, unilateral initiatives as challenges were posed to our core interests. Certainly the US worked closely with allies, especially NATO, but the threat perception, leadership, and the decisive troop and weapons commitment were dominated by the US. During the 1962 Cuban missile crisis, US decision makers formulated the response and then secured the approval of our allies. Allies played only marginal roles in the Vietnam War and in Operation El Dorado Canyon against Libya in 1986, and the US acted alone in the 1989 Operation Just Cause in Panama. During the cold war the Soviet enemy was formidable and nuclear equipped, which meant that US perceptions of threats to core interests would predominate as the US would bear the ultimate brunt of a full attack. But the proclivity towards unilateral action is well-grounded in America's isolationist tradition, which also extends into the economic realm.

The US has engaged in multilateral efforts, but such allied cooperation is often operationally only nominal although it serves a useful political purpose. This was the case in the operation against the Dominican Republic in 1965, against Grenada in 1983, and in the Vietnam War.[40] Against Iraq in 1991 the US assembled a significant alliance that included several major Arab states, but again the US initiated and managed the operation while also supplying most (not all) of the firepower. Certainly allied participation was not on the order of World War II. Generally, since 1945 US multilateral operations involved allies more for political than for vital military supportive purposes, often to satisfy US domestic constituencies. The absence of such militarily active allies would hardly have halted America's determination to prosecute those engagements.

The US has also been a major supporter and participant in efforts undertaken by the UN's, starting with the support extended by President Harry S Truman to the UN's police action in Korea in 1953. Various degrees of participation in United Nations–managed operations followed over the years as that organization came to be identified with global peacekeeping responsibilities. In 1993, the US had military troops stationed in Somalia, the Sinai, Macedonia, and small contingents in Western Sahara, Cambodia, Iraq-Kuwait DMZ, and Lebanon—all in support of the UN peacekeeping operations.[41] However, US troop commitments to UN operations are not without controversy, much of it reflecting our penchant for unilateral actions. America's major questions about the revitalized United Nations role concern the overextension of UN operations, paying for their costs, corruption, and inept military leadership, and there is very serious opposition to having any US troops under UN command.[42] Several US war deaths in the Somali intervention occurred while under UN-commanded operations.[43] Others argue that the United Nations is about to embark on a global nation-building offensive—for which the US military is not designed or trained.[44] Having the United Nations assume greater responsibilities for keeping the peace was an integral feature of the originally envisioned new world order, but this option needs considerable refinement.

Several factors will determine the choice among the options of unilateral, multilateral, and global cooperative responses. With the demise of the Soviet Union, major nuclear threats to the US have greatly diminished, which implies that more time is available to meet potential conventional challenges. This development also offers opportunity for building regional or global multilateral institutional capabilities with our established allies or with new ones. Some conflicts such as Just Cause or antinarcotics operations will be of little concern to others as their interests will not be at stake. But if the tranquil relations extant among the members of the first world are to be extended to a wider community, there may be advantage in greater security cooperation and multilateral approaches to conflict resolution. Wars may become depersonalized in the sense that they will not be viewed as disputes between only two parties, and instead they may assume a universalistic character: a crime against humanity—for which all nations have responsibility. Was not the welfare of the world jeopardized when, towards the end of the Gulf War, Iraq torched Kuwait's oil fields and that scarce resource was wasted and permanently removed from serving mankind?

Today the absence of an aggressive Soviet Union offers the opportunity to build such institutional links. Working with close allies will remain an attractive proposition, but the efforts to do so in Bosnia and Somalia have demonstrated lingering limits of such cooperative ventures. It is the further refinement of the United Nations's capability that still offers promising opportunities. That organization has been overtasked and is subjected to too many clashing perceptions, but we may argue that its full potential has not yet been tapped. The US may find great advantage in utilizing the UN's resources once they have been further developed. Until then, the US may be expected to retain its essentially unilateralist proclivities.

History, Leadership, and Power

In her influential 1976 article, "War and the Clash of Ideas," Professor Adda B. Bozeman observed: "It is much harder for Americans than for other peoples to accept [such] a world view because the United States, almost by definition, stands for the denial of cultural differences and the neglect or irrelevancy of the past."[45] And a celebrated article by Samuel P. Huntington, "The Clash of Civilizations?" appeared in 1993. He predicted: "The great divisions among humankind and the dominating source of conflict will be cultural. . . . The clash of civilizations will dominate global politics."[46]

Huntington exemplifies Bozeman's contention. She notes that the clash of ideas has prevailed since it was ". . . inaugurated by Herodotus when he explained the Persian Wars as a confrontation between the rival civilizations of Europe and Asia."[47] Huntington presents his thesis as if it were a new development—a new phase of sorts—but Bozeman argues that this is what war has been about throughout history. We may argue the merits of specific momentary strategic, economic, or political objectives being the motives for wars but ultimately, war is about ideas—the building blocks of civilizations. In this regard, Huntington offers little that is fundamentally new.

Huntington elaborates on the concept of civilization and identifies seven major ones, along whose cultural fault lines, which separate these civilizations, will occur the most important conflicts. Civilizations differ from each other on views concerning the relations between God and man; the individual and the group; citizen and state; and on matters of rights, responsibilities, liberty, authority, equality, and hierarchy.[48] He agrees with Bozeman that the nation-state is weakening as a source of identity. Huntington writes that the West is at the peak of its power and that this in turn may be responsible for the non-Western civilizations turning inward again. And Huntington also offers an interesting conclusion, that other civilizations are attempting to modernize without becoming Western—however, they wish to acquire the physical accouterments of Western societies.[49]

Huntington introduced a welcome—if controversial—element in the current studies of international relations, but he also encountered substantial criticism from several perspectives.[50] Realists argue that the nation-state still remains the focal point of war as entire civilizations don't fight, but nation-states do. And, they contend, the fight is for some sensible interests which all cultures value. In other words, all states operate within the context of core, intermediate, and peripheral interests, but they differ with respect to the specific content of these categories. But idealists, or globalists, maintain that there is a common bond that cuts across all civilizations and that its ideological expression is evolving in the United Nations. This view underlies the debate on the universalization of human rights, which is also represented by the work of organizations such as Amnesty International. In the same vein, Seyom Brown notes: ". . . the increasing mobility of persons and information assures that, like it or not, human rights conditions in all countries will be globally monitored."[51]

Neither Bozeman nor Huntington, nor realists and idealists, have pronounced the final word on this fascinating debate, which is important because the debate has forced the US to go beyond its traditional ethnocentric concerns. Such xenophobia may be tolerated in the case of marginal states but certainly not for a global power. The cold war served to "deisolate" the world's civilizations as the US and the Soviet Union explored every obscure conflict for its strategic impact. Today, with only the US having such interests and capabilities, leadership requires more than only the pursuit of national advantage but also the willingness and the ability to ameliorate clashing views of civilizations. A lesser power may pursue only parochial interests, but a global power must go beyond mere realist policies lest the evolving community of civilizations steers an undesirable course.

It remains to identify the nature of the leadership that is required. The US learned in the cold war that military leadership costs money—and does not necessarily guarantee preferred results. Yet the investment cannot be avoided. Military leadership required the outlay of huge expenditures on arms and forces and it also made the US the prime target of war should a global war have broken out. The goal of global military leadership must ultimately be global stability by ensuring that the inevitable wars that will break out will remain contained and not spiral out of control.

Similarly, economic leadership also requires sacrifices. A global power cannot simply approach the global economy from only the perspective of profit maximization, for soon it will be calculated that its preponderant military might can be impressed in pursuit of economic objectives. A global economy could not survive on such an exploitative foundation. Global economic leadership requires the creation of appropriate institutions that will further the maximum welfare levels for the greatest number by positively incorporating all states into the great international division of labor. Also, the use of economic instruments as preferred alternatives to force has not yet realized its full potential. And again, leadership in developing this instrument is likewise the preserve of responsible global powers.

Leadership must also concern the formulation of ideas, appropriate to the evolving relations between global cultures. Inevitably this will mean leading the historical synthesis of civilizations. In this regard the US has not been inactive and has proffered models of liberal democracy and human rights. However, much more remains to be developed. Specifically, it must not be assumed that the ideological structure of the leader's own domestic context is necessarily appropriate for all states—regardless of their developmental level. Sensitivity to historical differences among cultures and civilizations must also be demonstrated. The US must accept that most other cultures see the US as but the most recent ambitious Western power, dressing age-old economic interests in the garb of universal moral precepts. It is not the formulation of moral precepts that they find objectionable, but the inconsistent policies implemented in their pursuit—which may be driven by economic criteria. Some conflicts are addressed while others—often much more grave—are ignored. No one power will soon preside over the final synthesis of the world's great civilizations, but global leadership today ought to offer the base of moral commonalty to diminish the clashes between them.

Finally, power has been transformed. Throughout history, power has been evaluated in its military context and more recently, power has come to signify economic capacity. Yet these bases of power are ephemeral as we observe the rise and fall of history's great empires. Much more lasting and far more influential have been ideas—the very foundations of civilizations. We need to remember that empires, like nation-states, have short life spans compared to civilizations which in human culture remain eternal. Whether Confucius or Plato, Christ or Mohammed, Kautilya or Machiavelli, we today debate their ideas and we will continue to do so long after their and our nation-states have given way to new political configurations. Their ideas emerged out of civilizational contexts, which give them their respectability. Hence the power of ideas is ultimately the greatest power if the criterion is building lasting cultures and civilizations, rather than the possession of material capacity to influence events.

Notes

1. Such views tend to inspire skepticism. See Adam Roberts, "A new age in international relations?" *International Affairs* 67, no. 3 (1991): 509. Similarly, Richard Falk suggests that there might have been a new world order, but it was short lived. "In Search of a New World Model," *Current History* 92, no. 573 (April 1993): 145.

2. Writing about the new world order, Douglas Simon notes: ". . . it was a little naive, built more on hope than reality." *USA Today*, 11 October 1993. Also, Michael T. Klare, "The New Challenges to Global Security," *Current History* 92, no. 573 (April 1993): 155.

3. Although there has been a significant reduction in global arms expenditures, there were more war-related fatalities globally in 1992 than since the height of the Vietnam War. *Christian Science Monitor*, 14 December 1993.

4. The attributes of the new world order are summarized well by Mahmood Monshipouri and Thaddeus C. Zolty, "Shaping the New World Order: America's Post–Gulf War Agenda in the Middle East," *Armed Forces and Society* 12, no. 4 (Summer 1993). Of course not everyone agrees on the facts of a new world order. See C. G. Jacobsen, "Myths, Politics and the Not-So-New World Order," *Journal of Peace Research* 30, no. 33 (1993).

5. This theory is based on my graduate studies with Professor George Liska. It is elaborated in Karl P. Magyar, "Low-Intensity Conflicts: The African Context," in *Responding to Low-Intensity Conflict Challenges* (Maxwell AFB, Ala.: Air University Press, 1990), 172.

6. See "Toward a Two-Tier Commonwealth," *Christian Science Monitor*, 13 October 1992.

7. Wolfgang Ramonat, "Microstates in the United Nations," *Aussen Politik* 32, no. 3 (1981); John C. Caldwell, Graham E. Harrison, and Pat Quiggin, "The Demography of Micro-States," *World Development* 8 (1980); and Michael Ward, "Dependent development: problems of economic planning in small developing countries," in Percy Selwyn, ed., *Development Policy in Small Countries* (London: Croom Helm, 1975): 115.

8. S. N. Sangmpam distinguishes between empirical and juridical, or soft types of statehood. "Neither Soft nor Dead: The African State Is Alive and Well," *African Studies Review* 36, no. 2 (1993): 74.

9. "Talks to Restore Haiti's Democracy Proceed," *Christian Science Monitor*, 29 June 1993. Also, Foreign Broadcast Information Service, *Daily Report,Sub-Saharan Africa*, 28 October 1993, 1.

10. See Kenichi Ohmae, "The Emergence of Regional States," *Vital Speeches of the Day* 58, no. 16 (June 1992): 487.

11. Karl P. Magyar, "Northeastern Africa's Strategic Role in the Expanding Middle Eastern Conflict Zone," unpublished manuscript (Maxwell AFB, Ala.: Center for Aerospace Doctrine, Research, and Education, 1992).

12. Francis Fukuyama, "Have We Reached the End of History?" *The National Interest* (Summer 1989).

13. Daniel Bell, *The End of Ideology: On the Exhaustion of Political Ideas in the Fifties* (Glencoe, Ill.: Free Press, 1960).

14. Adda B. Bozeman, "War and the Clash of Ideas," *Orbis* 20, no. 1 (Spring 1976): 83–87.

15. Walter S. Jones and Steven J. Rosen, *The Logic of International Relations*, 4th ed. (Boston: Little, Brown and Company, 1982): 515–17.

16. *Christian Science Monitor*, 6 October 1993.

17. *Christian Science Monitor*, 29 September 1993.

18. *New York Times*, 17 June 1993.

19. *Christian Science Monitor*, 18 and 25 June 1993.

20. The discouraging data is offered in the annual report by Freedom House. *Montgomery Advertiser*, 17 December 1993.

21. The myth of capitalism as the road to global prosperity is raised by Paul Kennedy, "The Forces Driving Global Change," *Christian Science Monitor*, 9 April 1993.

22. Myron Weiner notes that traditionally scholars had been reluctant to list ethnicity as a major factor in international relations. "Peoples and states in a new ethnic order?" *Third World Quarterly* 13, no. 2 (1992): 317.

23. "Clinton Pushing Business With Asia," *New York Times*, 11 November 1993.

24. "Clinton Team Shifts Toward Trade Activism," *Christian Science Monitor*, 5 February 1993.

25. *Christian Science Monitor*, 29 September 1993.

26. *USA Today*, 11 October 1993.

27. "US and China Try to End Bar to High-Tech Trade," *New York Times*, 12 November 1993.

28. *Christian Science Monitor*, 29 September 1993.

29. "Some Question Legality of Yeltsin's Actions," *Christian Science Monitor*, 24 September 1993.

30. The White House, *National Security Strategy of the United States* (Washington, D.C.: US Government Printing Office, 1993), 1.

31. A broadened concept of national security is also offered by Joseph J. Romm, *Defining National Security: The Nonmilitary Aspects* (New York: Council on Foreign Relations Press, 1993), 1.

32. White House, *National Security Strategy*, 1.

33. Ibid.

34. Ibid., 21.

35. Ibid., 1.

36. Robert Pegaro, "Help for Central Asia," *Christian Science Monitor*, 27 October 1993.

37. Sheila Tefft, "When China Speaks, Asia Listens," *Christian Science Monitor*, 17 November 1993.

38. Stephen John Stedman elaborates on selective intervention in "The New Interventionists," in Eugene R. Wittkopf, ed., *The Future of American Foreign Policy*, 2d ed. (New York: St. Martin's Press, 1994), 322.

39. The literature on the classic realism-idealism debate is voluminous. Introductory readings are offered in John A. Vasquez, ed., *Classics of International Relations*, 2d ed. (Englewood Cliffs, N. J.: Prentice Hall, 1990), chapters 1–2.

40. John M. Collins, *America's Small Wars: Lessons for the Future* (Washington, D.C.: Brassey's US, Inc., 1991).

41. *USA Today*, 11 October 1993.

42. "Dial Emergency," *The Economist*, 14 August 1993.

43. Jeane Kirkpatrick, " 'Multilateralism' Deadly in Somalia," *Montgomery Advertiser*, 14 October 1993; and "Multilateralism's Obituary Was Written in Mogadishu," *Christian Science Monitor*, 27 October 1993.

44. Trent Lott, "UN Must Not Direct US Troops," *Christian Science Monitor*, 16 November 1993.

45. Bozeman, 79.

46. Samuel P. Huntington, "The Clash of Civilizations?" *Foreign Affairs* 72, no. 3 (1993): 22.

47. Bozeman, 79.

48. Huntington, 25.

49. Ibid., 49.

50. "The Summoning," *Foreign Affairs* 72, no. 4 (1993): 2.

51. Seyom Brown, *International Relations in a Changing Global System: Toward a Theory of the World Polity* (Boulder: Westview Press, 1992), 137.

PART I
THE CHALLENGE

Regional Study 1
Conflict and Confrontation in the Post–Cold-War Middle East

Dr Lewis B. Ware

With the defeat of Saddam Hussein and the collapse of the Soviet Union, some observers thought that the Middle East would recede from public view, shrinking to a space in the national consciousness appropriate to our preoccupation with more pressing domestic issues. But the Middle East already reoccupies a commanding position in post–cold-war American policy deliberations. In fact, since the collapse of Saddam's ambitions in the Gulf, the region has exercised an even more tenacious grip on the attention of the American public.

The reasons for the enduring presence of the Middle East in the American perception of global politics are not difficult to discern: oil is still considered a strategic commodity; far from being formalized in a peace treaty, the unprecedented agreement in 1993 between Israelis and Palestinians to recognize each other has caused yet a new round of inter-communal violence; the demographic shift to Western Europe of large numbers of Middle Eastern laborers represents an unwelcome intrusion of the global suburbs into the inner cities of the industrialized West with all the social disequilibrium that accompanies the inequities of unequal development; and the region boasts new political actors who have access to arms in quantities large enough to challenge the Middle Eastern secular state system and to disturb the tenuous regional balance.

In a word, everything in the Middle East is still geopolitically connected to everything else. For that reason the region will be a potentially volatile zone of conflict for the foreseeable future. We may therefore be certain that US security concerns will be enmeshed in the politics of this changeable part of the world. Taking that assertion as a given of the American strategic perception of the region, I propose to analyze the extent to which, and under what circumstances, the nature of Middle Eastern regional conflicts has actually changed. I will examine a number of issues in the context of this analysis.

First, this study looks at selected cases of the increasing trend toward religious and ethnic nationalism in the region. The impact of this trend on several Middle Eastern states will then be analyzed and while it is certainly too soon to make any definitive judgment about the future of the regional secular state system in general, readers may discern a pattern of political action in these movements that points to an acceleration in the fragmentation of other vulnerable regional regimes.

Second, several examples of intergovernmental organizations (IGO) will be chosen and their value for the future integration of the region will be assessed. By so doing, this paper does not aim to establish the IGO as an antidote to the above trend but to indicate in what ways Arab cultures and political economies often conspire to make integration as risky a proposition for regional stability as is fragmentation of the secular system.

Third, the study speaks to the need for a redefinition of the Middle East in terms of the realities that reflect a post–cold war regional security environment where fragmentation and integration play an increasingly important political role. In that context, this paper also examines a typology for conflicts which may arise in the Middle East as a consequence.

The Process of Regional Fragmentation

Some Observations on Hamas and the Kurds

Since the beginning of the decolonization process and the extension to the region of the Soviet-American rivalry, the secular nation-state model in its various forms has been applied to the problem of Middle Eastern regional organization and development. These models assumed that the evolution of the secular state went hand in hand with the theory and practice of political and economic modernization. The United States and the former Soviet Union promoted their respective versions of modernization under the rubric of the capitalist and Marxist-Leninist model of nation building. By so doing, the US-Soviet competition complicated the already formidable problems of sociopolitical consolidation that the countries of the contemporary Middle East were undergoing in the 1960s following independence from colonial rule. These countries tended to exhibit the kinds of conflicts that pertained to this particular stage in their national growth; conflicts with neighbors over sovereignty, territory, natural resources; conflicts with the former colonizing powers over political autonomy; and conflicts with Israel, a country that the regional states assumed was the West's neocolonial proxy.

While it deplored these regional Middle Eastern conflicts, the West dealt with them within the framework of a system of international law that the Middle Eastern states inherited from their colonial past. The cold-war superpower rivalry tried to accommodate these regional conflicts and tried to contain them within a pattern of alliances whose anticipated equilibrium was designed to preclude the domination of a single regional actor. In this way the regional countries were integrated, however imperfectly, into a global bipolar international political system. But it was the imposition of this system that masked the unfinished task of sociopolitical and economic integration within the Middle Eastern secular state itself. In the present post–cold-war Middle Eastern environment, the forces of religious and ethnic nationalism propose that only they can complete the process of integration at which the regional secular state has so manifestly failed. In making this claim, these nationalists are not only hostile to the secular state, but they have also rejected the principles upon which the regional political system of secular states was founded.

These nonstate actors act in the name of eternal religious and/or ethnic "truths." Some observers tend to think that the propagation of these "eternal truths" is an ideological phenomenon new to the region. Nothing could be farther from the truth. Throughout its classical history, the Middle East has been susceptible to the challenge of religious and ethnic alternatives to the organizing principles of empire and state. When the Middle East was integrated into the contemporary bipolar global system in which modernization was the dominant socioeconomic ethos, it became axiomatic in the West that such traditional historical factors as religion and ethnicity could not function as elements of progress and, therefore, would be eliminated as categories of national consolidation. This unfortunate misperception blinded the West to the fact that underneath the political superstructure of modernization and development, enthusiastically embraced and promoted by the Middle Eastern secular state, a suppressed current of religious and ethnic nationalism has always been patiently waiting to reassert itself. Hence, when religious nationalism reappeared in Iran in 1979, it took the West entirely by surprise.

Both ethnic and religious nationalisms reject the secular state for a number of reasons: religious nationalism—in this case, the various forms of the radical political ideology we call Islamism—considers the secular state illegitimate because it has betrayed its obligation under Islamic law to protect, defend, and provide for the prosperity of God's chosen community, the *ummah*. And yet at no time in Muslim history has the conflation of the temporal and the spiritual, in the form of the secular state acting as executor of God's plan for universal salvation, attained a satisfactory standard of practical application. Historically, the absence of integrated interests between Muslim states and societies has always existed and in times of increasing socioeconomic malaise has led to serious tensions.

The Islamists' strike at the secular state from within is an effort to replace it with governments according to holy writ; the secular state responds vigorously in an attempt to end the Islamist challenge to its power. Present-day Islamists are leading a concerted attack against the Egyptian and the Algerian governments where the gap between state and society is still ominously large; but this is not where the most ominous danger from Islamism lies. It lies in the Arab-Israeli arena where a struggle between the Palestine Liberation Organization (PLO) and Hamas (Organization of Islamic Resistance) for the right to dominate Palestinian independence politics portends serious future disequilibrium.[1]

Hamas is the acronym in Arabic for "zeal," and Hamas has shown considerable zeal in directing and sustaining the activities of the Palestinian revolt against Israeli occupation (the intifadah) that began in the winter of 1987. Active in Gaza because of the post-1948 Egyptian administration of the Strip, Hamas was initially an offshoot of the Egyptian *al-Ikhwan al-Muslimin* (the Muslim Brothers). Originally a group of Islamic reformists, the Brothers turned to a more active form of radical political protest after Gamal Abd al-Nasser's 1952 revolution when they challenged Nasser's Pan-Arab vision in the name of encouraging the Egyptian secular state to adopt a more Islamic character. Both Nasser and the Brothers claimed that Israel was the proxy of the West. But whereas Nasser raised the struggle against Israel to the pantheon of Pan-Arab political virtues to end the Western presence in the Middle East, the Brothers pursued their desire to free the Muslim personality from its dependence on neocolonial patterns of thought by mounting a sociocultural crusade against Zionist domination in Gaza where they were already well represented. Ironically, Israel cooperated in this crusade when, to impede the spread of PLO influence, Jerusalem encouraged countervailing Islamic tendencies by permitting the construction of new mosques in the occupied territories. As religious sanctuaries, the mosques were off-limits to Israeli authority. Consequently, the mosques became a focal point for the gradual creation of an Islamist movement as the Brothers began to turn gradually to the politics of radical religious nationalism. It was in the Gazan mosques that Hamas extremism was born.

The catalyst for the subsequent growth and maturity of Hamas, however, was the spontaneous outbreak of the intifadah. The intifadah took the PLO by surprise. The PLO had done nothing to precipitate the uprising and could do even less to control it. The natural beneficiary of this situation was Hamas which, with the self-help institutions created by the Brothers already in place, offered a powerful alternative focus to the PLO for the mobilization of Palestinian political loyalty. To Hamas the PLO's declaration of a future secular and democratic Palestinian state was incompatible with their Islamist political worldview. But Hamas made a temporary truce with the PLO to ensure the success of the intifadah. Now that the PLO has been recognized by Israel as the political interlocutor for the Palestinian people, Hamas has moved further toward the rejectionist camp. It is quite likely then that this fragile truce will no longer hold and that a civil conflict will erupt among Palestinians for control of the statehood process. Should an Islamist Palestinian state come to share a contiguous border with Israel and Jordan, the situation would be inimical to Israeli and Jordanian security, to say nothing of the security of other neighboring secular Arab regimes.

Because Hamas is antisecular is not to suggest that its antisecularism will be generalized to the entire region and that as a result the Middle Eastern secular state is doomed to extinction. It is only to assert that increasing internal fragmentation has sapped the secular state of its vigor to the extent that the threat may cause, under conducive circumstances, a number of the weaker states to disintegrate. The Islamic political worldview, one should remember, lacks a sense of sovereignty that coincides with defined territory. Wherever the believer is, the *ummah* is; hence, the *ummah* theoretically does not recognize the sanctity under law of national borders. This makes Islamism a transnational phenomenon *par excellence* with all that implies for the security of regional regimes.

Despite its tendency to cause political fragmentation, Islamism is inclusivist. Islamism abhors anarchy because the unity of the *ummah* is the supreme social value in Islam. So Islamism seeks to reintegrate the fragmented secular system into a reconstituted political community based on the broader allegiance of faith. The exercise of brute power in its creation notwithstanding, Islamist inclusivism demonstrates a concern for social improvement. It is ethnic nationalism that is truly exclusivist.

It is commonly assumed that ethnic nationalism is dependent on some visible, observable characteristics that separate peoples into national groupings—such as language, culture, history, territory, and so on. There is ample evidence that ethnic nationalism in fact may be grounded in the psychological perception of historical wrongs woven over time into the fabric of a community's social mythology.[2] The anachronistic belief in historical wrong passed along atavistically from the culture of one generation to the culture of the next defines the enduring identity of a community vis-à-vis the outside. Once frozen into uncompromising political attitudes, this belief perpetuates the distinction between *we* and *they*. Whereas religious nationalism aspires to the largest possible political community because of its universalizing ideology, ethnic nationalism maintains an aloof position toward the outside because of its typical minority attitudes of distrust, fear, apprehension, secrecy, demonization of the "enemy," and so on. For this reason, ethnic nationalism usually manifests itself in separatist and/or irredentist activities against the state.

But this does not mean that ethnic nationalism necessarily considers the secular state illegitimate per se. Rather, the secular state is viewed as an emanation of historical oppression. Ethnic nationalism seeks therefore to shelter the "nation" from secular depredations by claiming sovereignty over parts of the secular state which it designates an ancestral "homeland." And so it is clear, from the ethnonational point of view, that ethnicity provides the fundamental condition of nationhood upon which the nation bases its inalienable right to self-determination in its territorial homeland.

On the other hand, ethnic communities may also form national minorities within a state. While national minorities may possess the potential for a separate political identity, their designated status as such satisfies the immediate communal need for sociocultural autonomy within a larger secular unit. And so ethnic nationalism may also exist within a state without necessarily demanding the attendant accoutrements of political power.

The present tensions between the Kurds and the Turks over the question of Kurdistan illustrate one such case where the incompatibility of the concepts of nation and national minority has exacerbated an ancient historical conflict and may have serious repercussions for future regional stability.[3] In the post–Gulf War period the Kurds appear to be taking two major political directions in the four-state border area (Iraq, Iran, Syria, and Turkey) where they represent a demographic majority: they have either agreed to continue to live under Iraqi sovereignty as national minorities with guarantees to their clan leaders of communal autonomy; or they have agitated, through the quasi-Marxist PKK (Kurdish Workers' Party), for an independent Kurdistan to be carved out of Turkish territory.

The separatist thrust of the PKK is particularly troubling to the Turks. The Turks do not recognize the Kurds as a national minority, because they do not recognize a distinct Kurdish ethnicity. Such is the heritage that modern Turkey owes to Mustafa Kemal Atatürk, the founder of the Turkish republic who, by disavowing all claims to former Ottoman possessions after World War I, took the first important step toward the establishment of a secular, civic nationalism; that is, he declared that republican Turkey comprised one nation—the Turks—within one territorial boundary. For this reason Atatürk was loath to recognize the special position of Turks living outside the Turkish republic lest a recrudescence of the "myth" of ethnic nationalism cause the new Turkish republic to be accused of neo-Ottoman imperialism. Historically, republican Turkey has considered the ethnic Turks of the post-WWI Balkans national minorities of the countries in which they resided, a status they were not willing to apply to the Kurds within their own borders.

For the past several decades, Turkey has been seeking full membership in the European Union (EU).[4] Turkey believed that, by virtue of its participation in the 1991 Gulf War, it would finally obtain that goal. Instead Turkey earned yet another rebuff. Since that time Turkey has been actively courting compensatory markets among the Black Sea countries and the Central Asian republics of the former Soviet Union. But more important than the commercial aspect of these demarches, Turkey believes these new relationships also serve politically to stabilize a potentially volatile region. To express the desire for closer political relations with Central Asia, Turkey emphasizes common Turkic affinities. In other words, by treating the Turkmen, Azeri, Kazakh, Kirghiz, and Uzbek peoples as "nations," Turkey uses ethnopolitics for the purpose of stabilization, a policy not substantively different in intent from the one applied to the same region by late nineteenth-century Ottoman Pan-Turkists. In present times, however, this policy has created an internal debate in Turkey concerning the meaning of nationality, which the Kurds, who demand that the Turks also treat them politically as a nation, have begun successfully to exploit. Operation Provide Comfort—called irreverently Statehood by Stealth—certainly enhanced the Kurdish self-perception as a nation when Turkey let the Kurds from Iraq seek shelter in Turkey from Saddam Hussein. To put the predicament in more precise political terms, were Turkey to let the Kurds into the country as a national minority, then it would be open to the same pressure from Balkan Turks. And, since in the Kurds' case, this admission could lead potentially to separatist demands, such a situation would surely compromise Atatürk's concept of civic nationalism, which put the accent on the unitary nature of state and people. So Turkey has hardened its stance against Kurdish ethnonationalism. Moreover, the Kurdish border problem exacerbates the already tenuous conflict over water rights in the Tigris-Euphrates valley with Iraq and Syria, both of which have felt the impact on their foreign relations of a historically festering Kurdish minority problem. Hence, Turkey must face the possibility of conflict with a nonstate actor and/or with one or more contiguous states, two scenarios which threaten the regional stability Turkey seeks so avidly to construct.

The Kurdish PKK aspires to create a state from adjoining Kurdish territories carved out of four contiguous states. Islamism is not interested, on the other hand, in political separatism nor in coexistence with the secular state. Islamism is totalistic. The secular state is an alien body in a purposeful universe, the introduction of chaos into order. The secular state cannot be allowed to exist if God's plan for the universe is to be realized. Whether the challenge emanates from religious or ethnic nationalism, the consequences for the secular state remain essentially the same. Deprived of its legitimacy by the former or of its sovereignty by the latter, the secular state would be unable to operate autonomously in the regional or international system. Under these conditions, the secular state is bound to defend itself against ethnic and religious nationalism, since no state voluntarily commits "politicide."

It is interesting to note that many sociologists, anthropologists, and social psychologists contend that both ethnic and religious nationalism make no essential distinction in the way they act in the world or view their relationships with those who do not share their ideas. One could argue from the psychosocial point of view that religious and ethnic nationalisms have both adopted a similar Manichaean, conspiratorial, and reactionary approach to secular political society. And yet, any similarities between ethnic and religious nationalism in the Middle East are in the long run superficial. Inasmuch as Islamism recognizes no higher form of sociopolitical organization than the *ummah*, it considers all ethnic identification a form of degraded tribalism that submission to the higher values of Islam is supposed to supersede and destroy. Ethnic nationalism of any kind and Islamism therefore cannot coexist because they are mutually exclusive on the ideological level. This signifies that, practically speaking, if ethnic nationalism and Islamism give the impression of sometimes making common cause against a secular enemy, they will end up, in the final analysis, competitors for political power.

The Process of Integration
Some Observations on the Gulf Cooperation Council and the Arab Maghrib Union

The very same states whose integrity is presently being threatened by the process of fragmentation are vigorously pursuing the antidote of regional socioeconomic integration. The Arabs have traditionally conceived of the process of socioeconomic integration both as an instrument of mutual benefit and as a way to attain some of the political goals of Pan-Arab unity. And yet socioeconomic integration, like the process of fragmentation, may lead to unexpected stress on the Middle Eastern secular state system and could, under propitious circumstances, lead also to conflict.

Integration has come to have a definite and rather restricted meaning in the contemporary Middle East. It has always been a tenet of Pan-Arabism, and in particular its Baathist variant, that the independent Arab states should endeavor to merge politically by yielding their individual sovereignties in the service of forming a union of Arab nations. The notion that the Arabs are one people, one society, and one body politic, upon which this tenet is based, draws its special force and direction from the vision of the Muslim universe in which the Arabs' place as messengers of the Islamic revelation was a privileged one. Yet, apart from the fictive unity of the classical Arabo-Islamic empire, there is no historical precedent for the integration of the Arabs into a superstate. The most prominent Pan-Arab unionists, of whom Gamal Abd al-Nasser represented the zenith and Muammar Qadhafi the nadir, desacralized the Islamic content of this vision to put it at the service of the reconstitution of the postcolonial Arab political order. Throughout its checkered history, Pan-Arab unionism has been subjected to a competition among its most powerful advocates to determine which would have the honor of organizing political integration under the aegis of its own one-state nationalism. The winner temporarily enjoyed the privilege of directing the Arab politico-military effort against the former colonial powers and Israel, their imputed surrogate. Romantic and negative, Pan-Arab unionism served, in secular terms, the same purpose Islamism served in religious terms: it protected the *ummah*, however narrowly conceived in the secular sense, from its enemies and defended it from further disintegration, rather than providing the foundation for progressive, forward-looking sociopolitical policies; thus, it has furnished the basis for a regional political culture around which Arab regional aspirations as well as frustrations have rallied at the expense of the nation-building enterprise. In the final analysis, the weight of the Pan-Arab cultural baggage and the internecine struggle between the major Arab players (Egypt, Syria, Iraq, and Libya) for the right to control the Arab destiny did more to impede Arab progress than to promote it.

Political unionism has certainly failed to meet its objectives despite random attempts to revive it. As a result, the last decade has witnessed a decided turn toward maximizing the power of Arab economic resources in the interest of unity. This shift of emphasis was presaged by the initial success of the Organization of Petroleum Exporting Countries (OPEC) when in 1973 it used petroleum as a weapon of coercion against the West for its perennial support of Israel. The resulting wealth that began to accumulate presented a number of unforeseen problems to the oil-rich Arab nations, particularly in the realm of migratory labor practices, internal and Gulf security, regional and international aid, territorial disputes, and so on, and required coordination on levels previously deemed inappropriate to countries usually highly suspicious of each other. The Gulf Cooperation Council (GCC) was created in 1981 to satisfy this need for coordination. But once again, the impulse of this initial integrative effort was directed inward rather than outward and was more an effort to redefine the status of each individual country vis-à-vis the other in a regional arrangement than it was to establish the grounds for a definition of new relationships with the industrialized world. Still, the GCC was the start of a new and important direction for the Middle East.

Since the creation of the GCC the Middle East has undergone some very important transformations. The glut of oil on the global market after 1985 brought the price of petroleum products to an all-time low from which the region has not yet recovered. The weakness of prices forced a severe curtailment of Saudi internal development plans, which in turn affected the economies of those countries most dependent on exporting labor to the Saudi market. In addition to these factors, the Saudi political decision to furlough Arab workers from countries that took a pro-Iraqi position during the Gulf War further exacerbated already critically high levels of regional and global unemployment. The loss of revenues from repatriated workers, accelerating unemployment, the depression of prices for domestic oil production, and a failure politically and economically to react positively to these challenges have threatened the stability of many regional countries, especially Egypt, Tunisia, and Algeria because of their particular vulnerabilities to outside economic conditions.

In Arab North Africa (the Maghrib) the immediate response to the dilemma of the oil-rich Gulf Arabs was increased waves of emigration toward the EU countries and especially France, an emigration which the North African governments endeavored to control since emigration represented for the North African Arab countries a further deterioration in their hard currency balances and a strain on their fragile European economic and political relationships. These governments turned belatedly to liberal economic reforms.

An important reform was put into effect in 1989 when Morocco, Algeria, Tunisia, Libya, and Mauritania agreed to an integration scheme called the Arab Maghrib Union (UMA).[5] Like the GCC, the UMA fulfilled primarily a need to defend the North African regimes collectively from internal dissension and to bargain in strength with the resurgent forces of European unity through a coordination of their foreign policies. The UMA proposed that as an institution only, it could make North Africa more attractive for European trade and investment once the Maastricht Treaty went into effect, lest the EU deny North Africa access altogether to the potentially huge European market. The UMA also proposed that only together could its member nations be in the best position to negotiate emigration policies with the European Union. Furthermore, expanded access to outside markets could be complemented by the creation of an internal market for goods and services in which North African know-how, labor, and manufactures would move unimpeded across national frontiers. Thus, the UMA was meant both to imitate the EU and to protect North Africa from its competition.

Superficially, such movements toward integration appear to be mutually advantageous for their partners. But imbedded in these schemes are some problems which could lead to just the opposite effect. The UMA process implied that the political process be opened to plural political interests for the purpose of national mobilization, not the least of which were the inimical interests of the Islamists, whose charge that the secular state could no longer protect the *ummah* immediately gained a receptive audience. From their unique perspective the Islamists make no distinction between such integrative schemes and the neocolonial conspiracy of the secular West to dominate the Muslim world. To the Islamists, the West uses integrative economic schemes to spearhead further penetration of Arab political structures and to degrade Muslim society under the guise of economic improvement and aid. The Islamists point out that secular regional regimes consent to this conspiracy because they believe that by enhancing the waning political power of their secular, Western-trained and

-oriented elites, these integrative schemes will ultimately forestall the inevitable Islamic revolution. Everything to the mind of the Islamist is a sinister emanation of this collusion. According to the Islamists, secular regimes are reluctant to Arabize their educational curricula completely, for example, not because Arabic does not meet the need for technical training in an economically interdependent world dominated by the EU, but rather because it would advance the Islamization of society. By the same token, the commercial codes that governments must amend to encourage the uniformity of economic exchange are evidence to the Islamists of the regimes' desperate attempts to promote secular law over Islamic law and therefore to cast aspersions on Islam's ability to deal with issues of modernization and socioeconomic progress.

If these problems of domestic stability were not enough to give secular regimes pause for reflection, there exist other issues that beggar the endeavors of these regimes to integrate. Often, the accommodation of vastly different political economies is a daunting task both in terms of the scale of commercial exchange and the compatibility of institutions. Tunisia, for example, has an economy caught up in the throes of privatization but constrained by limited political pluralism under a dominant single party; Algeria, once a guided economy classified as a single-party Arab social democracy, is today also trying to liberalize as the single party withdraws from the public economic domain in the face of strong Islamist pressure; Morocco has a laissez-faire economy as an aspect of the flexible relationship between king, urban bourgeoisie, and a multiparty system; and Libya still flounders under the effect of the anarchy engendered by Colonel Qadhafi when he imposed an extreme decentralization of the economy in the name of the people's "Jamahiriyyan" democracy.

It is unfortunate that such countries cannot afford the luxury of permitting market forces to determine the evolution of a direction and of a pace to their cooperative economic enterprise. Although there are pressing reasons of economic health why these regimes should liberalize by withdrawing from the public domain and thereby make the state more attractive to Western capital, such action is neither congruent with their political cultures nor with the structure of their political economies.

Nor is there much hope that the reforms associated with liberalization will actually take hold. The state will continue to define the necessities of economic restructuring. And the Middle Eastern state, like present-day China, will do so in the belief that economic restructuring can be accomplished without significant political change. This restructuring will oblige the state to push its "internal" boundaries further and further out toward its actual "territorial" borders by means of an even more strenuous mobilization of the population for these new economic structures. And such mobilization has always meant an increase, politically speaking, in the imposition of the state over society. And so the state, through the means of a dominant party, will surely impinge more rather than less on national economic activity.

If the Middle Eastern state succeeds in its mobilizing effort—and there is no guarantee that it will—its success will translate immediately into greater legitimacy at a time when the state needs legitimacy the most. The Islamists, who themselves have an alternative Islamic economic program to promote, will contest this legitimacy because they cannot fail to interpret any return of the state to vigorous economic intervention as a new form of internal colonialization, a sinister way to exploit the people in the name of rationalizing the process of extracting national resources. Hence, it is not difficult to appreciate the wide range of possibilities for conflict that the process of economic integration might some day pose.

Conclusions

To say that the issues presented in this study are being posed in a new and radically different political context is to understate the gravity of the problem, especially with respect to the Middle East. During the past 150 years, the Middle East has been progressively organized under a system that reflected none of its territorial, cultural, social, economic, religious, ethnic, or political realities. The imposition of a Western concept of territoriality, law, and political organization and demeanor on the Middle East was meant to serve the imperial requirements abroad of the colonial powers for stability at home. It was not meant to serve the needs of the colonized peoples for sound government and administration. The result was that even after decolonization, inasmuch as the structures put in place by the West have been largely left intact but not politically and culturally internalized, the problems of the Middle East continue to be analyzed within a frame of reference that pertains solely to the Western nation-state. Hence, it remains both alien to the region and to its political culture. For the West this signifies that our Eurocentric concept of the Middle East is no longer valid. Where once we viewed the Middle East as an extension of our own political worldview, we are now obliged to view the Middle East in its own terms and to rethink its meaning accordingly. Where once the Middle East was defined solely in terms of the relationship between the nation-state and the alliance systems of the two global superpowers, today the disintegration of the Soviet Union and the resurgence of ethnic and religious nationalism have restored a degree of autonomy to regional politics. Ethnic and religious nationalism has weakened the hold of the nation-state on Middle Eastern society, given Middle Eastern boundaries a new functional and psychological equivalence, and has thus enlarged those boundaries to include areas such as Central Asia, which hitherto had been subsumed under other definitional rubrics.

The cases of fragmentation that this study has analyzed represent only the most salient examples of a trend that appears to be growing progressively more disruptive since the Soviet Union collapsed. Fragmentation is today proliferating with particular vehemence in such areas on the periphery of the contemporary Middle East as in the Caucasus, where Abkhazians are fighting Georgians, in Nagorno-Karabakh, where Azeris and Armenians continue to murder each other, and in the former Soviet Central Asian republics, where tensions are high between the local Turkic peoples and the minority Slavs. In these selfsame areas, we not only find that the imposition of Soviet rule has masked older, more historically entrenched rivalries, but also that Islamist movements are making a bid to play a predominant role in the political disposition of the now newly independent ex-Soviet republics. Yet, anybody who has studied Islamic history cannot find this phenomenon particularly odd. The student of Islamic history knows that these areas were once frontier provinces of the classical Arabo-Islamic empire. And, he knows also that no matter which imperial power happened, by dint of circumstance, to impose its power on the peoples of these areas, these people nevertheless underwent the same continuous cycle of ethnoreligious revivalism that has marked the political and cultural history of the traditional Middle Eastern heartland. If then, in the post–cold-war era, we propose, as this study implies, to redefine a region geopolitically according to the specificity of its historical political culture and to the problems particular to that culture rather than to the specificity of contemporary superpower politics, we will have good reason to suggest that the Middle East is in actuality geopolitically expanding.

But the issues of ethnic and religious conflict are not simply problematic for the Middle East; Western Europe will have to face the potential for confrontation among its own ethnic minorities that Serb, Croat, and Muslim ethnic nationalisms today portend, to say nothing of the impact that Muslim religiocultural issues are now presently having on the concept of pluralism in France and Germany, where the concentration of Middle Eastern Muslim immigrants is the highest on the European continent. Moreover, we would do well to assess in the light of its global impact the most recent instance of religious nationalism in Asia, where pressures between Muslims and Hindus over the political disposition of Kashmir has been building ever since the retreat of the British from the subcontinent. In a word, the entire global system is presently being shaken—and more vigorously than in times of superpower competition—by the continuation of instability in peripheral areas. And such instability can have important repercussions for the understanding of future US security requirements in a political environment that has yet to be satisfactorily defined.

Neither is the hope by any means assured that the integrative process will lead to a lessening of tensions. For if the fragmentation of the Middle East poses imponderable quandaries, the same can be said for the process of integration since we cannot be certain that the inevitable relinquishing of national sovereignty necessary to make supranational, nongovernmental organizations of economic unification function efficiently will actually produce the stability we anticipate. The consolidation of European unity through the implementation of the Maastricht Treaty will certainly be a formidable task. Can such a task be any less formidable for the North American Free Trade Agreement or for other nascent organizations of economic union in less advantaged parts of the world?

The simultaneous fragmentation and integration of the Middle Eastern environment point to a substantially different typology of regional conflict. The chances are extremely slim that the US military may have to fight future classical conventional actions of limited duration against Middle Eastern rogue states such as Iraq. It is much more probable that US forces will be engaged in protracted operations against nonstate actors whose religious or ethnic nationalism threatens to destroy states such as Saudi Arabia or Egypt, the survival of which is a core interest of the United States. Such operations will present the same kind of problems that the US military had to face in Somalia—operations that will be conducted without the benefit of front lines, clearly identifiable enemies, or a well-defined end-state.

There is no doubt that such nonstate actors are prepared to make maximum efforts to obtain their ends. Under these conditions, it is axiomatic that US responses be predicated on appropriate and accurate analyses and that these analyses be free of the kind of thinking that depicts Middle Eastern conflict in monolithic, civilizational terms.[6] Monolithic thinking fits well the paradigm of a Jominian military that seeks to concentrate its force against the enemy in the belief that the existence of a single center of strategic gravity presupposes a single node of tactical pressure and therefore the possibility of a decisive engagement. But it will not suffice as an answer to the requirement that the United States military adjust itself to the new political environment in this volatile part of the world. The Middle Eastern conflictual environment is simply too complex and too rich in contradiction to be managed by reducing conflict to monocausal factors. Each manifestation of conflict in the Middle East must be dealt with on its own merits. And before any successful response to conflict can be made, flexible examination of the issues must be renewed with vigor and paired to an appropriate configuration of military force.

Notes

1. For an analysis of the Hamas organization in the context of the Arab-Israeli political arena, see Lewis Ware, "LIC in the Middle East," in Stephen Blank et al., *Responding to Low-Intensity Conflict Challenges* (Maxwell AFB, Ala.: Air University Press, 19 December 1990), 5–22.

2. An excellent discussion of these points may be found in D. B. Vought, "Ethnic Conflict: The Invariable in the Human Condition" (Unpublished paper, International Studies Association-South, Maxwell AFB, Ala., October 1993).

3. The consequences of Turkish ethnopolitics toward the Kurds and other Balkan peoples are well documented in Gareth M. Winrow, "Turkey and the Balkans: Regional Security and Ethnic Identity" (Unpublished paper, 27th Middle East Studies Association annual meeting, Research Triangle Park, N.C., 11–14 November 1993). My discussion of this issue is based on Professor Winrow's analysis.

4. For purposes of this paper, I will use "EU" to include members of the European Economic Community, the European Community, and the newly named European Union.

5. For a general introduction and appraisal of the UMA, see Oussama Romdhani, "The Arab Maghrib Union," *American-Arab Affairs*, no. 28 (Spring 1989): 42–49. An excellent analysis of attempts at regional unification prior to the creation of the UMA may be found in Mary-Jane Deeb, "Inter-Maghribi Relations Since 1969: A Study of the Modalities of Unions and Mergers," *The Middle East Journal* 43, no. 1 (Winter 1989): 20–34.

6. See the article by the distinguished political scientist Samuel P. Huntingdon, "The Clash of Civilizations," *Foreign Affairs*, Summer 1993. Lauded by some as "the 'X' article of the post–Cold War era" and condemned by others, Huntingdon's views were the subject of a collective response by a number of well-known scholars. See Jeane Kirkpatrick et al., "The Modernizing Imperative," in *Foreign Affairs*, September/October 1993, 22–26.

Regional Study 2
Security Issues in the Former Warsaw Pact Region

Dr Paul Hacker

Few events of our time have caught the imagination and had such profound significance as the collapse of the communist system in Eastern Europe and the USSR. The democratic revolutions of 1989 in Eastern Europe, the disintegration of the Warsaw Pact in early 1991, and the breakup of the USSR later that year were developments that profoundly altered the security picture in Europe. This essay considers some of the most significant problems faced in the former Warsaw Pact region. Considered broadly, these include the following: (1) most crucially, how to consolidate democracy in Russia and to promote a new set of relations with the former Soviet republics in conditions of internecine wars, perceived threats from Islamic extremists, and economic breakdown; (2) how to achieve the coexistence of different nationalities occupying the same territory in many countries in the region; and (3) how to overcome the legacy of over four decades of communist rule and subservience to the former USSR in Eastern Europe while developing a new set of ties to the West that will enhance security throughout the Continent.

Russia

Developments in Russia will continue to exert significant influence not only in the former Soviet republics, but in Eastern Europe as well. Upheavals, marked most graphically by the military assault on the Russian White House on 4 October 1993, have yet to take their course. Russia faces all the problems of its former East European allies—including the need to develop stable democratic structures, transform to a market economy, clean up the environment, reorient and downsize its military, and correct other problems. While Russia's immediate postindependence orientation seemed to be heavily slanted toward the West, subsequent developments suggest that a more nuanced and balanced policy has evolved. Russian president Boris Yeltsin has appropriated some of the rhetoric of his nationalist rivals in championing the interests of the 25 million Russians inhabiting the other republics, especially regarding such issues as citizenship in the Baltic states. Russia has also asserted a leadership role in preserving security in the republics. The foreign policy doctrine released in December 1992 calls for cooperation with the West but notes that Western states may have interests that diverge from those of Moscow.[1] The document even suggests that the US might seek to replace Russia as the principal security guardian over the Commonwealth of Independent States (CIS) under the guise of "mediatory and peacekeeping efforts."[2] Russia's shying away from meaningful action against Serbia in the Bosnian conflict is also a sign of its reluctance to become too closely associated with Western views.

Future Role for the Russian Military

A major problem for the Russian military has been to restructure for a world of peace and to find a new mission. The prospect of fighting a war in Western Europe or of using military force to keep control of Eastern Europe has been superseded by the need to protect Russian interests in the former Soviet republics. Rapidly deployable airborne troops and peacekeeping units, rather than the vast tank armies assembled in the past, are the order of the day. This section looks at some of the major issues involving Russia's armed forces.[3]

Under Soviet rule, Russia's armed forces had a proud tradition. As one analysis described it, the Soviet Union, like Prussia before it, was not so much a country with an army as an army that used the entire country as its own billeting area.[4] With its good pay, prestige, and perks the officer profession was highly sought after. Five million strong at its peak in 1988 (all Soviet forces), the Russian army has dwindled to an estimated 1.5 million members, with another 770,000 now serving in the armed forces of the various republics.

The Russian military today suffers from postempire hangover. Its officer corps has been reduced to an impoverished, disunited, and often homeless mass. Some 595,000 troops have been pulled back from Eastern Europe and the Baltic states since 1989; of these, some 180,000 have no permanent housing. By the end of 1993, according to one estimate, the number of officers (630,000) will actually exceed the number of enlisted (544,000) because of difficulties in meeting draft requirements.[5] The military industry that supported the Soviet military has been confronted with the need to massively restructure for civilian use. Military spending, in real terms, has fallen 78 percent since 1989; arms procurement fell 68 percent between 1991 and 1992 alone, while military research and development (R&D) was reduced by half.

One of the most important problems that Russia must face is the lack of real civilian control over the military. The army has been drawn into politics by the unsettled circumstances of the country, especially its weak institutions. A kind of praetorianism has developed in which the military acts on its own rather than as an agent of civilian authority. The army is also affected by the fact that it has been stripped of its mission—it is no longer the "defender of socialism against world imperialism," it is distrusted by its own people, and it lacks political guidance. Senior military officers, feeling that the Russia they are sworn to defend has been debased to a second-rate power and, maintaining a residual fear of the capabilities of the US and its allies, have demanded an end to certain concessions that have included hasty withdrawals from the Baltic states, the idea that the East European states could easily join NATO, and especially, surrender to Japanese demands to surrender the four Kurile islands occupied by Soviet troops in 1945.

New Military Doctrine

Russia has revised its military doctrine, but in a way that is consistent with the military's view of the world and its needs therein.[6] The new doctrine abandons the first use of nuclear weapons, which had been a declared Soviet policy for decades and is a bow to the fact that Russian conventional forces are not as overwhelmingly superior to those of potential adversaries as they once were. The doctrine denies that Russia is faced with any specific threats or enemies and redirects military efforts to dealing with local wars and regional conflicts (i.e., those on Russia's borders) through smaller, mobile units. Significantly, among the threats to Russian security that the doctrine foresees are not only such traditional ones as territorial claims on Russia, local wars, attacks using weapons of mass destruction, and the proliferation of such weapons but also the "suppression of the rights, freedoms and legitimate interests of the citizens of the Russian Federation in foreign states."[7]

Monroesky Doctrine

Blueprint for Future Intervention?

There is ample evidence that current Russian officials persist in thinking about their country and its security situation in classical terms of spheres of influence—a notion that has been referred to as a Russian "Monroesky Doctrine." No less an authority than Foreign Minister Andrei Kozyrev, writing in the *Washington Post* just a week after the bloody events in Moscow that nearly toppled his president, argued that the West must accept the legitimacy of a Russian role in the "near abroad" countries of the CIS:

> Protection of legitimate rights of the millions of Russian-speaking minorities in the former Soviet republics, the economic reintegration of the republics and peacemaking activities in conflict areas: All of these are an objective necessity. Just as a relapse into imperial politics would lead to a repetition of the Yugoslavia scenario in the former Soviet Union, so too would renunciation by Russia of its proper role. . . . [A]ssistance to Russia in implementing its peacekeeping mission in the post-Soviet space—is precisely the formula for partnership with Russia.[8]

A more forthright view was voiced by Professor Andranik Migranyan, Russian foreign affairs expert and Yeltsin advisor, who argued that in view of the Russian presence in the new republics and the arbitrary nature of borders and questionable legitimacy of some of the regimes, "Russia should declare to the world community that the whole geopolitical space of the former USSR is a sphere of its vital interests and should say openly that it is opposed to the formation of any closed military-political alliances by the former Union republics, either with one another or with those countries that have an anti-Russian orientation and that it would regard any steps in this direction as unfriendly."[9] Migranyan defended this concept against charges that it represented a form of great power chauvinism by recalling that the US itself has stated that many regions of the world constitute a zone of vital interests. Yeltsin himself also suggested that the UN should grant Russia special powers to protect peace and stability in the region of the former Soviet Union.[10]

One Russian military writer noted that the idea is widespread in the military that some sort of Russian-dominated union will be reconstituted in the near future and that it is unnecessary to withdraw behind Russian borders since the military will simply be moved back in the near future. He also quoted Defense Minister Pavel Grachev as having told his colleagues in an internal briefing that a decision had been made not to pull back to Russia's borders but to maintain forces outside them, especially in Central Asia and the northern Caucasus.[11] Thus, the issue of whether Russian forces are truly engaged in peacekeeping—a function that is acceptable to the West—or in finding a thin veneer to reconstitute Russian domination over the former Soviet republics remains an open question. As one journalist summed it up, "Russian forces are regarded as saviors in Tajikistan, revanchists in Moldova, occupiers in the Baltic nations, and interventionists and liars in Georgia."[12]

The Former Soviet Republics

In his own country, Gorbachev's reforms released forces he was unable to control, resulting in the aborted coup against him in August 1991, which was followed shortly thereafter by the breakup of the USSR into separate republics. While the coup was the immediate cause of the breakup of the USSR, that process was a long-term one made inevitable by conflicts among various nationalities that became more apparent as the lid was lifted and by resentment against Russian domination.

The breakup of the USSR was sealed by the 1 December 1991 referendum in Ukraine in which voters overwhelmingly approved independence. Without Ukrainian participation, both Russian president Boris Yeltsin and Soviet president Mikhail Gorbachev agreed that the continuation of the USSR would be impossible. On 8 December 1991, meeting in the Belarusian capital of Minsk, Yeltsin, Ukrainian president Leonid Kravchuk, and Belarusian president Stanislav Shushkevich agreed to form the new Commonwealth of Independent States as a loose coordinating body for the former Soviet republics. Later that month, in Almaty, Kazakhstan, a total of 11 of the original 15 republics (without Georgia and the Baltics) signed a protocol making all the 11 republics cofounders of the CIS.

Collective Security in the Former USSR

In Minsk, the issue of disposition of the Soviet armed forces was addressed. It was agreed that each republic could found its own army and that nuclear weapons would remain under unified command. It was agreed that the Russian president would maintain primary authority over nuclear weapons—then based in Ukraine, Kazakhstan, and Belarus, as well as Russia. The other three states, expressing their intention to become nonnuclear powers at a future unspecified date, would have veto power over Russian use of those weapons. Each of the republics, starting with Ukraine, then moved to build their own armies.

The question of the security system encompassing the CIS is still an evolving one. Initial Russian attempts to retain control over unified armed forces failed by early 1992 (except for Russian control over strategic nuclear forces belonging nominally to the CIS). By May of that year, a Treaty on Collective Security was signed in Tashkent by the republics of Russia, Kazakhstan, Tajikistan, Armenia, Uzbekistan, and Kyrgyzstan. This was followed up by the CIS charter signed January 1993, to which Belarus and Turkmenistan also acceded. The charter contains a number of obligations in the field of mutual assistance and cooperation in the field of defense and security, but could not be characterized as a new defense alliance.[13] Ukraine remained "noticeably absent," fearing that the arrangement might become a fig leaf for reimposition of Russian control. In October 1993, Georgia, under duress of civil war, also joined the collective security arrangement. The treaty provides for coordination of efforts in the defense field.

Ukraine

Ukraine, with 54 million inhabitants, about a fifth of whom are ethnic Russians, and with the largest nuclear arsenals in the world after those of the US and Russia as well as substantial parts of the former Soviet military industrial complex, is a special case of post-Soviet security. As described in the *New York Times*, the country has a total of 1,656 nuclear warheads and 176 strategic missiles—more than France, the United Kingdom (UK), and China combined. The newspaper also noted that Ukrainian president Leonid Kravchuk had decided to retain 46 SS-24 missiles left over from the Soviet arsenal (the republic also has 130 SS-19 missiles and 41 nuclear bombers with about 600 warheads). Kravchuk had first agreed to dismantle all nuclear weapons on Ukrainian territory, ratify the 1991 Strategic Arms Reduction Treaty (START), and become a nonnuclear state, then hedged on his promises and finally signed an agreement in Moscow with visiting US president Bill Clinton and Russian president Yeltsin on 12 January 1994 committing his country to dismantle its nuclear arsenal in return for economic compensation. Kravchuk has stated that he would try to convince the Ukrainian Parliament to take up the issue again, but the final outcome remains uncertain.[14]

Another area of contention was the Crimea, which was transferred from Russia to Ukraine in 1954. Under former vice president Aleksandr Rutskoi, the Russian Parliament passed a resolution demanding that the Crimea be returned to Russia. Adding to the tension is the fact that the majority of the area's population is Russian (the Crimea voted by a small majority in favor of Ukrainian independence in 1991). Closely related to the Crimea issue is dissonance over the disposition of the Black Sea fleet. In 1992, the Russian and Ukrainian presidents agreed to split the fleet, but this measure has proved difficult to implement in practice. Because of the lack of a suitable Russian harbor in the region, some have suggested that the Russians lease the Crimean port of Sevastopol, which is the fleet's home port. The Russians rejected the idea. There are also tensions with the Crimean Tatars, deported in 1944 by Stalin as "security risks," over Russian failure to provide essential oil deliveries, and Russian fears over Ukrainization of the schools.

The nuclear issue is a reflection of larger insecurities in Ukraine's relationship with Russia, as well as the feeling that possession of nuclear weapons (even without the codes necessary to launch them) makes Ukraine (which nominally has the third largest nuclear arsenal of any state in the world) a force to be reckoned with. Retention of nuclear weapons is seen as a bargaining chip that will not be given away cheaply. These insecurities include uncertainty over the loyalty of the 60,000 Russian officers (out of 100,000 officers in the Soviet army stationed in Ukraine) who remained with the new Ukrainian army and took a loyalty oath to it.[15] While US officials, from President Clinton down, have urged the Ukrainians to proceed with earlier-announced intentions to give up the weapons (which some experts suggest are a wasting asset that is difficult to maintain and dangerous to store), some other observers have countered that only by keeping its own nuclear weapons can Ukraine provide an effective deterrent against a potential nuclear or conventional Russian attack.[16]

Ukraine in early 1994 was also a country in difficult economic straits; inflation was running at a rate of up to 100 percent a month, energy production had nearly collapsed, and many factories were idle or operating at under 30 percent of capacity. Before independence, about 30 percent of Ukraine's gross domestic product (GDP) came from the defense industry. It is heavily dependent on Russian energy imports. Its exports (chiefly coal and steel) are collapsing under the weight of bureaucratic red tape, and it is therefore unable to pay the high prices demanded by Moscow for oil.[17]

The Baltic States

The Baltic states were incorporated into the Soviet empire in 1940 by brute force and remained there until the collapse of the attempted coup in August 1991 in Moscow allowed the declaration of independence of all the republics of the USSR. Thus, it is not surprising that as Atis Lejins of the Latvian Institute of International Relations recently put it, "It must be clearly stated that the Baltics see the greatest threat to their security emanating from Moscow."[18] In his view, this threat is not simply historical but represents a continuation of previous policies adapted to new circumstances. Lejins noted that the official Russian foreign policy conception published in the *Diplomatichesky Vestnik* in February 1993 stated that while Russia seeks good relations with the Baltic states, it will need to retain strategic sites in the Baltics and must defend the rights of Russians living there. In negotiations in Jurmala, Latvia, for example, the Russians proposed in May 1993 that the Skrunda early warning site remain until the year 2003 (supposedly to allow time to build a replacement), the Ventspils Sigint station until 1997 (ostensibly for the same reason),[19] and the Liepaja naval base until 1999. This determination to keep the sites was reportedly repeated by Russian defense minister Grachev in an internal briefing to officers on 14 September 1993.[20] Russian leaders depict the Latvians and Estonians as violators of human rights because they are trying to restrict the political rights of the Russian-speaking population, most of which moved in after the 1940 annexations.

Lejins also quoted with some trepidation the paper of Dr Karaganov, deputy director of the European Institute of the Soviet Academy of Sciences at a seminar in Moscow on 6 October 1992. Karaganov set out the thesis that Russia must protect not only Russians living in the republics but also those members of the indigenous population who are eastern rather than western oriented. Russians should not be allowed to emigrate to Russia from the republics, an investment program should be instituted that would create Russian political and economic enclaves in the new states, the Russian language should be actively promoted in schools and media, and the Baltic states should immediately grant Russians full citizenship rights.[21] He argued that Russia should have the right to intervene to restore order in the ex-Soviet republics.[22]

One legacy of the half-century of Soviet occupation of the Baltic states is the influx of Russian settlers and their offspring. While in Lithuania the percentage of Russians in the local populace has been held to about 10 percent, the figure goes to some 30 percent in Estonia and over a third of the population in Latvia. Attempts of the indigenous governments to limit the voting rights of mainly Russian outsiders, while understandable from the historical viewpoint, have been harshly criticized not only by Russian officials but also by Western human rights organizations. An estimated 25,000 Russian troops remain in Estonia and Latvia; those in Lithuania were withdrawn at the end of August 1993.[23]

Moldova and the "Trans-Dniestr Republic"

When elections were held in December 1991 in Moldova (much of which was the Romanian province of Bessarabia until annexed by the USSR in 1940), they had no effect in the areas of Dniestr Moldova (on the left bank of the Dniestr River abutting Ukraine) and Gagauzia, between Ukraine and Romania in the south. Separate elections were held in these areas and a breakaway republic in Dniestr Moldova declared its independence. A major concern of the Russians who form the basis for the separatist movement is fear that Moldova will rejoin with Romania and that Russians will face second-class status. Clashes erupted in March and June 1992 when Moldovan president Snegur attempted to reassert Moldovan authority in Trans-Dniestr. The Russian side received the support of the Russian Fourteenth Army stationed in the republic. While the Russian government publicly supports the territorial integrity of Moldova and has sent a separate peacekeeping force to the area, it has been unable or unwilling to control the activities of the popular Lt Gen Alexandr Lebedev, the Fourteenth Army's commander, who was previously praised by Russian president Boris Yeltsin but who fiercely criticized Yeltsin's decision to use force against his political opponents in Moscow in October 1993. Lebedev would like to see the Moldovans recognize the independence of the breakaway Trans-Dniestr republic. That he has been able to maintain himself despite his opposition to Yeltsin's policies suggests that there are definite limits to Moscow's control over some of its more assertive military leaders in the field.[24] When Snegur visited Moscow a few days after Yeltsin crushed the hard-liners in Moscow, he was snubbed by the Russian president, one of whose aides added salt to the wounds by announcing that Trans-Dniestr had received about $30 million in cheap energy and raw material imports from Russia during the first nine months of 1993.[25]

Georgia

Georgia declared its independence as early as April 1991, even before the breakup of the USSR. An outspoken nationalist, Zviad Gamsakhurdia, was elected president the following month, but he soon lost support when he began to use dictatorial methods to deal with opponents. He also attempted to tamper with the political autonomy granted the Moslems of South Ossetia in the north. When tensions rose, riots, shootings, and demonstrations took place, ending with the president's departure from the country in January 1992. He subsequently returned, however, to his power base in western Georgia and attempted to stage a comeback. When Eduard Shevardnadze took over as Georgia's head of state later that year, he was faced with insurrections by forces loyal to Gamsakhurdia and separatists who took over South Ossetia (wanting to join it with North Ossetia in Russia) and the Abhkazia region that abuts it on the Black Sea. Shevardnadze reluctantly appealed to Russia for military assistance. The assistance was granted, but the price Shevardnadze reluctantly paid—bringing Georgia into the CIS on 8 October 1993—was too much for many of the 5.5 million Georgians to bear. Some, such as Defense and National Security Parliamentary Committee chairman Nodar Natadze, called the action "treason." Many other Georgians regard their country's independence as strictly limited, with foreign and especially defense policy under strong Russian influence.

Agreements on mutual defense that were signed with Russia will allow Russian troops to remain in Georgia indefinitely, despite the fact that the Georgian parliament had voted earlier in 1993 to send all Russian troops out of the country by 1995.

The agreements allowed Russia the right to maintain bases in key areas, including the Black Sea port of Poti. There is strong suspicion that the Russians were aiding separatist elements in order to have their own say over events in Georgia. It is certain that some of the separatists involved were aided by Russian troops with manpower and equipment, but it is not entirely clear whether that aid was given at the direction or with the connivance of Moscow. One can also recall the fact that Russian defense minister Grachev, speaking in 1993, had said flatly that Russia could not risk leaving Abkhazia because this would mean "losing the Black Sea."[26] Meanwhile, the fighting has been great in its economic and human toll, as hundreds of thousands of refugees fled the fighting (250,000 were driven out of Abkhazia).

Armenia and Azerbaijan

Armenia and oil-rich Azerbaijan have been fighting over the disposition of Nagorno-Karabakh, a mostly Armenian enclave inside Azeri territory, since 1988. When riots in the area did not induce a demanded transfer of the territory to Armenian control, it was placed under direct rule by Moscow from July 1988 to December 1989. A drive then began to push Azeris out of both Armenia and Karabakh. In 1991 Armenia offered to give up claims to Nagorno-Karabakh in exchange for free elections in the enclave and additional autonomy. Fighting flared up again in early 1992; thousands of people from both sides have been made into refugees. At that time, Armenian forces fighting in the enclave not only extended control over areas formerly held by the Azeris but also carved out a corridor to Armenia allowing direct access between Armenia and the enclave. In late October 1993 Armenian forces seized the last strongholds of Azeri forces in southwestern Azerbaijan; some 20,000 Azeri refugees are estimated to have crossed into Iran.

Azerbaijan's strongly nationalist and anti-Russian president, Abulfez Elcibey, was ousted in 1993 in a bloody coup and replaced by former Politburo member Heidar Aliev. Before he was ousted, Elcibey came under increasing pressure from Russia, which gave aid to Armenian separatists in Nagorno-Karabakh. Surprisingly enough, the Russians in this case helped engineer his ouster not through direct use of their forces but by withdrawing them in May 1993. Their withdrawal emboldened the Armenians to resume the offensive and thus pave the way for Elcibey's replacement by a more pro-Russian leader. Aliev was formally elected president in October. Aliev, who expressed readiness to join the CIS in September 1993, has also tried to use economic inducements to Russia to intervene in the Nagorno-Karabakh dispute with Armenia, including a reduction in the share of oil fields to be prospected by Western firms in order to give more of a share to Russian companies. Some reports suggest that Aliev has also assured the Russians the right to base troops in his country, including on the border with Iran, in return for support against Armenia.[27]

Tajikistan

Situated as it is on the northern border of Afghanistan, Tajikistan represents the southern outpost for Russian security in stopping the influx of militant Islam. Since December 1992, Tajikistan has been controlled by a government led by former Communists.[28] The government took over after a bloody civil war with tens of thousands being killed. The strife was motivated more by clan and regional loyalties than by interethnic disputes or a fight between Communism and Islamism. All parties were banned, including the Islamic Renaissance Party, a moderate partner in a previous coalition. More radical Islamic fundamentalists are continuing a guerrilla campaign against the government and receive support from Saudi Arabia, Sudan, and Pakistan, but especially from Afghan guerrillas wanting to avenge the Russian occupation of their country in the 1980s. Some 20,000 Russian troops of the 201st Motorized Rifle Division and a border guard unit are based in the republic of 5.7 million inhabitants. Russia pays 70 percent of the republic's budget (25 percent more than before 1991).[29] Russian foreign minister Andrei Kozyrev explained that the reason for the presence of Russian forces was to provide a "shield against the spread of regional and clannish Islamic extremism in Central Asia." While Russian fears that Tajikistan will become the first domino to fall to Islamic extremism are not groundless, the larger issue is whether the cure is appropriate to the illness—in other words, whether the choice is simply to succumb to radical Islamic forces or to agree to a restoration of Russian military domination. Meanwhile, the pro-Communist forces have been ruthless in dealing with their opponents, jailing or executing many and closing opposition newspapers.[30]

Kazakhstan

While Kazakhstan president Nursultan Nazarbayev has said his country persists in its intention to go nuclear-free, he has expressed some misgivings afterwards, asking for US, Chinese, and Russian security guarantees. Kazakhstan, however, has signed the Strategic Arms Reduction Treaty (START I) and nonproliferation treaties. The START I treaty was ratified overwhelmingly by the country's parliament during a December 1993 visit by Vice President Al Gore, who also gave Nazarbayev what he wanted—the promise of a summit meeting with President Bill Clinton in 1994 in Washington.

Relations with the Middle East

Relations with Middle Eastern states at the end of 1993 seemed to be developing slowly, being driven primarily by basic economic interests, although with some special circumstances as well. The major players appeared to be Turkey and Iran.

Due to the fact that both countries are neighbors, Iran and Azerbaijan have had what may be the most active contacts in the region between the central Asian republics and Middle Eastern states. Iranian interest stems from the fact that some 15 million of its citizens are of Azeri extraction. Remarks by former Azeri president Elcibey in speaking about a "southern Azerbaijan" in 1992 raised Iranian hackles. The Iranians have not tried to cultivate Azerbaijan as an ideological bridgehead, despite the fact that the republic is predominately Shiite Muslim as is Iran. Iranian interest now is predominately directed at finding a solution for the conflict over Nagorno-Karabakh, given the fact that the dispute has forced thousands of Azeri refugees to flee into Iran as Azeri territory is occupied by Armenian forces, and at promoting economic cooperation, as is the case with other states in the region. Thus, during a visit to Azerbaijan in late October 1993, Iranian president Heshemi-Rafsanjani condemned Armenian actions in the dispute over Nagorno-Karabakh but in subdued tones, calling the "continued aggression . . . regrettable and a source of anxiety."[31] In the economic field, the Iranian president concentrated on promoting economic integration. He carried a similar message to the capitals of other states in the region. The Azeris, for their part, were interested in obtaining as much active support from Iran as possible to stop the Armenian offensive.

While Turkey has a natural interest in promoting ties with the Turkophone countries of the trans-Caucasus and Central Asia, Turkish policy has also been low-key in this regard. Given Turkey's historical enmity to Armenia, it is understandable that the Turkish government has tilted toward Azerbaijan in its dispute over Nagorno-Karabakh. However, the Turks have rejected appeals for a more overt role that would involve committing military force.[32]

Cooperation with other states has developed more slowly. Israel, for example, has extended diplomatic ties to the Central Asian republics and is interested in promoting commercial ties. It has been suggested that if peace should develop in the Middle East, some joint ventures between Israeli and Saudi businessmen in such fields as agriculture and agricultural machinery are not out of the question.

East European States

Beginning with Hungary in mid-1989, the East European states one by one overthrew the Communist regimes that had dominated every aspect of life in the area since the 1940s. The Hungarian case was unique inasmuch as the Communist regime itself began the process of liberalization that it hoped would allow it to return to power in a free election. In Poland, a series of roundtable discussions in early 1989 led to semifree elections later that year. Due to Communist miscalculations, the Communist-led coalition collapsed and non-Communist forces were able to establish Poland's first free government in a half century in the latter half of 1989. In October 1989, as a direct result of its inability to control the flow of its citizens beyond the borders of the Warsaw Pact (Hungary decided in the summer of 1989 not to turn back East German citizens wanting to travel to Austria), the East German regime tried to prolong its vitality by forcing long-time Communist leader Erich Honecker to step down. However, on 9 November, it was forced to open the Berlin Wall and soon lost control of the situation, leading to further changes and the absorption of the country into the Federal Republic of Germany (FRG) on 3 October 1990. In Czechoslovakia, brutal police intervention against a student demonstration on 17 November 1989 commemorating the closing of Czech universities by the Nazis 50 years earlier was the spark that led to a massive outpouring against the regime and forced it to enter into discussions with opposition forces that resulted in the formation of a coalition government the following month, and soon afterward, the removal of all Communists from higher office. In Albania and Bulgaria, the process was similar as ruling Communist parties first replaced their leaders and then engaged in talks with opposition elements that led to the gradual replacement of former leaders by non-Communists. Only in Romania did the process end violently when President Nicolae Ceaucescu was overthrown in a bloody revolt that led to his and his wife's execution by reformist Communist elements constituting a National Salvation Front that remains in power.

Problems of Transformation

The East European states are beset with a number of problems in making the transition to a democratic market-oriented economy. Many voters in East Europe, accustomed as they are to a modicum of social welfare and guaranteed employment, have punished governments that have sought to introduce economic reforms that have placed hundreds of thousands out of work and caused sharp price rises and falls in the standard of living. Movements that piloted their countries from Communist dictatorship toward Western-style democracy have themselves fragmented. The need to restructure economically has been brought home especially in defense industries, whose products no longer find a market. Slovak sensitivities to decisions by the Czech-dominated federal government in Prague to end arms production and exports was one of the factors that contributed to a sense of estrangement that led to the 1993 breakup.

Security and Military Issues

In the security sphere, the East Europeans face a new security equation, both because of the political and territorial changes that have taken place in the past four years as well as the direct impact of the mandate of the Conventional Forces in Europe (CFE) Treaty to reduce conventional armaments and the dictates of economic exigencies. In 1988, for example, Poland had 406,000 of its own troops, a secure eastern border, 58,000 Soviet troops on its own soil, and a western "buffer" comprised of 172,000 East German troops in 11 divisions and 380,000 Soviet troops in 19 divisions. Poland's forces are to be cut to 200,000, facing over a million troops in Russian Kaliningrad (some 400,000 by the end of 1992 and growing), Germany (370,000), Ukraine, Lithuania, and Belarus.[33] The heavy concentration of Russian forces in the Kaliningrad salient causes headaches for the Poles. The area, in the words of one specialist, "has become a giant armed camp with greater combat power than the entire Polish armed forces."[34] While Poland is not even in potential conflict with any of its neighbors, sensitive issues do persist, which include protecting the Polish minority (200,000) in Lithuania and in Belarus (500,000), as well as finding middle ground between Ukraine and Russia.

Czechoslovakia, before its January 1993 separation, had a 10-division force of some 200,000 troops, which was in the process of being cut in half. In late 1993, the Czechs had an estimated 106,000 and the Slovaks 47,000 troops in their separate armies. Five Soviet divisions of 75,000 have now left the country. Hungary had 120,000 troops in 15 brigades in

1988 and four Soviet divisions of 64,000 troops. Hungarian strength is being cut to 75,000. The East European states have sought to deal with their new security situation through mutual consultation and discussions with the West through the European Community (EC)—known since 1 November 1993 as the European Union (EU)—and the North Atlantic Cooperation Council (NACC), which was organized in 1991. They have to deal with the legacies of the past—domination by the USSR, government control of the economy, and closed societies while dealing with issues that have been buried for years. Bulgaria in 1992 signed a friendship treaty with Russia that provides for, among other things, consultations in the event of a crisis threatening their security and pledges not to support aggression against each other.

Nationalities and Minorities

One problem that is widespread throughout the region is that of treatment of minorities and nationalities.[35] None of the states in the region has used the "Yugoslav approach" of civil war to deal with the issue, but it remains a sensitive one in several cases.[36] The Hungarians are the largest minority in the region, with an estimated 3.5 million in Romania alone, including 2 million in Transylvania, 700,000 in former Czechoslovakia (most in Slovakia), 450,000 in former Yugoslavia (most in Serbian Vojvodina), and Ukraine (about 200,000 in Transcarpathia). On the one hand, Hungarians are sensitive to the position of their brethren abroad; on the other hand, neighboring governments are suspicious of Hungarian motives, wondering whether they hide irredentist aims of restoring a greater Hungary that existed before the end of World War I.

In Bulgaria, the Turkish minority of about 1 million (out of 8 million people) was subject to discrimination and repression by the Communist government of Todor Zhivkov from 1984 to 1989. Its right to use its native language was severely restricted, and its people were forced to change their names to Bulgarian ones. After the political turn in the country, the legislation was rescinded and a Turkish-based party, the Movement for Rights and Freedoms, for a time held the balance of power in Parliament. The Bulgarian Socialist Party (ex-Communist) has continued to use the Turkish issue to inflame the public. While the Bulgarian government has tried to remove obstacles to good relations with Turkey, the fear of the former colonial master still exists just below the surface, currently aggravated by the feeling that there is a military imbalance between the two states in Turkey's favor, aggravated by Turkey's close ties to NATO. In Moldova, some 2.8 million persons of Romanian extraction are joined with 600,000 Russians and 562,000 Ukrainians in the Moldovan republic. Another 450,000 Romanians are living in a part of Ukraine that was originally the southern portion of the pre-1940 Romanian province of Bessarabia, then annexed to the USSR. There are also some 200,000 Romanians living in Hungary. Minorities are also scattered elsewhere in the region. In Estonia they amount to 38 percent and Latvia 47 percent of the population (predominately Russians). Some Germans remain in all the Central European countries.

Attempts at Cooperation

Visegrad

The heads of state of Poland, Hungary, and Czechoslovakia in 1990 met in the Hungarian town of Visegrad to discuss a regime of informal collaboration among their countries later called the Visegrad cooperation.[37] The Visegrad Group has established no formal structure or linkages but discussions have ranged over cooperation in economic, political, and security areas. One possible attraction of the Visegrad Group is that it would provide an umbrella under which its members could enter European security or economic cooperation institutions. To be sure, within the participating countries, there is no consensus as to the degree to which the Visegrad cooperation should be advanced. For example, Czech prime minister Vaclav Klaus has been a less-than-enthusiastic supporter, arguing that his Czech republic, independent since 1 January 1993, needs to look west, not east. On the other hand, one Polish observer suggested a number of areas for fruitful cooperation, including military production, and furthering links with Ukraine.[38] Another area of collaboration, in his view, is the increasing problem of illegal immigration; in

Poland, for example, 32,292 illegal aliens were arrested in 1992, compared with 2,407 three years earlier. Poles and Slovaks, in general, place the greatest hopes in the Visegrad process, the Czechs the least, with the Hungarians somewhere in the middle.[39] While the Czechs are looking west, the Slovaks have not settled a simmering problem with Hungary over the construction of the Gabcikovo-Nagymaros dam project on the Danube River. The issue has been mediated by the EC, and its legal aspects will be decided by the Hague Court.

Some Tentative Conclusions and Implications for the US

The security situation in the former Warsaw Pact and ex-USSR region is in a state of transition. The former domination by the USSR of the international environment (as well as the domestic politics) of the East European states has been replaced by a highly uncertain landscape devoid of firm military, political, or economic alliances. The East Europeans are searching for new ways to promote their political and economic stability and to find new guarantees for their security. Throughout the region, there has been a rush to join Western institutions, and disappointment in finding that such organizations as NATO or the EC are not welcoming new members from the East with open arms.

Quite obviously, the security situation in the former USSR is somewhat differentiated from that in Eastern Europe. Russia holds and will continue to hold a dominant position by its size and power. This reality will require a nuanced Western policy that recognizes legitimate Russian interests but seeks to warn Russian leaders away from the tried and tested path of using military force to maintain their sway over the newly independent states. While there has been strong sympathy for the people of the Baltic states, some have criticized the West for putting out of its collective mind less blatant examples of the use of force (or those further from the locus of Western attention) such as Georgia.[40]

As of now, it does not seem that the Russian maximum objective amounts to a full recovery of the strategic losses suffered by the breakup of the USSR and the Warsaw Pact. Its aims in Eastern Europe appear to be more defensive than offensive at this juncture—ensuring that no states join a pact that could be directed against Russian interests rather than seeking to reimpose control over them. As for the ex-Soviet republics, Russia seems more determined to take unilateral measures that will reestablish a strategic presence, although again the desire to guard against destabilization from outside seems to be a strong motivating force, especially in the case of Tajikistan. The Russians, however, have not been reluctant to intervene in other situations where they feel some advantage will accrue—especially in such cases as Georgia. The victory of the protofascist Liberal Democratic Party in the December 1993 elections has made prediction of developments even more obscure. The Western certainty that the country was headed toward democracy and a market economy now deserves rethinking. Indeed, as has happened more than once in the past in other states, Russian developments may also show that market reform and development do not automatically promote political stability, and indeed, may cause a contrary trend.

There will be a fine line for US policy to walk in the future. On the one hand, the US recognizes that the former Soviet republics still constitute an area of important strategic interest for Russia, somewhat in the way Latin America does for the US. The US is by no means unsympathetic to concerns such as the seepage of militant Muslim fundamentalism through such portals as Tajikistan, where the Russian army is already heavily involved. Given the fact that the US public is reluctant to support a US peacekeeping role in Bosnia, in an area much closer to the consciousness of Americans, it is doubtful whether the US could become actively involved in peacekeeping operations in the former Soviet periphery. The obvious response is likely to be "let the Russians do it" and to try to circumscribe the rules of the game as far as possible to preclude a resurgence of imperialism under the guise of peacekeeping. In this connection, however, US levers are likely to be limited, and more in the economic sphere than in the political or military sphere.

While the US is not ready to respond to the plea of the East Europeans for full NATO membership, the security concerns of those states are very much in the minds of American policymakers. While there is no scenario on the horizon for a return to Communist rule of the past (which historically was initiated, by the march of Soviet military power), there is no certainty that these states will have a smooth transition to democracy and a market economy. An activist US policy in the region will be required to ensure that events do not overtake us and get out of hand.

Notes

1. See S. Neil McFarlane, "Russia, the West, and European Security," *Survival* 53, no. 3 (Autumn 1993): 14.

2. Ibid.

3. Michael Gordon, "As Its World View Narrows, Russia Seeks a New Mission," *New York Times*, 29 November 1993, A1.

4. "Russia's Armed Forces: The Threat That Was," *The Economist*, 28 August 1993, 17.

5. Serge Schmemann, "Russia's Army: Now a Shriveled and Volatile Legacy," *New York Times*, 29 November 1993, sec. 1, 7.

6. Serge Schmemann, "Moscow Outlines Doctrine for its Military of the Future," *New York Times*, 3 November 1993. What is described as a "detailed account" of the new doctrine was published in *Rossiskoye Vesti*, which is translated in *Foreign Broadcast Intelligence Service (FBIS)-SOV-93-222-S*, 19 November 1993.

7. Ibid., 3.

8. Andrei Kozyrev, "And Now: Partnership with Russia's Democrats," *Washington Post*, 10 October 1993.

9. Quoted in Milton Kovner, "Russia in Search of a Foreign Policy," *Comparative Strategy* 12, no. 3 (October 1993): 313.

10. Ibid., 314. For an excellent analysis of the evolution of the Russian view of the relationship with the former Soviet republics stressing integration and a "first among equals" role in security matters see John Lough, "Defining Russia's Relations with Neighboring States," *RFE/RL Research Report* 2, no. 2 (14 May 1993): 53–60.

11. Gordon, A6.

12. Steven Erlander, "Troops in Ex-Soviet Lands: Occupiers or Needed Allies?" *New York Times*, 30 November 1993, A6. For a Russian view critical of "neo-Clausewitzian thinking" on the use of military force, see Pavel K. Baev, "Peace-keeping as a Challenge to European Borders," *Security Dialogue* 24, no. 2 (1993): 137–50.

13. See "Russia's Security Concerns to be Met in Cooperation with Newly-Independent States in the Territory of the Former USSR, a Generalized Overview," by Ambassador Shustov (Unpublished paper prepared for the Conference on Europe's Security Futures [subsequently

COESF], Garmisch, Germany, 3–5 June 1993). Shustov depicts the collective security mechanism evolving in the CIS as one which is compatible with cooperation with "Euro-Atlantic security mechanisms" (page 6). See also Ronald M. Bonesteel, "The CIS Security System: Stagnating, in Transition, or on the Way Out?" *European Security* 2, no. 1 (Spring 1993): 115–38.

14. For a discussion of this issue, see "Ukraine President Now Plans to Keep Some Nuclear Arms," *New York Times*, 20 October 1993; and Peter Greier, "U.S. Anxiously Eyes Ukraine Atomic Arsenal," *Christian Science Monitor*, 2 December 1993, 3; also Mary Kaldor, "Everyone Needs Good Neighbors," *The Statesman and Society*, 6 August 1993, 14–15; and Sergi Kiselyov, "Ukraine: Stuck with the Goods," *Bulletin of the Atomic Scientists* 49, no. 2 (1993): 30–33.

15. See Raymond Bonner, "Ukraine: A Nuclear Power but Not an Army of Untested Loyalties," *New York Times*, 2 December 1993, A1.

16. Greier, 3.

17. See Jane Perlez, "Economic Collapse Leaves Ukraine with Little to Trade but Its Weapons," *New York Times*, 13 January 1994, A4.

18. Atis Lejins, "The Baltic Security Dilemma: How to Secure Restored Independence?" (Unpublished paper prepared for the COESF), 2.

19. Ibid., 3.

20. "In Ex-Soviet Lands, Troops Now Find a Mixed Reception," *New York Times*, 30 November 1993, A6.

21. Lejins, 12.

22. Ibid., 13.

23. Michael Gordon, "To Latvians a Single Russian Soldier is Still One Too Many," *New York Times*, 30 November 1993, A6.

24. See discussion in Stuart Kaufman, "The Politics of Russian Military Policy: Continuities and Contrasts from Brezhnev to Yeltsin" (Unpublished paper delivered at the ISAS/South Conference, October 1993), 21–22.

25. See "Bessarabian Homesick Blues," *The Economist*, 30 October 1993, 62.

26. See "Tricked and Abandoned," *The Economist*, 2 October 1993, 56; Daniel Sneider, "Georgia on the Brink as Shevardnadze Turns to Russia," *Christian Science Monitor*, 1 November 1993, 3; and Raymond Bonner, "Pact with Russia Bedevils Georgian," *New York Times*, 9 December 1993.

27. See "The Bear Pauses," *The Economist*, 11 December 1993, 62.

28. See Raymond Bonner, "Why All Eyes Are on a Place Called Tajikistan," *New York Times*, 7 November 1993, sec. 4, 5.

29. See Bonner, "Ukraine," A1.

30. See Raymond Bonner, "Asian Republic Still Caught in a Web of Communism," *New York Times*, 13 October 1993.

31. "Iranian president Heshemi-Rafsanjani Visits; Holds Talks with Aliev," quoted in *FBIS-SOV-93-207*, 28 October 1993, 57. A Russian analysis of Rafsanjani's visit was that "Tehran appears to have decided not to strive to spread its thinking in the Central Asian region, but to forge reciprocally beneficial economic cooperation. . . . The Central Asian governments . . . are very cautious about any efforts to import any ideological influence or thinking from abroad." See "Iranian President's Visit to Central Asia Viewed," quoted in *FBIS-SOV*, 20 October 1993, 90. For a Turkish view of

the region, see Seyfi Tashan, "Caucasus and Central Asia: Strategic Implications" (Unpublished paper prepared for COESF).

32. For an overview of the Azeri-Armenian connection with the Middle East, see William Ward Magos, "Armenia and Azerbaijan, Looking toward the Middle East," *Current History*, January 1993, 6–11. Magos points out that Armenia has been isolated internationally over the Nagorno-Karabakh dispute, but notes that established Armenian communities throughout the Middle East act as an important source of influence in these states.

33. See Jeffrey Simon, "Central Europe: 'Return to Europe' or Descent to Chaos?" *Strategic Review*, Winter 1993, 18–25.

34. Ibid., 20.

35. For a broad overview of the problem of East European minorities, see "That Other Europe," *The Economist*, 25 December 1993, 17–20.

36. See Georg Brunner, "Minority Problems and Policies in East-Central Europe," in John R. Lampe, ed., *East European Security Reconsidered* (Washington, D.C.: Woodrow Wilson Press, 1993), 145–54.

37. For a fuller discussion of East European attempts at cooperation, see David Shumaker, "The Origins and Development of Central European Cooperation," *East European Quarterly* 27, no. 2 (September 1993): 351–73.

38. Henryk Szlajfer, "Central and East European Security Perspectives: Polish View" (Unpublished paper prepared for the COESF), 15.

39. See Miroslav Polreich, "Central European Security Perspectives," (Unpublished paper prepared for the COESF), 9.

40. See Melor Sturua, "Yeltsin's Newest Proconsul" and John R. Hannah, "The (Russian) Empire Strikes Back," both in *New York Times*, 27 October 1993, A13. Quite typically, this fear of Russian intentions extends to Eastern Europe as well. In a 10 December 1993 interview, Polish foreign minister Andzej Olechowski sought a clearer commitment from the US and the West on Poland's request for NATO membership, arguing that the West is "playing into Russia's hands by not seeing the signals of imperial thinking." See Jane Perlez, "NATO Commitment Sought by Poland," *New York Times*, 12 December 1993, A3.

Arms Control and Proliferation

Bradley S. Davis

Over the centuries there have many sincere attempts by mankind to stop, or at least to erect some boundary, to the horrors and lunacy of war. Nations, governments, and religions have built ethical and religious barriers against war; they have outlawed it and set up councils to arbitrate settlements through international law. Countries have tried to withdraw from the threat of war behind the walls of neutrality, or to escape it by practicing isolationism. When these stratagems did not work, they joined with other nations for the collective defense of their peace and security. The rare attempts to control the manufacture, distribution, and use of weapons were seldom successful or lasting. Arms control in its infancy was chiefly the imposition of the will of the victor over the loser of a conflict.

In today's world the spread of nuclear, chemical, and biological weapons, referred to as weapons of mass destruction (WMD), presents a national security challenge of unprecedented proportions for the United States. This challenge is especially true today since the demise of the former Soviet Union and the resulting birth of numerous, independent republics, each searching for its unique identity and an equal place among the world of nations. Without the former Communist government's tight security and positive controls over their WMD, the black market in those weapons is flourishing as third world countries and terrorist organizations around the world acquire them or their components. What possible reason could be advanced to justify a country's pursuing the acquisition or development of WMD, especially newly emerging countries with such fragile economies? Some of the reasons seen from the point of view of the states acquiring these weapons are to counter a perceived threat to their homeland security, to respond to a lack of positive security guarantees, to gain world status and prestige, to heighten a power projection capability within a certain regional area, or to counter a greater power's influence.

The security challenge facing the United States today is twofold. How do we attempt to reduce and eventually eliminate through arms control treaties the number of WMD currently held or being developed by nations around the globe and at the same time strengthen the nonproliferation regimes for arms of all types? This essay briefly reviews the history and the current activity of arms control treaties and agreements and then moves on to a discussion of nonproliferation regimes today. Possible solutions to the problem of WMD proliferation are offered. While WMD include nuclear, chemical, and biological weapons, the emphasis during this discussion, unless noted, is on nuclear weapons.

Arms Control

The activity of arms control can be traced at least as far back as 1817 when the United States and Great Britain concluded one of the most distinguished examples of a voluntarily negotiated and highly successful agreement to control armaments. The Rush-Bagot agreement limited the naval forces each side could have stationed and patrolling on the Great Lakes and Lake Champlain.[1] The International Peace Conferences at The Hague in 1899 and 1907 were the first attempts to approach the problem of war and peace on a worldwide scale. The participating nations recognized that the interests of all nations required their collective action to control modern weapons of war and their ever-increasing and devastating consequences.

The stupendous power unleashed by the use of nuclear weapons at the end of World War II shattered all the old concepts of war and weaponry and imposed a new urgency and demanded new perspectives on international efforts to control nuclear armaments. Since that time there has been a nearly continuous attempt on the part of the United States to limit nuclear armaments. The cold war's superpowers have had an adversarial relationship ripe for arms control agreements since the time the Soviets detonated their first atomic device in 1949. However, a combination of factors has recently brought the problem of arms control to the top of the international priority list. The disintegration of the Soviet Union and subsequent reorganization into new, independent republics frantically searching for recognition and respect in the commonwealth of nations have drastically increased the membership in the infamous "Nuclear Club" (fig. 1).

NUCLEAR CLUB
1994

Acknowledged Members:	United States, Russia, Ukraine, Kazakhstan, Belarus, United Kingdom, France, China
Suspected Members:	India, Pakistan, Israel, South Africa
Past/Present Suspected Aspiring Members:	Algeria, Argentina, Brazil, Iran, Iraq, Libya, Taiwan, North Korea, South Korea

Figure 1

By June 1982 both the United States and the Soviet Union had initiated talks on further agreements beyond the old Strategic Arms Limitation Talks to limit offensive strategic nuclear weapons. Although the early negotiations were somewhat tumultuous, especially after President Reagan's "the Soviet Union is an evil empire" pronouncement, the Strategic Arms Reduction Treaty (START) was finally signed by President Bush and General Secretary Mikhail Sergeyevich Gorbachev in July 1991. Once implemented, START will be the first treaty to actually reduce operational strategic offensive arms and will lead to stabilizing changes to the composition of, and reductions to, the deployed strategic armed forces of each party. The overall strategic nuclear forces in both countries will be reduced 30 to 40 percent, with an accompanying reduction of 50 percent in the most threatening and destabilizing weapon systems. In his letter of transmittal to the Senate for its advice and consent on the newly signed treaty, President Bush commented,

> The START Treaty represents a nearly decade-long effort by the United States and the Soviet Union to address the nature and magnitude of the threat that strategic nuclear weapons pose to both countries and to the world in general. The fundamental premise of START is that, despite significant political differences, the United States and Soviet

Union have a common interest in reducing the risk of nuclear war and enhancing strategic stability.[2]

The United States had several objectives in pursuing this treaty. First, the agreement was intended not simply to limit or cap the number of strategic offensive weapons but to significantly reduce them below current levels. Second, the treaty was designed to allow equality of American forces relative to those of the Soviet Union. Essentially, this meant that equality of military numbers did not require identical force structures; rather, it demanded limits that allowed each party equivalent capabilities. Finally, and perhaps a cornerstone to the entire agreement, was the exacting verification regime specified in the treaty. This verification regime includes exchanges of intercontinental ballistic missile (ICBM) test-launch telemetry tapes, permanent on-site monitoring of mobile missile ICBM assembly facilities, 12 separate types of on-site inspections, cooperative measures, and data exchanges to complement our national technical means of verification.[3] This system of safeguards, confirmed through the use of an extensive list of inspections to intrusively verify Soviet treaty compliance, was absolutely critical to ensure that American national security was not jeopardized. The Soviets, too, would have the right to conduct these inspections to ensure the "wicked" Americans were not cheating.

Unfortunately, the road to peace is very rocky and never easy to accomplish. In August 1991 General Secretary Gorbachev barely survived the abortive coup attempt by Communist party traditionalists, but it did spell the death knell to their crumbling empire. By early 1992 the Union of Soviet Socialist Republics was a part of history. A hope the Americans had held dear for nearly 50 years had unbelievably come true, almost before the nation could react to it. The United States was politically ill prepared for the aftermath of the Soviet Union's demise and for the mad scramble by the newly independent republics to assert their newfound identity. The situation also caused the proverbial wrench to be thrown into the works of the treaty process because the freshly signed START treaty was a bilateral agreement between the United States and a country that now no longer existed! International law permitted the new republics to repudiate and not accept the treaty, something the US government desperately wanted to avoid. Somehow the Bush administration needed to engender a solution to the problem of salvaging the treaty. The first step was actually taken by the new "nuclear republics"; Russia, Kazakhstan, Belarus, and Ukraine. During a 23 May 1992 meeting in Lisbon, the four leaders of the new states, along with the United States, signed a protocol to the START treaty, committing the four states to "make such arrangements among themselves as required to implement the treaty's limits and restrictions, to allow functioning of the verification provisions of the treaty, and to allocate costs."[4] The final part of the protocol stipulated that Russia would accede as the successor of the former Soviet Union to the Non-Proliferation Treaty (NPT) as a nuclear state, while the other three republics would sign and ratify the NPT as nonnuclear states in the "shortest possible time." (This last point will be very important as the discussion unfolds concerning proliferation.) In separate, legally binding letters to President Bush, the leaders of the three nonnuclear countries further guaranteed the total elimination of nuclear weapons from their soil within the seven-year implementation period of START. This meant all tactical nuclear weapons in Ukraine, Belarus, and Kazakhstan would be returned to Russia for decommissioning, and these three republics would also assist in dismantling and removing to Russia all strategic offensive weapon systems and weapons. To complement these steps, the United States signed with each of the new republics individual protocols, which effectively altered the previous bilateral START treaty between the United States and the Soviet Union into a multilateral agreement between the United States, Russia, Belarus, Ukraine, and Kazakhstan.

There will be extremely difficult times ahead as the newly independent republics of the former Soviet Union begin the process of START treaty implementation. The division into republics of all that was the Soviet Union for 70 years will be stressful to the new national identities, to emotional ties to the old ways, to each economy, to the new republics' infrastructures and natural resources, and to their cultural values. The most harrowing problem these states will deal with is the disposition of the former Soviet nuclear arsenal and its support and production infrastructure. All of the tactical nuclear weapons are supposed to have been withdrawn to Russia in accordance with the Lisbon Protocol. Of the close to 11,000 strategic nuclear warheads in the old Soviet arsenal, less than 1 percent is located in Belarus, 14 percent in Ukraine, 13 percent in Kazakhstan, and 73 percent in Russia.[5] Ukraine and Kazakhstan could respectively become the third and fourth largest nuclear powers in the world, each superior to Britain, France, and China combined, if they chose to repudiate the Lisbon Protocol. The prospective failure to maintain centralized control over these forces during the dismantlement and removal makes the rest of the world break out into a cold sweat and not without reason. The new republics are experiencing the wrenching internal economic and social calamities of any new nation. Violent collisions of national minorities with the predominant ethnic population in the republics and the potential rise of Islamic fundamentalism in Central Asia and Kazakhstan could lead to a change of leadership in some republics. A change to an unknown leadership could greatly affect relations among the republics and with outside states and lead to a revision of their commitments with unpredictable consequences for their previously stated position on nuclear weapons.

All is not bleak though since the further arms control initiatives, going beyond those of START I announced by President Bush and General Secretary Gorbachev and then by Russian President Yeltsin, were ultimately codified into the START II treaty and signed by the United States and Russia on 3 January 1993. During the two-phase drawdown, both sides will reduce their present-day arsenals by approximately two-thirds. After completing these reductions, projected for the year 2003, the aggregate ceilings for nuclear weapons allowed to be operationally deployed by either side will be a maximum of 3,000 to 3,500. Of particular note for the United States was the article in the treaty banning all multiple independently targeted reentry vehicles (MIRV) on ICBMs. The ban on MIRVed ICBMs has been a centerpiece of American arms control initiatives because these weapon systems were the very strength of the Soviet Union's nuclear might. This treaty achieves a major breakthrough in the scale and scope of nuclear reductions, but it still focuses on the means of weapon delivery, not the dismantlement of warheads.

A clarification should be interjected at this point concerning the intent of the two START treaties. They were designed and negotiated to emphasize the reduction of deployed delivery vehicles (missiles and bombers) in place of the reduction of the actual nuclear weapons themselves. START I and II limit the number of *deployed* weapons and delivery vehicles, but not the total number of weapons allowed in each party's arsenal. Once removed from their associated delivery vehicles, an unlimited number of warheads can be stored indefinitely by either country. The underpinning logic to this approach is that if the delivery vehicles with the corresponding weapon(s) were not operationally deployed (and this would be confirmed under the verification regime using on-site inspections and national technical means [satellite imagery]), then the nuclear weapons themselves could not be used against the other party.

There is a corresponding negative impact to this process of reducing the US and Russian nuclear arsenals to drastically lower levels since it inevitably brings the problem of third nuclear powers to the forefront of strategic policies. Nuclear third parties clearly have to join as equal partners in future arms control talks at some point in time. This is not necessarily the biggest problem facing the United States and Russia now, but it definitely will complicate any further negotiations on additional reductions. Continued nuclear proliferation around the world will continue its impact on the future of multilateral arms control. A direct consequence will be the raising of the perception level for strategic requirements of the other nuclear powers, and perchance those of Russia and the United States. New, inexpensive, extremely accurate strategic and tactical delivery systems, increasing targeting flexibility, and the development of subkiloton munitions may force decisions by these nations away from force structures of minimal deterrence. Indirectly, proliferation could encourage the development and deployment of antiballistic missile systems by the nuclear powers, a culmination that would inadvertently affect their own strategic relations and force postures. With the emerging Russian-US friendship, the codevelopment of a more effective policy of nuclear proliferation prevention must take priority, and it must be joined by the other nuclear powers. Failure in this regard will greatly jeopardize nuclear weapons reduction beyond START II.

Eventually, other nuclear powers should not only be invited to join this regime, but they should be strongly compelled through whatever incentives the United Nations, the United States, and Russia can enforce to ensure full participation. The new and friendly political relations between Russia and the United States allow an expanding regime such as this, and should not be mistaken by the other nuclear powers for a lack of trust, as in the past, but as an effort to promote greater transparency and predictability in their strategic relationship. The purpose of the regime would be to gradually transform the strategic relationship of all parties from the balancing of the present-day retaliatory capabilities against one another to the joint management of a strategic stability based on decreasing weapons numbers and alert levels.

Chemical and Biological Weapons
The Rest of the Story

Chemical and biological weapons are just as damaging and capable of inflicting horrible pain and suffering as are nuclear weapons, and their control and eventual elimination have also been a priority goal of the United States. The extensive use of poison gas during World War I (over one million casualties and over 100,000 deaths) led to the Geneva Protocol of 1925 prohibiting the use of both poison gas and bacteriological methods in warfare. During World War II even though new and more toxic nerve gases were developed, President Roosevelt's stern warning against their use may have persuaded the Axis powers not to employ them.

> Use of such weapons has been outlawed by the opinion of civilized mankind. This country has not used them, and I hope we never will be compelled to use them. I state categorically that we shall under no circumstances resort to the use of such weapons unless they are first used by our enemies.[6]

After the war the United States tried unsuccessfully for years to complete separate agreements banning the use, production, and stockpiling of these weapons, but the Soviet Union repeatedly blocked each proposal because they demanded these agreements must be linked together. In late 1969 President Nixon declared that the United States unilaterally renounced the first use of lethal and incapacitating chemical agents and weapons and unconditionally renounced all methods of biological warfare. This diplomatic "kick in the pants" forced the Soviet Union finally to alter its position and support the separate agreements approach. An agreement banning biological weapons was signed in 1972 and ratified by the United States in 1975. The terms of the convention mandated the signatories not to undertake the development, production, stockpiling, or acquisition of biological agents or toxins, to include the weapons and their means of delivery. Within nine months after the entry-into-force date, all parties to the agreement were to have completed the total destruction of all material. On 26 December 1975 all executive branch departments and agencies certified to the president that they were in full compliance with the convention.

It took almost 20 years from that date for the world to agree to a comprehensive agreement concerning chemical weapons. The Chemical Weapons Convention (CWC) was signed in Paris in January 1993 by 130 states and by 17 others since then. This convention is the first truly global disarmament treaty with extensive verification provisions. Unlike the NPT, the CWC reflects a post–cold-war era of improved, enlightened north-south relations providing equal rights and obligations among all parties, clearly defined procedures for cooperation and assistance among member states, and strict export controls aimed at states that are not parties to the convention. The CWC is the first experience for many signatories with an arms control treaty with such extensive reporting requirements and intrusive verification provisions. CWC's ratification and implementation during the next several years will affect in a major way how the signatories of the Non-Proliferation Treaty feel about arms control in the future. Their analysis on whether to rely on cooperative international security regimes, or to follow their knee-jerk, reflexive reliance on unilateral arms races will be greatly influenced by their experience with the CWC. To delay for any appreciable length of time the implementation of the treaty within their territories may jolt their confidence in multilateral disarmament agreements, and this loss of confidence could have very detrimental consequences at the crucial NPT Review and Extension Conference in April 1995 and at the Fourth Review Conference of the Biological Weapons Convention in 1996. The CWC's credibility will be strengthened immeasurably when the United States and Russia, the two states possessing the largest chemical weapons stockpiles, ratify the conventions.

When one considers that the objective of the CWC is to eliminate a major weapon of mass destruction and to lay the groundwork for new global security relationships, the resources required to implement the CWC are comparatively small indeed. While it is not without flaws, and while important issues that must be resolved quickly remain unresolved, the work under way in The Hague has nonetheless provided generally auspicious signs that chemical disarmament can soon be transformed from dream to reality. Perhaps the biggest challenge and potential stumbling block just ahead is that the power and responsibility to make that happen has now passed from an elite group of negotiators to a much broader group of lawmakers, technical experts, industry officials, and public organizations throughout the world and across the political spectrum.[7]

Proliferation of Weapons of Mass Destruction

Britain, France, and China are likely reassessing their nuclear postures and arms control attitudes because of the continuing hesitancy of Ukraine to remove all strategic nuclear weapons from its territory in accordance with the START I treaty and Lisbon Protocol. Despite the January 1994 signing of an accord by presidents Clinton, Kravchuk (Ukraine), and Yeltsin (Russia) in Moscow outlining the agreement to dismantle and remove all the strategic nuclear weapons from Ukraine and return them to Russia, the reaction by the

British, French, and Chinese to the potential sudden refusal by Ukraine to adhere to this agreement and to its emergence as the world's third greatest nuclear power might very well be a rapid buildup of their forces and rejection of further limitations. However, the heaviest blow would be struck upon the process of nonproliferation for nuclear weapons. The chances of extending the term of the NPT at the Review and Extension Conference scheduled for 1995 would be close to zero. If Ukraine can have them, then why not India, Pakistan, Iran, Iraq, and Israel, let alone Germany, Japan, and North Korea?

President Kennedy warned in 1962 that "fifteen or twenty or twenty-five nations may have these [nuclear] weapons by the middle of the 1970s."[8] The world is very lucky that President Kennedy was wrong in his prediction. Although nuclear proliferation has not kept pace with his schedule, there seems no reasonable means to impede the proliferation of these weapons and technology. Today there are nearly 500 civil nuclear power plants in operation or under construction in 32 countries.[9] The world is recognizing that the spread of the technology and comprehension required to build nuclear weapons is running far ahead of any international control. The stories of Iraq's secret nuclear weapons program have rejuvenated world fears that the nuclear club membership is growing, resulting in a correspondingly decreasing confidence in traditional nonproliferation procedures. President Bush announced in his 1992 State of the Union message, "We must have this protection [reference to the Strategic Defense Initiative] because too many people in too many countries have access to nuclear arms."[10]

From the technical standpoint the only stumbling block to fashioning a nuclear weapon is procuring the fissile material to create the chain reaction of a nuclear explosion. It takes a minimum of 25 kilograms (55 pounds) of highly enriched uranium or eight kilograms (17.6 pounds) of plutonium to make a weapon. Weapons-grade fissile material is produced by enriching the concentration of U-235 in natural uranium to 90 percent or higher. Plutonium, on the other hand, is gleaned by chemically separating (reprocessing) spent (irradiated) reactor fuel. The world's concern over nuclear proliferation has caused most countries not to build plutonium-fed "breeder reactors," but when the world's finite supply of natural uranium reserves is exhausted, these same countries have no current alternative but to go to these reactors for additional fuel. By one estimate there could be 300 tons of weapons-grade plutonium by the year 2000.[11] New British and French reprocessing plants may account for the production of over 200 tons in the next decade. Japan wants to acquire 100 tons of that amount, which equals the total sum in the entire United States nuclear arsenal. Japanese plans for the acquisition of so much plutonium has alarmed the world, North Korea being very vocal in its concern over a possible Japanese weapons program. There is no doubt the Japanese could build a nuclear weapon quickly with their technical expertise and that much material.

The list of countries having nuclear weapons, those probably-have, and those want-to-have countries is clearly growing. "Club Nuke" has nearly doubled its numbers with the disintegration of the Soviet Union. The original members coincidentally are the same permanent members of the United Nations Security Council. The new members are the newly independent republics of Belarus, Kazakhstan, and Ukraine, as well as India. The most obvious way to show one's nuclear weapons capability is to detonate a nuclear device. Six countries have accomplished this feat since the nuclear age began: the United States (960 explosions since 1945), the former Soviet Union (715 since 1949), Britain (44 since 1952), France (192 since 1960), China (36 since 1964), and India (1 in 1974).[12] The first five countries have "declared" nuclear arsenals, while India's 1974 explosion was described by the government for peaceful demonstration purposes only to aid in the civilian nuclear program. Along with India, the additional probable Club Nuke members include Israel, Pakistan, and South Africa, all widely feared either to have clandestinely assembled an undisclosed number of nuclear weapons or to have the ability to build them quickly once the decision is made. Other nations have displayed dubious intentions of trying to join the ranks of nuclear ownership. These nations include Algeria, Iran, Iraq, Libya, and North Korea. An encouraging note though is a recent Reuters news report from Algeria which states,

> Algerian Foreign Minister Salah Dembri said, "I formally announce today in the name of the country's ruling authorities Algeria's intention to adhere to the nuclear Non-Proliferation Treaty. Algeria is against military uses of the atom," Dembri said while inaugurating the country's second nuclear reactor, built with Chinese assistance 90 miles south of Algiers.[13]

The ongoing dispute between India and Pakistan in South Central Asia has triggered simultaneous nuclear programs capable of producing weapons by both countries. By one official estimate India has the components with which to assemble 40 to 60 weapons on short notice, while Pakistan could produce five to 10 weapons.[14] Why would countries who could redirect the enormous resources required for a nuclear program into other sorely needed programs want to pursue these WMD? India almost assuredly wants to increase its prestige in the international arena and to be seen as the dominant state in the area. This is more true today as its once major political and military ally, the Soviet Union, broke up into a number of separate republics, and its biggest and potentially most aggressive foe, China, has been expanding its influence into the region. Pakistan probably pursues its nuclear program not for world prestige, but from a regional standpoint. It is the first Islamic country with a nuclear capability anywhere in the region of the Islamic Crescent. To Pakistan's credit and the world's relief, it has requested that the United States mediate at regional nuclear disarmament talks and has jointly pledged to sign the NPT along with India. India has objected to this proposal since it is of the opinion the NPT is discriminatory and believes nuclear weapons proliferation should be addressed on a global versus regional basis. Progress is occurring though, because both countries agreed to lessen the risk of nuclear war by pledging not to attack each other's nuclear facilities.

Israel allegedly manufactures up to 40 kilograms (88 pounds) of weapons grade plutonium annually in addition to other necessary components for thermonuclear weapons. One hundred to 200 nuclear weapons, with a high estimate of more than 300 weapons may be currently in the Israeli arsenal, even though officially Israel pretends to have no weapons, and the United States supports this charade with a "see no evil, hear no evil" attitude. Even the most conservative potential number of weapons in the region should cause the world to recoil in horror. South Africa's program (probably with extensive Israeli assistance) was shrouded in as much secrecy as Israel's until the summer of 1993. At that time South African president F. W. de Klerk announced to the world that South Africa had indeed established a nuclear program. However, the political bombshell of his announcement was that South Africa had actually assembled a small number of complete weapons. President de Klerk declared these weapons would be dismantled and the South African nuclear program would subject itself to the UN's International Atomic Energy Agency's (IAEA) safeguards and inspections to verify that no nuclear material, equipment, or facilities in its possession would be misused for military purposes in the future.[15]

Iran, Iraq, and North Korea lead the list of nuclear weapon "want-to-haves" and are attempting through various means to acquire them. Iran is a signatory of the NPT, but Iranian leaders have nonetheless reiterated Iran's right to possess nuclear weapons and believe Muslim nations should balance Israel's suspected capabilities. Before the Gulf War in 1991 Iraq was believed to be five to 10 years away from constructing a nuclear weapon. In postwar IAEA inspections estimates have Iraq less than two years away from having the bomb. Iraq, as an NPT signatory, had as early as 1972 concluded a full-scope safeguards agreement with the IAEA. Yet, while openly participating in the international nonproliferation system, Iraq was able to clandestinely violate the system, as we have witnessed during the post–Gulf War United Nations–mandated inspections of their nuclear facilities.

Recent intelligence disclosures of North Korea's nuclear program and its assumed ability to produce nuclear weapons have dampened the recent warming trend in North Korean relations with South Korea and Japan.

> The prospect of an uncontrolled North Korean nuclear weapons program leading to an arsenal of hundreds of nuclear weapons early in the next century would have profound impact on the strategic stability in Northeast Asia. South Korea and Japan might reassess their nuclear futures and China would be much less likely to consider reducing its own nuclear forces. Any retreat from the IAEA's newly

> established authority for special inspections would drastically weaken the agency's future effectiveness.[16]

Threats by North Korea of abrogating its NPT membership unless South Korea and the United States make concessions have done nothing to stabilize this region of the world. Hopefully, recent indicators are that a solution may be in the offing,

> . . . in what amounted to a diplomatic breakthrough, North Korea said it was willing in principle to allow full access to its reactor and reprocessing plant. Given the right package of incentives, like diplomatic recognition, security assurances and economic ties, Pyongyang might be persuaded to trade away its nuclear program, just as South Africa and Belarus already have.[17]

The world will look to the United States for continued leadership in settling this tricky situation, and its solution may be an example of how the NPT treaty can and should work in the years to come.

It must be strongly noted though that the finger of world condemnation for pursuing weapons of mass destruction cannot be pointed solely at the above countries. The economic laws of supply and demand force us to backtrack to the ultimate suppliers of nuclear knowledge as well as fissionable material. Assistance from profit-minded governments, businesses, and individuals around the industrialized world share in the blame. France has provided nuclear assistance to India, Iraq, Israel, Pakistan, and South Africa. Germany has supplied nuclear technology to Argentina, Brazil, India, Iran, Iraq, Libya, and Pakistan. The United States is also to blame. Israel supposedly acquired 100 kilograms (220 pounds) of American weapons-grade uranium in the 1960s and followed this coup with further smuggling of krypton triggering devices in the early 1980s. Nuclear test data from the United States also mysteriously showed up in Israel. The situation most alarming the world right now is the suspected brain drain of Soviet nuclear scientists and weapons technicians who are finding employment opportunities in the third world. An estimated 1 million Soviets are working in various third world countries, 1,000 to 2,000 having the knowledge to design and manufacture nuclear weapons and their components.

It is gravely evident that immediate action is required to plug the holes in this leaking ship of proliferation. The cornerstone to the world's nonproliferation activities today is the treaty on the Non-Proliferation of Nuclear Weapons. As early as the 1960s the use of nuclear reactors to generate electricity was becoming a vast source of reactor by-product: plutonium. Enough plutonium is being produced now to produce 15 to 20 nuclear weapons daily.[18] An organized international system is required to prevent diversion of these nuclear materials as well as to lessen the risks of nuclear war, accidental detonation, unauthorized use, and regional conflict escalation. The United Nations has sponsored various proposals from the United States, the Soviet Union, and a variety of nonnuclear states. The biggest stumbling block was the Soviet insistence that collective security organizations (like NATO) should not have access to any member's weapons. An agreement was eventually finalized after intense negotiations. The treaty entered into force in 1970, and since then it has been signed by more than 140 countries. The NPT is essentially a bargain between the nuclear weapons haves and the have-nots. For their pledge not to acquire nuclear weapons, the have-nots received a reciprocal pledge from the haves to provide nuclear assistance suitable to the development of peaceful uses of nuclear energy and for the haves to slow and reduce vertical proliferation or growth in the sizes and capabilities of the existing nuclear arsenals.

Other blocks in the international wall of nonproliferation include the International Atomic Energy Agency established in 1957. It serves as the primary verification tool for the NPT, monitoring compliance with the treaty's legal obligations and norms and as a facilitator for the transfer of peaceful nuclear materials and technology. The IAEA safeguards are designed to provide timely warning of proliferation problems by detecting any diversion or misuse for military purposes of significant quantities of declared peaceful nuclear materials, equipment, and facilities. The Zangger Committee is a voluntary group of nuclear materials major suppliers, who developed a list of dual-use items whose export is designed to trigger the application of IAEA safeguards. The list includes nuclear reactors, reactor components, and certain nuclear materials such as heavy water. The Nuclear Suppliers Group, or London Club, developed guidelines adhered to by more than 25 countries and includes provisions of physical security for transferred nuclear facilities and materials, the acceptance of safeguards, and the prohibition of third-party retransfer of nuclear exports. It also established Nuclear Weapon Free Zones (NWFZ) where certain regions of the world have been declared through treaties to be off-limits to nuclear weapons (further discussion on NWFZ later).

One of the NPT's stipulations is that review conferences must be held every five years. The past conferences (1975, 1980, 1985, 1990) all reaffirmed the treaty's arms control success, but there are problems still to be hammered out. The planned conference in April 1995 is considered extremely important by most countries because there is a required vote on whether to continue the treaty for an indefinite period, while at the same time there have been grumblings by more than a few of the nuclear have-nots that the treaty is discriminating against them. There is a prevailing sense in the world community that time is running short to stem the tide of nuclear proliferation.

Failure by the United States, Russia, and the world community to persuade Ukraine to abide by its political commitment to join the NPT and ratify START I makes it impossible to speculate on any development that will further imperil the indefinite extension of the NPT. The January 1994 agreement signed between the United States, Russia, and Ukraine to remove the strategic nuclear weapons from Ukraine's territory is now only a promise to be fulfilled, with no substance as yet. A majority vote on the indefinite extension will be defined by the two issues of how well the NPT has worked up to the date of the conference and whether a reduction of the nuclear arsenals, required under Article VI, has been faithfully pursued. If Ukraine still is maintaining nuclear weapons, the foundation of the NPT will be shaken, forcing the major countries to reanalyze their strategic and security concerns. Additionally, without entry-into-force of the START I and II treaties, Article VI of the NPT will not have been honored by the United States and Russia since not one formal, internationally recognized agreement would exist between the two countries limiting their nuclear armaments. With that in mind other nations may decide for only a short extension of the treaty pending further developments. This argument also leads to the belief that the START I treaty implementation and signing of the NPT by Ukraine would be a giant leap forward, cementing the spirit of NPT as an effective nonproliferation tool requiring indefinite extension.[19]

If the unthinkable situation occurs in which one of the successor nuclear republics decides to commit a deliberate act of proliferation and maintain its nuclear weapons, this decision would cause severe repercussions around the world. Widespread possession of nuclear weapons in various regions of the world would decrease the relative military and political power of the United States and other nuclear powers. It could frustrate United Nations peacemaking/peacekeeping operations and slow the emergence of a world security system capable of keeping organized violence to a minimum. Tragically, it could also convince some nonnuclear industrial states that the time is not right to trust their individual security to multilateral security systems perceived to be weak and ineffectual. Countries like Italy, Germany, Japan, Taiwan, and South Korea all have strong military potential that includes a rapid nuclear weapons production capability. Their perception that the nonproliferation regime is untrustworthy and unable to provide basic security against proliferation may force them to begin their own nuclear development programs in self-defense.

Solutions

The Zangger Committee, the Nuclear Suppliers Group, and most importantly the IAEA and the NPT have done a better-than-average job of slowing the proliferation of nuclear weapons, but they have not stopped or even reduced the development, manufacture, or stockpiling of these weapons. What else can be done? What other actions can individual countries, regions, the superpowers, the United Nations, or the entire world do to stop the flow of nuclear arms? First and foremost, *the will to do something further* must be stronger, and the participants in any further nonproliferation actions must be disposed to transform their collective will into positive action. One solution would be to strengthen current peaceful nonproliferation norms, specifically the detailed inspection regime or safeguards used by the IAEA. Any country that owns nuclear weapons and is serious about stemming continued proliferation must take the lead by lessening its reliance on such weapons. By maintaining huge arsenals of these weapons such countries are attesting to the rest of the world their importance, and it should come as no surprise that other countries may also want them. Once this giant political hurdle has been crossed, there are a variety of actions that can be taken in addition to the current nonproliferation regime. These steps are of varying magnitude and will present difficult political, economic, and military obstacles to those nations willing to find a solution.

One enhancement to the strengthened IAEA safeguards would be to include all nuclear installations of all UN member states. If the five declared nuclear powers agreed and were backed by a Security Council resolution requiring all other United Nations members to do likewise, this action could freeze both the declared and undeclared nuclear arsenals. Concurrently, the United States and Russia could dismantle the reduced warheads resulting from current and future arms control agreements, transferring the fissile material to monitored storage areas under IAEA safeguards. The reductions in the US-Russian nuclear arsenals should be made permanent for long-term effectiveness, and they should agree not to continue the current treaty-allowable practice of withdrawing nuclear warheads from the field and storing them. The current START I and II treaties allow retaining the capability to produce new warheads without limit. Both countries, therefore, must negotiate a verified, bilateral agreement to dismantle all strategic warheads reduced under START and subsequent agreements or negotiations and include a provision prohibiting reuse of fissile material mined from old warheads for the production of newer weapons. The United Nations Security Council would, at the same time, start a program to entice the handful of states not currently NPT members to join the NPT or any similar regime of multilateral controls which would end their capability, present or future, to produce weapons-grade fissile materials, as long as IAEA safeguards could be implemented. The bilateral agreement between Brazil and Argentina, who are not current signatories of the NPT, outlines an agreement to adhere to the safeguards of the IAEA and to terminate their individual nuclear programs.

The pending START treaties between the United States and Russia cover only a portion of the nuclear club membership. The full implementation of the proposed US-Russian actions should be contingent upon the agreement of the other declared nuclear weapon states—Britain, France, and China—to voluntarily follow the stated limits by freezing the numeric level of their warheads, restricting missile production to a bare minimum, phasing out nuclear warhead testing, stopping all fissile material production, and allowing all their nuclear facilities to come under IAEA supervision. A Security Council decision would enjoin the council to take any necessary joint action against states or terrorist groups initiating the use of nuclear weapons. Such joint action decided upon by the Security Council is authorized under chapter 7 of the United Nations Charter and could include features like economic sanctions against any United Nations member state refusing to submit all nuclear installations under their control to IAEA safeguards, or some other multilateral equivalent.

The reductions and restrictions upon the nuclear capabilities of the five declared nuclear powers, who are also the permanent members of the Security Council, would assure continued tough council supervision of this broader system for control over nuclear weapons. For example, the council could decide to obligate supplier countries to report to the IAEA sales and transfers of all components and items on a list prepared by the suppliers group.[20] This action is now carried out on a voluntary and incomplete basis.

Another nonproliferation concept, which currently has two shining examples of success in Latin America and the South Pacific region is the establishment of Nuclear Weapon Free Zones. NWFZs are internationally recognized regions of the world that have been created by formal treaties that include verification provisions to stop the migration of nuclear weapons and assist in efforts to roll back proliferation where it has already occurred. NWFZs also could help defuse regional tensions and instability that increase the incentive for countries to opt for nuclear weapons, and they offer an attractive alternative to states that have rejected the NPT membership because of its perceived discriminatory nature. Both existing NWFZ treaties, Tlatelolco in Latin America and the Treaty of Rarotonga in the South Pacific, express a desire to remove the threat of nuclear war from their respective regions, to contribute to global elimination of nuclear weapons through regional measures, and to prevent the proliferation of nuclear weapons. Both agreements highlight the value of NWFZs in building regional confidence and security.[21]

The current NPT embodies a double standard legitimizing nuclear weapons in possession of some but not by others. This is the crux of the claim by many countries without a nuclear capability that there is no equality in the treaty. The NPT's nonproliferation tenets should be applied equally both to nuclear weapon nation haves and have-nots. Members of the nuclear club, to maintain their credibility and effectiveness on nonproliferation matters, must practice what they preach. De-emphasizing and devaluing the possession of nuclear weapons by agreement of all the nuclear states, along with permanent reductions in their arsenals, will show the resolve these countries have to ensure the safety of the world. The constraints of the NPT, linked with sufficient authority, resources, and backing, plus the IAEA safeguards system are the best hope for preventing the continuing proliferation of nuclear weapons.

All the aforementioned ideas are proposed to prevent the acquisition of nuclear materials and weapons or the production of them from current civilian-use programs. What happens after a country or other actor is already in possession of weapons and begins to rattle its nuclear sabers? Until now nonproliferation efforts have encompassed only political and economic activities and sanctions in an attempt to stop the proliferation or at least stop the intent to use or threaten to use nuclear weapons. Political and economic sanctions may or may not be fully effective in forcing that country or actor to freely and voluntarily curb the threats of use or even relinquish their "claim to fame." To physically prevent the use of this weapon or weapons is when the military option should be considered for possible employment. We are now stepping into the realm of the "twilight zone" of counterproliferation—a coherent strategy to prevent countries from acquiring any WMD through a combination of nonproliferation regimes, export controls, and political persuasion, or should efforts to prevent the acquisition of these weapons fail, to deter or destroy them prior to their use. The estimation of the adversary's potential threat and intent by the United States or United Nations will help determine the level of military response. The threat is a combination of factors including the type of weapon or proliferation that has occurred, the delivery capability, the adversary's intent of use, and the inherent regional instability. The willingness to take military action (unilaterally, bilaterally, or multilaterally) in response to this threat is also a combination of factors, including US/UN military capability, our knowledge of the adversary, what US/UN interests are at stake, and the domestic and international support perceived for the use of the military option. If willingness to act by the United States or the United Nations is not commensurate to the level of threat, the military option is simply not available because it will fail.

One fact predominates: the use of military force should not and cannot be the first option explored in response to a threat. It must follow and be totally integrated into a unified response using political, economic, and military options. If the military action is then to be used, two outcomes must occur. First, the military action must inflict the minimum requisite punishment to ensure the adversary is worse off than before. Second, the action must establish a credible reputation through its results to discourage future proliferators from triggering like actions. If the intended military action does not succeed, not only will it not remove the specific threat that precipitated the military response, but the entire world will assume that military action is futile as a solution to the problem of proliferation.

An effective and efficient nonproliferation regime (and possibly a counterproliferation option) will send a clear and precise message to any current or potential proliferator. This message must be carried forward by a unified, coordinated effort of the political, economic, and possibly the military elements of the world body. First, the acquisition of WMD will not be easy or cheap. Second, any attempts to threaten or use WMD will be dealt with rapidly and severely by the United States and the international community. There are many potential pitfalls to using a military option in a counter-proliferation regime, and their effects must be balanced when contemplating the use of military force. A military response is only a stopgap measure at best. Israel's surprise attack on Iraq's Osiraq reactor in June 1981 only temporarily slowed Iraq's nuclear program. Second, military strikes are likely to produce unintended consequences. For example, Israel's attack on Osiraq only drove the program underground into hardened facilities. An attack on an operating reactor could also risk a Chernobyl-like disaster. Third, military strikes set a precedent for other countries to launch their own attacks against suspected sites on the territory of adversaries. (South Korea has made some provocative statements about knocking out North Korea's nuclear facilities in the wake of the Gulf War.) Finally, military strikes against nuclear facilities are a clear violation of international norms against such action. In fact in December 1990 the United Nations General Assembly voted 141-1 to condemn attacks against nuclear reactors. The lone dissenting vote was cast by the United States.[22]

The current nuclear nonproliferation regime does nothing but maintain the nuclear status quo, and inherent to that situation are secret and unchecked proliferation activities by a variety of state and nonstate actors. If the world is scared enough and sane enough to really desire an end to this nuclear madness, it is absolutely essential that the nuclear haves practice what they preach to the have-nots and that all rules of nonproliferation and nuclear weapons reduction and elimination apply equally to all participants across the board. There have been many who have proclaimed their ideas in this arena to be the panacea, and it is a sure bet there will be others in the future with a better mousetrap. There are though certain logical precepts and common-sense steps which, if applied, will have a constant positive force on the nonproliferation regime.

No progress will be possible though without the active participation and unanimous agreement of the present members of the declared nuclear states. In this respect, progress will not be possible under any circumstances without the foresight and the initiation of strong, enlightened leadership on the part of the United States. This is the premier national security challenge the United States faces in the arms control and proliferation arenas today. Will America recognize its responsibilities to step forward and provide the requisite leadership critical to undertake this task?

Notes

1. United States Arms Control and Disarmament Agency, *Arms Control and Disarmament Agreements, Text and Histories of the Negotiations* (Washington, D.C.: Government Printing Office, 1990), 3.

2. Treaty Document 102-20, *Message of the President of the United States transmitting the Treaty between the United States of America and the Union of Soviet Socialist Republics on the Reduction and Limitation of Strategic Offensive Arms* (Washington, D.C.: US Government Printing Office, 25 November 1991), iv.

3. Ibid., v–vi.

4. Alexei G. Arbatov, "Russian Nuclear Disarmament: Problems and Prospects," *Arms Control* 14, no. 1 (April 1993): 105.

5. Ibid., 103.

6. Ibid., i, 131.

7. Peter Herby, "Building the Chemical Disarmament Regime," *Arms Control Today*, September 1993, 19.

8. Oscar Luire, "Stopping the Spread of Nuclear Weapons: Still Time to Act," *The Defense Monitor* 21, no. 3 (1992): 1.

9. Ibid.

10. Ibid.

11. Ibid., viii, 3.

12. Ibid., 3.

13. "Algeria to Sign Arms Treaty," *Reuters News Service*, 22 December 1993.

14. Ibid., viii, 3.

15. Ibid., 4.

16. Spurgeon M. Keeny, Jr., "The North Korean Crisis" (editorial), *Arms Control Today*, May 1993, 2.

17. "If North Korea Has Bombs," *New York Times*, 28 December 1993.

18. Ibid., i, 89.

19. Spurgeon M. Keeny, Jr., "It's Ukraine, Stupid!" (editorial), *Arms Control Today*, September 1993, 2.

20. Jonathan Dean, "Comprehensive Control over Nuclear Weapons," *Arms Control* 14, no. 1 (April 1993): 250.

21. Jon B. Wolfsthal, "Nuclear-Weapon-Free Zones: Coming of Age?," *Arms Control Today*, March 1993, 3.

22. Ibid., viii, 6.

The Changing Nature of Alliances

Maris McCrabb

The final decade of the twentieth century marked a dramatic change in the relationship between the United States and the rest of the world.[1] America's security, traditionally defined as preserving the United States as a free nation with its fundamental values and institutions intact, seemed as assured as at any time in the post–World War II era.[2] For 40 years America knew what national security meant—protection against the overarching threat of communist expansion. Furthermore, America knew the means to counter this threat—a series of alliances like the North Atlantic Treaty Organization (NATO) with like-minded states oriented against the Soviet threat. With the demise of the Soviet Union and democracy breaking out in the former communist states of Eastern Europe, the threat to America's security seems tangibly diminished. Likewise, the role of, and indeed the need for, its alliances has undergone a substantial transformation.

The purpose of this study is to examine the changing nature of alliances in light of the changed nature of the international environment.[3] It describes current alliance characteristics and discerns emerging trends within alliances. It examines the changed motives for membership and under what conditions the alliance will either act or not act. It describes the formal and informal decision-making apparatus within the alliances. Fundamentally, this is an attempt to uncover the objectives of these alliances. The thesis of the study is that alliances are moving from traditional balance-of-power and external-threat orientations toward mechanisms for resolving conflicts internal to the alliances or among their participants.

To show how the changed nature of the international environment is changing the nature of alliances, this study looks at three cases: NATO, the Western European Union (WEU), and the Visegrad Group. NATO and the WEU are alliances that have roots in the very origins of the cold war. They allow us to examine the impact that the new international environment has on existing alliances. The Visegrad Group (Poland, Hungary, Slovakia, and the Czech Republic) barely fits the definition of an alliance. However, there is some argument that this group carries the seeds of what future alliances may well look like and why and how they may be formed.

The relevancy of this study lies in the impact that these changes will have on US military options and contingency planning. It is almost becoming a cliché that America will no longer engage in unilateral military operations—Panama, El Dorado Canyon, and the antidrug efforts notwithstanding.[4] Likewise, it is becoming redundant to speak of the malaise of NATO and its search for an identity and mission in the "new world order."[5] This "NATO-sclerosis" has in some ways occurred parallel with the rebirth of the WEU as a competing military security institution and poses questions concerning the link between NATO and the WEU such as whether they can coexist in the same manner they have done so over the past 40 years and, if so, what roles and missions each will play. Finally, while much of the concern has been over the security needs and aspirations of the Commonwealth of Independent States (CIS), a potential US security concern must also include the other former Warsaw Treaty Organization (WTO) states. An important question deals with the security arrangements of Poland, Hungary, and the Czech Republic, for example, fitting into the larger NATO (or WEU) universe.

This study begins an examination of these concerns, with a brief historical background on the two previous upheavals in the realignment of alliances: the nineteenth-century attempt by the Congress of Vienna to institutionalize the Grand Coalition after the defeat of Napoléon and the post–World War II point-counterpoint of NATO and the WTO. The attention then rapidly turns to the twenty-first century by looking at the future of NATO and the role the European Union (EU)[6] and the WEU will play in US security calculations. The study examines opportunities and pitfalls that an organization like the Visegrad Group presents to the US. Finally, it closes with some conclusions and recommendations for US policy.

Historical Background

Napoléon's opponents formed coalitions whose members fluctuated according to the perceived self-interests of the individual nations.[7] Their fundamental outlook was determining if the greatest threat was Napoléon or those who opposed him. The only nation consistently opposed to him throughout the Napoleonic Wars was Great Britain.

Post–Napoleonic Nineteenth Century

Napoléon's fall began with his establishment of the Continental System on 21 November 1806.[8] This system was Napoléon's attempt to close continental Europe to British trade. Britain needed those markets. She exported metals and textiles and imported naval stores and cereals. Napoléon's attempt to force Spain and Portugal into the system (through invasion) started the Spanish War of Independence. To support the Iberian nations (and to tie down French forces), Britain landed troops in Portugal on 21 October 1807, and the Peninsular War began. It became Napoléon's "Vietnam" quagmire. Likewise, the French invasion of Russia on 24 June 1812 was directed at stopping Russian trade with Great Britain.

The first attempt at semiformal collective security was the Quadruple Alliance of November 1815, which consisted of Austria, Prussia, Russia, and Great Britain. Bourbon France was admitted in 1818. Its purpose was to control threats from within Europe. The alliance, which met irregularly in congress, prohibited intervention in internal affairs,[9] but it did not stop war between nations (or even member states), nor was it a forum to resolve conflicts. The continental keeper of the peace was Austria under the leadership of Prince von Metternich. After 1850, the role of Russia in European stability was also central. These two states provided the "backstop" for other, more regional partnerships such as Britain protecting Belgium, Austria protecting Italy, and Prussia protecting the Rhineland. Continuing the arrangements solidified by the Battle of Trafalgar, Britain remained hegemonic on the seas.

It would be a mistake to believe that the Congress of Vienna stopped war between the major powers or that it was successful in eliminating revolution (which the rulers equated with a desire to eliminate autocratic rule) from Europe. The ancien régimes that existed before 1789 were gone forever. Thus, this early attempt at the use of an alliance for collective security failed.

Post–World War II

Point-Counterpoint—NATO and the WTO

The next major realignment of alliance powers occurred after World War II. The entry of the United States into NATO marked a watershed in the history of US security policy. Since the days of the Founding Fathers, America had studiously avoided entanglement with foreign alliances. With the founding of NATO, not only had the US entered into a permanent security alliance with other states, but the US pledged itself to playing a leading role in ensuring the stability of the Western world.

While there is scholarly debate on the origins of the cold war, there is some agreement on the precipitating events.[10] Two of the most significant events occurred in Turkey and in Greece.[11] Traditionally, that part of Europe had been protected by Great Britain, but Britain, weakened by the war and unable to provide assistance to either Greece or Turkey, turned to the United States. President Harry S Truman, in a historic reversal of US policy, announced on 12 March 1947 that the US would "support free peoples who are resisting subjugation by armed minorities or by outside pressure."[12] This Truman Doctrine was interpreted by the Soviet Union as an intrusion into the internal affairs of other states.

The wartime amity between the Soviet Union and the United States was on fragile ground. By 1947, Poland was ruled by the Communist party. In February 1948, the pro-Western party in Czechoslovakia was expunged. Then in June 1948, the Soviets blocked all overland access to Berlin, which, while under four-power (US, Soviet, British, and French) administration, was completely surrounded by the Soviet zone of occupation. Truman immediately instituted the famous

Operation Vittles—the Berlin airlift. That same month, the US Senate passed a bipartisan resolution supporting collective defense in Western Europe, and on 4 April 1949, the North Atlantic Treaty was signed in Washington. Its original 10 European countries[13] plus Canada and the US were expanded by Greece and Turkey in 1952, West Germany in 1955, and Spain in 1982.[14]

To counter NATO, Stalin institutionalized Soviet control over Eastern Europe through the WTO, which was founded on 14 May 1955 when eight European states[15] signed a Treaty of Friendship, Cooperation and Mutual Assistance.[16] The cold war was on, and Europe was divided into two camps. Alliances now formed a dominant, though not exclusive, overarching framework for international relations between states.

This brief historical review has highlighted three important considerations to bear in mind when analyzing future alliance characteristics and models. First, for the US and for most nations, alliances have been the exception. Second, alliances have been formed to counter a known external threat. Finally, prior to the current situation facing NATO, alliances fell apart soon after the common threat was gone; they did not evolve into lasting arrangements, nor did they necessarily expand to include nondefense security issues.

Towards the Twenty-first Century

The following case studies on NATO, the WEU, and the Visegrad Group are avowedly Eurocentric. There are three reasons for this.[17] First, only in Europe has the US pursued multipartner alliance ties. The other defense security alliances are more traditional bilateral alliances and/or multilateral coalitions. Second, it is in Europe that the specter looms of long-standing US alliance partners framing their own alliance without the US. Finally, the issue of central and eastern European countries poses a significant dilemma for both the US and other European nations, notably whether there should be Western security guarantees to these states and, if so, what form should they take. Some argue that these guarantees should be expressed as bilateral arrangements with EU/WEU and/or NATO. However, if there are not security guarantees to these states, the question remains whether they will form a multilateral security arrangement among themselves. This last issue has been at the heart of the proposed "Partners for Peace" initiative launched at the January 1994 NATO summit. According to Anthony Lake, President Bill Clinton's national security advisor,

> Through [the Partnership for Peace], former members of the Warsaw Pact will be able to plan, train, exercise, and, if necessary, operate with NATO forces. . . . NATO itself will be better prepared for possible contingencies in the east and the new democracies will be better prepared to play their role in building a secure Europe.[18]

The US, Europe, and the Future of NATO

It is not the purpose of this study to explore in any depth the origins of NATO.[19] As outlined above, NATO was primarily formed to counter the perceived threat of Soviet expansion in Europe following World War II. It is important to note that NATO followed efforts by individual European states to form a collective defense (discussed in more detail below). It is also important to note that NATO's defense security orientation was only part of the US plan for ensuring the security of Europe. The Marshall Plan was as much a part of the US moves in Europe as was the Washington Treaty codifying the Atlantic Alliance.

The future of NATO largely depends upon the future role the US is willing to play in the alliance. That, in turn, depends mainly on what role the alliance will play in maintaining European defense and political security. Obviously, then, the role of the alliance will be determined by what challenges NATO foresees in these two areas. This has much wider implications. It also concerns NATO joint force planning. Prior to the collapse of the WTO, NATO joint force planning was a means by which NATO countries coordinated their military capabilities and policies. Without a common threat, NATO has no obvious need for joint force planning. This therefore frees individual nations to develop their own force structure and employment policies.[20] The first key question concerns the possible threats to European security. Once that concern is answered, the next step is to determine what US interests are in Europe. From these interests, we can then determine what role, if any, the US will play in the NATO alliance. Finally, these changes in NATO's perceptions of threats will affect the decision making in the alliance.

There are three possible defense security threat scenarios in Europe.[21] The first is a resurgent Russia threatening stability in Europe by directly threatening the West. While the probability of this occurring may be quite low, the costs of a major power war in Europe would be quite high. Under this scenario, NATO provides a transition insurance policy. NATO and US forces committed on the Continent exist perhaps for decades as Russia completes its transition to political democracy.[22]

The second scenario is war in Eastern Europe that threatens the West. This scenario has two aspects. The first is the spread of war to the West. This would most likely occur if the West (or even a single Western state) appears to one of the belligerents to be actively (or covertly) aiding their adversary. The second aspect involves the West being drawn into a war in the East when Russia enters on the side of one of the belligerents. This ties the second scenario back to the first. Again, NATO would act as a balancer of forces in Europe.

The last scenario involves Russia going to war against a neighboring Eastern state, such as the Ukraine.[23] This scenario would be considered threatening to the West as a prelude to the first scenario (i.e., a resurgent Russia threatening the West). In this case, NATO acts as a guard against the conflict spilling over into the West. Given these threat scenarios, the next fundamental issue posed concerns the US security interests in Europe.

There are two important parts to the discussion over American interests in Europe. While there are some "Fortress America" advocates who argue that the US should return all its forces stationed overseas back to the US, most adhere to the notion that the US must remain engaged in Europe. The issue, though, is what is meant by "engagement" and what is the extent of that engagement. Some argue that with the demise of the Soviet Union and the WTO and the end of the cold war, the US no longer has any defense security concerns in Europe. They are optimistic that the likelihood of major power war in Europe is small and that outbreaks of wars within and among small powers, while regrettable, are not of concern to the US. Others argue that the US must remain militarily engaged in Europe for defense, political, and economic security reasons. Essentially, they argue that America could be excluded from a prosperous and stable Europe based around the EU and extending into Eastern Europe and possibly Russia. A second argument revolves around an unstable Europe leading to a renewed great-power rivalry.[24]

Another rationale for NATO is that it maintains stability within Western Europe.[25] This line of argument centers on the fear of a militarily resurgent Germany. With the movement of Western Europe's forward defense line away from the German border, these fears center on two potential outcomes. The first is a Germany that seeks defense security in nuclear weapons or at least in an expanded military. Ironically, the second is the fear of a militarily impotent Germany.

The nuclear Germany scenario envisions Europe, stripped of the US nuclear umbrella, reverting to pre-World War II security policies when each nation viewed its security as being based upon its own capabilities. Here Germany, faced with a nuclear France and Great Britain in the west, and a nuclear Russia and perhaps Ukraine in the east, abrogates the 1955 Paris Agreements that prohibit Germany from possessing nuclear weapons. This scenario is not dependent upon Germany actually possessing the weapons, only that it might obtain them. The argument rests on the belief that a nuclear (or even a militarily strong) Germany will be perceived as a threat to other Western European (indeed, perhaps all European) nations.

The latter scenario, a militarily weak Germany, is based upon the argument that in the absence of US forces in Europe other Western European states need a bulwark to the instability of Eastern Europe that a militarily strong Germany could provide. In light of the three threat scenarios postulated above, the reductions taking place in the German military are of increasing concern to other European states.[26]

In sum, while the US distinctly has defense security interests in NATO, the likely scenarios point to much more murky threats than in the past. Consequently, the US will no longer play the role of "first among equals" in NATO decision making. Therefore, it is important to consider some of the ramifications for policy-making in an alliance of equals.[27] The first is that a given situation is less likely to be identified as a problem requiring action when responsibility is dispersed among alliance members. This creates a bias towards avoidance of issues. Second, issues tend to be framed narrowly, again reflecting the uncertainties, particularly those caused by the uncertainties of collective actions, over which actor is expected to do what. Third, the absence of a compelling threat tends to make government leaders more susceptible to fickle public opinion. This is exacerbated by elections that are not synchronized, leading to at least one of the member states facing electoral concerns. Thus, the nature of "the West's welfare-minded, inward-looking societies, leads to risk-averse, self-protective thinking."[28] Finally, weak political leaders, sensitive to public opinion, looking at ambiguous issues will be less likely to commit themselves to decisive action without a high degree of consensus among the alliance members. The result tends to be decision by committee and the attendant possibility of inaction and groupthink.

The EU and the WEU

The WEU shares common roots with NATO. Those roots stem from a recognition by the Western European nations following World War II for a need for collective defense. The first act began with a Treaty of Defense Alliance (known as the Dunkirk Treaty) between France and Great Britain signed on 4 March 1947. Its intent was to prevent further German aggression. This arrangement was extended to include Belgium, the Netherlands, and Luxembourg on 17 March 1948 (the Brussels Treaty).[29] This alliance formed the nucleus for the Atlantic Alliance and NATO. Furthermore, these nations, with the exception of Great Britain, formed the nucleus for discussions that led to the creation of the European Coal and Steel Community (ECSC).[30]

The ECSC was the brainchild of French foreign minister Robert Schuman. It was concerned with high politics. The reindustrialization of Germany was a great concern to the other nations of Western Europe. They were committed to finding a way of preventing another central European war.

Germany, on her part, was searching for a way of regaining control over the Ruhr and Saar areas that had been under French jurisdiction since the end of the war.[31] The ECSC filled each party's requirements. Germany regained sovereignty over the areas while the other nations, through the ECSC High Authority, retained some control over the outputs and uses of these regions (as well as the outputs and uses of all ECSC member states). The idea that integration would lead to increased regional security had a distinct scholarly basis. David Mitrany, a leading theorist of this school that came to be called "functionalism," believed that the close collaboration inherent in economic integration would eventually "spill over" into other areas, thus building a "web of interests" that would foster increased political cooperation and hence provide a firm basis for regional security stability.[32]

The success of the ECSC led to further negotiations on establishing a European political community and European defense community. These were designed to further integrate Germany into Europe. However, both of these proposals failed in the French National Assembly in 1954. This led to negotiations to broaden the Brussels Treaty Organization. The ensuing Western European Union came into force on 6 May 1955 when Germany and Italy joined the original five signatories of the Brussels Treaty.[33]

There are three interconnected decision-making bodies in the WEU. The Council is the executive and policy-making organization with general competence over all questions relative to the application of the treaty. It meets twice a year and the presidency is held for one-year terms on an alphabetical rotation. It has a subcouncil Permanent Council consisting of ambassadorial-rank ministers that meets biweekly. The Assembly, composed of 108 parliamentarians, while largely consultative, is empowered to make binding decisions concerning questions about its internal functioning. It usually meets twice a year. The final organization is the WEU Institute for Security Studies, which carries out research for the Council and Assembly, promotes greater awareness of European security issues, and organizes meetings with other European institutes.[34]

From the early 1960s to the mid-1980s, the WEU was somnolent. This was due to the entry of Britain into the EU and the "civilian power" approach European states took to harmonize external policies. Thus, the primary rationales for the WEU—to provide a forum for Britain to discuss common issues and to cooperate on security issues—were assumed by other organizations. In the mid-1980s, the WEU, under French initiative, was revitalized for three reasons. First, it was increasingly clear that the EU was unable to assume a common defense and security identity. Second, the specter of a "reheating" of the cold war between the US and USSR made many Europeans realize that they required a forum for defense cooperation divorced from a superpower. Third, there was increasing concern that the German peace movement might lead to German neutrality. The catalyst was the Reykjavik Summit of October 1986 between President Ronald Reagan and General Secretary Mikhail Gorbachev. The proposals put forth at that summit concerning elimination of nuclear ballistic missiles led to a fear in European circles that they might no longer be able to rely on America's nuclear umbrella.

The WEU Council issued the "Platform on European Security Interests" in October 1987, reaffirming the WEU's primary objective of preventing war through deterrence. It did, however, mark the first appearance of a distinctive "European identity" in security matters.[35]

The second significant event was the EU's Single European Act (SEA) that came into force on 1 July 1987 and established the European Political Cooperation (EPC) with responsibility for coordinating the external foreign policies of the EU. However, the SEA was silent on coordination of security matters. Such matters were explicitly left to WEU and NATO. The primary reasons for this are reluctance by the member states to relinquish sovereignty over defense matters to the supranational EU Commission or EPC, suspicion by the US over the effect on NATO, and the weakness of the WEU institutions.

There are two differing views on the WEU's relationship with NATO. The first, often referred to as the "Atlanticist" view, argues that the WEU should be the "European Pillar" within NATO. This view rests on five overlapping arguments. First, the Atlanticists, despite the end of the cold war, believe that

NATO remains essential to the defense and wider security of the European continent. Second, they believe that NATO is better able to adopt a more political orientation to accommodate moves towards a greater European security identity. Third, the Atlanticists believe that a US military presence in Europe is needed for the foreseeable future and that only NATO can achieve this. Fourth, they see NATO as a bulwark against renationalization of security policies. Finally, they see NATO as a means of managing the political and security evolution of Europe in the post–cold-war era.[36]

Those who have an opposite view see the WEU as a means of fostering increased European integration. They foresee the WEU as the security arm of the EU. As the EU moves to closer economic integration (via the SEA and the European Monetary Union) and greater foreign policy integration via the EPC, they argue that the natural evolution for a common security voice is via the WEU.[37]

The most telling arguments against the WEU playing a central role in European security involve the WEU's inability to coordinate actions in both the Gulf War and in Yugoslavia (at least as of January 1994). Further, while the WEU is becoming more integrated with the EU, it has the fatal flaw of not containing all the EU's members.[38] This is a particular concern in light of the addition of Sweden, Austria, and Finland by the mid-1990s. The first two are traditional neutral states, and the third is still faced with the delicate balancing act of not appearing to be a threat to Russia. Despite the collapse of the WTO, Russia still does not have a western security alliance state directly on her borders save Norway at the Kola Peninsula.[39]

The Visegrad Group

Any security arrangement in Europe must address the problem of the former WTO states. For the purposes of this study, the discussion is limited to the Central and Eastern European states and does not include the former Soviet republics. Since the end of World War II, the West has used a perimeter strategy to ward off threats to its security. Is such a strategy, moved further east, still viable? Some argue that the most promising European strategy is collective security and the best means to accomplish that is through the Conference on Cooperation and Security in Europe (CSCE).[40] Others argue that the best means to ensure security to Eastern Europe is through some sort of accommodation in which the West provides security guarantees to the East. This can be accomplished either through formal or informal arrangements with NATO or the EU/WEU or through verbal guarantees without any structural ties.[41] One option not often explored is the viability of Eastern states forming their own collective defense security arrangement.

There is a fundamental tie between democracy, economic liberalization, and security. It is not a matter of providing democratic institutions first, followed by market economy antecedents such as private property rights, then adding security regimes later. Rather, it is the establishment of all three systems, in a balanced manner, that secures the twin goals of peace and prosperity. This is the central challenge facing the states of Eastern Europe. There are key obstacles facing these postcommunist states in their first few decades of protodemocracy. First, political apathy of the populace, born of long authoritarian rule and a cynicism that current politicians cannot solve their problems, is a direct result of the high political costs of marketization. Second, the political and bureaucratic opposition to reforms by the remnants of the former communist *nomenklatura* and the uncertain civil-military relations is a source of internal instability. Finally, the explosion of ethnic identity and the long-standing irredentist problems facing many Eastern European states has both external and internal instability dimensions.[42] A real danger is that a combination of these factors may cause the collapse of the fragile governments and their replacement by demagogic and potentially rogue governments.

To solve these security problems, Eastern European governments have pursued various strategies. The most prominent have been attempts to gain some sort of association with Western states, either through NATO or the EU.[43] However, these states have also formed associations among themselves, based upon the common perception that while restructuring, redeploying, reducing, professionalizing, depoliticizing, and developing new arms sources and the like were essential steps in transforming their military forces, they were not going to achieve security solely through their national armed forces. The main source of East European security will be a combination of bilateral, regional, and multilateral schemes.

Focusing on the regional attempts, the experiences of Hungary, Poland, and Czechoslovakia[44] (the Three) is instructive. Immediately after achieving their independence from Soviet domination in 1989, these three states viewed cooperation among themselves as a transitory phase, as a test of preparedness, toward eventual EU membership. However, by mid-1992, the international as well as regional climate had changed significantly. First, following the turmoil over the Maastricht Treaty ratification, the EU turned decidedly inward and focused more on the implications of deepening rather than the prospects of widening. Furthermore, any expansion of the EU was viewed more in favor of the more prosperous European Free Trade Area (EFTA) states of Sweden, Finland, Austria, and Norway than the poorer East European states. Thus, the Three recognized that full EU membership was not going to occur this century. The second significant event was the August 1991 coup attempt in the Soviet Union. This forced the Three to undertake serious consultation of common security concerns. However, the past record of relationships among the Three argued against substantial cooperation in the present.

Therefore, the Three took immediate steps to lay to rest some of these past conflicts. First, they agreed to forgo any attempt to reopen territorial issues. Second, they attempted to defuse the volatile irredentist issue. This had been a particular concern of Hungary, who pledged to renounce sovereignty claims over other states with large Hungarian populations in return for guarantees of ethnic minority rights. The Three have pursued cooperation along several separate paths. The broader Central European Initiative[45] brings together the Three with the neighboring states of Italy, Austria, and the former Yugoslav republics of Slovenia and Croatia.

The Visegrad Group, which is confined to the Three, has proceeded along the lines of pursuing greater economic integration and joint security efforts. The Three, through experiences in coordinating a joint response to the August coup, the civil war in Yugoslavia, and the protracted EU negotiations have realized that they carry more weight when speaking with a single voice. Hence, at their Prague summit in May 1992, they decided on a joint application to the EU. Likewise, they pursue common interests within NATO's newly formed North Atlantic Cooperation Council.[46] In accomplishing these tasks, however, the Three have explicitly stopped short of formalizing their efforts institutionally. This is because some, Hungary in particular, believe that such an institution may be used as an excuse by the EU to delay full membership in the community.

In sum, the Central European states of Hungary, Poland, and the Czech Republic have used many different, but complementary, avenues to increased cooperation. They have done so primarily in response to the diminished prospects for fuller integration into existing Western European structures. It is too much to call the Visegrad Group an *alliance* in the traditional meaning of that term. There is no formalized structure, for example. However, in terms of using cooperative frameworks to achieve lasting goals, the Visegrad Group offers many insights into future arrangements. First, the group covers a broad range of issues, from economic and defense security concerns to migration, borders, and external-relation issues that traditionally fall under political-security discussions. Second, the Three realize that more can be gained by joint action than can be achieved unilaterally. Despite past disagreements, they do recognize common grounds. Finally, they have learned much from other similar type arrangements. The Three have held numerous meetings with representatives of Belgium, the Netherlands, and Luxembourg—the so-called Benelux countries—about building regional cooperation along the Benelux lines.[47]

Conclusions

The fundamental cause of the changing nature of alliances is the end of the cold war. This changed the international environment from one characterized by predominantly bipolar, defense security concerns to a multipolar arena in which defense security issues are receiving competition from other security concerns, mainly economic security. Furthermore, the internal relationships of the post–World War II alliances are significantly changed. When defense security issues dominated, the United States and the Soviet Union were the hegemonic powers in their alliances. As John Spanier notes,[48] these unequal power arrangements within alliances had two significant outcomes. First, due to the differential in power, each bipolar superpower was, in effect, a unilateral guarantor of their allies' security. Second, this dependency of the lesser powers on the dominant power reduced the freedom of movement of the lesser powers. For example, the US response to the Soviet stationing of missiles in Cuba in 1962 was taken unilaterally, even though any war that might have resulted would surely have affected America's NATO allies. Likewise, when the Nationalist Chinese wanted to invade mainland China, the US stopped them. The Soviets exercised similar restraint on the Communist Chinese invasion of Taiwan in 1958 because the Soviets believed such an action would risk wider war with the United States.

The changed international environment has significant impacts on US security concerns and the role alliances will play. First and foremost, the bipolar (or now unipolar) defense security world is being supplanted by a multipolar economic-security world. This is not to say that defense security concerns have been eliminated. The world is still a dangerous place.[49] What it does imply is that for the major industrialized nations of the world, defense-security concerns follow economic-security concerns, a complete reversal from the 40-plus years following World War II when economic-security concerns were often subordinated to defense-security concerns. This transformation of the international arrangements have two ramifications. First, if the theories of international relations theorists are correct, this multipolar world will be more stable. This is because each major power views all other actors as both potential adversaries and potential allies. This gives the state greater mobility to align and realign itself. The second ramification is that such alignments will tend to be short-lived and issue-specific. This too should lead to greater stability because issue disagreements will be resolved by compromise instead of conflict. Much like domestic political actors, each state will recognize that an opponent on one issue may be an ally on another. More important, each actor recognizes that each opponent, as potential ally, must not be forced to total capitulation on any one issue that may preclude cooperative action on another issue.

This comparison with the domestic political process leads to the second implication that the changed international environment has on US security concerns and the role of alliances—the increasing role that domestic policies and the political process will play in alliances. It has been an American tradition that foreign policy was the province of the executive branch and enjoyed bipartisan support from the legislative branch. On the other hand, economic policy, seen as domestic policy, was very much subject to the vicissitudes of the political process, particularly the interplay of domestic interest groups. As economic-security issues take the fore in international relations, the boundary between foreign and domestic politics becomes blurred.

These two forces—the emergence of economic-security over defense-security issues and the increasing role of domestic political process in international relations—are affecting all the alliances that remain from the cold-war era. They are also shaping new alliances as they form. These changes will significantly affect US security policies in the twenty-first century.

First, NATO will remain but only as a means of consultation between the US and Europe. While maintaining its ostensibly defense-security veneer, it will become more involved in issues dealing with economic-security matters. The US will pursue defense-security policy through unilateral determination of issues under a United Nations umbrella. Likewise, the Europeans will pursue collective defense policy through the wider-mandated European Union—expanded to include Central and Eastern European nations in at least associate status—that will use the WEU as its defense security arm.

Second, pure defense-security alliances will lose their vitality if not outright disappear. Nations will still cooperate, however, but the alliances will be issue-specific and immensely more flexible. The relaunching of the WEU in the 1980s and subsequent development is a case in point. The impetus for a revived WEU was a new awareness that serious discussion of a

European external identity and a defense capability could not be postponed in a changed global environment. Equally important, however, was the awareness that the WEU was no more than a transitional institution, albeit a critically important one. The final product will be a EU-based political-security and defense-security arrangement. To get to this state, the WEU provides a forum for senior defense and foreign affairs officials of nine European nations to meet regularly outside the NATO framework. Recognizing this, the NATO heads of state, at their January 1994 summit, authorized the establishment of a Combined Joint Task Force headquarters to coordinate the efforts of NATO and the WEU.[50]

Finally, alliances will supplement cooperative agreements between the states in these issue-specific arrangements. These alliances will be used to resolve wider conflicts. In other words, alliances, instead of being either specifically defense-security oriented (as is NATO and the WEU) or economic-security and political-security oriented (i.e., EU), will be forums for discussion and resolution of all three agendas. The model will be more like the European Council of the EU than the North Atlantic Council of NATO.

The primary policy implication for US decision makers is to recognize these changed international environmental conditions. Second, US policy makers must not try "new wine in old bottles." For example, the US should not attempt to refocus NATO to achieve nondefense security goals. The US should look to other multilateral organizations to fulfill the continuing need for global engagement. Recognizing that security in the twenty-first century will be predominately, though not exclusively, economic-security based, the US needs to refocus on building and maintaining its economic base.

Finally, those involved in planning military options in the twenty-first century must likewise change their horizons. The familiar scenarios are gone. The new scenarios are murky at best. American leadership in European security matters can no longer be taken for granted. Thus, military officers must become even more aware of the geopolitical environment. They must be attuned to the political ramifications of their plans and, reflecting the ambiguous defense-security arena, be sensitive to requirements laid on by their political masters that may involve less than clear and concise objectives. In the past, a concrete plan against a known threat only required "fine-tuning" around the edges. This situation no longer exists. Just as diplomats in this changed world must relearn the art of statecraft, so too must military professionals rediscover the art of planning under conditions of ambiguity.

Notes

1. For one senior military leader's view on the changing role of the US in the post–cold-war era, see US Army Chief of Staff Gordon R. Sullivan's "Power Projection and the Challenges of Regionalism," *Parameters* 23, no. 2 (Summer 1993): 2–15.

2. See William G. Hyland, "Reexamining National Strategy," in *The Nature of the Post–Cold War World* (Carlisle Barracks, Pa.: US Army War College Strategic Studies Institute, 1993).

3. First, though, some definitions are in order. The Department of Defense defines an *alliance* as a formal arrangement to accomplish broad, long-term, objectives. This is in contrast to a *coalition*, which is an informal agreement between two or more states for common action. Balance of power refers to the state system in which any shift away from equilibrium leads to countershifts through mobilization of countervailing power. That is, power begets opposing power; the best antidote to power is power. External threat orientation as used in this study refers to the core objective of an alliance. It means that the purpose of the alliance is to counter some other identified state. For example, NATO clearly stated that its purpose was to counter the Soviet Union in Europe. Likewise, the WTO was formed precisely to counter NATO. Conversely, internal conflict resolution means that the purpose of the alliance is to provide a forum to mediate policy conflicts *among the alliance member states*. Additionally, these conflicts are not limited to defense issues but may embrace wider concerns such as economic or political conflict.

4. For a discussion of the times when the US will engage in unilateral actions and the desire for collective action, see US Secretary of Defense Dick Cheney's *Annual Report to the President and the Congress* (Washington, D.C.: Government Printing Office, 1993), 1–23.

5. For a countering argument that claims NATO is still relevant and indeed essential to US security, see Capt William F. Hickman, "NATO: Is It Worth the Trouble?" *Naval War College Review* 46, no. 3 (Summer 1993): 36–46.

6. The evolution of the European Union is beyond the scope of this paper. For our purposes, "EU" will be used to include members of the European Economic Community, the European Community, and the newly named European Union.

7. For an insightful analysis of the coalition wars against Napoléon, see Russell F. Weigley, *The Age of Battles: The Quest for Decisive Warfare from Breitenfeld to Waterloo* (Bloomington, Ind.: Indiana University Press, 1991).

8. See Paul Kennedy, *The Rise and Fall of the Great Powers* (New York: Vintage Books, 1987), 129–39.

9. Ibid., 184–90. This was a fundamental problem for nineteenth-century geopoliticians.

10. This section is based mainly on John W. Spanier's *Games Nations Play* (Washington, D.C.: CQ Press, 1991), 140–45; and David W. Ziegler, *War, Peace and International Politics*, 9th ed. (New York: Harper-Collins, 1993), 53–61.

11. Following the end of World War II, the Soviets requested Turkey to relinquish some territory that the Soviets believed the Turks had falsely appropriated following the Bolshevik Revolution in 1917 when the Soviet Union was weakened by civil war. Turkey refused the Soviet request. In Greece, the government found itself in a civil war with communist guerrillas that were believed to be controlled by the Kremlin.

12. Ziegler, 58.

13. Great Britain, France, Belgium, the Netherlands, Denmark, Norway, Luxembourg, Iceland, Portugal, and Italy.

14. *The North Atlantic Treaty Organisation: Facts and Figures* (Brussels: NATO Information Service, 1989), 11.

15. Albania, Bulgaria, Czechoslovakia, East Germany, Hungary, Poland, Romania, and the USSR.

16. *The North Atlantic Treaty Organisation: Facts and Figures*, 207.

17. Obviously, this is not all inclusive. See Gregory Treverton, "America's Stakes and Choices in Europe," *Survival* 34, no. 3 (Autumn 1992): 119–35.

18. Anthony Lake, "How Partnership for Peace Will Build Security in Europe," *Boston Globe*, 12 January 1994, 11.

19. For those interested in a deeper understanding of the NATO origins, see *The North Atlantic Treaty Organisation*, chapter 1.

20. See Ted Greenwood, "NATO's Future," *European Security* 2, no. 1 (Spring 1993): 1–14.

21. These scenarios are based upon an analysis done by Charles L. Glaser, "Why NATO is Still Best: Future Security Arrangements for Europe," *International Security* 18, no. 1 (Summer 1993): 8–13.

22. Treverton, 123. He writes, "NATO has the great virtue of existing."

23. Some may argue that there is a fourth possible scenario—a war between Western states.

24. See Phil Williams, Paul Hammond, and Michael Brenner, "Atlantis Lost, Paradise Regained? The United States and Western Europe after the Cold War," *International Affairs* 69, no. 1 (1993): 1–17.

25. See Paul Bracken and Stuart Johnson, "The Changing Framework of European Security," *Defense Analysis* 9, no. 2 (1993): 227–30.

26. The *Bundeswehr* (Federal Armed Forces) are scheduled to be reduced from the pre-unification level of 515,000 (which included East German forces) to 370,000 by the end of 1994. See Thomas-Durell Young, *The "Normalization" of the Federal Republic of Germany's Defense Structures* (Carlisle Barracks, Pa.: US Army War College Strategic Studies Institute, September 1992), 8–17.

27. For a complete analysis of the consequences of NATO's emerging consensual decision-making process, see Michael Brenner, "Multilateralism and European Security," *Survival* 35, no. 2 (Summer 1993): 138–55.

28. Ibid., 149.

29. For a more detailed examination of the roots of the WEU, see Alfred Cahen, *The Western European Union and NATO: Building a European Defense Identity within the Context of Atlantic Solidarity* (London: Brassey's, 1989), 1–4.

30. The Brussels Treaty was designed to be more than a defense treaty. Its complete title, "Treaty of Economic, Social and Cultural Collaboration and Collective Self-defense," highlights the diverse nature of this alliance.

31. Ziegler, 263–64.

32. See James E. Dougherty and Robert L. Pfaltzgraff, Jr., *Contending Theories of International Relations*, 2d ed. (New York: Harper & Row, 1981), 418–21.

33. The Paris Agreements, signed on 23 October 1954, actually consisted of six documents in four areas: (1) West German sovereignty and the termination of the occupation regime there; (2) the revision of the Brussels Treaty and the creation of the WEU that included Germany and Italy; (3) German rearmament; and (4) French-German agreement on the Saar. See Julia A. Myers, *The Western European Union: Pillar of NATO or Defence Arm of the EC?* (London: Centre for Defence Studies, 1993), 3.

34. Ibid., 7–8.

35. Ibid., 17–18.

36. Ibid., 23–27.

37. Ibid., 32–36.

38. The Maastricht Treaty on European Union, signed on 7 February 1992 by the 12 EC members, invites the members of the EC who are not in the WEU to become either members or observers. Likewise, it invites non-EC European members of NATO (Iceland, Norway [who subsequently has applied for EC membership] and Turkey [whose EC membership application is on hold]) to become associate members of the WEU. See Anand Menon, Anthony Forster, and William Wallace, "A Common Defence?" *Survival* 34, no. 3 (Autumn 1992): 98–118.

39. It is interesting to note that Norway is the only NATO member that has no plans to cut its defense budget. They fear that much of the equipment brought out of Central Europe under the Conventional Forces in Europe agreement has been relocated in the Kola Peninsula. Hickman, 45.

40. Charles L. Glaser argues that collective security will not work. His argument is based on fundamental flaws in collective security, not any specific flaws in a European system. The two key flaws are that states will fail to meet their commitments and that collective security only works when it is unnecessary. Glaser, 27–29.

41. German Minister of Defense Volker Rühe argues that Eastern Europe should be tied structurally to the West. See his "Shaping Euro-Atlantic Policies: A Grand Strategy for a New Era," *Survival* 35, no. 2 (Summer 1993): 134. Glaser argues that NATO can prevent instability in the East through security guarantees not requiring formal or informal structural ties. Glaser, 19–23.

42. See Daniel N. Nelson, "Democracy, Markets, and Security in Eastern Europe," *Survival* 35, no. 2 (Summer 1993): 159–64, for further elaboration on these obstacles.

43. Perhaps reflecting the desperation born of the fear of violence in the former Yugoslavia spilling over their boundaries, Albania formally applied for NATO membership in early 1993. The application was turned down. Ibid., 166.

44. On 1 January 1993, Czechoslovakia peacefully separated into separate Czech and Slovak Republics. The Slovak Republic, under Prime Minister Vladimir Meciar, is generally seen as the most recalcitrant state. See David Shumaker, "The Origins and Development of Central European Cooperation: 1989–1992," *East European Quarterly* 27, no. 3 (September 1993): 355.

45. The Central European Initiative started as the Alpine-Adria Working Group in 1977. Ibid., 357–60.

46. This council was formed in November 1991 specifically to foster security cooperation between the 16 NATO members and former WTO states.

47. Shumaker, 365–66.

48. Spanier, 143.

49. It is worth noting that the issue that brought France back into NATO's integrated command structure for the first time since its withdrawal in 1966 was the threat of proliferation of weapons of mass destruction.

50. "NATO Leaders Enjoy Rare Accord on Arms," *Defense News*, 10–16 January 1994, 1, 8.

The Military's Changing Sociological Concerns

Rali M. Dobberstein

America's most pressing sociological concerns include rapidly changing demographics, a growing percentage of women in the work force, and increasing efforts toward gaining civil rights and social acceptance for homosexuals. The US population is becoming more diverse by race and by ethnic origin. By the year 2000 proportionally more Americans will be members of a minority group. Additionally, there has been a greater acceptance of women and gays in the workplace. A study conducted by the United Nations (UN)-sponsored International Labour Organization noted women will represent a majority of the work force by the end of the decade. As for gays we can expect changes in society to reshape the nation's political agenda, creating advocacy groups for new legislation and altering the consequences of existing laws.

The United States armed forces as a reflection of the nation in microcosm has the same sociological concerns. In the future, a number of questions of sociological concern will come to the attention of the United States military. The armed forces of the twenty-first century will be challenged on demographic, homosexual, and gender issues. The most important issue we will face is changing demographics. Within the realm of changing demographics lies the issue of language. We may have in our armed forces a situation similar to that of the Canadian armed forces—essentially an awareness of the importance of making the forces more representative of a multicultural nation. New policies may include expansion of language training, recruiting, and promotion policy to achieve proportional representation through rank structure, separate training for non-English-speaking personnel covering most specialist trades, and non-English-speaking personnel in ships, flying squadrons, and ground-force units. These types of initiatives, coinciding with sharp reductions in overall strength and a weak budget coupled with political interference would no doubt be acutely unpopular with the English-speaking majority. The non-English-language units would make the armed forces look as multicultural as the country they serve. Time, patience, and new generations of personnel will gradually make bilingualism seem more natural. As we will see, these issues are the subject of intense debate. This issue of changing demographics alone deserves a separate study—one that goes beyond the scope of this paper. My paper will discuss the secondary issues we as an armed force will face in the twenty-first century. These issues center around the question of equal rights and opportunities for both gays and women, the collective good of society, and concern for the overall performance of the armed forces in terms of the effect gays and women will have on the military's morale, good order, discipline, and ability to fight. This study intends to analyze the homosexual and women-in-combat issues that, as we will see, have already caused some changes; and, given the intense debate surrounding them, will continue to cause changes for years to come. How will these challenges affect the military? The answers are to be determined.

Homosexuality in the Armed Forces

Department of Defense (DOD) policy concerning homosexuals in military service has recently changed. Prior to 1993 personnel policy barred homosexuals from entering or serving in the armed forces. Under this policy individuals who stated they were homosexual, who engaged or intended to engage in homosexual behavior, or who married or attempted to marry someone of the same sex were administratively discharged from the military service. In addition homosexual or heterosexual acts of sodomy or disorders and neglects to the prejudice of good order and discipline in the armed forces were punishable by court-martial.

In July 1993 President Clinton announced a compromise plan, commonly referred to as the "don't ask, don't tell, don't pursue" policy. President Clinton's policy stated that sexual orientation was not a bar to military service. It also proposed to end the practice of questioning recruits and service members about their sexual orientation but allowed the military to continue to discharge those who engage in homosexual acts, state that they are homosexual or bisexual, or marry or attempt to marry someone of the same sex. President Clinton's compromise also called for even-handed enforcement of the *Uniform Code of Military Justice* for heterosexuals and homosexuals and an end to witch-hunts to force homosexuals out of the military.

In fall 1993 the House and Senate both countered President Clinton's compromise plan with new legislative policy. The new legislative policy approved in November 1993 states that Congress has the constitutional right to make rules for the military, that the armed forces are unique, and persons who demonstrate a propensity or intent to engage in homosexual acts would create an unacceptable risk to the high standards of morale, good order and discipline in the military. Under this new policy, making a statement about one's sexual orientation is considered an "act." The legislation makes no mention of orientation, witch-hunts, or the code and says a future defense secretary could reinstate the policy of asking recruits their sexual orientation.

As we implement this new don't ask, don't tell, don't pursue policy it is useful to examine the attitudes and policies of other countries. A number of countries have tackled the issue of whether homosexuals should be allowed in the military. NATO acceptance of gays runs full spectrum "from that of the Dutch—where gays in the army are represented by a union—to that of the Greeks—who flatly ban gays from service" (see Table 1).[1]

Although numerous countries have policies that are more liberal than the current US ban, nations that allow homosexuals to serve openly have not resolved the problem of fully integrating them into their armies. The Dutch, Germans, and Israelis are but several examples, and their experiences foretell some of the problems the US can expect if it too allows homosexuals to serve in its armed forces.

For nearly two decades the Dutch military has been open to homosexuals under a governmentwide edict that makes discrimination on the grounds of sexual preference illegal, and yet research found widespread discrimination against gays. There were few cases of physical assault but many examples of

Table 1

NATO Policies on Gays in Uniform

Belgium	Not acknowledged as a relevant issue. Neither conscripts nor volunteers are asked about their sexual orientation. Homosexuality itself does not exempt Belgians from the draft unless there are accompanying psychological disorders as determined by clinical evaluation. Homosexual conduct between consenting adults off duty is not punished, but inappropriate homosexual and heterosexual behavior can lead to dismissal from military duty or exclusions from certain units and jobs.
Britain	Homosexuals are officially barred from service, but unofficially the British Defence Ministry says the practice of prosecuting gays simply for being gay is rare. Homosexual acts among consenting adults have been decriminalized in military as well as civilian law as long as it is off duty.
Canada	Was ordered by the Federal Court of Canada to drop its ban on gays in the Canadian Forces in October 1992. Canadian service members were not required to certify they were heterosexual when they enlisted, but openly gay persons were often discharged or had their transfer or promotion opportunities limited. The files of service members who were either discharged or denied promotion because of their sexual orientation are being reviewed for reconsideration by military authorities.
Denmark	No law or policy. Neither conscripts nor volunteers are asked about sexual orientation. Treated as a personal, private matter.
France	No legislation or written codes. Gays are allowed to serve in the French military as long as they do not harass other members of their units. But gays and lesbians can avoid being drafted by claiming their homosexuality is incompatible with service life.
Germany	Homosexuality cannot be used as a reason not to be drafted, although potential gay conscripts who claim service would be psychologically injurious are evaluated and frequently given alternative mandatory service. Career members of the military who are openly gay do face discrimination, frequently finding promotions blocked and access to top-level classified information denied.
Greece	Homosexuals are banned from military service.
Italy	Homosexuals are deemed unsuitable for military service. During medical examinations, homosexual conscripts will be declared ineligible if found to have behavioral "anomalies" caused by sexual deviations.
Luxembourg	Homosexuals are not precluded from service. Military service is voluntary and enlistees are not asked about sexual orientation. Improper conduct—whether homosexual or heterosexual—is punishable by discharge or court-martial.
Netherlands	Basic law prohibits all discrimination, for any reason. A union represents homosexuals in the military. Unwanted advances are treated as improper behavior. Courses in human relations are conducted for commanders and include homosexual issues. Legislation is pending for homosexual survivor benefits.
Norway	Not considered a relevant issue and no one entering the service is asked about their sexual orientation. Unwanted advances by either homosexual or heterosexual service members are treated as improper behavior contrary to good order and discipline.
Portugal	Not seen as a relevant issue. Homosexuals may serve in the armed forces, although conduct may be punishable.
Spain	There are no codes regulating homosexuals in the military. Like religion, sexual orientation is considered a person's own choice.
Turkey	Homosexuals are not permitted to serve openly in the armed services, although they are not asked about their sexual orientation upon entering the service.

Source: Reprinted courtesy of *Army Times*, 11 January 1993. Copyrighted by Army Times Publishing Company, Springfield, Virginia.

verbal abuse. Although lesbians were found to have experienced fewer problems than gay men, homosexuals of both sexes faced an "unfriendly" military environment.

Although the German armed forces' (Bundeswehr) prohibition on gays ended in 1969, the Bundeswehr also has experienced problems in fully integrating homosexuals into their army. For example, "gay German officers find paths to promotion blocked, and in some cases have been blocked from access to classified material."[2] Gay conscripts often find life in the Bundeswehr unpleasant.

Israeli policy states homosexuals are not to be denied promotion because of their sexual orientation, that they are allowed to become career soldiers, and that they may serve in the most elite fighting units, even those on critical frontiers. Reality however is quite different. Israeli soldiers found to be gay or who proclaim their homosexuality must undergo psychological testing. Their files are annotated, and they are usually barred from positions requiring top security clearances. Known gays rarely are assigned to combat units and do not serve without stigma regardless of the position they hold.

David Burrelli, in his examination of homosexuals and US military policy, believes "the question confronting policy makers remains, To what extent, if any, would open homosexuality be disruptive to morale, cohesion and readiness in the ranks, and to what extent does any such disruption justify discrimination?"[3] Other problems to keep in mind are public opinion, including the views of current active duty military personnel and the scientific literature on group cohesion, sexuality, and related health issues. Lastly, legal and enforcement issues must be addressed. Ronald Ray notes "DOD and the services have commissioned two major efforts that focused on whether homosexuals were more of a security risk than heterosexuals and concluded that there was no factual data to substantiate that premise."[4]

The Rand Corporation has conducted many studies for the Department of Defense. Recent research into the issue of acknowledged homosexuals serving in the military concluded that acceptance by the public and by the people serving in the US military is critical. A review of various surveys indicates that US public opinion is divided over this issue. Until recently roughly half of the population believed that homosexuals should not be allowed to serve. However, a very recent poll indicates that the percentage who believes they should not be allowed to serve under any conditions has dropped to less than 25 percent. Clearly the public has become more accepting of homosexuality and of homosexuals serving in the military.

In a study undertaken by Rand's National Defense Research Institute, researchers found that "military opinion is overwhelmingly against allowing homosexuals to serve. In surveys and Rand-conducted focus groups, a minority of service members expressed indifference to or approval of the policy change, and women were less opposed than men."[5] The debate has centered around concern about the effect that an acknowledged homosexual would have on "combat effectiveness and unit cohesion." Most military leaders argue that introduction of a known homosexual into a unit, no matter how discreet his or her behavior might be, would seriously undermine the cohesiveness of that unit. Unfortunately, the subject has not been studied specifically, and no controlled experiments or other research bears directly on this issue.

The Rand Corporation also discovered that a large body of applicable research exists in the fields of industrial organization, social psychology, sports psychology, and group behavior. Other potentially relevant material can be found in the ethnographic and biographical military literature. The principle conclusion from this literature is a commonsense observation: It is not necessary to like people in order to work with them, so long as members share a commitment to the group's objectives.

The new US policy emphasizes actual conduct, not behavior presumed because of sexual orientation, and holds all service members to the same standard of professional conduct. Rand Corporation found that four features of this standard are central:

- A requirement that all members of the military services conduct themselves in ways that enhance good order and discipline. Such conduct includes showing respect and tolerance for others. While heterosexuals would be asked to tolerate the presence of known homosexuals, all personnel, including acknowledged homosexuals, must understand that the military environment is no place to advertise one's sexual orientation.

• A clear statement that inappropriate personal conduct could destroy order and discipline and that individuals are expected to demonstrate the common sense and good judgment not to engage in such conduct.

• A list of categories of inappropriate conduct, including personal harassment (physical or verbal conduct toward other, based on race, gender, sexual orientation, or physical features), abuse of authority, displays of affection, and explicit discussions of sexual practices, experience, or desires.

• Application of these standards by leaders at every level of the chain of command, in a way that ensures that unit performance is maintained.[6]

Our new conduct-based policy does not require extensive revisions to existing military rules and regulations or to personnel policy. Rand Corporation concluded that on issues such as recognizing homosexual marriages or conferring benefits on homosexual partners, there is no reason for the DOD to change current policy or to become the lead federal agency in these areas.

Women in the Armed Forces

America is experiencing a growing percentage of women in the workplace. Women will represent a majority of the work force by the end of the decade. We will now focus our attention on a hotly debated gender issue—that of women in combat.

Current laws and policies regarding the assignment of women in the armed forces have recently changed. Prior to 1991 public laws and policies prevented women from serving in combat positions in any of the four services. The old laws that restricted the assignment of women in the Navy, Marine Corps, and Air Force were enacted in 1948 when the women's auxiliary components were made part of the permanent military structure. Under these statutes women in the Navy and Marine Corps could not be assigned to duty on ships or in aircraft that were engaged in combat missions, nor could they be assigned to other than temporary duty on vessels for the Navy except hospital ships, transports, and vessels of similar classification not expected to be assigned combat missions. Similarly, Air Force women, except those in designated medical, chaplain, and judge advocate functions, could not be assigned to duty on aircraft engaged in combat missions. There have never been any statutory restrictions on the utilization of Army women in combat. Rather, the Army Department policy paralleled the statutes and restricted women from assignment to those skills and positions that through doctrine, mission, or battlefield location invited the highest probability of direct combat.

In December 1991 public laws were amended and repealed thus allowing the Air Force and Navy to use women as combat pilots. Although the statutory ban was lifted, each service maintained regulations and/or policies governing the assignment of women. Women continued to be excluded from serving in direct ground combat positions (infantry, armor, artillery, and combat engineers), combat aircraft, or on combatant ships. In April 1993 Defense Secretary Les Aspin announced a policy that allows women to fly combat aircraft. The Air Force immediately changed to a gender-neutral pilot training and aircraft assignment system. New legislative policy approved in November 1993 allows women sailors to serve permanently on combat vessels.

As we begin to break the combat barrier it is also useful to examine the attitudes and policies of other countries. Although most Western Alliance countries allow women to serve in some capacity in the armed forces, only a few have opened combat posts to women (see Table 2). Policy on employment of women in combat has developed independently within each country. Northern European and North American members have tended to be more open earlier than their southern partners. In Denmark, Canada, and the Netherlands, for instance, women are ready, willing, and legally able to fill combat roles. Although some women presently serve in combat positions in Denmark, Canada, and the Netherlands, none have actually served in a direct combat unit under wartime conditions. In all cases the decision to integrate women into combat positions was based primarily on equal opportunity. These countries have pursued a gender-neutral policy in assigning women to military specialties. "Although

Table 2

NATO Policies on Women in Combat

Belgium	Unrestricted employment of women. Allows women in combat.
Britain	Under British law, women are not allowed in any combat roles and may be armed only for self-defense and certain guard duties.
Canada	A 1989 decision by the Canadian Human Rights Tribunal opened all combat positions in the Canadian Forces except submarines to women.
Denmark	First NATO country to introduce full equality between the sexes in its armed forces. Frontline combat units have included women since 1988; however, the Ministry of Defence prohibits women from flying combat aircraft. The Danish Air Force is receiving considerable pressure to reevaluate this policy.
France	Does not allow women in combat.
Germany	Does not allow women in combat. Limited primarily to the medical services.
Greece	Does not allow women in combat. Greek policy limits participation to certain arenas of military warfare, primarily the medical services, as well as clerical and secretarial duties.
Italy	Only NATO country to bar women from serving in its armed forces in any capacity. Recently (1989) began to debate legislation that would open up its military services to women.
Luxembourg	Allows women in their armed forces. Limited primarily to the medical services.
Netherlands	Allows women in combat. All combat assignments are open to women with the exception of submarines and the Dutch Marine Corps.
Norway	Unrestricted employment of women in all branches of the armed forces.
Portugal	Very restrictive rules governing the employment of women in the armed forces. Limited primarily to the medical services. No longer (as of 1989) recruits women.
Spain	Recently (1988) adopted legislation opening up its military services to women.
Turkey	Does not allow women in combat. Women serve primarily as administrators, doctors, nurses, and instructors.

Note: Table information not obtained from a specific source but written by the author and adapted to the format of Table 1.

the goal of these countries is a 20 percent 'critical mass' for women in the naval, air and ground forces, all are willing to operate at a minimum level of five percent."[7] It has been difficult, however, for any of these countries to attract and retain women in any significant numbers. Debate and criticism continue to plague their efforts. Similar circumstances can be expected in the United States armed forces as they take on the monumental task of integrating women into combat roles.

In 1988 Denmark became the first NATO country to allow women in combat units. David Fouquet in his article notes that "in addition to aiming for equal rights, the decision was to some degree motivated by difficulties in obtaining enough young men for the forces."[8] Despite Danish attempts to introduce "full equality" between the sexes in its armed forces, women are not permitted on submarines or in deep-sea diving. Additionally, Danish Air Force women are experiencing difficulty integrating because of reservations in the air force as to the piloting capabilities of women in high G-force aircraft like the F-16.

In 1987 the air arm of the Canadian forces opened all of its jobs to women, including flying single-seat fighter aircraft. Two years later, the Canadian forces were ordered to end their combat-exclusion policy. The Human Rights Tribunal in Canada gave the armed forces 10 years to achieve "full integration for women." This decision, which gives women the right to join men in combat units such as artillery and infantry continues to exclude them from submarine duty. Although the full integration of women into the Canadian forces is well ahead of schedule, it too is not without controversy. The vast majority of Canadian women lack the stamina and endurance to serve in the infantry. Also, for reasons unknown, the four women trained as fighter pilots are no longer assigned to tactical fighter squadrons.

James Hyde, in his examination of women in combat, notes that the Netherlands, with one of the most liberal NATO policies, not only permits women to serve in combat roles but in some cases they are chosen before men if considered to have the same abilities. In his words, "the Dutch want women to defend their country."[9] All Dutch training institutes are open to women as are all military posts. The Dutch have found however, that women generally don't qualify for marine, submarine, engineer, or other duties with heavy physical requirements. With only two exceptions, Royal Dutch marines and submarines, women are permitted in every combat role.

At the root of the controversy about women in combat roles is the issue of individual rights conflicting with the collective good for society and concern for the overall performance of the armed forces. The questions and concerns confronting policymakers are the same as those surrounding the homosexual issue.

In 1992 The Presidential Commission on the Assignment of Women in the Armed Forces researched the issue of women in combat. In doing so, they made a great effort to determine the attitudes of the public toward women in combat and the effect of such assignment on the public. They concluded that military readiness should be the driving concern regarding assignment policies; there are circumstances under which women might be assigned to combat positions. Overall, they found that one of the strongest sociological arguments in favor of women in combat focused on selecting the best-qualified person for a position, regardless of gender. It was their belief that under some circumstances, American society not only allows, but actually encourages and approves the further integration of women into combat roles. Specifically, public and military opinion varied depending on the combat role studied. In terms of ground combat, they found that members of the military are strongly against women serving in all branches of ground combat. The public, on the other hand, has mixed views on service in different ground combat specialties. When it came to combat aircraft, "69 percent of all pilots (Air Force, Navy, and Marines) believed that women should not be assigned to combat aircraft."[10] The question of assigning women to combatant vessels received the least objection.

> When asked in the national public survey whether women should be assigned to combat ships, 83 percent of the public surveyed said that women should be assigned. Among those who had prior military experience, 72 percent said that women should be assigned to combatant ships. The results of the military poll showed that in today's Navy, 73 percent of those surveyed felt that women should be allowed to serve on combatant ships. In fact, one-half of Navy respondents felt that women should be required to serve on combatant ships.[11]

Despite recent changes in the United State's combat-exclusion laws, American military women are prohibited by service policies that preclude them from serving in direct ground combat positions. The specialties that fall under the exclusion are grouped into four major areas: infantry, armor, artillery, and combat engineers. Scientific studies clearly show that unit cohesion can be negatively affected by the introduction of any element that detracts from the need for such key ingredients as mutual confidence, commonality of experience, and equitable treatment. Cohesion problems might develop around physical standards of endurance and stamina, forced intimacy/lack of privacy, traditional western values, dysfunctional relationships, and pregnancy.

Legal issues also pose a special problem for the United States. Concerns exist regarding the effect of changes in combat exclusion laws and policies on women's current exemption from conscription and registration obligations.

Conclusions

What will the American society look like in a generation? All indicators point toward a population that is becoming more diverse by race and ethnic origin. The growing presence of minority groups nationwide will be evident in the workplace, especially among young entrants to the work force. "During the remainder of the century, three of every five of the new entrants to the nation's labor force will be a member of a recognized ethnic or racial minority."[12] The US Department of Commerce projects that Black; Asian and Pacific Islander; American Indian, Eskimo, and Aleut; and Hispanic-origin minorities will comprise 37.9 percent of the population by 2025. Additionally, there has been a greater acceptance of women and gays in the workplace. Women will continue to increase in the work force. C. Edward Wall notes that "for the rest of the 1990s, some studies project: Two out of three new workers will be female."[13] By 2000 women are expected to make up more than half of the labor force. Ronald Ray notes "general public attitudes in the United States about homosexuality appear to be changing."[14] National polls, conducted by Gallup and Penn and Schoen Associates, Inc., "indicated that more Americans now say they believe that homosexuals should be allowed to participate in various occupations, including the armed forces. A Gallup survey conducted in March 1991 of a cross section of the American population of adults aged 18 and over showed that 69 percent of those interviewed felt that homosexuals should be allowed to serve in the armed forces, whereas only 51 percent felt that way in 1977."[15] The number of homosexuals in society is always difficult to determine. Ronald Ray, in his examination of the homosexual issue, notes "the limited data currently available (largely Kinsey Institute studies) suggests that the primary sexual orientation of between 5 and 10 percent of the general US population is homosexual."[16]

What will the United States armed forces look like in a generation? The United States armed forces as a reflection of the nation in microcosm will experience similar changes. Although the changes may not be extreme within the military, trends in the same general direction are anticipated. Given the "young" average age of the military, we can expect the same and quite possibly an even greater increase in the number of minorities serving in our armed forces. Remember, C. Edward Wall stated "three of every five of the new entrants to [the] nation's labor force will be a member of a recognized ethnic or racial minority."[17] Race and ethnic relations will take on greater importance than at any time in our military's history. We may even face the same situation Canada did in 1970, that is, having to make our armed forces more representative of a multicultural nation.

A growing percentage of women in the work force will be paralleled by a growing percentage of women in the military. With the integration of women into selected combat units under way, we will no doubt see more women exposed to combat, captured, and killed in defense of our nation. We will accumulate more data on how women perform in combat and the effect they have on a unit's morale, good order, discipline, and ability to fight. We may eventually evolve to the point where there will be unrestricted employment of women in the military. Secretary of Defense Les Aspin's decision to lift the combat barrier poses new questions. Would we ever go so far as to draft women in time of national crisis? The Supreme Court ruled in 1981 that women were excluded from registering for the draft. Rationale behind the decision was that any reinstated draft would be intended to increase the pool of people available for combat. Now that combat planes and ships are open to women, might they too be considered part of the available personnel pool in a major conflict?

If the armed forces are a microcosm of society and the Kinsey Institute is correct, we can expect between 5 and 10 percent of the military to be homosexual. Keep in mind that the number of homosexuals in any given group is hard to define. DOD's exclusion policy that involved a screening-out process and a lack of acceptance of homosexuality in the military probably limited the number of homosexuals in the military. Consequently, we can expect a slight increase in the number of gays in the military now that DOD has ended the practice of questioning recruits and service members about their sexual orientation. US policy has taken the middle ground—discouraging homosexuals from joining the military but not automatically discharging those who are already in it.

Information in this essay points to pending sociological concerns for the United States armed forces. The issues of homosexuality and women in combat will pose challenges; but, as mentioned earlier, the real challenge will be grappling with changing demographics. As we have seen, we are already experiencing pressure to remove the barriers. It is only a matter of time before the inevitable occurs. The manner in which the new US policy is implemented will have a decisive impact on whether these problems are managed with minimal disruptions or undermine the effort to change. US policy must be clear and consistently communicated from the top with emphasis on behavior and conduct. Leadership at all levels must send messages of reassurance to their subordinates and be empowered to implement the policy. A continuous improvement process should be established to identify and correct any problems.

Notes

1. Tom Philpott et al., "NATO Acceptance of Gays Runs Full Spectrum," *Army Times*, 11 January 1993, 20.
2. Ibid.
3. David F. Burrelli, *Homosexuals and U.S. Military Personnel Policy* (Washington, D.C.: Library of Congress, 1993), i.
4. Ronald D. Ray, *Gays: In or Out?* (Washington, D.C.: US General Accounting Office, 1992), 5.
5. Rand Corporation, *Sexual Orientation and U.S. Military Personnel Policy: Options and Assessment* (Santa Monica, Calif.: 1993), xxi.
6. Ibid., xxv.
7. Robert T. Herres, *The Presidential Commission on the Assignment of Women in the Armed Forces* (Washington, D.C.: US Government Printing Office, 1992), C-21.

8. David Fouquet, "Growing Role for Women in the Forces," *Jane's Defence Weekly*, 29 July 1989, 166.

9. James C. Hyde, "Gender Gap Narrows in Allied Services, but Women Still Fight for Combat Roles," *Armed Forces Journal International*, June 1989, 28.

10. Herres, 29.

11. Ibid., 32.

12. Rand Corporation, *Congress and the Year 2000: A Demographic Perspective on Future Issues* (Santa Monica, Calif.: 1991), 15.

13. C. Edward Wall, *A Matter of Fact* (Ann Arbor, Mich.: The Pierian Press, 1993), 225.

14. Ray, 6.

15. Ibid.

16. Ibid., 10.

17. Rand Corporation, *Congress and the Year 2000*, 15.

US National Security Strategy

Dr Paul Hacker

Because of the momentous changes in the international area resulting from the breakup of the Warsaw Pact and the dissolution of the Soviet Union, it is useful to take stock and examine the implications of these transformations. This essay examines some of the major trends in the 1990s and shows how they are necessitating a rethinking of the priorities for US national security policy. It begins by identifying the concept of national security, noting how that concept is evolving over time into a broader one than the purely military. It then considers the current international system and some elements that provide the basis for consideration of our national security strategy. It then focuses on the agencies of government that exist to sort out security issues and delineates their responses to recent trends. It proceeds to explore the consequences of the breakup of the Warsaw Pact for the future structure of European security, especially the implications of internal developments in Russia. Finally, it concludes that potential threats to US security have been transformed, but by no means dispersed, in the new international environment.

The Concept of National Security

Many writers have attempted to define national security. While they often differ in their focus, there is a general consensus on what the concept entails. Thus, Harold Brown, former secretary of defense, explained the concept as "the ability to preserve the nation's physical integrity and territory; to maintain its economic relations with the world in reasonable terms; [and] to protect its nature, institutions and governance from disruption from outside."[1] Other writers include the notion of retaining the core values of one's nation (Walter Lippmann), the absence of both threats to those values and fear that they will be attacked (Arnold Wolfers), or the enrichment of life in all its spheres (Michael Louw).[2]

National security should also be considered from the viewpoint of such dimensions as military versus nonmilitary or external versus internal. While the original postwar concept of national security primarily focused on its military dimensions, writers in the past two decades have broadened the notion to include access to raw materials (especially petroleum), the fight against drugs and terrorism, and the environment. National security has also been seen as having an important internal component that includes economic competitiveness, high literacy, and the sense of personal safety.[3] Brown, for one, saw slackening of economic growth; declining productivity; a dissipation of natural resources; a loss of domestic cohesion from ethnic or other conflicts; an erosion of the educational system; a decline in the work ethic; the alienation of the poor, aged, or minorities; and the loss of confidence in the national leadership as trends that could sap America's own security. Surely, the borders between the internal and external aspects of national security are blurring. Not untypically, President Bill Clinton has made it clear that domestic concerns—especially job creation—will have a strong impact on shaping his administrations's international policies. The public debate over the North American Free Trade Agreement (NAFTA) was played out primarily in terms of NAFTA's likely impact on American jobs. While some have criticized this "dollar-oriented" foreign policy, it does point up one basic political reality—a president's policies are only as viable as the public support he can gain for them. The other part of this reality is that it is becoming more and more difficult to separate economic policy from foreign and defense policy because all of our relationships with other major powers involve mixes of competition and cooperation.[4]

To be sure, a certain realism must pervade the discussion. Surely, without a healthy economic base, no nation can shoulder the burdens of military defense. On the other hand, military options must be available to counter military threats, as it is by no means sure that nonmilitary means alone can do the job.

The Structural Framework of National Security

The organizational system of national security that exists today was established by the National Security Act of 1947, as amended. The act created the National Security Council (NSC), headed by the president, with the vice president and secretaries of state and defense as members; and the director of Central Intelligence Agency (CIA) and the chairman of the Joint Chiefs of Staff (JCS) as advisors. It also created the first peacetime intelligence agency, the CIA; a unified Defense Department; and a JCS headed by a chairman and vice-chairman, with each of the uniformed service chiefs as members. The purpose of the JCS is to plan unified military strategy and reduce rivalry and duplication among the armed services in areas such as military procurement, research, and weapons development. Besides the armed services, the State Department, and the intelligence community, other agencies with important roles to play include the Department of Commerce, primarily responsible for helping American firms find overseas markets; the Treasury, responsible for our financial dealings with other nations; and Energy, which controls our nuclear testing program. No less important in this regard is the Congress, with its power of the purse over expenditures (especially foreign aid and the military), the Senate's ability to approve senior appointments, and the possibility of determining by legislation the structure of national security-related agencies and overseeing their activities through investigations and hearings.

Effective coordination of all aspects of national security policy among the various agencies of government is surely a crucial one. Each president has brought his own style into the picture. Some presidents have chosen to use the NSC and its staff more heavily than the Department of State to carry out particular activities (e.g., note the tension between National Security Advisor Zbigniew Brzezinski and Secretary of State Cyrus Vance in the Carter administration). Some have relied on small groups of trusted individuals not associated with either body. In some cases, senior NSC staff have been brought into the Department of State to take over policy-making positions. In the Clinton administration, indications are that the NSC is reverting to its classical function of coordination among the relevant federal agencies rather than taking an independent role for itself.

Intelligence Operations

Throughout the cold-war period, the primary responsibility of US intelligence agencies was to protect US security by gathering information about threats of surprise attack and subversion from the Soviet Union, its allies, and clients. In this connection, it is useful to review what has changed and what remains the same in the post–cold-war era.

The fact that Russia alone retains the capability to destroy the US, combined with the importance of events in Russia to the security concerns of its neighbors, means that developments in Russia and the former USSR will continue to be of prime concern to US strategic planners and thus to the intelligence community as well. This attention will monitor arms modernization programs, as well as Russia's future political landscape—its leadership and its intentions both at home and abroad.[5] Intelligence priorities will also focus on verification of arms control treaties, including strategic weapons, conventional forces in Europe, and chemical and bacteriological weapons.

In the post–cold-war environment, while the threat of a Russian surprise attack is almost nil, the need to provide lead-time warning of any attack will not end. As US military assets draw down, the US will be more vulnerable to surprise attack against itself or its friends and allies. As former House Intelligence Committee chairman Dave McCurdy pointed out, the question of intelligence data sharing will become more important in the future, as major US military actions are likely to be undertaken as part of a coalition.[6]

Another priority will be to keep track of attempts to proliferate weapons of mass destruction and missile technology. Intelligence sharing will be an issue not only vis-à-vis allies and future coalition partners, but also in regard to international organizations such as the International Atomic

Energy Agency (IAEA), whose work is crucial in the area of nonproliferation.

Other priority areas include support for future contingencies such as peacekeeping operations, drug interdiction, monitoring social unrest arising from population growth and international conflicts, assistance to insurgents or counterinsurgents, depending on which side they are fighting.[7] Last, but not least, in the list is the need to monitor terrorists and to assist in antiterrorist operations.

The Post–Cold-War World
Implications for American Policy

In the post-1945 period, the US has pursued an activist foreign policy involving the projection of American power abroad. The fundamental goal of American security policy was summed up in one word—containment—meaning the use of force and other instruments to stop the expansion of Soviet power. This expansion was seen as threatening in its ideological challenge to the basic precepts of Western democracy, its propaganda conducted against America's friends and allies, and wars of national liberation that aimed at overthrowing regimes depicted as being colonial or being closely associated with major Western powers. The USSR and its East European allies conducted espionage and forgery campaigns against the West and provided training and support to individuals and groups characterized as terrorists in the West. With the collapse of the USSR and the democratization of its former allies, these threats have effectively vanished and the need has arisen to consider the attributes of the post–cold-war international system that will determine future security policies.

Attributes of the New International System

With the collapse of the USSR, some writers suggest that a new unipolar system has emerged, with the US being the only relevant superpower. As Charles Krauthammer has put it, the US is the "only country with the military, diplomatic, political, and economic assets to be a decisive player in any conflict in whatever part of the world it chooses to involve itself."[8] While some may question that view, he does make an important point in noting that in discussions of collective security, dealing with such episodes as the Gulf War, one should not lose sight of the fact that without active American prodding and involvement, there would have been no UN or other response to Iraqi aggression.[9]

A second attribute is that, even though the ending of East-West confrontation has made the threat of a deliberate nuclear attack on the West highly improbable, the continued existence of massive nuclear arsenals means that arms control is still a relevant issue. As one specialist pointed out, even after the implementation of the Strategic Arms Reduction Treaty (START), both sides would retain some 12,000 strategic nuclear warheads. The START II treaty, assuming it is implemented, would reduce warheads to 3,000-3,500 for each side by the end of the century. Along with the START agreements, a comprehensive test ban—a measure strongly opposed by the Reagan-Bush administrations but favored by the Clinton administration—is more likely to be realized and should help reduce incentives for modernization of nuclear weapons.[10]

The main area of concern over former Soviet nuclear weapons is not so much the threat that they would be used against the West as it is uncertainty over the disposition of the former Soviet nuclear arsenal. For one, those weapons were contained on the territory of three other republics besides Russia (Kazakhstan, Belarus, Ukraine), and Ukrainian leaders have indicated reluctance to part with all of the weapons on their territory without firm security guarantees from Moscow (but also the US) and payments for the costs involved in dismantling those weapons. Another issue is whether Soviet nuclear weapons or expertise will be sold to the highest bidder in third world nations desiring to become members of the nuclear club.

Along with the reduction in the threat from our old adversary comes the likelihood that new states will join the nuclear club over the next few years. Iraq's nuclear program was in an advanced stage at the time of the Desert Storm operation, which set it back but cannot be guaranteed to have ended it. North Korea has refused IAEA inspection and has engaged in bellicose behavior over its nuclear program; it is likely that the country is on the verge of crossing the nuclear threshold if it has not done so already. Nations that have acquired or are in the process of developing nuclear weapons include India, Israel, Iran, Pakistan, Taiwan, Libya, Brazil, and Argentina. South Africa, which had its own nuclear weapons program, has voluntarily given it up. A number of other states have engaged in research on chemical and biological weapons. By the year 2000, some 20 states may also have the capability of building their own ballistic missiles. According to former defense secretary, Dick Cheney, by the year 2000, "more than two dozen developing nations will have ballistic missiles, 15 of these countries will have the scientific skills to make their own, and half of them either have or are near to getting nuclear capability, as well. Thirty countries will have chemical weapons, and ten will be able to deploy biological weapons."[11]

Proliferation of missiles from North Korea to such customers as Syria and Iran is becoming an increasing headache. So too are less-than-responsible Chinese policies that have allowed Chinese Silkworm missiles to be shipped to Iran in 1987 and sold other weapons to Iraq that were used against coalition forces in 1991. The crux of the problem with China is not merely the shipping of the weapons themselves; China has also assisted in the transfer of missile technology that will allow other states to begin their own missile manufacturing. China has also furnished nuclear information to a number of third world states aspiring to their own nuclear weapons.[12]

With such a combination of factors, the US ability to mount an operation such as Desert Shield/Storm looks increasingly problematic in the future.[13] As Frederick Strain, a proliferation expert, put it, "The possibility that the United States may face nuclear blackmail or assault has never been greater. When nations are ruled by despots who have little experience in crisis resolution and have a tendency to confuse personal ambition with the national interest, the likelihood of disaster increases dramatically." For this reason, he concludes that the US, more than ever before, needs to develop a defense against ballistic missiles.[14]

Another reality with which policymakers will have to deal is the fact that the US military can expect to have much more limited resources available in the years ahead; indeed, by 1995, military spending as a percentage of the gross national product (GNP) is expected to be under 4 percent—less than at any time since before Pearl Harbor.

In terms of the consequences of the above trends, one needs to reconsider the concept of deterrence. If containment has been one of the key concepts of postwar US policies, deterrence has surely been the other. Most of US strategic thinking was governed by the mutual assured destruction (MAD) doctrine that postulated that the Soviets would not attack the US and its allies as long as they were convinced they would suffer a counterattack that would destroy their society. With the expectation of a Russian nuclear attack discounted by most analysts, the question now becomes one of whether deterrence has a continuing utility as marginal insurance or whether it is still valid as a concept in the conventional arena.

The credibility of a deterrent is only as great as the ability to convince a potential aggressor that his actions will be met with a counterforce sufficient to destroy him and his military forces. Clearly, in the case of the Iraqi invasion of Kuwait in 1990, conventional deterrence failed, mainly because Saddam Hussein was unconvinced that the US and its allies would go to Kuwait's rescue. The concept of deterrence can work when one is dealing with an adversary who proceeds from the same psychocultural postulates as our own. The US may be faced with more cases like that of Saddam Hussein in the future that do not easily lend themselves to this sort of persuasion.

The reader should also be aware that one of the four key concepts of the Bush administration's final concept paper on national security strategy—reconstitution—has been criticized by some specialists as downgrading our ability to offer a credible deterrent. As defined in the strategy, reconstitution means the ability to recreate a global war-fighting capability, including training and fielding new fighting units from cadres, mobilizing previously trained or new manpower, and activating the industrial base on a large scale.[15] However, there are many uncertainties in such a scenario. Will there be sufficient warning? Will the US be capable of acting in time? Will our industrial plants be capable of returning to military production or will they already have gone over to other activities? Will needed expertise be irretrievably lost? US reconstitution may also be regarded as a casus belli for another power and might hasten the spiral of conflict rather than dampen it.[16]

The Gulf War of 1991 has also caused a rethinking of national security strategy in the wake of lessons learned from the conflict. First of all, Iraq's use of the Scud B missile in the Gulf War has affected the way in which we perceive strategic defense, particularly against ballistic missiles. The Scud attacks did not achieve their desired intent to terrorize the populations of Israel or Saudi Arabia or to bring Israel into the war. They did, however, cause a renewed emphasis in US thinking on the need to counter theater missile attacks. The focus of the Strategic Defense Initiative (SDI) program, consequently, is more toward meeting limited threats than its initial direction against strategic missile attacks (the program is now known as GPALS, or global protection against limited strikes).[17]

The Gulf War also underscored the importance of forward military presence. US forces were not prepared for forward defense of either Kuwait or Saudi Arabia but had a limited forward presence in terms of a moderate naval force and a ready Saudi infrastructure. Where infrastructure assets are being reduced elsewhere, we must increase the mobility of our forces, including sea lift for heavy-armored ground forces, a naval presence, and deployable, sustainable tactical air strike forces to provide for future contingencies. Having the consent of Saudi Arabia to field the half-million-plus coalition force was crucial to its success. However, future conflicts may not provide such a clear-cut enemy as Saddam Hussein and may require more convincing than was even the case in 1990 when US representatives needed to push a reluctant Saudi king to agree to large-scale deployments on his territory.[18] Moreover, the buildup time provided in the Kuwaiti situation may be much shorter or nonexistent in possible future conflicts.

There are also some political lessons to be learned. Public support was sustained because US military strategy allowed for a quick resolution of the conflict rather than an endless quagmire. Secondly, coalition support for such operations can be essential not so much because of the additional war-fighting capabilities it gives as for the legitimacy it lends the operation in the eyes of the US public, Congress, and foreign countries.

NATO and US Policy
What New Role?

For four decades, NATO remained the core of the US alliance system. The US sought to preserve the freedom of the people of Western Europe and to provide a system of collective security, through the alliance, against Soviet-led attacks from the east. The issue facing us today is what to do about NATO now that its original raison d'être no longer exists. The collapse of the Warsaw Pact, followed by the breakup of the Soviet Union, has vastly changed the East-West balance of power. The East European militaries can no longer be counted on to be the spearhead of a westward invasion. The Soviet Union that controlled them is no longer in existence, and the Russia that replaced it is not in position to reassert that control. The level of military forces is also decreasing in Europe, with substantially more cuts in conventional forces inflicted on the former Eastern bloc militaries than those of NATO, in order to keep the forces of the former East and West in rough balance.

Some basic questions arise. First, does NATO have a viable role to play in the future given the collapse of its adversaries? If so, how might its role be transformed from the present? Second, what should NATO's posture be vis-à-vis demands for inclusion from East European states and the former Soviet republics, including Russia itself?

While no decisions have been made, some indications are already apparent. First, enough uncertainty about Europe's future still exists to ensure that NATO will continue, albeit within changed parameters. A continuation of the alliance will increase its members' security by providing a hedge against backsliding in Russia and possible instability in Eastern Europe. It could also provide the glue that would ensure that

Western Europe stays together and that tensions do not erupt among West European states.

Decisions on the future of NATO will be made after careful assessments of Western security interests and how they might be best served. Scenarios other than a now unlikely Russian attack on the West could exist: if a war were to break out in the East, resulting in Russia expanding its present zone of control—say over Ukraine—and Russia were to consequently consolidate its military hold westward back into Eastern Europe, the threat situation for the West could arise that resembles more and more the pre-1989 scenario. Conflict in the East—most likely internal in nature—does have a possibly destabilizing impact for the West in its potential to cause massive refugee flows.[19]

The question of East European inclusion in NATO is more complex. Already, the issue has become an emotional one for some East European leaders who are alarmed over what they see as both a return to old ways in Russian strong-arm tactics in some of the former Soviet republics, as well as over the victory of ultranationalist Vladimir Zhirinovsky in the December 1993 elections.[20] East Europeans argue that the West should not let the issue of expansion of NATO membership be subject to a Russian veto. However, recent forthright statements by Russian president Boris Yeltsin on the subject, including the warning to NATO Secretary-General Manfred Worner that Russia would have to take countermeasures in case of NATO expansion eastward, have strengthened the already considerable wariness of allied leaders over the expansion issue. For now, the new slogan will be "Partners for Peace"—a program approved at the January 1994 NATO summit that will offer increased common activities between NATO and the former Warsaw Pact members but will sidestep the issue of membership with the security guarantees that it entails.[21] The issue is not simply the desire not to provoke Russia into a counterproductive response. It also includes the fear that some NATO members have over the effect enlargement will have on the alliance, the realization that NATO was unable to have an effect on the Bosnian war, the fear of being drawn into future national conflicts in Eastern Europe, and finally, the inability of the organization, especially in times of severe budget cuts, to implement the security guarantees to its new members that would be part of an enlargement decision.[22]

US Military
Projections for the Future

While it is not the purpose of this chapter to focus in detail on US military force planning for the future, a few highlights are certainly relevant. Perhaps the core document in planning to meet national security needs in the post-cold-war era is the Bottom-Up Review, presented by Secretary of Defense Les Aspin, on 1 September 1993. In formulating the framework within which military planning takes place, Aspin postulated four categories of dangers to US interests: (1) nuclear weapons and weapons of mass destruction; (2) regional threats of large-scale aggression by local powers, but also smaller, internal conflicts based on ethnic or religious animosities, state-sponsored terrorism, and subversion of friendly governments; (3) dangers to democracy and reform in the former USSR and Eastern Europe; and (4) economic dangers which would result if the US failed to build a strong, competitive, and growing economy.

Postulating that US forces must be sufficient for the contingency of fighting up to two major regional conflicts (MRC) simultaneously, Aspin projected a cut of US forces to 10 divisions (plus five more in reserve) for the future Army; 11 aircraft carriers (with one in reserve, 45–55 attack submarines, and 346 ships) for the future Navy; 13 active and seven reserve Air Force fighter wings (with up to 184 bombers); and three Marine Expeditionary Forces. These plans also include a cut of US forces in Europe by nearly half to about 100,000, with the retention of about that number in Northeast Asia as well in South Korea, Japan, and Okinawa. Cuts in the 45,000-strong troop levels in Korea are likely to be postponed pending the resolution of the issue of North Korea's nuclear capability. In Southwest Asia, heavier reliance will be made on naval forces and periodic force deployments rather than ground bases. Prepositioning of equipment to be used in possible ground conflicts is also to assume increased importance. Taken another way, whereas active duty US military forces numbered 2.1 million in 1990, this figure was reduced to 1.9 million by 1992 and is expected to fall by about a quarter to 1.4 million by 1997. About a third of the projected reduction of up to 700,000 troops—some 250,000—is expected to come from the Army.[23]

Thus, the search for a national strategy to replace containment and strategic nuclear deterrence will continue. The new watchword of "peacetime engagement" may not fully capture the essence of the new era, but it is intended to convey the notion that the US expects to use its military forces more for peaceful purposes (e.g., humanitarian relief) than for warfighting, even if that contingency must be prepared for. It does involve more use of diplomatic and economic instruments to deal with states and situations which may be hostile to our interests. It also means that more reliance will be placed on military forces based in the continental US, with the possibility of rapid deployment to deal with future regional crises. Finally, dealing with those crises will compel us to determine whether to act alone or whether to assemble the kind of ad hoc coalition that proved so successful in the Gulf War.[24]

Peacekeeping Operations

The issue of how to mold UN peacekeeping operations into a larger framework compatible with US interests is also a question that is high on the agenda. While the US shied away from most direct involvement in such operations during the height of the cold war, it has made important financial contributions and has been responsible for much of the logistic support necessary for these operations to succeed. Peacekeeping has been a growth industry—in 1987 there were five peacekeeping operations (PKO) with a manpower allocation of 10,000 and a budget of $233 million; today the number of operations is up to 18 and the annual cost has skyrocketed to $3 billion. More recent events, such as the killing of US servicemen in Somalia, have made participation in PKOs less palatable to the American public and to

Congress. Current US thinking, as contained in a draft National Security Decision Directive (NSDD), would sanction operations approved by the UN Security Council in dealing with a threat to international peace and security as contained in the UN charter. These threats, under the American definition, could include "one or a combination of the following: international aggression, a humanitarian disaster requiring urgent action coupled with violence, a sudden and unexpected interruption of established democracy or gross violation of human rights coupled with violence or the threat thereof."[25] At the same time, the document requires that each operation have a clear objective, strategy for completion, political support, and must serve US interests. Particularly hazardous missions would have to have a US commander or a US officer near the top of the chain of command. As President Clinton succinctly phrased it during his address to the UN General Assembly in September 1993, "If the American people are to say yes to peacekeeping, the United Nations must know when to say no."

Conclusion

The Certainty of Uncertainty

While it may seem a banality, one of the most important conclusions emerging from a discussion of future US national security strategy is that we are dealing with a much less certain world than we have been accustomed to. The previous opponent—world communism and its leader, the USSR—was well known, and the strategy for dealing with it has joined the "trash heap of history." In its stead has come a series of lesser and more uncertain threats. Security was defined in primarily military terms, and the prevention of surprise attack on the US and its allies was the apogee of its efforts.

While military preparedness will always be essential if only as an insurance policy against threats that may be coming down the road but are not evident today, it is also a given fact that the amount of resources dedicated to protecting the national security will be a function of how the American public perceives that security and threats to it. Characteristically, a 1990 survey of American attitudes regarding security threats identified drug trafficking as the most serious, followed by nuclear proliferation. Soviet nuclear weapons and Soviet aggression came at the bottom of the list of 14 items.[26] One survey of post–cold-war national security strategy put it this way: "As we look ahead, the threat is more diffuse, the institutions more varied, and the roles and missions of the players more diverse, while the consensus of the American public over what the primary issues really are, at least for the real term, will be much looser."[27]

Thus, national security strategy will be formulated in a much more complex environment in the future. Paradoxically, as the US remains the only real superpower, it finds itself restrained in its ability and willingness to use that power in troubled situations such as Haiti, Somalia, and Bosnia; and it lacks the ability it once had to dominate its allies. It will need to deal with Russia in a new framework, balancing the desire to keep that country developing down the road to democracy and peaceful engagement with the West, with the understanding that Russia remains a potentially powerful adversary that has its own views of how it should behave. It will also need to enlist Russia in common efforts that may not be successful to ensure that weapons of mass destruction and their delivery means do not fall into the wrong hands. It will have to deal with the outbursts of nationalism and hatred so apparent today and will have to determine the resources available to back up our policies, whether they entail the use of military force or political/economic instruments. It will need to foster a robust economic and spiritual base at home to keep America a vibrant society that continues to provide leadership in uncertain times. It will need the support of its own people and their representatives if it is to be successful.

Notes

1. Harold Brown, *Thinking about National Security* (Boulder: Westview Press, 1983), 4.

2. In Cecil V. Crabb, Jr., and Kevin V. Mulcahy, *American National Security: A Presidential Perspective* (Pacific Grove, Calif.: Brooks/Cole Publishing Co., 1991), 4–5.

3. Former secretary of state Henry Kissinger, for example, remarked in 1975 that "the problems of energy, environment, population, the issues of space and the seas now rank with the questions of military security, ideology, and territorial rivalry which have traditionally made up the diplomatic agenda." See Roger Cary and Trevor C. Salmon, eds., *International Security in the Modern World* (New York: St. Martin's Press, 1992), 2. For a complete work focusing entirely on the nonmilitary aspects of national security, see Joseph J. Romm, *Defining National Security: The Non-Military Aspects* (New York: Council on Foreign Relations Press, 1993).

4. See Dave McCurdy, "Glasnost for the CIA," *Foreign Affairs* 73, no.1 (January–February 1994): 127.

5. See Loch K. Johnson, "New Directions for US Strategic Intelligence," in James E. Winkates, Jr., J. Richard Walsh, and Joseph M. Scolnick, eds., *US Foreign Policy in Transition* (Chicago: Nelson Hall Publishers, 1994), 82–83, 89.

6. McCurdy, 135.

7. Thomas B. Grassey, "US Intelligence and the New National Security Strategy," in James J. Tritten and Paul N. Stockton, eds., *Reconstituting America's Defense: The New US National Security Strategy*, 36–37.

8. Charles Krauthammer, "The Unipolar Moment," in Graham Allison and Gregory M. Treverton, eds., *Rethinking America's Security: Beyond Cold War to New World Order* (New York: W.W. Norton & Co., 1992), 297.

9. Ibid., 297–98.

10. See Robert A. Hoover, "Old Business, New Business: US Arms Control Policy in the Post Cold War World," in Winkates, Walsh, and Scolnick, 52–75.

11. Quoted in Krauthammer, 302.

12. See Monte R. Bullard, "US-China Relations: The Strategic Calculus," *Parameters*, Summer 1993, 86–95.

13. See David Hughes, "Regional Nuclear Powers Pose New Risks to US Military," *Aviation Week & Space Technology*, 13 January 1992, 65.

14. Frederick R. Strain, "Nuclear Proliferation and Deterrence: A Policy Conundrum," *Parameters*, Autumn 1993, 85–95.

15. In George Bush, *National Security Strategy of the United States* (Washington, D.C.: The White House, 1993), 15.

16. See introduction by Paul N. Stockton in Tritten and Stockton, 4–6.

17. Michael N. Pocalyko, "Riding on the Storm: The Influence of War on Strategy," in Tritten and Stockton, 57.

18. Ibid., 60–63.

19. For a far-reaching analysis of possible threat scenarios in the future and the conclusion that NATO's continuation is the best alternative to deal with all of them, see Charles L. Glaser, "Why NATO is Still Best: Future Security Arrangements for Europe," *International Security* 18, no. 1 (Summer 1993): 5–50.

20. See, for example, comments by Polish foreign minister Andrzej Olechowski, quoted in Jane Perlez, "NATO Commitment Sought by Poland," *New York Times*, 12 December 1993, sec. 1, 6. See also Craig Whitney, "Russian Vote Stirs Uncertainty for NATO Talks," *New York Times*, 15 December 1993, 8. Whitney quotes Olechowski as saying, "We were

concerned up to now; now [after the nationalist victory in the Russian elections] we are worried."

21. For example, a comprehensive proposal for expanding the activities of the North Atlantic Cooperation Council (NACC), a coordination body in which the former Warsaw Pact and newly independent states of the former USSR are linked to NATO without actual membership, was made by the former deputy commander in chief of the US European Command, Gen James P. McCarthy. His proposals included participation in alliance humanitarian and relief operations, consultations on security matters of concern to NACC members, expertise in nuclear security and safety, in inspection information sharing, defense conversion, refugees, and peacekeeping cooperation in negotiations on conventional armed forces in Europe (CFE). See James P. McCarthy, "Strengthening Security in Central and Eastern Europe: New Opportunities for NATO," *Strategic Review*, Spring 1993, 60.

22. For a further discussion of the problems entailed by NATO enlargement, see, for example, "The World Sends NATO Back to the Drawing Board," *The Economist*, 25 December 1993, 61–62; and Justin Burke, "Eastern Europe Presses Its Case for Speedy NATO Membership," *Christian Science Monitor*, 7 January 1994, 6.

23. See James E. Winkates, Jr.,"US Defense Policy in the 1990's," in Winkates, Walsh, and Scolnick, 41.

24. Ibid., 48–49.

25. See Paul Lewis, "Reluctant Warriors: UN Member States Retreat from Peacekeeping Roles," *New York Times*, 13 December 1993, I-9.

26. Gregory F. Treverton and Barbara A. Bicksler, "Conclusion: Getting from Here to Where?" in Allison and Treverton, 421.

27. Ibid.

Conquest and Cohesion
The Psychological Nature of War

Martin L. Fracker

This is the theory of "weapons decide everything," which is a mechanistic theory of war. . . . In opposition to this view, we see not only weapons but human beings. Although important, weapons are not the decisive factor in war; it is man and not material things that decide the issue.

Mao Zedong

The recent crises in Bosnia, Somalia, and Haiti have stumped American foreign policy and stymied US military planners. Not coincidentally, these are also complex crises with roots buried deep in the history and population of each region. While we are not currently at war, the policy difficulties that these situations have posed raise the question of just how we would go about winning if we were at war. The recent US-led victory over Iraq has reinforced a traditional American view that war is about destroying the other side's physical war-making capacity. Historian Russell Weigley has called this mind-set a preference for "wars of annihilation," a preference that he says prevented Americans from being able to cope with the Communist strategy in Vietnam.[1] Mao Zedong, intellectual father of America's Vietnam defeat, derided this mechanistic mind-set. He argued, and the Vietnam War seemed to prove, that real war is not about destroying physical capacity. Rather, real war is about destroying the desire to keep fighting. War, in other words, is a problem in psychology.

Central to the psychological nature of war is what Carl von Clausewitz called the "wonderful trinity" embodied in the people, the army, and the government. The people, he said, provide the passions that ignite the conflagration of war. The army provides the talent and courage that interact with chance to determine the outcome of battles. The government provides the political objectives that give the reasons for war and determine what conditions will constitute victory.[2]

The population plays a special role in the psychological nature of war. Even undemocratic governments ultimately rule with at least the passive acquiescence of those governed. And virtually all modern militaries draw themselves from their larger populations. This dependence of both government and military on population therefore suggests that a state's population is the fulcrum upon which war rests. This conclusion, in turn, suggests that the enemy's population should be the key target in war. This does not mean attacking the population with bombs and bullets or even necessarily attacking the things upon which the population's quality of life depends. Military theorist Robert Pape has argued convincingly that such attacks on civilians are fruitless.[3] Rather, the psychological object of war is the population's conviction that the war is in their interest. When the population turns against the war, the government must redirect energies toward safeguarding its position at home. And the army, knowing that it no longer fights for family and friends, loses its fighting spirit.

To develop this theme, we begin by looking at why the political leadership is not the proper target once war has begun. We will then examine wartime populations themselves, explore the mechanisms by which populations influence the outcome of wars, and see that the proper target should be the internal cohesion that binds them to their rulers. Finally, we will examine military forces and see that successful psychological operations do much more than merely play on soldiers' fear of death. Rather, successful campaigns are integrated into larger efforts aimed at undermining the enemy society's cohesion; these campaigns convince the combatants that they are fighting and dying for the wrong people.

Political Leaders

Reactance and Resistance

Clausewitz viewed war as a political decision based on a more-or-less rational calculation of the costs and benefits of war.[4] From this perspective, fighting may not always be necessary to achieve victory. Sometimes, it may be enough to convince the enemy's political leaders that acceding to one's demands costs less than trying to resist them. Hitler showed that this kind of persuasion is sometimes possible when he convinced the French and British in 1938 to accept his occupation of Czechoslovakia, first of the Sudetenland and then of the whole country, rather than fight another war. However, the recent Gulf War shows this Clausewitzian strategy sometimes fails. Even when faced with the overwhelming condemnation of the United Nations, the unprecedented and massive deployment of coalition military force, and the resolute determination of President George Bush to evict Iraq from Kuwait, Saddam Hussein could not be persuaded to accede to the coalition's wishes.

Political psychologist Philip Tetlock and his associates have suggested that persuasion attempts that rely on cost-benefit calculations often fail because nonrational factors exert more influence over human decisions.[5] For example, rational political leaders entering a conflict should reassess the conflict's costs and benefits as events unfold. But real political leaders, as most human beings, tend to ignore important developments that contradict their initial beliefs while paying too much attention to minor events that support them. Saddam Hussein, who apparently thought that American public opinion would cripple President Bush in the Gulf, may thus have found his belief buttressed by small, sporadic, and ineffectual antiwar protests in the US. At the same time, he seems to have discounted President Bush's continuing consolidation of international support.[6]

Perhaps a more important factor influencing Saddam was "reactance," the tendency to become more strongly committed to a course of action when faced with demands to change. Demands that people change their behavior threaten a basic human need for self-determination, and people respond with defiance in order to reestablish their independence.[7] In terms of the Clausewitzian model, reactance dramatically raises the amount of pain that the enemy is willing to suffer. Thus, President Bush's demands for Saddam immediately and unconditionally to withdraw from Kuwait likely sparked massive reactance within the Iraqi leader, guaranteeing that he would pay virtually any price to stand fast. The US-led coalition then had little choice but to fight, hoping that military pressure would succeed where diplomacy had failed.

Once war has started, the enemy leaders' reactance must be overcome before they can be persuaded to quit—a formidable challenge because the use of military force instigates even more reactance. Some researchers believe that repeated failures to restore one's freedom of action eventually causes reactance to collapse into helplessness.[8] If so, then consistently attacking and undermining the enemy's military strategy could eventually produce his psychological defeat, as Pape has recently argued.[9] Yet, history suggests that producing helplessness in wartime political leaders rarely succeeds. In World War II, both Germany and Japan fought well beyond the point at which they had any realistic hope of winning. Pape suggests that the Germans fought to a decisive conclusion because fighting seemed preferable to the costs they would suffer once they surrendered.[10] Japan also fought ferociously despite horrendous casualties and devastating setbacks, induced to surrender only by the confluence of economic strangulation, America's use of the atomic bomb, and Russia's entry into the war.

The aftermath of the Gulf War demonstrates a further difficulty in destroying a political leader's determination to keep fighting. Forced out of Kuwait, Saddam Hussein did not surrender until it was clear that he could not win. Yet not even that humiliation seems to have lessened his resolve to eventually prevail. Devastating losses inflicted by the coalition may have convinced him only that a different strategy was needed. The fact that he remains in power, continues to oppress Kurdish and Shiite minorities, and apparently still strives to develop weapons of mass destruction indicates that he yet hopes to one day dominate the region by force and intimidation.

A clearer example of this problem is the aftermath of US involvement in Vietnam. The North Vietnamese had seen at least two different military strategies fail in their efforts to annex the South: guerrilla strategies before 1968 and more conventional strategies thereafter. But the North's leaders never lost faith in their ability to eventually triumph. As events showed, they were convinced that winning only required letting the Americans declare victory and leave.

Yet, it is not impossible to produce helplessness in national political leaders. The North Vietnamese succeeded in fostering a sense of helplessness and incompetence among US leaders that extended well beyond Southeast Asia and even the cold war. In the years from 1972 to 1980, the United States passively endured Marxist victories in Vietnam, Cambodia, Angola, and Nicaragua. Growing Communist insurgencies in the Philippines, Peru, and El Salvador were met with little if any direct response from the United States. American helplessness continued to the depths of the 1979 Iranian hostage crisis, ending only with Ronald Reagan's ascendancy to the presidency. But the North Vietnamese had not defeated US forces in a single major battle. Rather, they had simply destroyed the cohesion of America's population, fracturing the essential unity of people and government.

Populations
Cohesion and Conquest

While most people recognize the role popular support played in America's Vietnam defeat, a common assertion holds that nondemocratic states are immune from such public pressure. Commenting on German discontent under the Nazis, the United States Strategic Bombing Survey concluded:

> If they had been at liberty to vote themselves out of the war, they would have done so well before the final surrender. In a determined police state, however, there is a wide difference between dissatisfaction and expressed opposition. . . . However dissatisfied they were with the war, the German people lacked either the will or the means to make their dissatisfaction evident.[11]

But if popular support counts only in democracies, one can hardly explain why Clausewitz put it on the same level as the government and armed forces. Clausewitz, after all, was writing about war as he knew it in late eighteenth- and early nineteenth-century Europe. Democracy, to the extent that it had existed at all, had flickered only briefly, and only in France, before collapsing into Napoléon's withering grip.

Neither can one explain Sun Tzu's concern with popular support in dynastic China more than two thousand years earlier: He had warned that wars should not overly burden the people lest they become impoverished and resentful.[12]

Yet, if we accept Clausewitz and Sun Tzu's insistence that popular support *does* matter in undemocratic states, we are challenged to identify the mechanism by which such support makes a difference. In democracies, of course, people can vote their leaders out of office. In nondemocratic states, where voting is either forbidden or irrelevant, there are still at least two other mechanisms. The first is that the people may revolt against their political leaders, as the Germans successfully did in the final days of World War I. This threat of revolt probably helped motivate Sun Tzu's concern because the wars of ancient China were commonly interrupted by popular rebellions and coups d'etat.[13] But revolts don't have to succeed in order to endanger dictatorial regimes. A failed rebellion or even just the threat of an uprising can still force governments to divert scarce war resources to the costly task of keeping themselves in power. Further, the fear of rebellion may preclude dictators from taking militarily necessary steps that could alienate the population. This fear, for example, may explain why Hitler failed to fully mobilize the German economy for war until well into the conflict when, as history proved, it was too late.

A second mechanism grows from the fact that the armed forces are drawn from the population. When Clausewitz insisted that the people provide the passions of war, he implied that the troops' commitment to a conflict reflects that of the people as a whole. John Spanier, in his book *Games Nations Play,* makes clear the relationship between popular support and military effectiveness. Undemocratic states, he says, must worry about mass support because

> a people's acceptance of military service, separation of families, and death measures its commitment to the nation. . . . The German armies fought very well in two wars, despite the Allied blockade in World War I and the heavy bombing in World War II; widespread support for Germany's government lasted until near the end in each instance. Japanese soldiers demonstrated a tenacious fanaticism during World War II, which led them to fight hard for every inch of territory, to sacrifice their lives freely in the process, and to impose heavy casualties on American marines.[14]

Sun Tzu said essentially the same thing writing of the importance of harmony between the people and their leaders. He spoke of the people and the army in virtually a single breath, as if one could hardly be distinguished from the other:

> When troops are raised to chastise transgressors, the temple council first considers the adequacy of the rulers' benevolence and the confidence of their peoples. . . . When one treats people with benevolence, justice, and righteousness, and reposes confidence in them, the army will be united in mind and all will be happy to serve their leaders. The Book of Changes says: "In happiness at overcoming difficulties, people forget the danger of death."[15]

From Sun Tzu, Clausewitz, and Spanier, it seems clear that the unity of the population with its military and government is key to victory in war. The Nazi propagandists understood this principle and used it to good effect in Austria and Czechoslovakia, so thoroughly dividing the civilian populations against themselves that the German army was able to occupy both countries virtually without resistance.[16] They achieved at least as impressive a feat against the French. In *To Lose a Battle,* Alistair Horne describes how Hitler identified social disunity within France as something he could use to render the French army all but useless. Otto Abetz, whom Hitler sent into France, carefully cultivated the anti-Semitic and antisocialist sympathies of the French elite. They were easily convinced that only Germany stood between Europe and Jewish bolshevism. Another line targeted the French socialists and asked why socialists should fight for the interests of fascists and reactionaries. Still another propaganda theme played on the French distrust of Britain. The Jews controlled Britain, so the line went, and this would be Britain's war against Germany—but it would be the French who die. The Nazi propaganda machine finally took aim at the average French soldier, asking why the soldier who lived in grubby barracks, ate from substandard canteens, and was paid only pennies a day should fight for pampered officers who lived in luxury. The outcome was all that Hitler had hoped for. France did not mobilize her forces, and when the invasion finally came, the French fought without enthusiasm. In just six weeks, Hitler defeated one of Europe's greatest armies.[17]

The Germans had perhaps learned from their experience in World War I during which the Allies deliberately used military pressure and propaganda to fracture German society. In 1917, British lieutenant general Sir George Macdonogh wrote:

> Although it may be argued that the German Armies can not be decisively beaten in the field, the German nation is very vulnerable politically. The best weapon to take advantage of this weakness is military pressure for it will *more than anything else* accentuate the internal dissentions and contribute more rapidly than any other measure to the undermining and final breaking of the German war-spirit which is our foremost war-aim.[18] (Emphasis added)

To further destroy German cohesion, the Allies supported indigenous radical socialists who feared that a German victory would make socialism in Germany all but impossible. At the same time, the Allies undertook a vigorous propaganda campaign aimed specifically at German social cohesion and designed to promote an anti-kaiser revolution. The propaganda emphasized that ordinary Germans were working, suffering, and dying for a greedy, capitalist elite. This line was well received among the German people who finally began to wonder "why they should go on being killed and starved for masters who [told] them only lies."[19] On 9 November 1918 following a period of civil uprising and several government resignations, the kaiser abdicated and the Socialist Party, by then in control of the Reichstag, proclaimed the German Republic. Two days later, the republic surrendered to the Allies even though the German army was undefeated, still fighting on foreign soil.[20]

Oddly, the lessons Germany learned in World War I and applied so well in France more than 30 years later were forgotten when the Nazis invaded the Soviet Union. A multinational empire as oppressive as any under the czars, the Soviet Union was ripe for an attack on its social cohesion. Indeed, when the Nazis first invaded the Ukraine, the civilian population welcomed them as an army of liberation. Stalin was so alarmed that he ordered any Soviet soldier who surrendered to the Germans to be considered a traitor. Yet Hitler failed to capitalize on the Ukrainians' hatred of Russia. Instead, he imposed a brutal occupation aimed at subjugating the Slavic people whom he regarded as inferior and at appropriating the Ukraine as land for Germans. By his inhuman treatment, Hitler welded the Ukrainians to Stalin, thereby assuring his own defeat.[21]

The United States likewise discovered the importance of national cohesion in Vietnam. For the North Vietnamese, the only serious obstacle to a united Vietnam was the United States. They knew that the People's Army of Vietnam (PAVN) could not defeat the United States in a purely military contest, but they understood that this fact was not decisive. At the heart of North Vietnam's strategy was the doctrine of protracted war. Sun Tzu had warned against such wars. "For there has never been a protracted war," he said, "from which a country has benefited. . . . War is like unto a fire; those who will not put aside weapons are themselves consumed by them."[22] His reasoning was that prolonged wars overtax the state treasury, exhaust the army, and overstress the civilian population. In the end, the people would rise up and overthrow their own government.

But what Sun Tzu saw as protracted war's danger, Mao saw as its opportunity. For by intentionally protracting a war against a militarily superior nation, one could inflict upon the enemy

> hundreds of thousands of casualties, consumption of arms and ammunition, *decline of morale of the troops, discontent of the people at home,* shrinkage of trade, an expenditure of [millions of dollars] and condemnation before the court of world opinion.[23] (Emphasis added)

Mao made the objective of protracted war especially clear when he wrote:

> Is it not self-contradictory to fight heroically and then abandon territory? Will not the blood of heroic fighters be shed in vain? *This is an incorrect way to pose the question.* One eats first and then relieves oneself; does one eat in vain? One sleeps first and then gets up; does one sleep in vain? I think not. . . . [W]e have gained time [and] realized our objective of . . . wearing down the enemy.[24] (Emphasis added)

The North Vietnamese therefore waged a war intended to break not American military might but American will. While there seems to be little evidence that the North Vietnamese conducted actual propaganda operations within the US, they didn't need to.[25] In any pluralistic society, numerous social rifts are bound to exist, and the United States has not been spared.[26] The stress produced by a seemingly endless war may have been enough to start and sustain the processes that would split and demoralize the American people. The universal draft may also have played a role, disrupting people's lives and putting families in fear for their loved ones gone off to war. Sun Tzu had warned that "if the war drags on without cessation men and women will resent not being able to marry."[27] Added to this disruption were moral qualms about the war that the strategy of protraction successfully exacerbated. Many Americans correctly judged the South Vietnamese government to be autocratic and opposed to liberal concepts of democracy and fairness. Did such a government merit the war's horrible costs? Grotesque images burned themselves permanently into the America psyche: a captured Vietcong guerrilla murdered on the street in front of cameras; a child terror frozen while being engulfed in exploding napalm; American soldiers gutted, dismembered, and poured into body bags.[28]

Fissures long latent in American society yawned open. No less a figure than retired Marine Corps general David Shoup, a Medal of Honor winner, proclaimed that the US armed forces had "relished" the war in order, as *Time* magazine put it, to "field test new weapons and season a generation of career soldiers," thereby transforming America into a "militaristic and aggressive nation."[29] President Dwight Eisenhower's nightmare of a military-industrial complex gone mad seemed to have come true. But in the public mind it was not these warmongers who bore the cost of the military's obsession; it was the 18-year-old innocent who should have had all his life to look forward to.

The war had pitted average Americans against military-industrial elites who seemingly cared nothing for the blood they spilled. That image erupted into brilliant colors when Ohio national guardsmen opened fire into a crowd of protesters at Kent State University, killing three students. It was reinforced by the My Lai massacre, for more than a year a darkly held Army secret. Lt William Calley, apparently following orders, murdered the innocent, child and adult, able and feeble, women and men—22 civilians in all. The military seemed to have violated everything that Americans cherished about themselves.[30]

The turning point had come in the form of the 1968 Tet offensive. The Vietcong, with the encouragement of the North, had sprung its most massive attack in more than three years of war. Though the United States beat back and destroyed the guerrilla army, the psychological shock had already done its job. Before Tet, Washington had been whispering foolish assurances that the end was just in sight; all that was left was a little mopping up. For many Americans, Tet seemed to prove that the president and the military had been lying all along. The following year, Americans rejected the Democratic leadership that had given them the war and elected Richard Nixon instead. Nixon accordingly changed America's war objectives. From that time on, according to military historian Mark Clodfelter, the United States fought mainly to achieve a face-saving withdrawal.[31] Though the shooting war would continue throughout Nixon's first term, the North had already won the only war that counted.

As Saddam Hussein approached the Gulf War almost 20 years later, he hoped to replicate North Vietnam's success against the United States. Accordingly, Iraqi propaganda emphasized that the United States was preparing to fight another imperialist war for oil designed to prop up a corrupt and repressive Kuwaiti regime. As usual, it would be the poor and the minorities who would die in this rich man's war. The war, the Iraqis said, would be another Vietnam, lasting many years and costing countless lives. The Iraqi propaganda machine, however, did little more than talk. Saddam believed that the US public already opposed sending its boys to die in an Arab war. He saw the few antiwar demonstrations that occurred and the debates in Congress as evidence of a wide rift between the Bush administration and the American population. Apart from maligning US intentions, all he really had to do, he thought, was to drag out the crisis long enough, and the rift would explode into a Vietnam-era antiwar movement that would hobble President Bush and force American acquiescence.[32]

The rift that Saddam Hussein perceived simply did not exist. A poll sponsored by *Newsweek* magazine taken only hours after the war began showed that the vast majority of Americans supported President Bush's actions. This was not a transient rally-around-the-flag support; a month later, fully 90 percent of the adult population supported the war effort.[33] What Saddam needed to do and did not do was to identify those social ruptures that actually existed in American society and actively exploit them, just as Hitler had exploited existing ruptures within Austria, Czechoslovakia, and France.

Interestingly, what Saddam failed to do, American antiwar activists attempted. The Georgia chapter of the National Organization of Women asked why women should support a male war for "gender apartheid," referring to Saudi Arabia and Kuwait's unprogressive treatment of women. The National African-American Network, noting that blacks make up 22 percent of the military but only 11 percent of the civilian work force, asked why African-Americans should shoulder the risk of death for a society that denies them other kinds of opportunity. Environmentalists in Missoula, Montana, asked why environmentally conscious Americans should fight and die for the great polluter, oil. Certain homosexual rights groups portrayed the impending war as a distraction from the fight against Acquired Immune Deficiency Syndrome (AIDS). Other activists, chanting, "We won't go for Texaco," implied that a war would somehow serve only the interests of big oil companies. There were even anti-Jewish appeals made against the war by groups such as Lyndon LaRouche's organization, Louis Farrakhan's Nation of Islam, and the Liberty Lobby.[34]

In the end, all of these attempts to divide American society and produce large-scale opposition to the war failed. Some of the appeals were not credible to their intended audiences. The National African-American Network's theme, for example, probably sounded strange to African-Americans who could not help noticing that the highest ranking officer in the military, Gen Colin Powell, was black. The idea that only the big oil companies cared about petroleum prices undoubtedly rang hollow to average Americans who put gasoline in their cars every week or who would use oil to heat their homes during the coming winter.

Jacob Weisberg, writing in the liberal *New Republic* magazine, suggests that the antiwar activists caused their own failure. The activists, he wrote, seemed trapped in a time warp, as if still focused on the Vietnam War, unable to adapt to the current situation. In one rally, young men even chanted, "Hell no, we won't go!" as if at risk of being drafted. The protesters seemed either not to know or care that Saddam Hussein had brutally invaded Kuwait, was looting its wealth, murdering its citizens, and threatening much of the world's oil lifeline. The protesters seemingly thought there could be nothing worth fighting for. To make matters worse, the antiwar rallies often became forums for extremist groups. Ramsey Clark's National Coalition to Stop US Intervention in the Middle East, one of the two major organizers of these rallies, was a front group for the Workers World Party that had approved of the Tiananmen Square massacre and now apparently endorsed Saddam's annexation of Kuwait.[35] A speaker at one of the coalition's rallies, not untypically, castigated the "illegal state of Israel" and cried, "Down with Zionism!" Another, representing the American Indian Movement, demanded that the United States withdraw from both Saudi Arabia and Arizona. The effect of these rallies was to alienate ordinary Americans who may have had doubts about the war but who lived their lives in the political center. It was hardly surprising, then, when a *Wall Street Journal*–National Broadcasting Corporation (NBC) poll conducted during the war found that 60 percent of Americans had lost whatever respect they once had felt for the protesters.[36]

In short, attempts to turn the US population against the Gulf War failed because they lacked credibility, were morally and intellectually bankrupt, and were ineptly executed. Whether an intelligent, well-planned, and carefully executed propaganda campaign could have succeeded is not known. Iraq's aggression in Kuwait was unmistakable; the war's morality was recognized even by many who opposed it.[37] In light of the economic disruption caused by the 1973 Arab oil embargo, the threat to American economic security seemed real.[38] Nevertheless, intelligent, well-informed, and patriotic Americans did oppose the war prior to its start. Among these were such notable figures as Ambassador Jeane Kirkpatrick, columnist Patrick Buchanan, and senators Mark Hatfield (R-Oreg.), Ernest Hollings (D-S.C.), John Glenn (D-Ohio), and Daniel Patrick Moynihan (D-N.Y.).[39] This observation, combined with the social discontinuities that exist within American society, suggests that a cleverer enemy than Saddam might have succeeded in destroying American cohesion and will.

Combatants

Cohesion and Fear

Saddam had adopted a more or less passive psychological strategy against the US population, but his efforts directed against the American military were much more active and direct. He launched a campaign intended to exaggerate threats of chemical attack and the hardships of desert war. He apparently believed that as Operation Desert Shield dragged on, these themes would eventually cause American troops to desert or refuse to deploy. Yet here too Saddam was inept. For example, an Iraqi propaganda broadcast warned American GIs that while they were suffering in the excruciating heat, their wives and girlfriends back home were dating movie stars like Bart Simpson (whom the Iraqis did not realize was a cartoon character).[40]

In contrast, such appeals had worked when the Germans used them against the French in 1940. Nazi propaganda, for example, warned French soldiers that while they were preparing to fight Britain's war, British soldiers were enjoying the favors of French women.[41] Within the context of French social resentments as well as historic French distrust of the British, the Nazi assertions seemed believable. Indeed, the Nazi effort was probably successful only because it was well integrated into a larger, brilliantly crafted campaign aimed at every segment of French society. Saddam could make no such claim.

But Saddam has company in propaganda ineptness in modern wars, for in Vietnam the United States likewise bumbled its way through the conflict. What the United States did in the psychological war was, for the most part, directed at the Communist fighters of both the Vietcong and the PAVN. Apparently, the intent was to exacerbate the psychological stress imposed on enemy fighters by the search and destroy missions upon which the United States had come to rely.[42] According to Lt Col Robert Chandler, an Air Force intelligence officer serving in Vietnam, United States psychological operations struck five major themes: (1) fear of death from US attacks, (2) the hardships of living and fighting in the jungle, (3) certainty that the communists were losing, (4) concern for families back home, and (5) doubt about North Vietnam's ultimate goals.[43] Though this campaign occasionally succeeded in inducing Vietcong soldiers to give up, it was an overall failure. The Vietcong generally did not surrender; instead, they fought to their death in the 1968 Tet offensive. Members of the PAVN didn't surrender either; rather, they achieved their goal of driving out the United States and finally uniting the country under communism.[44]

Why didn't the American psychological campaign work? Some writers blame the failure on poor execution. For example, Lt Col Benjamin Findley notes that the US dropped "fear leaflets" imprinted with the ace of spades, unaware that the Vietnamese didn't know that the ace of spades was supposed to signify death. Another fear leaflet gruesomely depicted human corpses, which the Vietcong took as American gloating over Vietnamese deaths.[45]

Execution was not the problem. Rather, the campaign itself was ill conceived. Campaigns that aim at merely frightening enemy personnel while leaving them essentially cohesive seem bound to fail. Threats of death merely provoke reactance and thereby stiffen determination. Prolonged stress could conceivably turn reactance into helplessness, but cohesion counteracts the effects of stress.[46] Returning to the five themes developed in the American psychological campaign, only the fifth attempted to divide the Vietcong from the North. Whatever good that appeal may have done was probably undone by the third, which tried to convince soldiers that the *government* of South Vietnam was winning. That was the worst possible message to send.

Consider that South Vietnam was fissured between rulers and the ruled. The communist victory in the North had forced the dispossessed Catholic elite to flee southward where they quickly gained control over the government. Historian Larry

Cable documents that Ngo Dinh Diem, president of newly formed South Vietnam,

> committed a massive and egregious error in 1956, when he prohibited the traditional and deeply cherished village elections and instead appointed as village chiefs fellow Catholic refugees from the North. This was a blunder which even the French and the Japanese had not committed.[47]

The following year, Cable continues, Diem made things even worse by launching a land reform program that, besides being corrupt, failed to redistribute any land. When the indigenous Vietnamese peasantry complained, Diem's brother, Nhu, led the security police in a brutal repression. Thus, South Vietnamese rural peasants, mostly poor and Buddhist, found themselves oppressively governed by an urban, rich, and corrupt Catholic ex-northern elite bent mainly on securing its own comfort. Little wonder that the peasants revolted, swelling the ranks of the Vietcong. Even less wonder that, as the United States stepped in to back up the elitist government, southern peasants saw America as their enemy.

As the United States undertook the war in Vietnam, it failed either to recognize or else to act on the recognition that the Vietcong expressed genuinely perceived grievances of the southern peasantry. Cable documents how the United States treated the Vietcong as merely an auxiliary to the North's PAVN when in fact the Vietcong constituted an independent insurgent force whose principle aim was to rid the South of its recently arrived ex-northern oppressors. While the North Vietnamese certainly welcomed the insurgency and would use it to achieve their own goals, the United States, by fighting to sustain the government that had caused the insurgency in the first place, only fanned the flames of rebellion.[48]

The American propaganda message that the government of South Vietnam was winning the war must therefore have only reinforced the peasantry's belief that it had no choice but to fight or continue living under oppression. The peasantry acted out Sun Tzu's dictum that "if they know there is no alternative they will fight to the death."[49] Thus, American psychological operations, as a whole, very likely cemented the Vietcong to the North.

Yet the ingredients were in place for a successful psychological war aimed at separating the insurgents from their Northern allies. The southern peasants resented the northern interlopers and through the Vietcong were fighting both for liberation and *independence*. Political unification was a principal goal of only the North Vietnamese who foresaw the Vietcong as a postwar political rival.[50] To win the psychological war, the United States needed to make itself the southern peasants' liberator and unmask North Vietnam as seeking only the South's subjugation. Col Horace Hunter, Army counterinsurgency expert, eloquently stated the point:

> The Communists identified with decent causes, which they perverted, while we, with the best of motives, shored up repressive and venal systems. . . . We talked about reform and democracy without assuring either reform or democracy. . . . As a result, we were sullied by association with reactionary and corrupt regimes and seemingly condemned to lose. . . . Winning require[d] making the revolution ours.[51]

Instead of fighting the Vietcong, the United States needed somehow to take its side and force a settlement upon the government. Yet because the US saw itself engaged with monolithic communism in a global zero-sum game, the political goals of the Vietcong seemed unacceptable. But by opposing the insurgents and in effect the aspirations of the southern peasantry, the US played into North Vietnam's strategy of using the Vietcong to wear down the United States and using the United States to destroy the Vietcong.[52]

In contrast to the failed US efforts in Vietnam, the coalition's psychological war against Iraqi soldiers was spectacularly successful. Following weeks of relentless bombing and the stunning mechanized blitzkrieg on the ground, Iraqi soldiers surrendered by the thousands without fighting; they were broken men, often shuddering in tears. Gen Charles Horner, who commanded the coalition's air forces, attributed the mass surrenders to the psychological impact of round-the-clock bombardment, a conclusion at least consistent with Israeli psychologist Zhava Solomon's studies of combat stress.[53] Nevertheless, it is not clear that the bombing alone could have produced the intense distress that the defeated Iraqi soldiers displayed. For example, British and American researchers studying soldiers' reactions to sustained shelling in World War II drew conflicting conclusions. Unlike their British counterparts, American investigators suggested that soldiers eventually become desensitized to continued attacks.[54]

Key to the demoralization of Iraqi soldiers may have been a basic sense that the war was not theirs. A *Newsweek* reporter quoted an Iraqi close to the government as saying at the time that "this is not our war. This is Saddam's war. He's put us back 40 years."[55] How widespread this feeling may have been among the Iraqi military is not known, but one suspects it may have been common among those on the front lines who were poorly trained and only recently mobilized from among the general population. If so, these soldiers' lack of personal commitment to the war, more than the bombing itself, may explain their quick surrenders.

Conclusion

Facing the New World Order

The United States can no longer count on winning wars by destroying the enemy's military, if it ever could. The world is not soon likely to forget that twice in this century nuclear-armed superpowers were defeated by much smaller, poorly equipped armies: the United States in Vietnam and the Soviet Union in Afghanistan. Saddam Hussein thought he could do the same and perhaps could have if he had been smarter about it. Others will undoubtedly try and some will probably succeed if the US does not learn to fight the psychological war as well as it fights the "mechanistic" one.

Psychological war focuses on Clausewitz's "wonderful trinity": the people, the army, and the government. The army, interacting with chance, determines the outcome of battles. The government sets the war's political objectives and defines what victory will mean. But at the heart of modern war is the population. Governments, democratic or not, rule with at least the acquiescence of the people. Modern militaries are drawn from, and are therefore subsets of, their larger populations. Populations, as Clausewitz said, provide the passions of war;

they are the fulcrum upon which war rests. The enemy's population, then, is the proper target in war—specifically, the population's conviction that the war is in its interest. When the population turns against the war, the government is forced to redirect scarce war resources toward safeguarding its power. The army is robbed of its fighting spirit.

The key to turning the population against the war is to divide the society against itself, breaking the unity of the masses with their rulers. To accomplish this division, one must identify and exploit those socioeconomic, religious, and ethnic discontinuities that exist among the enemy's society. Nazi Germany defeated France by setting rich against poor, capitalist against socialist, Christian against Jew. Each group came to see the war as serving only the other's interest and therefore no one really wanted to fight. North Vietnam defeated the United States because the average American likewise came to see the war as being in the interest of only the military-industrial complex. Americans, for their part, fought on the wrong side, fighting to prop up an oppressive, elitist government against peasants who saw Communist revolution as their only way out. Had we but realized that the Vietcong longed for independence from the North as much as for freedom from their oppressive rulers, we might have won—not by killing Communist soldiers but by turning the Vietcong against North Vietnam and welding them to ourselves. It is a lesson that we should remember as we face the new world.

Notes

1. Russell F. Weigley, *The American Way of War* (Bloomington, Ind.: Indiana University Press, 1973), 464–67.

2. Carl von Clausewitz, *On War,* trans. J. J. Grisham (London: Penguin, 1968), 121–22.

3. Robert A. Pape, Jr., "Coercion and Military Strategy: Why Denial Works and Punishment Doesn't," *Journal of Strategic Studies* 15 (December 1992): 423–75.

4. Clausewitz, 125.

5. Philip E. Tetlock, Charles B. McGuire, and Gregory Mitchell, "Psychological Perspectives on Nuclear Deterrence," *Annual Review of Psychology* 42 (1991): 239–76.

6. See Norman Cigar, "Iraq's Strategic Mindset and the Gulf War: Blueprint for Defeat," *Journal of Strategic Studies* 15 (March 1992): 1–29, for a discussion of what Saddam Hussein may have been thinking.

7. Jack W. Brehm, *A Theory of Psychological Reactance* (New York: Academic Press, 1966).

8. Joel Brockner et al., "The Role of Self-Esteem and Self-Consciousness in the Wortman-Brehm Model of Reactance and Learned Helplessness," *Journal of Personality and Social Psychology* 45 (1983): 199–209. For recent discussions of the learned helplessness theory, see Jay G. Hull and Marilyn Mendolia, "Modeling the Relations of Attributional Style, Expectancies, and Depression," *Journal of Personality and Social Psychology* 61 (1991): 85–97; and Mario Mikulincer, "Attributional Processes in the Learned Helplessness Paradigm: Behavioral Effects of Global Attributions," *Journal of Personality and Social Psychology* 51 (1986): 1248–56.

9. Pape, 423–75.

10. Ibid., 461–64.

11. *The United States Strategic Bombing Surveys (European War) (Pacific War)* (1945; reprint, Maxwell AFB, Ala.: Air University Press, October 1987), 12.

12. Sun Tzu, *The Art of War*, trans. Samuel B. Griffith (London: Oxford University Press, 1963), 73–74.

13. See Samuel Griffith's introduction to *The Art of War*, especially the footnote on page 7.

14. John Spanier, *Games Nations Play* (Washington, D.C.: Congressional Quarterly Press, 1993), 177.

15. Sun Tzu, 63–64.

16. Karl R. Stadler, *Austria* (New York: Praeger, 1971); J. F. N. Bradley, *Czechoslovakia* (Edinburgh: Edinburgh University Press, 1971); and B. Bilck, *Fifth Column of Work* (London: Trinity Press, 1945).

17. Alistair Horne, *To Lose a Battle: France 1940* (Boston: Little, Brown, and Company, 1969), 85–87, 103–4, 109–15. Also, see Larry H. Addington, *The Patterns of War Since the Eighteenth Century* (Bloomington, Ind.: Indiana University Press, 1984), 187–92.

18. Quoted in M. E. Occleshaw, "The Stab in the Back—Myth or Reality?" *RUSI: Journal of the Royal United States Services Institute for Defence Studies* 130 (3 September 1985): 49–54.

19. George Herron, quoted in George G. Bruntz, "Allied Propaganda and the Collapse of German Morale in 1918," in *Psychological Warfare Casebook*, ed. William E. Daugherty (Baltimore: Johns Hopkins University Press, 1958), 96–105.

20. Addington, 157. Both Occleshaw and Bruntz point out that the propaganda campaign alone probably could not have broken German will. The military campaign created the socioeconomic pressure that made Germans susceptible to propaganda, and the resulting socialist uprising precluded the German army from having time to regroup and carry on the war.

21. Paul Blackstock, "German Psychological Warfare against the Soviet Union, 1941–1945," in *Psychological Warfare Casebook*, ed. William E. Daugherty (Baltimore: Johns Hopkins University Press, 1958), 263–73.

22. Sun Tzu, 73.

23. Mao Tse-Tung, *On the Protracted War* (Beijing: Foreign Language Press, 1960), 53.

24. Ibid., 120–21. In this passage, Mao actually writes about "our objective of annihilating and wearing down the enemy." His use of the term

annihilate, however, does not necessarily imply the physical destruction of the enemy's force. Rather, as he says on page 75, it means to "disarm [the enemy] or to deprive him of his power of resistance."

25. Jeffrey P. Kimball, "The Stab in the Back Legend and the Vietnam War," *Armed Forces and Society* 14 (Spring 1988): 433–58.

26. See for example, Paul Luebke and John F. Zipp, "Social Class and Attitudes toward Big Business in the United States," *Journal of Political and Military Sociology* 11 (Fall 1983): 251–64; and A. Wade Smith, "Public Consciousness of Blacks in the Military," *Journal of Political and Military Sociology* 11 (Fall 1983): 281–300. The recent Los Angeles riots sparked by the Rodney King beating also attest to the rifts lying just beneath the surface of American society.

27. Sun Tzu, 74.

28. To say that the war itself produced all these effects is not to say that the North Vietnamese did not consciously abet or take advantage of them. On the contrary, the communists made every effort to publicize civilian collateral damage from US air attacks, for example, and permitted American journalists and sympathetic celebrities such as Jane Fonda to visit North Vietnam. For discussions of the role the media played in this process, see Gerald S. Venanzi, "Democracy and Protracted War: The Impact of Television," *Air University Review* 34 (January–February 1983): 58–71; and Michael Mandelbaum, "Vietnam: The Television War," *Parameters* 13 (March 1983): 89–97.

29. "The Military: Servant or Master of Policy?," *Time* (11 April 1969): 20, 22.

30. Guenter Lewy, *America in Vietnam* (New York: Oxford University Press, 1978), 326–27, 356–64. See also "Who is Responsible for My Lai?," *Time* (8 March 1971): 18–19.

31. Mark Clodfelter, *The Limits of Airpower: The American Bombing of North Vietnam* (New York: The Free Press, 1989), 148–49. Clodfelter quotes Nixon as later saying, "We were going to continue fighting until the Communists agreed to negotiate a fair and honorable peace or until the South Vietnamese were able to defend themselves on their own—whichever came first."

32. Frank L. Goldstein and Daniel W. Jacobowitz, "Psyop in Desert Shield/Desert Storm," in "Psychological Operations and Case Studies," ed. Frank L. Goldstein and Benjamin F. Findley, (Unpublished book manuscript, 1993); and Cigar, 1–29.

33. *Newsweek,* 28 January 1991, 36; and *Newsweek,* 25 February 1991, 25.

34. *Newsweek,* 28 January 1991, 38; *The Nation,* 1 July 1991, 8–9; *The Progressive,* February 1991, 13; and *U.S. News & World Report,* 4 February 1991, 20.

35. The other was the more moderate National Campaign for Peace in the Middle East, which Jacob Weisberg notes did condemn Iraq's invasion of Kuwait and called for continuing economic sanctions as long as necessary.

36. Jacob Weisberg, "Means of Dissent," *The New Republic,* 25 February 1991, 18–20.

37. "A Just Folly," *New Statesman & Society* 3 (11 January 1991): 4–5.

38. But see Shilbey Telhami, "Between Theory and Fact: Explaining American Behavior in the Gulf War," *Security Studies* 2 (Autumn 1992): 96–121.

39. *Time,* 10 September 1990, 27–28; and *Reader's Digest,* June 1991, 159–60. The *Time* article also identified Dr Edward Luttwak as initially opposed to the war.

40. Cigar, 4.

41. Horne, 111.

42. Weigley, 464–67.

43. Quoted in Benjamin F. Findley, Jr., "U.S. and Viet Cong Psychological Operations in Vietnam," in Goldstein and Findley.

44. For brief but insightful discussions of why the US lost in Vietnam, see Weigley, 455–70; and Spanier, 403–6. Some writers like U. S. G. Sharp in *Strategy for Defeat* (Novato, Calif.: Presidio, 1978) and Harry G. Summers, Jr., in *On Strategy* (Novato, Calif.: Presidio, 1982) have argued that a "conventional" or "mechanistic" strategy could have defeated the Vietnamese if properly applied. Mark Clodfelter, *The Limits of Air Power,* and Larry E. Cable, *Conflict of Myths: The Development of American Counterinsurgency Doctrine and the Vietnam War* (New York: New York University Press, 1986) strongly criticize that assertion.

45. Findley, "U.S. and Viet Cong Psychological Operations in Vietnam."

46. Robert H. Scales, Jr., "Firepower: The Psychological Dimension," *Army* 39 (July 1989): 43–50; Zahava Solomon, "Does the War End When the Shooting Stops? The Psychological Toll of War," *Journal of Applied Social Psychology* 20 (1990): 1733–45; Zahava Solomon, Mario Mikulincer, and Steven E. Hobfoll, "Effects of Social Support and Battle Intensity on Loneliness and Breakdown during Combat," *Journal of Personality and Social Psychology* 51 (1986): 1269–76; idem, "Objective versus Subjective Measurement of Stress and Social Support: Combat-Related Reactions," *Journal of Consulting and Clinical Psychology* 55 (1987): 577–83.

47. Cable, *Conflict of Myths,* 185.

48. Larry E. Cable, *Unholy Grail: The US and the Wars in Vietnam, 1965–8* (New York: Routledge, 1991).

49. Sun Tzu, 110.

50. Cable, *Unholy Grail,* 220.

51. Horace L. Hunter, Jr., "Capturing the Revolution," *Military Review* 70 (January 1990): 89–90.

52. Cable, *Unholy Grail,* 220–21.

53. Lt Gen Charles A. Horner, "The Air Campaign," *Military Review* 71 (September 1991): 16–27; and Zahava Solomon, "Does the War End When the Shooting Stops?," 1733–45.

54. Anthony Kellet, *Combat Motivation: The Behavior of Soldiers in Battle* (Boston: Kluwer-Nijhoff, 1982) 254–57. See also Martin L. Fracker, "Psychological Effects of Aerial Bombardment," *Air Power Journal,* Fall 1992, 56–67.

55. *Newsweek,* 18 February 1991, 32.

PART II
THE RESPONSE

The Diplomacy of Regional Conflict Management

Albert U. Mitchum, Jr.

Thinking about war termination in the rational-choice approach, by analogy to chess, assumes that during the terminal stage of a war, a state, pursuing its national interests or goals, will prudently calculate the probable consequence of alternative courses of action, choose the one that maximizes its interests, and act accordingly. . . . Indeed, the national interest could be operationally defined as the goals for which a state would prefer to keep waging a lost war rather than concede.

—Leon V. Sigal
Fighting to a Finish

This essay will explore the implications of regional conflict management. There are several concepts that have recently appeared in the literature on conflict management that deserve a more detailed discussion. Specifically, one such idea is the concept of establishing buffer zones in an attempt to ease tensions, much as the boxing referee does when he asks both fighters to return to a neutral corner. That might work well for the sport of boxing where both contestants in the sport acknowledge the jurisdiction and legitimacy of the referee. Imagine the complications, however, if one or both of the combatants in the arena refused to comply with the referee's instructions.[1]

The analogy is not so farfetched in the world of the realpolitik where the United States finds itself the only viable superpower. During the past 40 years the politics of containment have left the US deeply involved in wide and diverse parts of the world. Without the threat of communist expansion to contain, we have been forced to rethink our posture. As the 45-Years' War, the cold war, ends in the blink of a calendar, we find that the world has become accustomed to a US presence. Meanwhile the US has become accustomed to the primacy of US interests and dealing only with the specific and vital US interests being threatened. That may be a luxury we can no longer afford as we grapple with the reality of living in a world where US national interests may not be directly threatened but where US action is demanded by the world at large.

Many in the US would like to turn inward and leave these external conflicts to the United Nations. Secretary-General Boutros Boutros-Ghali has outlined four missions for the United Nations (UN) in "An Agenda for Peace." These missions, which form the basis of his vision, are preventive diplomacy, peacemaking, peacekeeping, and postconflict peace building.[2] We will use the secretary-general's outline as a starting point. Indeed it is one of the few models existing in the real world. In the next few pages, we will briefly explore the vision, the reality, and the implications of future costs and consequences of US activity as a constabulary force in regional conflict management.

The emergence of limited war has meant that military activity had to be conducted below the thresholds that would trigger a direct confrontation between superpowers.

> The use of force in international relations has been so altered that it seems appropriate to speak of constabulary forces, rather than of military forces. The military establishment becomes a constabulary force when it is continuously prepared to act, committed to the minimum use of force, and seeks viable international relations, rather than victory.[3]

The constabulary concept defines a military framework allowing it to be used as an instrument of power projection. Despite the capability to destroy the world, we theorize about the use of military force just as we would about the use of political influence, economic power, and information dominance as instruments of power projection. The obvious paradox is that the military professional who is trained and prepared for employment of force (force projection) on a grand scale may also be the best suited for a role in regional conflict management on a subnational scale.

This is in keeping with the vision that the secretary-general of the United Nations espouses for military forces. Boutros

Boutros-Ghali's foreword to the *Yearbook of the United Nations, 1991* gives us a glimpse of his vision for the future:

> The year 1991 saw the definitive end of the Cold War and the bipolar era. Political energies previously held captive to the super-power struggle were released; new states were born as people recovered their freedom; major steps forward helped to reduce the threat of nuclear war. A new spirit of hopefulness and a belief in the relevance of common action began to take shape. But it also emerged that the transition to a new pattern of international relations would be *neither* easy *nor* risk free.
>
> One of the most hopeful signs was the clear consensus among states that the age of the United Nations had come. The United Nations suddenly found that it was no longer paralyzed by the bipolar struggle; indeed, the world looked to the organization as never before. It was increasingly being asked to take on and fulfill its historic mission: that of the guardianship of peace and hope.[4]

Not two years after these words were written they began to lose some of their power. It is not the lack of interest nor the loss of direction but the harsh glare of reality that has begun to diminish the words' impact. What has also begun to tarnish is a clearly defined role for the US military in regional conflict management. The strategy of containing violence within a specified area as a confined regional conflict requires highly centralized control of the instruments of power projection by civilian policymakers. In these situations military combat forces are only one facet of an overall campaign of coercion through diplomacy.

Along these lines the secretary-general considers preventive diplomacy the most desirable and efficient method for easing tensions before they erupt into violence. As a subset of preventive diplomacy, he suggests preventive deployments of armed forces to unstable areas. In his vision these forces serve a diplomatic mission to deter cross-border predatory behavior as well as to stabilize internal hostilities. His vision also calls for the creation of demilitarized zones in this preventive context.[5] However, the introduction of armed forces capable of combat and the imposition of demilitarized zones could act to institutionalize a conflict. Taken to its logical extreme, preventive intervention could lead to the type of repression that sowed the seeds of conflict in Yugoslavia.

If the conflict cannot be prevented, the next step would be to bring the conflict to a peaceful resolution. This peacemaking role tasks the UN to bring hostile parties to agreement by peaceful means. If peaceful diplomatic means fail, the UN would deploy heavily armed peace-enforcement units.[6] While peacemaking and peace enforcement break new ground for the United Nations, the new plan also calls for increases in its other, more traditional role of peacekeeping. The secretary-general forces full participation of the General Assembly in supporting mediation, negotiation, and arbitration efforts, plus a greater reliance on the International Court of Justice for peaceful adjudication of differences.

As the international climate *has* changed in the last four years, the peacekeeping mission has evolved rapidly as a popular and viable concept, despite increased demands in logistics, equipment, personnel, and finance. Peacekeeping entails inserting lightly armed forces where a cease-fire has already been agreed to by the warring parties. Peacekeepers primarily monitor and encourage conformity of the parties to the cease-fire or armistice.[7] In an effort to capitalize on recent successes the secretary-general recommends a $50 million revolving reserve fund and a prepositioned stock of peacekeeping equipment for under-equipped troops. The implications are that member states should commit certain equipment to stand by for immediate use and that peacekeeping personnel would receive improved language training. The secretary-general sees peacekeeping as a short-term stability factor designed to improve the chances of long-term peace. Unfortunately, he does not present a plan to create the infrastructure and support base this would require.

He also believes that postconflict peace building would foster confidence between parties to an armed dispute. These national forces on loan to the UN would disarm the belligerents, repatriate refugees, monitor elections, protect human rights, and help reform/strengthen governmental institutions. They would undertake projects such as developing agriculture, improving transportation systems, sharing resources, and improving education to bring states together. The technical assistance of this UN's imitation of the peace corps is conceived as a way to transform deficient national structures and strengthen democratic institutions.[8] Boutros Boutros-Ghali's agenda assumes the UN has or can readily acquire the capabilities, the latitude, and the national will to use them. The secretary-general's plans for an enhanced role in the post–cold-war era are based on the assumption that the major powers generally agree and are generally equal in economic as well as military power.

The Reality

The end of the superpower and ideological rivalry has not meant the end of superpowers. There remains one lone superpower in the world today, the United States. Several writers have described the current world structure as being unipolar, with the United States sitting at the apex. For the near future, only the United States possesses the combination of political, economic, and military power to perform all the missions outlined in "An Agenda for Peace." The events of the 1990s lend credence to this assertion.

International peace and collective security have been primarily defined and shaped by the United States. In short, where the US has not led, neither has the UN nor the rest of the world. It was US action that prevented the predatory aggression of Iraq from continuing south of Kuwait and wresting control of the Arabian Peninsula. One could argue, as some states have already argued, that the UN served as a tool of US foreign policy. The Security Council resolutions to condemn the invasion, approve the economic embargo, and to use force were *de facto* consent to US policy. While the US could have acted unilaterally if needed, it was appreciably easier and politically more palatable to act in concert with other states. Admittedly, the use of force was much easier to sell to the American people and to Congress when "legitimized" through multilateral consensus.[9]

Desert Shield and Desert Storm represent, in fact, the first peacemaking and peace-enforcement operations in the post–cold-war era. The unprecedented cooperation of many dissimilar states fueled the emerging hope for the UN to take a more proactive role in international peace and security. But here the analogy breaks down because the reason for US involvement was that the US saw its own interests directly threatened. The US, therefore, immediately involved itself to rectify the situation.

The further evidence of the UN's inability to perform peacemaking operations is the literal disintegration of Somalia. The overthrow of President Siad Barre proved to be a quagmire for the UN. With the Somali government and infrastructures virtually nonexistent, conditions there seemed to provide the ideal challenge for the newly resurgent UN to test its mettle. The organization responded and established the United Nations Operation in Somalia (UNOSOM) in April 1992.

Current Perspective
Somalia

For more than two decades, the African nation of Somalia was a pawn in the global battle between communism and democracy. First the Soviet Union and then the United States poured millions of dollars' worth of weaponry into the sparsely populated Muslim nation in their struggle over what was called 'the strategic Horn of Africa.' When the cold war ended, Somali President Mohammed Siad Barre fell from power and the country slipped back into obscurity. But the killing only intensified as local warlords turned their Kalishnikovs and M-16s on aid workers and even on relief ships. Where man left off the killing, nature stepped in: Three years of drought have dried up water supplies, killed livestock and baked cornfields into concrete.

—Carla Robinson
"Waiting for America"

Somalia presents a unique set of challenges to be faced. The country has disintegrated into family-based tribes and coalitions of tribes that often lack central leadership. The principal thrust comes from groups of armed gangs referred to as "technicals." These technicals mix with the local population and owe their allegiance to local warlords. As the system of law and order broke down, the rest of the population armed themselves. The US ambassador to Kenya warned, in a cable to the US under secretary for international affairs, "Somalis, as the Italians and British discovered to their discomfiture, are natural-born guerrillas. . . . They will mine the roads. They will lay ambushes. They will launch hit-and-run attacks. They will not be able to stop the convoys from getting through. But they will inflict—and take—casualties."[10]

The first significant UNOSOM action was with the deployment of 3,500 troops to Mogadishu in September. Their peacekeeping mission was simply to protect humanitarian relief supplies.[11] The United States landed marines in early December and brought in approximately 25,000 combat, combat-support, and other troops to stabilize the internal situation and protect the relief supplies. The United States, in effect, engaged in a small-scale peace-enforcement action to disarm and separate the rival clans and to foster a mutually agreeable settlement between them.[12] The UN planners could take a lesson from the US experience. President George Bush provided assistance reluctantly to the Somalis and only after a UN resolution offering a coalition solution. The UN resolution specified "the US-led international force will be allowed to use 'all necessary means' to create a secure environment for humanitarian relief operations in Somalia."[13] In setting national objectives, President Bush declared Operation Restore Hope a humanitarian mission. He also warned the technicals, however, that the US would not tolerate interference.

Situations like the one in Somalia are not very satisfying, but are likely to be increasingly common in the years ahead. With that in mind, there is a lesson here to be taken from the Joint Doctrine Air Campaign Course (JDACC) *Air Campaign Planning Handbook*. This handbook directs the campaigner to gather information on the enemy's culture and religion as well as on health, social structure, food, public utilities, mass media, the monetary system, and finally significant ethnic and socioeconomic breakdowns.[14] In Somalia's case, culture and religion must be the foremost consideration in achieving the desired end state because all other elements of the governmental infrastructure are either destroyed or incapable of caring for the population.

I caution that in researching the Somali culture and formulating courses of action, we must guard against the pitfalls of ethnocentrism. The Somali Muslim is not likely to perceive our actions as we do from within our frame of reference. America is unique in assimilating a wide variety of people into a single society without distinct social classes, major ethnic divisions, or subnationalistic undercurrents.[15] Somalia, on the other hand, is a "fractured country, long molded by a culture of decentralization, where the basis for all political and social structure is genealogy."[16] The authority of clan elders, now more than ever, provides the foundation for Somali society. The national leaders of Somalia's recent postcolonial nationhood pitted one clan against another and this development, combined with the influx of modern small arms, severely weakened the traditional position of the clan elders. Now warlords and technicals wield authority at gunpoint. The society is in flux.

A UN resolution defined the end state in Somalia as a secure environment for humanitarian relief operations. The best means of restoring near-term security was to ensure that the Somali population identified US intervention as purely humanitarian and not favoring one tribe over another. In addition, any use of air power beyond airlift would only increase Somali misery and add to the cost of rebuilding. For example, if the US were to apply air strikes against warlord strongholds, we would only aid the consolidation of territory by other clans. Attacks on Somalia's already sparse infrastructure would further delay delivery of aid, thereby inflicting more suffering on the people and increasing the costs of rebuilding Somalia.

Current Perspective

Yugoslavia

We would be remiss not to mention the situation in the former Yugoslavia[17] where the United Nations Protection Force (UNPROFOR) consists of about 23,000 troops at this writing. This troop presence, however, has not deterred ethnic cleansing, detention camps, refugees, nor killing in Bosnia-Herzegovina.[18] One European diplomat familiar with the crisis commented: "What we've seen in Yugoslavia isn't peacekeeping, peacemaking or peace enforcing. It's been a case of watching as peace deteriorates."[19] As in Somalia, the UN has deployed peacekeeping forces with a peacekeeping mind-set into a peacemaking/peace-enforcing situation; there is no peace to keep, so the UN forces have been inadequate to the task.

The experiences in Iraq-Kuwait, Somalia, and the former Yugoslavia all point to one reality; there is a need for US leadership in a new world order of uncertainty and instability. The UN is not yet prepared to take the lead step in international peace and stability which Boutros Boutros-Ghali envisions.

Although the means to accomplish the ends are not exactly clear, nor universally acknowledged, the objectives seem clear enough. The UN's stated goal is to establish humanitarian relief to the besieged cities of Bosnia.[20] The more difficult objective is to bring the fighting to an end in order to establish a lasting peace between the warring factions. The first step toward this end would seem to be deciding which course to follow.

The difficulty is in determining the best course to follow and the most appropriate means to accomplish the desired end state. There has been much discussion of a bombing campaign against the Serbian forces. The danger is that there is a downside to a successful bombing campaign in which the Serbian forces could be driven to a guerrilla war that could, in turn, lessen the direct impact of air power. At that point we would be forced to choose between a continued bombing campaign against a highly mobile target or a mounted house-to-house assault that would require an enormous number of troops. Senator Sam Nunn (D-Ga.) gives us this stern warning:

> You need to know how to get out as well as get in. Whatever is done militarily ought to be carried out quickly without implying a long-range, continuing commitment by US forces . . . and I suspect the same thing by European forces.[21]

Even the option of an air campaign against Serbia is fraught with potential political, military, economic, and moral costs. There are no easy solutions and the costs are prohibitive.

Future Implications

Costs and Consequences

The reality of the world is that the United States enjoys certain technological advantages over most of the world's military forces, and these secrets are jealously guarded by an army of bureaucrats and legislation aimed at prohibiting the export of certain technologies. It seems the potential for compromise of some of these technologies increases as we become involved in less structured coalition force arrangements. While we all want our soldiers to be protected by our best and latest technologies, we do not want to see these same technologies used against them. Conventional wisdom would point to arms and parts left behind in Vietnam being used to repair US-made equipment in other parts of the world. Conventional wisdom and recent experience would point to Iranian pilots flying US-made fighter aircraft and terrorists threatening the US with US-made Stinger missiles originally intended for the Mujaheddin. The point here is to highlight the dichotomous situation where our servicemen and servicewomen might be denied our full range of technology because of the danger of technology transfer to temporary allies in a UN-sponsored coalition.

Unsuccessful involvement in UN-sponsored missions into world conflict zones can only hurt the United States's posture and prestige in the eyes of the world. The United States stands at the edge of a *pax americana technica* that no single nation in the world can challenge. We should be selective as to our involvement in military operations that do not directly support advancement of US objectives. The technological advantages we enjoy were paid for by US taxpayers in a hard-fought technology race with the former Soviet Union. US taxpayers, therefore, should have a voice in the use of those technologies, which they financed through sacrifice.

The alternative then is to recognize that US taxpayers have, and still are, footing much of the bill for military activity overseas. If the mandate the current administration claims is to be believed, US taxpayers are more interested in programs at home even if they are at the expense of programs abroad.

Domestic sentiment says that diplomats should be given the chance to resolve regional disputes without involving US military forces, and they should be held accountable if they do not. The Clinton presidency appears to be centered on domesticity, not on global interdependence and collective security. The reality of the world indicates that comanagement of regional conflicts has not performed as expected and that the US by default is in high demand to "make it work." The question that begs to be asked then is who picks up the pieces if the US fails? The caution, despite world opinion, is to be very selective as to the nature and depth of US involvement.

Summary

Clearly regional conflict management is a role at which the US could look in order to keep the hot spots in the international system from boiling over. In a recent statement before the House Foreign Affairs Committee, a State Department official commented:

> We have reached one of the three great junctions of 20th century history. We have won the Cold War, just as we have won the First and Second World Wars. Our prestige and influence are at an apogee, but in some ways, we are tired from the struggle and want to turn inward. Our domestic problems are myriad and cry out for attention. We want somebody—anybody—to take over the load overseas.[22]

During the early 1960s under former secretary-general Dag Hammarskjöld, peacekeeping operations were termed "preventive diplomacy" and were intended to keep the major powers out, especially the superpowers, by bringing in the smaller powers to stabilize a situation before the superpowers would feel compelled to intervene.[23] Today, the challenge will be just the opposite: to find a way to attract American interest, involvement, and leadership.

One of the potential problems is the concept of a continuum of UN actions, any of which can be chosen in response to a given situation.[24] The steps from preventive diplomacy to peacemaking, to peace enforcement, and finally to postconflict peace building all appear to follow a logical, linear flow of options which will fit almost any situation in some fashion.

However, there is a very fundamental and significant jump from peacekeeping to peace enforcement.[25] The difference is not just one of degree, but a near quantum leap in kind, and it reflects the fundamental interests of the conflicting parties. In peacekeeping situations, both sides have mutually agreed to a cease-fire, consider a cessation of hostilities to be in their best interests, and harbor the hope of at least a tentative agreement on future relations. In peace-enforcement situations, on the other hand, at least one side has something to gain from the conflict and is therefore reluctant to stop the fighting. Even if a peace-enforcement action is successful in terminating the open conflict between hostile parties, it will not necessarily eliminate the root cause of the conflict. The cause and ultimate resolution of conflict is a political process, not a purely military activity.[26] Therefore, a successful peace-enforcement action does not necessarily lead to a peacekeeping operation. The difference is not trivial, and carries significant implications in the type of forces the United Nations would need to deploy.[27]

Peacekeeping is the United Nations's most visible and prominent mission. It is also the mission which will continue to largely define the organization's role in international peace and security for the near future. It is the most practical and the most practiced of the UN's missions. Peacekeeping forces do not have to create peace, the warring factions have already agreed to a cease-fire or armistice. Peacekeepers are caretakers to a peace already agreed upon, and most importantly, their presence is desired by both sides. Hence nations are more willing to contribute forces for peacekeeping. Certainly, peacekeeping is a "growth industry" with a future for even further growth.[28] It is, however, also one of the most difficult missions[29] since it is essentially a diplomatic initiative but one that must be based on power. Suffice it to say that it is hard enough to build and coordinate activities within the political architecture of any individual nation state. It is an exponentially more difficult task for a coalition of states.

Postconflict peace building is a logical follow-on mission to peacekeeping. Postconflict peace building is also performed at the pleasure of both parties. This mission could be performed following the conclusion of a successful peacekeeping operation or in conjunction with an ongoing peacekeeping operation. Peacekeeping operations, however, will not necessarily build the foundations for a future peace; only the opposing sides can do that. Peace-building operations have a great potential as lubricants to the longer term peace process, not as the fuel for it.

In situations in which American national security interests are directly threatened as in the Persian Gulf, the United States will take the lead to secure them. This will be all the more true in a major peace-enforcement situation. The United States can be expected to build ad hoc coalitions and to seek legitimacy for actions in the international community as well as with the American Congress and the American people who have borne and will bear the majority of the expenses incurred in any such operations. From a US perspective the UN serves as a tool of American policy in situations where vital US national security interests are at stake.

In localized situations, however, where peripheral national security interests are involved, the US will be more reluctant to step in and more willing to support UN action. However, as the Somalia experience demonstrates, when a legitimate mission undertaken by the UN proves too tough for it to handle, the US may feel compelled to step in and get involved or even to take the lead. The UN cannot create the peace it seeks to ensure. Only the respective states in a conflict can really create the peace the secretary-general desires. The UN is far more likely to be nudged and pushed along by the actions of individual states in the international system than it is to shape the agendas for the states themselves. The new world order may not be so new. It may very well be the same old order with many of the same old players playing on a new field.

Furthermore, since the US is not bound to the UN, the potential for exploitation of regional conflicts by regional powers does exist. If the US is prepared to accept this potential, then we need do nothing. If we do not accept it then we need to take action, but the instruments of diplomacy and economic coercion should be exploited before we commit US lives where US interests are not clearly at risk. This may be the alternative paradigm for US force employment abroad—let the diplomats do their work and hold them accountable.

Notes

1 The boxing referee might be able to enforce his ruling and could even declare the center of the ring a no-man's land as a kind of buffer zone. Unfortunately, this might also serve to ensure the combatants do not come to agreement on the rules. Such a ruling might well serve to institutionalize the tensions it was intended to relieve.

2. One could argue that what these missions really form is a demand for military and diplomatic muscle that can be met by only one power on earth.

3. Morris Janowitz, *The Professional Soldier: A Social and Political Portrait* (New York: Free Press, 1960), 418.

4. United Nations, *Yearbook of the United Nations, 1991*, vol. 45 (New York: Martinus Nijhoff Publishers, 1992), foreword.

5. Boutros Boutros-Ghali, "An Agenda for Peace," *UN Chronicle*, September 1992, 3.

6. The stated purpose for these peace-enforcement units is to enter into a combat zone in order to forcibly create a cease-fire.

7. Peter R. Baehr and Leon Gordenker, *The United Nations in the 1990s* (New York: St. Martin's Press, 1992), 81.

8. Boutros Boutros-Ghali, 3.

9. Charles Krauthammer, "The Unipolar Moment," *Foreign Affairs* 70, no. 1, 26.

10. Carla Robbins, "Waiting for America," *U.S. News & World Report*, 7 December 1992, 26.

11. Russell Goekie, "US Commits Forces to Somalia, But for How Long?" *Africa Report*, January–February 1993, 5.

12. A glaring ineptitude of international proportions left the first contingent of 500 troops pinned down by local warring factions and unable to ensure their own safety, much less protect supplies. The situation continued to deteriorate and the remainder of the force could not be deployed. Then, the UN relief ship carrying 10,000 metric tons of food was shelled trying to enter Mogadishu's harbor and forced to turn back to sea. By November it was clear that the UN was not up to the task in Somalia. Only the US possessed the combination of political, economic, and force projection capabilities along with the national will to establish a positive presence in the country.

13. The plan called for the US to go in-country to stabilize the situation and pave the way for a larger, follow-on contingent of UNOSOM peacekeeping forces. The Somalia situation again suggests the US is the only country that can take on and lead peace-enforcement operations. It also suggests that UN peace-enforcement activities can occur only with the cooperation, involvement, and leadership of the United States.

14. Eric Randell and Carla Robbins, "Operation Restore Hope," *U.S. News & World Report*, 14 December 1992, 28.

15. Joint Doctrine Air Campaign Course (JDACC), *Air Campaign Planning Handbook* (Maxwell AFB, Ala.: College of Aerospace Doctrine, Research, and Education, July 1992), 2, 7.

16. Francis Fukuyama, *The End of History and the Last Man* (New York: Free Press, A Division of Macmillan, Inc., 1992), 118.

17. Jeffery Clark, "Debacle in Somalia," *Foreign Affairs* 72, no. 1 (1993): 110.

18. The main interest at the time of this writing is the region of Bosnia-Herzegovinia, which is slightly larger than the state of Tennessee (51,000 square miles) and has an extremely rugged topography. Bosnia is a net importer of food and can meet the needs of only about half of its approximately four million inhabitants. Only about 20 percent of the land is arable and the majority of it is in private hands. The region does, however, have some natural resources: coal, iron, bauxite, manganese, and timber. Bosnia's main industries before the war began were those linked to the Yugoslav arms production and exportation. The fighting has taken its toll, and the region now suffers from plummeting production, 28 percent unemployment, and an inflation rate that reaches 80 percent per month. This is exacerbated by various economic blockades that Serbia and Croatia have imposed in the areas where most of the industry is located. The country's infrastructure includes 13,000 miles of highway and 100 miles of pipeline for crude oil. The telephone system boasts over 700,000 subscribers, but it is woefully antiquated. There are only two television stations and only two major airports. At the risk of sounding glib, this was not a formula for economic success and growth, even before the conflict began.

19. Thomas G. Weiss, "New Challenges for UN Military Operations: Implementing an Agenda for Peace," *Washington Quarterly*, Winter 1993, 56.

20. Michael S. Serrill, "Underfire," *Time*, 18 January 1993, 32.

21. David A. Fulghum, "US Weighs Use of Nonlethal Weapons in Serbia if UN Decides to Fight," *Aviation Week & Space Technology*, 17 August 1992, 64.

22. Fulghum, 62.

23. US Department of State, *Dispatch* 3, no. 13 (30 March 1992): 246.

24. David W. Ziegler, *War, Peace, and International Politics*, 4th ed. (Boston: Little, Brown and Company, 1987), 326.

25. Donald M. Snow, "Peacekeeping, Peacemaking and Peace-enforcement: The U.S. Role in the New World Order," *U.S. Army War College Fourth Annual Conference on Strategy*, February 1993, 19.

26. Ibid., 21.

27. Ibid., 20.

28. There are wholesale differences between the requirements of peacekeeping and peace enforcement. Peacekeeping forces are not combat forces. The soldiers have traditionally been lightly armed for self-defense, inserted by mutual agreement of the parties in conflict, and viewed as neutral parties to the original conflict. The role of peacekeeping forces is analogous to national police forces rather than military forces. Peace-enforcement units, on the other hand, are combat units by necessity. Their purpose would be to engage in combat and their presence in a conflict would be opposed by at least one of the combatants. These units would not be viewed as neutral and could very well be regarded by one side as reinforcements for the other. They must be armed with exponentially higher capability than peacekeeping forces for at least two reasons. To achieve a decisive effect in the battle zone, they will want to get in fast and quickly

terminate hostilities to reduce the loss of life to the respective belligerents. Secondly, if the United Nations asks the US to contribute forces to a combat zone for something less than our own national interests, then the United Nations will have to take the necessary measures to ensure the greatest chance of survival of these troops: this necessarily means using decisive force. Decisive force means more than just firepower. It also requires strategic and tactical mobility, flexibility, precision, unit cohesion, and considerable amounts of training. Peace-enforcement units will require more than just ground troops; they will require air, space, and naval forces to be decisive. Since these are combat units, they will require the sophisticated logistics network to maintain them. Extensive, responsive transportation assets will be required to insert the units into or near the combat zone as well as support the logistics aspects of the operation. There are other requirements to building a decisive force, but they are beyond the scope of this discussion.

29. John Spanier, *Games Nations Play*, 8th ed. (Washington, D.C.: Congressional Quarterly, Inc., 1993), 542.

30. Currently there are 15 member nations that compromise the Security Council, and there is general agreement the composition of the Security Council needs to be changed. Many of the proposals include placing Germany, Japan, and third world potential members such as India, Brazil, and Nigeria as permanent members on the Security Council, expanding the body to 20 or more nations. While this might make the Security Council more representative of global and regional powers, it would most certainly hamper its ability to make quick or decisive decisions on the use of force. The inevitable debates might add legitimacy, but they would do so at the expense of mission accomplishment (e.g., preventive deployments or peace enforcement).

Forecasting Military Technological Needs

Anthony D. Alley

Time and again, we have seen technology revolutionize the battlefield. The US has always relied upon its technological edge to offset the need to match potential adversaries' strength in numbers. Cruise missiles, stealth fighters and bombers, today's smart *weapons with the state-of-the-art guidance systems and tomorrow's* brilliant *ones. The men and women in our armed forces deserve the best technology America has to offer.*

—Victor H. Reis
"Foundations for the Future"

Clearly, the political establishment in office at the time of Desert Storm saw technology as an important element in defense. The acquisition process that aimed to keep US military technologies five to 10 years ahead of those of the Soviet Union is even credited as a contributor to America's victory in the cold war.[1] Although cuts in defense spending will certainly alter the acquisition processes for high technology, the Clinton administration appears to be no less interested in technology.[2]

Moving from the broader, political perspective to the Department of Defense (DOD) opinion of the role of technology in the Gulf War, the DOD notes, "A revolutionary new generation of high-technology weapons, combined with innovative and effective doctrine, gave our forces the edge."[3] In the DOD's final report to Congress on the conduct of the war, former Secretary of Defense Dick Cheney also noted that capitalizing on the leading-edge technologies available during Desert Storm "promises to change the nature of warfare significantly."[4]

The potentially decisive nature of technology in warfare has been well stated. However, forecasting technological needs can be an especially challenging task. The spectrum of available technologies is quite broad, and the pace of technological change is swift. The Committee for Strategic Technologies for the Army (STAR) is predicting that

> the explosive rate of technological progress observed in the last three decades can be expected to continue, if not increase, during the next three decades. Weapons of 20 years from now will have completely outmoded those of today, just as those of U.S. forces outmoded the older weapons of Iraqi forces in the Persian Gulf war.[5]

Trying to understand the intricacies of the thousands of technological subsystems proposed for use in military operations is far beyond the capabilities of most. Still, the importance of technology in military operations and public/congressional interest in the military's high-dollar/high-tech expenditures compel us to understand what shapes and drives our procurement of technology. Each of us needs to be able to articulate the significance of technology in military operations. Consequently, it may be best to take a top-down approach and consider some of the influences and principles that drive the pursuit of technologies.

This essay is offered in response to this challenge. It will highlight some of the principles of military operations that can be extended with technology. Thereafter, a few of the major influences on technological procurement will be addressed. The view is purposefully broad, and the material is presented as an impetus to further consideration, study, and dialogue. The majority of examples used to demonstrate technology's impact on military operations is taken from Desert Storm. It should not be taken that Gulf War technologies represent the extremes of possibilities for technology nor that they will be sufficient to counter the next threat, but given the recent nature of the war and the unprecedented television coverage, most readers will be familiar with the systems and occurrences addressed.

Technology is a term that can be difficult to come to grips with. For the purposes of this essay, the term *technology* is assumed to mean a system or subsystem sought for practical application. That is, technology infers research and development with practical aims and objectives. Political and military aims, at least at strategic and operational levels, ought not to be dictated by technology. More appropriately, technologies should be pursued to meet, and are therefore subordinate to, political and military objectives.[6] Still, it must be noted that, "Strategy without suitable tactical instruments is simply a set of ideas."[7]

Technology as an Extension to Military Principles

Application of the principles of war, detailed in Air Force Manual 1-1, *Basic Aerospace Doctrine of the United States Air Force*, does not secure success in military operations. Instead, they "represent generally accepted *truths* that have proven effective for commanders employing forces in combat."[8] If we accept that technologies make up the vehicles of force employment, speaking both figuratively and literally, then technologies that extend the ability of commanders to fight according to the principles of war should prove most effective. That is, technologies that maximize a commander's ability to use force economically, concentrate power, maneuver, maintain the offensive, and so on, will pay greater dividends than technologies that make lesser contributions to the exercise of those principles. Consequently, an excellent framework for the consideration of technologies is in terms of their contributions to the employment of military forces under the principles of war.

For example, during World War II, it would have required 108 aircraft dropping a total of 648 1,100-pound bombs against a power-generating plant to achieve a 96 percent probability of striking the plant with two bombs. During Desert Storm, the same probability could be achieved with only one aircraft dropping two precision guided bombs.[9] Were we compelled to argue for one technology over the other, in this example, we would argue in favor of precision guided munitions and associated delivery systems, given their ability to offer the commander a greater opportunity to capitalize on *simplicity* and *economy of force.*

From this example, it can be seen that the technologies associated with precision guided munitions, as employed during the Gulf War, contributed directly to economy of force and simplicity, and indirectly to the exercise of other principles of war. Where this technological advantage was not available during Desert Storm, it can be seen that economy of force and simplicity were sacrificed. The DOD's final report to Congress on the conduct of the Gulf War notes that

> the lack of PGM [precision guided munitions] capability on many US aircraft required planners to select less-than-optimum attack options, such as delaying attacks or assigning multiple sorties with non-precision munitions. Operation Desert Storm results argue that a higher percentage of US attack aircraft should have PGM capability to increase the amount of target damage that can be inflicted by a finite number of aircraft.[10]

Of course, some of the same technologies that contributed to economy and simplicity also contributed to *surprise*. Most notably, the F-117 utilized stealth technology to bring firepower to Iraqi facilities inside Baghdad. "Platforms like the F-117 provided low-risk attack options that required neither the traditional imperative of air superiority nor electronic-warfare and fighter-escort support."[11] This assessment of stealth technology is especially significant. When Army AH-64 attack helicopters first struck Iraqi radar sites during the initial moments of Desert Storm, F-117s were already beyond those radar sites and well inside Iraq, providing that country's military a rather startling wake-up call. So, the stealth technologies of the F-117 greatly extended surprise, allowing commanders to employ weapon systems with little warning and attack where attack would have been traditionally awkward.

In order to support the principle of *maneuver*, technologies that allow for flexible power projection need to be pursued. This will become increasingly difficult as more and more US installations overseas are closed. Even after forces have deployed into the theater of operations, distances to strategic targets can restrict the numbers and types of assets that a commander can launch against an enemy. Power projection proved to be a focal point for effort during the Gulf War with nearly 17,000 tanker sorties flown in support of combat missions. Many aircraft required refueling support to and from targets inside Iraq, and it is estimated that nearly 60 percent of the sorties flown by air-refuelable aircraft required air-refueling support.[12] As our focus shifts from a major battle against the former Soviet Union and to regional operations in support of peacekeeping, humanitarian relief, and localized instabilities, power projection will need to be a factor considered with most technological purchases.

It should come as no surprise that operations out of area and coalition warfare will also confound efforts to operate under the principle of simplicity. Orchestrating integrated attack packages of multinational forces requires a lot of attention to detail and carefully communicated directions. For instance, during Desert Storm the daily air task order (ATO), the document which details targets, routing, support, and other particulars, grew to hundreds of pages. The long time required to plan the day's activities, generate the ATO, and then distribute it electronically using the Computer-Assisted Force Management System was significant. However, most units received details of that portion of the ATO pertinent to their unit via secure telephone long before they received the electronically distributed ATO.[13] Technologies that simplify the functions of communicating, planning, and executing tasks are a must, especially if we continue to operate as participants in multinational coalitions and away from well-established military facilities.

Of course, technologies that simplify operations need not reduce *security*. For instance explicit communications between units within theater and between Gulf-based units and agencies in the US were vital if information and material were to continue to flow. Spare parts were required, plans needed to be coordinated, and taskings needed to be generated in as direct and simple a manner as possible, but security could not be compromised. Secure telephone systems proved to be one of the most effective technologies of the war. An extension of this technology, secure fax systems, was especially useful. Target details, such as the layout of buildings, were faxed to attacking units to enhance mission effectiveness.[14] Commanders will continue to require technologies that foster this sort of simplicity without sacrificing security.

Few technologies contributed to the principle of *offensive* in the Gulf War as did those associated with high-speed antiradiation missiles (HARM). The *Gulf War Air Power Survey Summary* notes, "The use of HARMs effectively neutralized both elements of Iraqi ground-based defenses—antiaircraft artillery (AAA) and surface-to-air missiles (SAM)—by suppressing the SAMs and thereby allowing coalition aircraft to fly above the lethal range of AAA."[15] Consequently, commanders were able to prosecute the air war at the time and place of their choosing. This freedom of action was a prime contributor to the coalition's ability to maintain the initiative.

Influences on Technological Pursuits

These few examples demonstrate that links between technologies and war-fighting principles can be established. However, as we consider the suitability of various technologies for military applications, we are likely to find that choices are never as simple as selecting technologies solely due to their utility in exercising the principles of war. Instead, a variety of other factors will also influence our decisions.

First of all, we are likely to find that the exercise of the principles of war is frequently constrained by political concerns and ethical considerations. For instance, early in the Gulf War there seemed to be no pressing military need to target Iraqi mobile Scud missile systems due to their limited accuracy.[16] However, after a few Scud attacks against Tel Aviv and other Israeli cities, "many sorties were diverted or replanned from their intended targets to hunt and suppress the Scuds."[17] In this case, it could be argued that political considerations subverted the principles of mass, economy of force, offensive, and maneuver. The recorded history of our experiences in Vietnam is replete with similar contravening concerns. Another example that is more germane to the issue of technology acquisition focuses on the use of weapons of mass destruction. There are those who argue, for instance, in favor of the deterrent potential assumed to be characteristic of nuclear weapons versus large standing armies. However, political, social, and moral influences encourage a broader, more balanced perspective for weapons procurement.

Away from the battlefield, political and social issues will also influence our pursuit of technologies. The 25 March 1991 issue of *Fortune* magazine begins its article "How Defense Will Change" with the following note:

> When military historians look back on the 20th century, they may well call the war against Iraq the last big hurrah for America's awesome arms industry—an all-stops-out, razzle-dazzle, techno-killer grand finale. Normally a performance like that would guarantee future engagements or at least a rousing encore. But—for now—this show is over.[18]

Fortune may have overstated the point a bit, but clearly, defense spending is on the decline. Defense funds are being diverted into social programs and debt reduction. Some estimates forecast defense cuts to bring defense spending for 1997 down to the buying power levels of 1960.[19] Consequently, some degree of concession will need to be made as the best and most promising technologies are procured from among the growing number of very attractive alternatives.

This increasing number of technologies and restricted budgets will have another influence on technology procurement. In times past, the US was guaranteed a technological edge in military matters by virtue of the services' procurement procedures and our well-established and well-financed defense industrial base. Systems could be sponsored, from prototype through implementation, by the DOD. Exclusive control of research, development, and production could be tightly managed. Consequently, management of technology transfer and technological preeminence were relatively certain. Changes in the economy have diminished that certainty.

In response to budgetary pressures, the services may be compelled to buy systems *off-the-shelf* or, at least, ask defense contractors to field prototypes in a more open market. It has also been suggested that the US military will need to field systems derived from commercially available parts.[20] As Victor H. Reis, director of defense research and engineering, noted before the House Appropriations Committee, "we will produce weapon systems only when we have an identifiable need, *when the technology is in hand* and only when it is cost effective [emphasis added]."[21] There is no reason to believe that these commercially available subsystems could not make their way into the weapons of a future adversary. The implication is, in future battles, we could be challenged by technological systems on par with our own.

This problem is exacerbated by the globalization of production. Industry will continue to look for less expensive areas for manufacturing, and in some instances, those areas will be outside of the US. Consequently, research and development and advanced production technologies will be available to a wider audience.[22] An anticipated spin-off is that post-graduate students in technical fields, a dynamic source for military technologies, will relocate away from the US in order to complete their studies nearer research and development (R&D) centers.[23] Again, these factors are likely to contribute to the technological sophistication of our adversary in the next war. Our approach to technology will need to take this into account.

Budgetary restrictions also compel us to pursue power projection technologies more aggressively. As fewer weapon systems and personnel are strategically stationed near potential hot spots, we must seek technological solutions to power projection challenges. These solutions must include needs for global surveillance in preparation for operations out of our local area; enhanced precision for navigation and weapons delivery; minimization of collateral damage; employment of weapon systems across greater distances; and maintenance of air superiority from afar. Of course, each of these challenges is likely to generate additional expenses and technological complications of its own. Long-haul transport with the means of delivering materials into unprepared areas may be crucial. Air refueling seems to be a certain requirement. Virtual reality systems may provide aircrew and others with simulated in-theater training in advance of their deployment. Satellite-based, secure communication systems may need to be procured.

We can diminish some of the impacts of reduced budgets through a number of approaches to technological purchases. Pursuit of technologies with low failure rates could reduce support costs. If systems are purchased with extended longevity, upgradeability, and high reliability in mind, fewer personnel would be required to maintain these systems.[24]

The problem of limited funding for military hardware can be exacerbated in that fewer defense dollars typically means smaller production runs and higher costs per item. Of course, an increased awareness of the potential for developing systems and subsystems with sister services could help offset this problem. An emphasis on jointness can enhance effectiveness on the battlefield through commonality in communication, supplies, and spare parts. The benefits of jointly sponsored research, development, and procurement should be a primary consideration as we forecast appropriate technologies for future military operations.

Were the challenges to forecasting technologies offered by broader political agendas and reduced defense spending not enough, the evolution of the services' roles and missions is likely to demand new solutions supported by new technologies. Humanitarian relief, peacekeeping, drug interdiction, and other, as of yet unforeseen, roles and missions may demand more of our time, attention, and technology procurement dollars.

An easily overlooked element in technological procurement is the operator. The STAR committee notes, "The information explosion on the battlefield, and in preparation for battle, will continue as intelligence sensors, unmanned systems, computer-based communications, and other information-intensive systems proliferate."[25] Organizing this data in practical ways and presenting it for effective use by planners and operators will be especially challenging and require substantial technological investment. User interfaces will also have to account for the increased number of systems allocated to each individual in a shrinking military. Jeff Hecht of *New Scientist* appropriately notes, "as fewer soldiers come to control more systems, each one becomes a more valuable asset—making it increasingly important to communicate with and protect soldiers during a conflict."[26] Ideally, end-users would be actively involved in research and development to ensure technologies meet their needs for ease of use and effectiveness.[27]

A final point to consider as we try to forecast technological requirements: having stated that technology's contributions to military operations can have decisive effects, it is of immense importance to understand that superior technologies do not win wars on their own. "It is a supremely dangerous error to suppose that technology is a solution for the problems of war.

A strategy devised by technocrats, based solely on superiority in weaponry is not strategy at all. Machines do not win wars."[28] As noted earlier, the right technologies working together with an effective strategy made the difference in Desert Storm. Strategy, objectives, and technology are inextricably linked.

Summary

Hopefully, these few examples of applied technologies and factors that will impact our procurement of technologically sophisticated systems give some basis for the development of a framework for the consideration of such acquisitions. However, there is still a good way to go and many challenges ahead as we try to make decisions about the best and brightest technologies suitable for military applications. As Colin Gray notes in his book *Weapons Don't Make War*, "If one looks for works that seek systematically to explore the connections among policy, strategy, and weapons, the hunt is poorly rewarded indeed."[29] Instead, weapon systems, military plans, arms control, and other weapon-related issues are addressed as "technical subjects separate from broader strategic or policy meanings."[30] In many ways, the problem is similar to developing curriculum without an instructional systems development (ISD) philosophy. A lot of good education takes place without the benefit of ISD, but concerns about truly meeting students' needs, expense, and quality of instruction typically go unanswered. Likewise, investment in technologies without serious consideration of strategy or war-fighting principles may leave doubt about their suitability. We need to work toward a paradigm for technological pursuits that encompasses policy, strategy, objectives, principles of war, and budgetary constraints.

If, as stated earlier, we are to justify the expense of high technology, we need to be able to articulate the connections before Congress and the public. This essay has been written to prompt thinking about these connections; to encourage consideration of technologies with regard to principles of war;

and to note a few of the influences that will impact the way we procure technologies and which technologies we will pursue.

As noted, the principles of war do contribute to an effective framework for the consideration of technology requirements. As roles and missions evolve, we will still need to think in terms of power projection, economy of force, security, and so on. However, the officer charged with evaluating technologies for future operations will not be so fortunate as to be able to think solely in terms of military war-fighting principles. Budget cuts will have a significant impact on procurement. Smaller production runs will exacerbate the problems of fewer defense dollars. The globalization of commerce and the broadening alternatives of technological systems will mean that the US may meet a technologically sophisticated enemy in the future. We can alleviate some of the problems associated with budget cuts as they relate to technology procurement if we consider reliability, maintainability, and interoperability. It is also of great importance to remember that technology does not win wars on its own. Technology must be developed, procured, and employed with clear objectives in mind and as part of a sound strategy.

Notes

1. Victor H. Reis, "Refocused Science and Technology Supports U.S. Power Projection Needs," *Defense Issues* 7, no. 6 (19 March 1992): 1.
2. Ibid., 2–4.
3. *Conduct of the Persian Gulf War: Final Report to Congress*, prepared under the auspices of the Office of the Under Secretary of Defense for Policy (Washington, D.C.: Government Printing Office, April 1992), ix.
4. Ibid., xii.
5. *STAR 21: Strategic Technologies for the Army of the Twenty-First Century*, prepared by the Board on Army Science and Technology, Commission on Engineering and Technical Systems, and National Research Council (Washington, D.C.: National Academy Press, 1992), 256.
6. Colin S. Gray, *Weapons Don't Make War: Policy, Strategy, and Military Technology* (Lawrence, Kans.: University Press of Kansas, 1993), 2.
7. Ibid., 67.
8. Air Force Manual (AFM) 1-1, *Basic Aerospace Doctrine of the United States Air Force*, vol. 2, March 1992, 14.
9. Richard P. Hallion, *Storm over Iraq: Air Power and the Gulf War* (Washington, D.C.: Smithsonian Institution Press, 1992), 192.
10. *Conduct of the Persian Gulf War*, ix.
11. *Gulf War Air Power Survey Summary*, 29 March 1993, 212.
12. Ibid., 195.

13. Ibid., 199.
14. Ibid., 198.
15. Ibid., 196.
16. *Conduct of the Persian Gulf War*, 122.
17. Ibid., 224.
18. Nancy J. Perry, "How Defense Will Change," *Fortune*, 25 March 1991, 58.
19. Reis, 2.
20. *STAR 21*, 29.
21. Reis, 1.
22. *STAR 21*, 34.
23. Gray, 2.
24. *STAR 21*, 31–32.
25. Ibid., 8.
26. Jeff Hecht, "Weapons for the 21st Century," *New Scientist* 135, no. 1833 (8 August 1992): 21.
27. Reis, 1.
28. Barry S. Strauss and Josiah Ober, *Anatomy of Error: Ancient Military Disasters and Their Lessons for Modern Strategy* (New York: St. Martin's Press, 1990), 10.
29. Gray, 1.
30. Ibid., 5.

Constituting US Military Manpower Needs

Joseph W. Kroeschel

In the winter of 1991, people from around the globe witnessed the systemic destruction of the Iraqi military, arguably the fourth largest army in the world. News accounts of the US and coalition forces in Desert Storm showcased the incredible power, range, and accuracy of high-technology weapons and the extraordinary abilities of the soldiers, sailors, and airmen using those weapons. Indeed, these two elements, superb hardware and high-quality manpower, were the fundamental ingredients that led to success in the Gulf War, and these ingredients are the sine qua non to the preservation of peace in the future.

The central question in the post–cold-war era is how much of these ingredients are needed to protect US vital interests and in what combination. Complicating the issue is the need to move tax dollars from defense to revitalizing our economic infrastructure and reducing the budget deficit. Military personnel cuts, it is argued, provide immediate dollar savings, unlike weapon systems procurement dollars that are spread out over several years. Thus, large-scale manpower reductions have been implemented and the administration's national defense strategy is to rely on high-technology weapons, many of which are still in the planning stage.[1]

Such a strategy seems acceptable given the visual evidence the American public witnessed from the Gulf War. Precision guided weapons could hit enemy tanks in Iraqi territory. Laser guided bombs destroyed key targets, and Tomahawk missiles launched from ships demonstrated that they could destroy military structures hundreds of miles away without harming nearby civilian facilities. Given this experience, why shouldn't we develop a national defense strategy that relies on high technology? The answer is simple. The administration has no corresponding strategy to obtain the high-quality manpower to operate and maintain high-tech weapon systems of the future.

On the surface the development of a manpower strategy may appear unnecessary. After all, we are working very hard to reduce the size of our military forces, but we cannot get enough people to separate or retire. Selective early retirement boards have been the norm for years. Special benefit packages have been developed to provide incentives for midlevel personnel to separate or retire early. Early-out programs and involuntary separations have also been necessary, and we have cut accessions to the minimum level to sustain the future force structure. Even with all these programs, we still have more people in uniform than we need.

Why, one may ask, would we need a strategy to obtain manpower? There are three reasons. First, our 20 years of experience in manning the all-volunteer force (AVF) shows that high-quality manpower is not always easy to obtain or readily available. Second, the characteristics of the labor force from which we will recruit our future military will be dramatically different from the young people recruited in the seventies and eighties. Finally, we need a manpower strategy due to the time delay between recruiting shortfalls and the ability of the Department of Defense (DOD) to respond to those shortfalls. The programming, budgeting, and appropriation process is far too lengthy to respond quickly to manpower shortages.[2] Before elaborating on a manpower strategy, "quality" manpower must be clarified.

High-"Quality" Manpower

The issue of high-quality manpower for our high-technology military is not solely a question of whether or not the people can operate or maintain the equipment. To a certain extent, these problems can be offset by designing systems, albeit at increased costs, to be simpler, more user-friendly, and more reliable. Rather, the quality of military manpower is directly related to readiness. The question of how to define "quality" is debatable, but the services use two factors, high school diploma and aptitude test scores, as a measure of quality. The reason for this is that experience has shown that high school graduates, on average, are more likely to complete initial training, are involved in fewer disciplinary incidents, are promoted more rapidly, and are more likely to be eligible to reenlist. In fact, high school graduates are about twice as likely as non-high school graduates to complete their initial enlistment.[3] Thus, higher quality recruits translate directly to increased readiness due to reduced costs, lower disciplinary problems, and higher experience levels.

The second measure of quality, the Armed Forces Qualification Test (AFQT), helps to determine entry qualifications into the services. A subset of the AFQT is used to determine qualification for specific initial skills training. Again, the services have found that persons scoring in the lower percentile on the AFQT need more training and have greater disciplinary problems, therefore increasing costs and reducing readiness. For these reasons the need for quality manpower is not simply an issue of matching weapons and equipment with capable manpower. Rather, quality manpower is necessary to keep training costs to a minimum, increase experience levels, and reduce disciplinary problems. Quality manpower directly relates to readiness, and it has not always been easy to obtain in the AVF.

The AVF and Manpower Shortages

In 1973, after a lengthy national debate, the all-volunteer force began as military conscription ended, and DOD began competing for manpower with civilian industry. Despite an ample labor supply from the baby boom of the fifties, the military did not fare well in obtaining high-quality manpower. Recruiting goals could not be met, and the services had difficulty getting volunteers with high school diplomas or high aptitude test scores. By the end of the decade, many were claiming the AVF unworkable.[4] Faced with a poor image from the Vietnam era and lower pay relative to civilian workers, the military services could not compete for labor with civilian firms. At the same time, emerging technology was leading to the development of high-tech weapons. In short, America faced the same problem in the 1970s and early 1980s that we face in the future—attracting high-quality people into the military to maintain and operate high-tech weapons and equipment. In 1984 Martin Binkin said:

> When Virgil sang of arms and the man, words like "smart" and "friendly" characterized the warrior, not his weapons. Today, because of modern technology, these terms are more often used to describe the machine than the man. Dramatic advances have spawned a generation of weapon systems designed to tell friend from foe, to stalk the enemy with precision and stealth, and to destroy him with unprecedented efficiency. But can ordinary Americans operate and support these advanced systems, or have the emerging technologies pushed military hardware beyond the capabilities of the people the armed forces can expect to attract and retain?[5]

When Binkin wrote these words, the nation had for 13 years experienced dismal recruiting and retention with the AVF. The AVF that successfully prosecuted the Gulf War proved, without a doubt, that the military could attract and retain people with the skills necessary to staff our nation's forces. But the highly trained and highly skilled AVF that served during Operations Desert Shield/Storm was a product of the eighties—a decade with a president, a Congress, and a people who supported the notion that military service is an honorable endeavor worthy of fair compensation. We face a very different environment in the future when, political concerns aside, the supply of high-quality manpower available to serve in a high-tech military will decline, and competition for that manpower will increase. At the same time, our nation's young people are showing a waning interest in enlisting, and the recruiting environment is littered with the stories of drawdown casualties who have lost faith in the government.[6]

That is not to say, however, that we should maintain a large military force, in spite of the reduced threat, to forestall future personnel shortages. On the contrary, to maintain a youthful, responsive force we must have a personnel system that is dynamic. We need a viable recruiting program to bring in new accessions. Then we must have high-quality training programs, a fair and equitable promotion program, and a selective reenlistment program to retain high-quality personnel. In addition, we need a viable retirement program as both a recruiting incentive and a personnel-reduction program. Such a personnel system will allow new people to enter, serve, and ultimately leave through attrition or retirement and keep our armed forces youthful and responsive. The point is that we cannot rely solely on high technology as a panacea to our national security. We must also develop a strategy to obtain manpower in the changing environment ahead.

A Changing Labor Force

The cultural, demographic, and socioeconomic nature of our nation's labor force will change dramatically in the future. The recruiting environment will be characterized by shrinking numbers of young people entering the work force and a larger proportion of the population made up of racial and ethnic minorities experiencing high rates of poverty that will hinder their educational attainment and future productivity. In the next decade, 63 percent of people entering the labor force will be women. One out of every four children will be born to an unmarried woman, and 70 percent of our adolescents will not have lived in a two-parent family through their first 18 years.[7] These disadvantaged young people will also experience two or three times the percentage of developmental delays, learning difficulties, and emotional or behavioral problems than children living in intact two-parent families.[8] Educational attainment for persons 25 years and over is also a concern. In 1991, approximately 78 percent of all people 25 years and older had graduated from high school, but only 67 percent of African-Americans had completed high school. For Hispanics in the same age category only 51 percent had high school diplomas.[9] At the same time, we were seeing a dramatic decline in young people interested in enlistment. In January 1993 DOD reported a 10 percent decline in enlistment interest overall.[10] An Army study also identified a 30 percent decline in enlistment interest for 16- to 21-year olds, and a 45 percent decline among African-Americans.[11] These changes in the characteristics of the work force and the decline in interest towards serving in the military will have serious consequences for our ability to obtain high-quality manpower to meet defense needs.

The Management Process— Slow to Respond to Shortages

Our ability to resolve manpower shortfalls is hampered by a lengthy management process. This issue is particularly important with the reduced force structure and manpower requirements in the future. Lengthy time delays between actual labor shortages and our ability to fill those shortages will limit our surge capability to meet future contingencies. For example, in 1981 the Air Force had critical shortfalls in current and projected engineering requirements. Numerous programs such as engineering bonuses, scholarship programs, and increased recruiting budgets were developed to fill requirements. Nonetheless, it was not until 1986, five years later, that the engineering shortage ended. While much of the delay can be attributed to educational requirements, it still took approximately two years from the time a critical need developed before legislation and appropriations were made. Consequently, a reliance on high-tech equipment and weapons without the ability to rapidly overcome labor shortfalls may seriously limit military readiness. Gary R. Nelson, former deputy assistant secretary of defense, noted:

> The AVF is a volatile program, different in characteristics from the draft system it replaced. The AVF is far more sensitive to the movements of the business cycle, to relatively small but sudden changes in the demand for non-prior service enlistees, and to unexpected developments. . . . The management process by which the federal government responds to a decline in enlistment supply is totally inadequate to the problem at hand. The program-budget and appropriations process is two years from start to finish. We could go from surplus to disaster in that period of time—and in a much shorter period if there were a surge in demand.[12]

The problems in recruiting and retention in the first decade of the AVF, the changing characteristics of our labor force, and the long lead time before military labor shortages can be overcome suggest a strategy to obtain manpower in the future. Fortunately, our 20-year history with the AVF has also given us a wealth of experience in dealing with manpower issues. Before we can develop a strategy we must address some of those issues.

Recruiting

A Smaller Force Means Fewer Requirements

In the 1980s the DOD was recruiting about 300,000 young people each year to meet desired active duty enlisted strength goals.[13] One may argue therefore that our reduced force structure, which calls for about 200,000 active duty accessions per year, can easily be sustained, even in a highly competitive recruiting market. In June 1993 Secretary of Defense Les Aspin said that in the first half of 1993 only 94 percent of the new recruits had a high school diploma versus 97 percent in 1991. As a result he said he would spend more money on recruiting.[14] But such a simplistic approach to hiring manpower for the AVF ignores the changing manpower landscape as well as the complexity of obtaining military manpower. Taking a snapshot of the recruiting environment for one year and looking a little closer may help to clarify why this issue is not simply a function of recruiting.

In 1981 there were 4.3 million 17- to 19-year-old male high school graduates and seniors. Forty-one percent of those did not qualify for enlistment for physical, mental, or other conditions. Twenty-eight percent were in college and 8 percent were already in the service, leaving 23 percent, or 983,000 potential enlistees.[15] On the surface, the number of available 17- to 19-year-old males appears quite sufficient since we can recruit females or older adult males. But there are other limitations we must consider. First, according to the youth attitude-tracking study in the fall of 1982, 73 percent of those potentially eligible to enlist said they probably would not, or definitely would not, enlist in the armed forces.[16] Therefore, about 270,000 males in the 17- to 19-year-old category were available in 1981, but many of these would be ineligible for enlistment because they would not qualify on the AFQT. In fact, in any given year, only a portion of the labor force is eligible for enlistment. In 1984 only 61 percent of the 18- to 23-year olds were eligible for enlistment based on the services' aptitude and educational standards.[17] Also, while the percentage varies from year to year, approximately 20 to 30 percent of those who actually enter the service with high school diplomas fail to complete the first 36 months of service.[18] This is due to separation from basic or technical training, failing to maintain medical or behavioral standards, or other reasons.

Clearly, the available military manpower pool is directly related to the quality of the labor force and the qualifications for military service, as well as to interest in serving in the military. The labor force of the future may not have the interest, the qualifications, or the educational background of those we recruited in the 1980s. We should also remember that future leadership, recruited in the AVF environment of the 1980s, will not share the ethnic, racial, and cultural characteristics of the young people they are leading. As Assistant Secretary of Defense Christopher Jehn said:

> You have to remember that the military is a closed system with (no lateral entry) and recruitment is its lifeblood. The youngsters we recruit today are the sergeants, captains and majors of 2005. If we don't do a good job today, our military will be weaker in the future.[19]

The question of obtaining high-quality manpower is infinitely more complex and is not solely a function of recruiting an ample supply of people from our population. It requires careful analysis of future population demographics, the availability of qualified and interested people, the political and public support for the military, and the likely economic conditions in which DOD will compete for labor. For these reasons, a strategy for obtaining manpower should consider these complex issues, and contingency plans should be developed to counter the effects of possible labor shortages and surge requirements.

Minorities in the Military

Opportunities or an Unfair Burden?

During the period from 1961 through 1966, African-Americans represented 11 percent of the 19- to 21-year olds in America—and one out of every five Army combat deaths in Vietnam. When conscription was used to man our nation's military, African-Americans were more likely to be drafted than whites, so they were more likely to serve in combat units and be wounded or killed.[20] One of the primary arguments in favor of the AVF was the fact that volunteers, rather than draftees, would serve in the military. As a result, the services must compete for labor with the civilian economy, so pay and benefits must be attractive. Unfortunately, in the 1970s the nation was not prepared to devote such resources to the military, causing the services to lower standards and recruit many who had not finished high school. During this same period, to overcome economic or educational disadvantages in the civilian sector, African-Americans sought employment in the military. In the seventies 25 percent of African-Americans who turned 18 entered the military but 30 percent of them did not have a high school diploma.[21] The military became the major employer of African-Americans, and the military had a higher proportion of minorities than the population at large.

Many economists and social leaders began to question the wisdom of filling our nation's military with poor, disadvantaged youths who did not benefit from our economic system yet would die in disproportionate numbers in future wars. Other economists, political leaders, and manpower planners argued that the military was providing economic opportunities not otherwise available in the civilian world.

In the 1980s, higher pay and benefits made the military more competitive and attractive, leading to higher retention and a higher percentage of new enlistees with high school diplomas. Political and public support for the military also increased, leading to a greater number of middle class whites and minorities in the military. The debate over whether the military is providing economic opportunities or taking advantage of disadvantaged youths became academic. However, prior to our involvement in Desert Shield/Storm, the debate raged again. Fortunately, we did not suffer a great abundance of casualties in Desert Storm and thus repeat history from the early 1960s. But a growing proportion of minorities entering the labor force means that we will have more minorities entering the military. The issue as to whether the military is providing opportunities or exploiting disadvantaged youths will become more pronounced. Manpower planners must understand this issue and consider the problem in developing a plan to obtain military manpower.

The Institutional or Occupational Model and Military Pay

A discussion of military manpower in relation to military compensation invariably leads to a debate over whether or not military service follows an institutional or occupational format. Those who believe that military service follows an institutional model see military service as a calling requiring sacrifice and devotion to the institution. Compensation is less important in the institutional model because self-sacrifice and devotion to the institution characterize the people who serve. By comparison, the occupational model views military service as just another job in the bureaucracy. Consequently, competitive pay and benefits are critical to keeping an adequate labor force. To explain these viewpoints more clearly consider the following quote from Charles C. Moskos and Frank R. Wood:

> I go anywhere in the world they tell me to go, any time they tell me to, to fight anybody they want me to fight. I move my family anywhere they tell me to move, on a day's notice, and live in whatever quarters they assign me. I work whenever they tell me to work . . . I don't belong to a union and I don't strike if I don't like what they're doing to me. And I like it. Maybe that's the difference.[22]

The current military pay system, which evolved from the draft era, generally follows the institutional model. All service members are paid based on grade and years of service; therefore, the institution does not view some jobs as more important than others. The military pay system in the AVF environment has become replete with special pays and bonuses. But these are paid as inducements for retention, enlistment, or reenlistment; are changed based on manning levels; and are not part of military retirement. Some economists believe that the military pay system should be more efficient, following an occupational model. Payment for labor services, they believe, should be based on market forces like the civilian labor market. Using this approach, military members would be paid based on their specific qualifications, the job to be done, and the market wage derived from the civilian economy. For example, nurses may be paid a higher mean wage than, say, navigators, given the shortage of nurses relative to the supply of navigators. Compensating wage differentials would also be paid to induce people to work in undesirable places or accept other undesirable aspects of the job.[23] Therefore, sailors would be paid a higher wage than airmen with the same grade and years of service, the difference in wage being a compensating wage differential for sea duty. Further, a cook aboard a ship would be paid less than a radio repairman on the same ship because of the higher educational requirements for the radio repairman. These compensating wage differentials would be part of the sailor's wage package and would be included in retired pay computations.

As high-quality labor resources become more scarce and we have fewer tax dollars for defense needs, manpower planners should look to changing the DOD pay system to make it more efficient.

A Strategy for Obtaining Military Manpower

In November 1983, 275 economists, manpower experts, political and military leaders, and academicians met at the US Naval Academy to review, analyze, and discuss the AVF. The product of that conference was a complete review of the AVF successes, limitations, and suggested course for the future.[24] The first part of our strategy is to develop a DOD manpower planning group. This group would have three specific functions. First, manpower and personnel experts would evaluate current manpower shortfalls, recruiting problems, and demographic trends. Second, human-factor engineers would ensure that new, high-tech weapon systems are designed to be reliable and user-friendly. Third, economists on the group would develop changes to the DOD pay system when needed and complete econometric analysis and modeling to identify potential manpower problems.

The DOD planning group should host an annual conference, like the AVF conference held in 1983, to review demographic changes and discuss manpower issues and problems. Further, the manpower planning group should meet on a monthly basis to review and approve drawdown plans, discuss implications for the future, and consider other manpower issues. To meet future requirements and respond rapidly to changing manpower needs, the group should be able to seek legislative changes and appropriations to reduce the lengthy management process.

The military pay system should also be changed to reflect the changing nature of military service. The post–cold-war drawdown of our military forces has changed the institutional characteristics of the military. Forced retirements and separations are causing those in uniform to become more concerned with job security and benefits than with service to the institution. The military pay system should be changed to coincide with the occupational model allowing the services to compete for high-quality labor in the future. One service may have to pay a higher wage to compensate people for the undesirable aspects of the work, or different jobs within a service may require different wages.[25]

Developing a manpower planning group to resolve manpower problems and changing the pay system are two aspects of our manpower strategy that will help us work the manpower side of the equation. The third component addresses the hardware side. That is, DOD must ensure that new high-tech weapons are engineered to be user-friendly and reliable. Martin Binkin suggested this in 1986 when he said:

> Most worthy of special attention are those options that would diminish the need for large numbers of highly qualified people by reducing the complexity of military systems, by making them more reliable, or by facilitating their maintenance. . . . Affording manpower equal billing with performance, schedule, and cost early in the weapon development cycle would brighten the prospects that the systems fielded by the armed services in the future will be within the capabilities of their personnel and that the nation will realize a fuller return on its investment in military technology.[26]

Conclusion

After World War I, World War II, and the wars in Korea and Vietnam, our nation reduced the size of our military forces. In the post–cold-war era we must do the same. But we have not yet learned the most important lesson from past drawdowns. That is, a threat to our nation could come again. We cannot rely on future high-tech weapons and dismiss the need for high-quality men and women to field those systems. We must have a defense strategy for the procurement of high-quality hardware and a strategy to obtain high-quality manpower. A DOD manpower planning group will allow us to focus on key manpower issues and give us a better response to manpower shortages. Revising the military pay system will make DOD more competitive in the labor market and cut costs. Finally, developing high-tech weapons that are user-friendly and reliable will reduce the need for expensive manpower.

Notes

1. "Pentagon Culture Clash," *U.S. News & World Report* 115, no. 2 (12 July 1993): 32.
2. William Bowman, Roger Little, and G. Thomas Sicilia, *The All-Volunteer Force after a Decade: Retrospect and Prospect* (Washington, D.C.: Pergamon-Brassey's International Defense Publishers, 1986), 48.
3. James Kitfield, "Mustering," *Government Executive* 24, no. 5 (May 1992): 13.
4. Ibid., 15.
5. Martin Binkin, *Military Technology and Defense Manpower* (Washington, D.C.: The Brookings Institution, 1986), back cover.
6. "You're Out of the Army Now," *Time* 139, no. 10 (9 March 1992): 30.
7. Peter A. Morrison, *Congress and the Year 2000: A Demographic Perspective on Future Issues* (Santa Monica, Calif.: Rand Corporation, 1991): 4–12.
8. Ibid., 23.
9. U.S. Department of Commerce, Bureau of the Census, *Population Profile of the United States 1993*, series P-23, no. 185 (Washington, D.C.: Government Printing Office, 1993), 15.
10. Department of Defense, *Annual Report to the President and the Congress* (Washington, D.C.: Government Printing Office, January 1993), 50.
11. "Pentagon Culture Clash," 32.
12. Bowman, Little, and Sicilia, 11.
13. Ibid., 277.
14. "The Week," *Time* 141, no. 24 (14 June 1993): 12.
15. Bowman, Little, and Sicilia, 275.
16. Ibid., 280.
17. Binkin, 21.
18. Ibid., 12.
19. Kitfield, 15.
20. Martin Binkin, *Who will fight the next war?* (Washington, D.C.: The Brookings Institution, 1993), 68.

21. Ibid., 72.

22. Charles C. Moskos and Frank R. Wood, *The Military: More Than Just a Job?* (Washington, D.C.: Pergamon-Brassey's International Defense Publishers, 1988), xiii.

23. Joseph W. Kroeschel, *Compensating Wage Differentials and Military Labor Supply* (Monterey, Calif.: Naval Postgraduate School, December 1988), 47.

24. Bowman, Little, and Sicilia, vii.

25. Kroeschel, 46–47.

26. Binkin, *Who will fight the next war?*, 131.

Military Responses in Nonpolitical Conflicts

Steven W. Zander

The purpose of this essay is to investigate the feasibility of the use of military assets in nonpolitical conflicts. It concentrates primarily on antidrug operations, given the fact that other uses of military force in nonpolitical conflicts (such as peacekeeping and humanitarian operations) are dealt with elsewhere in this volume. I begin by offering a definition of nonpolitical conflicts, and discuss how the national drug control strategy will affect future use of military assets to support law enforcement agencies and foreign governments in the conduct of antidrug operations. Next, I offer an overview of the major military commands and law enforcement agencies as a prelude to discussing how the military is used in counter-drug operations in three locations—in the drug-producing countries, in the transit zone, and within the US. Finally, I believe past experience suggests that the military can play an important role in waging the "drug war," even if its success is limited by a number of caveats.

Nature of Nonpolitical Conflicts

While there is often no clear division between political and nonpolitical conflicts, the latter term commonly refers to those instances requiring the use of military forces to solve issues that are other than political in nature. Thus humanitarian assistance commonly involves using military assets to save lives and assists survivors after natural disasters. Peacekeeping operations are intended to facilitate a peaceful settlement of disputes by separating warring parties, but they do not normally have political objectives.

This essay concentrates on another kind of operation—the interdiction of the flow of drugs to the US. One might argue whether drug interdiction operations qualify as "nonpolitical" since they often entail disagreements with supplier nations over how to eradicate the drug traffic, and because in some states drug traffickers have made an alliance with indigenous political forces to threaten stability in their home countries. Certainly, the United States has brought tremendous pressure to bear to influence these nations to increase their counter-drug activities.[1]

However, the US has gone to great lengths to ensure that it does not become involved in the internal politics of such nations; it sends troops or other forms of assistance only upon the request of host nations.[2] Although a primary focus on the eradication of drug-trafficking elements can contribute to instability in the target nation, a policy of simultaneous institution building can help achieve antidrug objectives.[3]

Elements of Drug Control

Conduct of the drug "war" comes down to a matter of strategy. Most agree that the war is waged on two fronts[4]—a supply front that targets drug-producing nations and indigenous underground drug organizations and a demand front that targets Americans who do not "just say no to drugs."

Many disagreed with the Bush administration's focus on interdiction (approximately 70 percent of a $11.7 billion budget in 1992) instead of on demand-reduction programs focusing on education, treatment, and prevention.[5] Bush's National Drug Control Strategy was based on the view that interdiction programs were more costly than demand-reduction programs due to the costly military and law enforcement equipment the former required—radar, helicopters, aircraft, computers—for domestic and foreign military and law enforcement agencies.

With a change of administrations, many saw an opportunity to raise the portion of the budget directed to demand reduction to about 50 percent.[6] Surprise was expressed when the new administration suggested a drug policy that seemingly would continue to favor interdiction.

Surely there will be more allocation of resources to demand reduction programs. President Bill Clinton stated as much in his recent State of the Union address. Indeed, much has been learned since the military became actively involved in various stages of the war, whether in Latin American countries, interdicting drugs in transit, or trying to arrest the problem within our national borders.

Wisely, the Clinton administration has embraced a policy that targets the true center of gravity in the drug war: drug production. Although the formal National Drug Control Strategy for 1994 is yet to be released, administration spokespersons have presented a consistent view of the future strategy.

State Department counselor Timothy Wirth has stated that the "new" drug strategy will focus on drug organizations, convincing drug-producing nations to stop production operations, and eradication of drug crops[7]—key steps that have proven essential to disrupt drug-trafficking activities.

Those who say that this policy is nothing new are in many ways right. A review of the national drug control strategies, published since 1989 to present, reveals a comprehensive knowledge of all facets of the drug problem. Therefore, there is nothing new that can be tried; however, what is new is that the policies initiated during the Bush administration are bearing fruit.

The policy of institution building, based upon providing economic and military assistance, has reinforced democratic governments now prevalent in Latin America. These governments have newfound ability to counter not only revolutionary movements within their countries, but to focus on the drug-trafficking organizations.

Further, these governments have evidently come to recognize that the drug-trafficking organizations within their countries have a destabilizing effect both economically and socially. Proof is in the growing number of drug seizures, destruction of cocaine processing laboratories, arrests, and the growing number of indigenous military and police operations conducted since 1991.[8]

Assistant Secretary of State for International Narcotics Matters Melvyn Levitsky in 1992 noted that while the situation is improving, many problems remain. He told a Senate subcommittee that there are

> inherent difficulties which must be overcome in trying to deal with an underground, illicit, violent, and economically powerful adversary . . . [and there] are barriers that must be overcome in assisting governments in the region—many of which have multiple problems of economic recession, under development, indigenous guerrilla subversion of democratic institutions, internal corruption, and weak judicial and penal institutions—in order to respond to this threat.[9]

However, what is also "new" is that the countries have the will to combat drug traffickers (not to be confused with possessing the capability, which some do not yet have)—will that for years was not evident. Its absence was ascribed to governmental corruption stemming from the drug trade and the weak institutions Levitsky mentioned.[10] It is because of this new will that the Clinton administration's continuance of past policies may succeed. For with the will and the US-provided resources, the foreign governments will have the ability to disrupt the drug organizations and accomplish drug crop eradication programs—programs that in the past have failed if for no other reason than the time-consuming, labor-intensive characteristics associated with past operations.

Eradication will succeed much as was prescribed by Gary Williams in his paper, "The War on Cocaine: Strategy and Tactics," released in March 1991. There are herbicides available (including one he advocates in his paper or another presently under study) that will, after delivery by aircraft, eradicate coca plants, and given that these plants require 18 to 24 months to grow from seedlings into a viable crop, this time will provide the necessary break in the drug cycle.[11] This break will enable winning the drug war by addressing the demand front in the US. Williams offers the historical precedence of a similar drug epidemic that was successfully arrested between 1920 and 1960.[12] As further proof that there are no new strategies, Williams also suggested that there are essentially three centers of gravity in the drug problem: the drug organizations in Colombia;[13] eradication of the drug crop—because it is slow moving and therefore much easier to hit than the fast-moving drug trafficker in jet aircraft or high-speed boats;[14] and using the military to provide security for police engaged in the interdiction of the drug traffickers' transit lines.[15]

Finally, another reason the new drug strategy will succeed is because the previous administration made wise investments in the military portion of the drug budget. Indeed, of the $12.7 billion estimated for counterdrug efforts in 1992, only $1.3 billion was specifically identified for the Department of Defense (DOD).[16] Of this relatively small share of the drug budget, half was used to acquire needed improvements to detection and monitoring, and command, control, communications, and intelligence (C^3I) systems. This amounted to a side benefit since the antidrug role was an extension of the military war-fighting capability; an improvement that proved useful in support of drug interdiction operations also improved military capability.

With the detection and monitoring systems in place, or soon to be so, and the integrated C^3I systems that have been established or are in the pipeline, the Clinton administration would be ill advised to deemphasize this important element of the National Drug Control Strategy. For as Wirth has stated, "the new policy does not mean that narcotics will be allowed to flow unhindered into the United States. . . . The United States will continue to engage in more selective and flexible interdiction programs near the US border, in the transit zone, and in source countries."[17] To this end, the US military and leading law enforcement agencies (LEA) have built a comprehensive, at times complex, network of cooperation between themselves and with producer nations to interdict the flow of drugs. To better understand this network, the following discussion will focus on elements of the military and law enforcement agencies that play major roles in waging the drug war.

Major Military Commands and Law Enforcement Agencies

The US has a comprehensive drug control strategy that, over time, has provided for an increase in the military forces and equipment used for antidrug activities. Starting with the National Defense Authorization Act for fiscal year (FY) 1989, the military has played a leading role in detection and monitoring of drug activities in the air, on sea, and on land; providing improved C^3I support for law enforcement agencies and host nations, and increased support of domestic operations primarily through the National Guard.[18] The secretary of defense directed in 1989, through a series of guidance letters, that the military support efforts to attack the drug problem in three areas: at the source—host nations, in transit to the US, and within US borders.[19]

The military response takes advantage of existing military command structures established to counter military threats in their respective areas of responsibility. Efforts have been under way since 1989 to take advantage of inherent capabilities within these commands to target the drug trade and improve interoperability with civilian law enforcement agencies that are leading or have a major role in counterdrug efforts in a particular command's area of responsibility. A brief discussion of the major military commands and LEAs follows. This will be followed by discussions on how joint operations have been or could be conducted to meet the drug interdiction threat.

Military Command Structure

Four war-fighting commands have responsibility for supporting counterdrug operations within their areas of responsibility. They are Southern Command (SOUTHCOM), Atlantic Command (LANTCOM), Pacific Command (PACOM), and North American Aerospace Defense Command (NORAD).[20]

SOUTHCOM, headquartered in Quarry Heights, Panama, is responsible for counterdrug efforts from the Guatemala-Mexico border to Cape Horn. As Gen George A. Joulwan stated before the Senate Armed Services Committee in 1993, "Trafficking in illegal drugs adversely affects every nation without exception in the [SOUTHCOM area of responsibility] AOR.[21] It includes operations in Central America; the Andean-ridge countries of Peru, Bolivia, and Colombia; and the southern-cone countries of Argentina, Chile, and Venezuela. Given its location it plays a key role in the support of the Andean Strategy aimed at curbing the illicit drug trade. It exercises control over a Special Operations Command (SOCOM), Joint Task Force (JTF) Bravo, located at Soto Cano Air Base, Honduras, and security assistance organizations located in 16 of the region's countries.[22]

USACOM, formerly LANTCOM, has primary responsibility for counterdrug efforts from the North Pole, through the north Atlantic, to the waters surrounding South America. This includes detection and monitoring of air and sea smuggling in the Atlantic Ocean (west of the 17th parallel), Gulf of Mexico, Caribbean Sea, and portions of the eastern Pacific (up to the 92d parallel). Counterdrug operations in the Caribbean are planned and coordinated through its subordinate command, JTF 4, headquartered at Key West, Florida. Common to all military functions established to support drug interdiction, information obtained regarding drug trafficking is shared with the appropriate LEA responsible for interdiction.[23]

USACOM has delegated to the US Army Forces Command (USFORSCOM) responsibility for drug interdiction efforts along the 2,000-mile southwest border, which includes the border states of California, Arizona, New Mexico, and Texas. The subordinate JTF 6, primarily a command and control headquarters, coordinates the activities of National Guard forces of these four border states. JTF 6 was located at Fort Bliss, to better coordinate the activities of Operation Alliance (a law enforcement coalition of federal, state, and local law enforcement agencies providing coordinated interdiction efforts along the southwest border) located in El Paso, Texas, near the El Paso Intelligence Center (EPIC).[24]

PACOM has responsibility for over 105 million square miles covering the Pacific and Indian oceans (up to the 17th parallel) and as such overlaps SOUTHCOM responsibility in tracking cocaine and marijuana from Mexico. Adm Charles R. Larson described the drug threat facing PACOM before the Senate Armed Services Committee in 1993: "As was the case last year, more than 75 percent of the world's estimated opium production continues to take place in the Golden Triangle of Burma, Thailand, and Laos. Although cocaine remains the most serious threat to Americans, the heroin threat is growing most rapidly, and the Andean cartels are beginning to cooperate with the warlords of the Golden Triangle."[25] To meet this threat, counterdrug activities are coordinated and implemented by JTF 5, headquartered at Alameda, California. These operations include command, control, communications, and intelligence assistance for host nation; operations planning support; intelligence support; training of host-nation counterdrug forces; and tracking cocaine and marijuana from Colombia and Mexico, and marijuana from Hawaii.[26]

NORAD employs its network radars (originally designed for high-altitude airspace penetrations but parameters were changed to track slower routine traffic) to detect aircraft attempting to penetrate US borders. This is done in partnership with Canada on the northern border and includes over-the-horizon backscatter radar, based aerostats (blimps carrying radar antennae), and E-3 airborne warning and control system (AWACS) aircraft to detect aircraft along the north American coast and the southern US border. Alert aircraft are also employed to assist the US Customs and US Coast Guard with their interdiction missions.[27]

These major commands are provided assistance as needed by the unified commands of Special Operations Command; Central Command (CENTCOM); European Command (EUCOM); and Transportation Command (TRANSCOM).[28]

Law Enforcement Agencies

All of the military commands must work closely with the various LEAs to ensure integrated counterdrug operations. The federal agencies that have major drug-interdiction responsibilities include the Drug Enforcement Agency (DEA), the Federal Bureau of Investigation (FBI), the US Coast Guard (USCG), the US Customs Service (USCS), and the US Border Patrol (USBP). John Ahart and Gerald Stiles provide concise discussions of these agencies in their paper, "The Military's Entry into Air Interdiction of Drug Trafficking from South America." They note that the primary role of the Drug Enforcement Agency is to combat drug trafficking. DEA agents have powers of arrest, search, and seizure and are engaged in both foreign and domestic efforts. "DEA personnel may be assigned to a particular US mission abroad . . . and [DEA] is the lead agency responsible for collection and maintenance of worldwide drug intelligence information."[29]

The FBI antidrug jurisdiction overlaps with that of the DEA due to its responsibilities as the lead agency for investigating interstate and international drug cases. This overlapping area of responsibility offers the potential for (and has in the past) led to confusion in the conduct of counterdrug operations.

The USCG has primary responsibility for drug interdiction on the high seas and navigable waterways and, with the US Customs Service, has joint responsibility for air interdiction. In its law enforcement role (during war it also has a military role), the USCG has broad authority to inspect vessels and regulate maritime commerce.

The US Customs Service is the lead agency for drug interdiction on land and is supported in its efforts by the US Border Patrol—an agency under the Immigration and Naturalization Service (INS). As mentioned it has joint responsibility for air interdiction with the USCG, and also supports the USCG in maritime interdiction. The Customs Service has broad powers in that it may board any vessel or enter any vehicle at any place within US territory. However, their capabilities are restrained in that most Customs Service personnel are located only in the major ports and airfields of the United States, Puerto Rico, and the Virgin Islands.

As mentioned the US Border Patrol of the INS supports USCS drug-interdiction efforts on land, primarily as an extension of its efforts to enforce laws relating to the control of illegal aliens. In this role Border Patrol agents have the authority to conduct searches at the border even without suspicion of criminal activity.

As can perhaps be imagined, given the number of major players in the drug-interdiction effort and overlapping areas of responsibility, there is an inherent complexity associated with coordinating the counterdrug activities of the various agencies. There are many other agencies (approximately 40 if counting only federal agencies) which have a role in the drug war, such as the State Department's Bureau for International Narcotics Matters which has responsibility for coordinating the US international supply reduction strategy. However, the foregoing serves to establish a basis for discussing the complexity of counterdrug operations, and how these agencies must integrate their activities to provide a coordinated response to the drug threat.

Three Stages of the Drug War

As previously stated, the military is used to support law enforcement efforts attacking the drug problem in three phases. These include counterdrug operations within a foreign country; interdiction of drug shipments in transit in the air, at sea, and on land; and operations within US borders.

Operations in Foreign Countries

The National Drug Control Strategy identifies the point where the drug trade is most susceptible to disruption—the (drug) organization's center of gravity—as the drug trafficker's home country base of operation.[30]

This, then, is the basis of the Clinton administration's "new" policy of institution building, for by strengthening local government, police, and military institutions, these countries will then possess the capability to curb production and stop trafficking. The question then becomes a matter of whether they possess the will.[31]

The answer to this question appeared wanting until relatively recently (1992) when the Andean countries of Peru, Colombia, and Bolivia, apparently realizing that the effects of drug trafficking were contributing to internal instability, began waging major counterdrug operations that have resulted in the seizure of coca, destruction of processing labs, and the arrest of major criminal figures.[32]

As part of the Andean Initiative, the US signed military assistance pacts with six Andean countries. These pacts provided for economic and military assistance and equipment and help in mounting of more effective counterdrug operations.[33] Some, however, suggest this policy has failed, and wonder what has changed to make institution building a viable policy.[34]

In reality, lack of commitment still exists. Of primary concern in Peru and Bolivia is the desire to establish "economic and political stability . . . [after years of] suffering from high unemployment, political instability, low wages, and social unrest."[35]

Against this backdrop, the Peruvian coca crop was estimated in 1990 to bring in $1 billion annually and employ 15 percent of the national work force. Similar figures for Bolivia are $600 million annually and 20 percent of the adult work force.[36]

With these economic realities in mind, the US military is used to support LEAs and the host nations in drug interdiction activities. Levitsky explained US policy regarding the use of the military as follows:

> We have involved the military in supporting roles to provide sophisticated assets for detection and monitoring, transport, training, and delivery of military assistance hardware and in providing communications, logistical, and intelligence expertise to missions abroad. Host government militaries provide air intercept, transport, and airlift capabilities to their own police, security for law enforcement personnel; [and] riverine capabilities; and [these] are sometimes used directly for operations against outlying drug production complexes.[37]

In fact, the US military has been used to support DEA-led counterdrug efforts in Latin American countries since the 1980s. William W. Mendel provides a good summary of operations conducted in his article, "Illusive Victory: From Blast Furnace to Green Sweep." Initial operations conducted in Bolivia in 1984 with US-supported Bolivian troops "were unpopular locally, and peasant demonstrations . . . [eventually led to] the withdrawal of troops."[38] A more notable effort—Operation Blast Furnace—was conducted in Bolivia in 1986. During the course of this operation 160 US-support personnel with six US Black Hawk helicopters arrived in Bolivia in July 1986 to "provide air mobility to Bolivian antidrug forces."[39] The operation was considered unsuccessful for a variety of reasons including poor intelligence, poor prior planning, poorly trained US personnel, and lack of secure communications. Publicity alerted drug traffickers who fled prior to the arrival of law enforcement agents, and antagonism of the peasant populace led to an uprising against the drug operation. This further led to condemnation of US actions by nations in the region and protests within Bolivia that threatened the stability of the government.[40] However, the operation did prove the effectiveness of targeting the lab-production capabilities as a center of gravity because approximately 90 percent of the coca flowing from Bolivia was interdicted.[41] More importantly, since the drug traffickers decided to wait until the US left before resuming coca processing operations, this removed the source of revenue from the region. The resultant drop of coca prices led peasants to seek governmental support of alternative crop production. Although any positive effects were reversed once US-led operations did cease, the operation successfully proved that destruction of the coca labs combined with crop eradication could successfully disrupt drug operations and induce peasants to seek alternative crops. This then became the basis for future operations.

According to Mendel, "Since 1988, DEA has continued its efforts to suppress cocaine trafficking in the Andean Ridge [the Upper Huallaga Valley in Peru and the Chapare region in Bolivia] under a program called Operation SNOWCAP."[42] This operation used temporary-duty agents assigned to US ambassadors to assist police in Peru and Bolivia in counter-drug operations.

An operation that typifies the difficulties of mounting counterdrug operations similar to Snowcap in this region is the more recent Operation Ghost Zone. Mendel described how this operation began March 1993 and, attempting to use lessons learned during Operation Blast Furnace, targeted the drug-trafficking organizations in the Chapare region in Bolivia. "It involved about 750 Bolivian counterdrug personnel under a Special Narcotics Force that was . . . supported by 35 Americans from the Army, Coast Guard, and US Customs with DEA as the lead agency."[43] The objectives of the operation included reinforcement of a Bolivian crop-eradication effort and suppressing export of coca base via air, land, and sea from the growing fields to distant labs for processing and keeping precursor chemicals from coming in. The operation was intended to last through two growing seasons, thereby seriously restricting availability of this region as a source of supply to Colombian traffickers. These operations showed early indications of success. In anticipation of the expected drop in coca prices, the Bolivian agency DIRECO (Coca Eradication Directorate responsible for rural development with alternative crops) attempted to encourage crop substitution by offering $2,000 for each hectare of coca destroyed.

During the active counterdrug operation the US military group also supported Bolivian goals of strengthening governmental control over the region and inspiring economic growth by providing assistance in the form of 16 major engineering projects at eight different locations. These projects were considered essential in convincing the farmer of the long-term benefits of accepting alternative farming.

Although the final results of the operation are yet to be evaluated, there was concern noted as in past operations that social tension resulting from the disruption of drug profits would spark armed struggle. Some of this unrest could have been avoided had a responsive alternative crop development program been available. However, DIRECO failed to provide such a program. This led to allegations of corruption within DIRECO and eventually resulted in the Bolivian government's removing the chairman. An important lesson learned was that lagging support of an alternative crop program contributed to social unrest by allowing the seeds of desperation to set in among the peasants who now lacked a source of income. This desperation was subsequently fanned by fledgling revolutionary elements that attempted to organize the peasants against the US presence and the counterdrug operations.[44]

Positive aspects of the operation included the demonstrated will of the Bolivian government to target illicit drug operations. The operation also provided the US military an opportunity to enhance the professional development of the Bolivian police and military. Lessons learned likewise paved the way for future cooperation.[45]

Operations in the Transit Zone

As mentioned, the DOD has been tasked with the leading role in detection, monitoring, and C^3I in antidrug operations. A typical drug-interdiction scenario could see employment of a combined interdiction force comprised of Navy ships, USAF aircraft, US Coast Guard and Customs Service aviation units, and state and local law enforcement agencies among others. This need for interoperability of various agencies engaged in counterdrug operations serves to highlight various aspects which constrain military support efforts.

First, the extent of the interdiction problem is enormous when considered within the context of the total number of potential ways to smuggle drugs into the US. Based upon 1991 US Customs Service data, over 46 million people enter the US each year by air, another 374 million by land, and 7 million by sea. Air traffic includes over 560,000 commercial-sized aircraft and 158,000 smaller aircraft. Also there were over 8 million cargo shipments by land and sea. The sheer volume of traffic represents an enormous detection and interdiction work load.[46]

Second, the military is restrained from serving in a law enforcement role by the Posse Comitatus Act (PCA) of 1878. Although the act was modified in 1988 to enable the military to fulfill its support roles, as a result of this act, the military cannot apprehend or arrest suspects—although there are exceptions for the National Guard in-state status.[47] These functions must be performed by one of the law enforcement agencies. This means that while the military is engaged in detection, monitoring, and communication activities, when suspect drug activity is detected, a member of a LEA must be present to accomplish the search, seizure, and arrest. This includes intercepting suspect vessels or aircraft outside the US. In cases where a law enforcement agent is not present, the military must direct the suspects to a location "designated by appropriate civilian officials."

The constraints of the PCA place an even greater burden on cooperation between the military and the LEAs, to ensure that a police officer is on board a vessel or aircraft or nearby to provide a timely response. This burden gives rise to concerns that while a ship or aircraft supports a suspect to a "designated location," a gap will occur in the surveillance coverage, enabling another smuggler to slip through.[48]

A third factor affecting the ability to conduct air intercepts is the lack of authority to compel suspected smuggler aircraft, operating over the high seas or US territorial waters, to land. This is an important constraint given that smuggling by noncommercial aircraft is considered a major means of transporting drugs to the US from foreign countries. The Bush administration tried each year since the 1990 National Drug

Control Strategy Implementation Act to gain congressional approval for this authority.[49] As of February 1994 it was still not granted. However, debate revolves around what is "reasonable" use of force and how to avoid mistaking legitimate aircraft for criminal activity. As a result, when smuggler aircraft are detected, they can ignore directions to land, jettisoning their drugs—at times to high-speed boats waiting below—and fleeing the area.[50]

Finally, there are gaps in the radar coverage necessary to detect and monitor drug traffic. The previous administration responded by including the funding for aerostat radar that would be deployed along the southwest border and in the Caribbean, and for radar systems in the Andean countries to support counterdrug operations. While aerostat radar systems are a cost-efficient means to create an effective network, there are inherent problems associated with terrain masking and poor operability in various weather conditions—they must be lowered during rough weather.[51] Further gaps are created when an aerostat must be lowered for maintenance. This results in the need for greater coordination of air-based coverage. Thus, on the one side is the drug smuggler who is proving more inventive in circumventing the interdiction network; on the other side are the military and LEAs who are working aggressively to plug the gaps and deter smugglers.

The following composite scenario is based upon one described by Ahart and Stiles in "The Military's Entry into Air Interdiction of Drug Trafficking from South America."[52] It helps to explain the complexities associated with conducting successful drug interdiction operations with an integrated military and LEA response. Notification of an impending drug shipment could come from an in-country Drug Enforcement Agency agent. Such messages are relayed through the joint USCG and US Customs C^3I Center East in Miami, Florida. The center balances the information against the interdiction assets available.

Once a decision has been made to act, C^3I East requests the JTF 4 in Key West, Florida, to realign surveillance assets—frigates, airborne warning and control system, and E-2 aircraft—into position for best detection of a suspect smuggling flight. JTF 4 controls military assets.

AWACS monitors the suspect aircraft from takeoff until it can pass tracking responsibilities to a US Navy frigate on patrol in the area. AWACS also employs its data-link communications to broadcast information regarding the suspect to forces assigned interdiction tasks.

As the suspect aircraft continues its flight, monitored by the Navy frigate, US Customs Service aircraft are scrambled to intercept. Equipped with special night-viewing sensors, a Customs Service jet aircraft closes upon its target, attempting to stay above and behind in the suspect's blind spot as its progress is monitored. If the aircraft tail numbers are discernible, this information is passed to the El Paso Intelligence Center to check against its intelligence data base for prior involvement in drug activity.

If the aircraft crosses into the US, its flight is monitored until it touches down, and DEA, FBI, Customs, and local law enforcement authorities are directed to intercept. However, successful air interdiction operations have led smugglers to drop their drug cargo from the air to high-speed boats waiting offshore. The aircraft, still over international waters and essentially safe from interdiction, can then reverse its course unhindered.

If an airdrop does occur, chase of the smuggling vessel ensues, perhaps by a Customs Service aircraft equipped with ocean-scanning radar, while directing the operations of Customs and USCG surface craft. If the smuggler craft approaches the shore and lands, it can then be met by a coterie of law enforcement authorities.

However, if the smugglers have realized that they are being monitored and in danger of capture, they can attempt to escape. Often equipped with high-speed boats quicker than the LEA surface craft, the smugglers may escape unless the USCG vessel is one equipped with a UH-60 Black Hawk helicopter, which can be launched and continue pursuit until capture can be effected.

A variation on this scenario might include the aircraft's avoiding a sea drop but continuing on to Mexico and landing at an isolated airstrip. (This can bring C^3I West and JTF 5 into the operation if the flight drifts into their area of responsibility.) On the ground, the illicit cargo can be unloaded and prepared for shipment overland or overseas into the US. However, the aircraft could have been tracked by AWACS and ground-based aerostat radar, and intercepted by Mexican authorities with DEA advising on the operation.

Drug detection, monitoring, and C^3I activities comprise the bulk of the drug control budget for the military. By taking advantage of the inherent capabilities within the military commands, an effective detection, monitoring, and C^3I network now exist. Success in air interdiction has actually resulted in greater attempts by smugglers to ship drugs overland or by sea. These interdiction efforts give credibility to US demands upon foreign governments to increase counterdrug operations within their borders. Certainly a foreign policy based upon foreign interdiction of illicit drugs appears hypocritical if a like effort is not mounted by the US within its borders. This has led to greater use of military forces, particularly the role the National Guard has played in the eradication of the large marijuana crop grown in the United States.

Operations within the US—Crop Eradication

In addition to crop eradication, the National Guard has been used to aid the Customs Service in the inspection of commercial conveyances and cargo containers, which continue to be a major means of shipping drugs into the country.[53]

As discussed in the 1992 National Drug Control Strategy, the LEAs are attempting to take advantage of "the unique skills and expertise of military personnel to provide assistance and training and are integrating these personnel into support functions. This allows agents and inspectors to devote a greater percentage of time to their border control mission."[54]

The 1992 strategy also states that "in Fiscal Year 1991, National Guard personnel performed marijuana eradication operations (nearly 21 million plants eradicated and over $47 million in cash confiscated). Eradication of domestically grown marijuana resulted in the virtual elimination of the Hawaiian crop and 87 percent of marijuana production in California.[55] This success supports the Clinton administration's emphasis on eradication. Logically, stopping the production of the drug would seem more economical than trying to stop it after entry and dissemination in an increasing widespread and complex network of middlemen and street dealers.

This concept was reflected in comments by State Department counselor Wirth, who stated, "Very aggressive eradication efforts may offer the most cost-effective approach. Although this has produced strong opposition by Peru and Bolivia because of the dependency of rural growers on the drug crop for livelihood. This administration would attempt to address these concerns through alternative crop-production programs."[56]

As a matter of fact, there are parallels to crop eradication in the US and Latin America. In both countries, marijuana usage has varying degrees of support by the civilian populace. Fields are often located in remote areas requiring considerable expenditure of resource to detect and destroy, and the profits generated by the crop ensures the grower will resist, perhaps violently, any eradication efforts. Indicative of eradication efforts, the following discussion is based upon Mendel's "Illusive Victory" which helps convey various aspects of the eradication efforts within the US.[57]

In the summer of 1990, Operation Green Sweep was conducted on federal land in part of northern California's Emerald Triangle, the King Range Nature Conservation District. A joint eradication task force was formed under the lead of the Bureau of Land Management and consisted of 110 California National Guard, 60 law enforcement agents, and 60 regular Army personnel. Eradication efforts were met by hostile growers who did not want to lose their piece of the $500 million generated annually by this area. Resistance took the form of negative press coverage and a local radio station and Citizen's Oversight Group which discouraged support for the operation and attempted to organize civilian demonstrations. Resistance was also offered by the local sheriff, originally part of the operation but who subsequently withdrew and became a harsh critic of the "invasion."

The 11-day operation overcame these difficulties and resulted in destroying marijuana plants valued at over $2.8 million, removal or destruction of 28 tons of growing equipment, and returning 26 growing sites to their natural state. As a short-term effort the operation can be considered a success; however, to be truly effective (parallel to operations in Latin America), a continued governmental presence was required.

Conclusion

The foregoing discussion has served to highlight the complex situations in which the military must respond to accomplish its drug-interdiction duties. These include providing support of drug-interdiction efforts in foreign countries, attempting to stem the flow of drugs through transit zones, and supporting crop-eradication efforts. Although there have been lessons learned en route to achieving successful counterdrug operations, the military has inherent capabilities required to support the new administration's national drug control strategy—a strategy based upon institution building, disrupting the drug organizations, and crop eradication.

As mentioned, institution building has begun to pay dividends in drug interdiction. Military training, equipment, and intelligence has led to disruption of major drug cartels in Colombia and arrests and seizures in all the major drug producer nations. The military plays a key supporting role in helping these countries conduct successful antidrug operations as part of the overall national drug control strategy. Our future strategy, as General Joulwan has stated,

> demands a long-term commitment on both supply and demand, at the source, in transit, and at home, to be successful. We need to invest in the long-term goals of the nations involved with the United States as a partner and ally in the fight. . . . I have met with the heads of state of these nations multiple times, and I am convinced of their determination in the counterdrug effort. They are committed.[58]

Although drug-eradication efforts in Andean countries have not always been successful in the past, as operations Blast Furnace and Ghost Zone suggest, if crop eradication is conducted, concurrent with long-term interdiction efforts, then the price paid for coca will go down. Williams stated that it took 10 years for the drug organizations to develop extensive coca crops in the Huallaga Valley. This implies that it could take a like effort to eradicate it (unless an environmentally safe herbicide is used).[59] Any eradication effort mandates that the US and the host nation must be prepared to provide economic assistance to support alternative-crop production, otherwise the incentive to develop alternative crops (a key step in dismantling the drug organizations) will evaporate and ultimately result in social unrest.

Until such times that the drug organizations are dismantled and crop fields are eradicated, the military must continue to play a major role in operating systems that detect, monitor, and track drug intruders. As the Clinton administration's 1993 Interim National Drug Control Strategy states:

> Interdiction . . . keeps many tons of cocaine, heroin, and other dangerous drugs from crossing our borders. This important effort attacks the traffickers' critical transportation networks to deny them easy access to this country. . . . Success in keeping the traffic from significantly increasing drug availability supports the treatment, prevention, and local law enforcement elements of our strategy.[60]

This then brings us to the future role the military will play in the drug war. The national drug strategies of the past, since 1989, have set the bounds of this role: the military supports the antidrug efforts of foreign countries and the major law enforcement agencies. Given the provisions of the PCA the military will continue in a supporting role. Within these bounds, the Clinton administration has good reason to continue the past policies of the previous administration for they are beginning to produce success. While this success can be measured in the tons of drugs seized or arrests made, the one true measure of success in the drug war is whether drug usage has declined. DOD coordinator for Drug Enforcement Policy and Support, Stephen M. Duncan, offered the following measures of success to a House subcommittee:

> Without claiming specific credit, the Department of Defense can fairly share in the success enjoyed since 1988. That success includes:
>
> – A 13 percent reduction in the current overall national use of illegal drugs;
> – The fact that more than 1 million fewer Americans are current users of cocaine, a drop of 35 percent;
> – The fact that occasional use of cocaine has dropped 22 percent and that adolescent use has dropped 63 percent;
> – The fact that the number of marijuana users has dropped by about 2 million, or more than 16 percent; and

– The fact that among persons ages 12 to 17, the current use of any illicit drug is down more than 25 percent.

The best evaluation of the department's counterdrug support is the judgment of those who are suited to evaluate that support—the law enforcement agencies themselves. Those agencies continue to give the department high marks.[61]

Notes

1. Peter R. Andrews et al., "Dead-End Drug Wars," *Foreign Policy*, no. 85, (Winter 1991–1992): 107.

2. Melvyn Levitsky, "International Narcotics Control: Andean Strategy Update" (Statement before House Foreign Affairs Committee Task Force on International Narcotics Control), *US Department of State Dispatch*, 15 July 1991, 510. This was restated with examples of major international cooperation initiatives by the Office of National Drug Control Policy, *National Drug Control Strategy: Progress in the War on Drugs 1989–1992* (Washington, D.C.: Executive Office of the President, January 1993), 27–29.

3. Thomas W. Lippman, "The US Takes New (Old) Path in Narcotics Battle," *The Washington Post*, 12 January 1994, A8.

4. The actual reference is "There are some who believe the Federal effort should be evenly divided among what are loosely called 'supply reduction' and 'demand reduction' activities." Office of National Drug Control Policy, *National Drug Control Strategy* (Executive Office of the President, February 1991), 2. Later, two fronts are identified in domestic terms of "casual drug use" and "chronic drug use" by the Office of National Drug Control Policy. See *National Drug Control Strategy: A Nation Responds to Drugs* (Washington, D.C.: Executive Office of the President, January 1992), 4.

5. Joseph B. Treaster, "Pentagon Plans Shift in War on Drug Traffickers," *New York Times*, 8 October 1993, A4.

6. Ibid.

7. Lippman, A8. There is ambiguity on what the Clinton administration's policy will be on drug interdiction. Office of National Drug Control Policy, *Breaking the Cycle of Drug Abuse: 1993 Interim National Drug Control Strategy* (Washington, D.C.: Executive Office of the President, September 1993), 22, offers that, "In a country with borders as vast and as open as our own, however, interdiction is a costly undertaking that requires the cooperation of numerous federal agencies and the source and transit nations. We will review existing interdiction organizations, resources, and methods to ensure they are operating in the most effective manner. Programs that are proven effective will be continued." This was further addressed by Lee P. Brown, director, Office of National Drug Control Policy, during an interview on "Meet the Press," 23 January 1994, where he stated there would be increased focus on domestic drug-prevention efforts; and focus on drug-producer nations and eradication efforts, while citing interdiction in the transit zones as too costly.

8. For a good summary of counterdrug efforts waged by Colombia, Peru, and Bolivia, see Melvyn Levitsky, "Progress in the International War Against Illicit Drugs" (Statement before Subcommittee on Terrorism, Narcotics, and

International Operations of the Senate Foreign Relations Committee), *US Department of State Dispatch*, 2 March 1992, 158–60.

9. Ibid., 156.

10. Why Latin American countries lacked the will to pursue antidrug activities is discussed by Andrews et al., 111–19.

11. Gary Williams, "The War on Cocaine: Strategy and Tactics," Center for the Study of Foreign Affairs, Department of State Publication 9849, March 1991, 11.

12. Ibid., 6–8.

13. Ibid., 16. In this paper, Williams discusses crop eradication through the use of tebuthiuron. To enable this operation he proposes that, "American military trainers can help keep narcotics police alive by giving them some paramilitary training." Although he later qualifies it when he states, "The crackdown in Colombia, if it can be sustained, and the proposed eradication in Peru, if it can be implemented, attack the supply problem at the root. Neither action requires the deployment of military forces by the US." Ibid., 19.

14. Ibid., 13.

15. Ibid., 16.

16. Office of National Drug Control Policy, *National Drug Control Strategy* (Executive Office of the President, January 1992), 144. For a more detailed, historical perspective of the total National Drug Control Budget, 1981–1992, by a major agency, see Office of National Drug Control Policy, *National Drug Control Strategy: Budget Summary* (Washington, D.C.: Executive Office of the President, February 1991), 216–19. More detailed descriptions of specific budget line items are at pages 175–82.

17. Lippman, A8.

18. Joint Publication 3-07, "Joint Doctrine for Military Operations Other Than War," final draft, April 1993, VI-3. Authority for military involvement started with the Defense Authorization Act for 1989 and was further codifed in guidance letters from the secretary of defense during 1989, ultimately included in the *National Military Strategy of the United States*, January 1992 (Washington, D.C.: The Pentagon, 17 September 1992), 15; with like inclusion in service doctrine such as *The Air Force and US National Security: Global Reach—Global Power* (June 1990), 15. Also for comprehensive counterdrug joint doctrine see JCS, Joint Publication 3-07.4, "Joint Doctrine and JTTP for Counterdrug Operations," initial draft, 15 August 1992.

19. Ibid.

20. Army-Air Force Center for Low-Intensity Conflict, "The Role of the Department of Defense in the National Counterdrug Effort," (Langley AFB, Va.: 10 June 1993), 58–73. Note the document is not cleared for public release. This discussion is based on Joint Publication 3-07.4, initial draft, A-1 though A-4; and VI-1 through VI-60. For a concise summary of the major commands and counterdrug activities accomplished in foreign countries, see Stephen M. Duncan, "DOD's Counterdrug Efforts" (Statement to Defense Subcommittee, House Appropriations Committee, 1 April 1992) *Defense Issues* 7, no. 29, 1–8.

21. Gen George A. Joulwan, USA, commander in chief, US Southern Command, "Continued Engagement Needed in Southern Command Region" (Statement to Senate Armed Services Committee, 21 April 1993) *Defense Issues* 8, no. 24, 1.

22. Ibid., 3.

23. Army-Air Force Center for Low-Intensity Conflict, 63. On 15 April 1993, the secretary of defense directed JCS to expand the responsibilities of LANTCOM, changing its designation to USACOM. In the process of the reorganization, FORSCOM was aligned under USACOM; however, it retained its operational responsibilities for counterdrug operation. Details regarding this realignment were taken from the Implementation Plan for Establishing United States Atlantic Command as the Joint Force Integrator, final draft (Norfolk, Va.: Headquarters USACOM, September 1993), 1-1 through 1-7.

24. Ibid.

25. Adm Charles R. Larson, commander in chief, US Pacific Command, "Pacific Command Cooperative Engagement Advances US Interests" (Statement to Senate Armed Services Committee, 21 April 1993) *Defense Issues* 8, no. 17, 3–4.

26. Ibid., 4.

27. Becky Colaw, "War on Drugs: Keeping Watch on the Golden Road," *Airman*, May 1993, 35.

28. *National Drug Control Strategy*, February 1991, 107.

29. John Ahart and Gerald Stiles, "The Military's Entry into Air Interdiction of Drug Trafficking from South America," Rand Corporation, 1991, 11.

30. *National Drug Control Strategy*, February 1991, 77.

31. Andrews et al., 111–19.

32. See comments by Melvyn Levitsky, assistant secretary for International Narcotics Matters, "Progress in the International War Against Illicit Drugs," *US Department of State Dispatch*, 2 March 1992, 158–60.

33. Andrews et al., 110.

34. Lippman, A8.

35. Andrews et al., 113.

36. Ibid.

37. Levitsky, "Progress in the International War Against Illicit Drugs," 161.

38. William W. Mendel, "Illusive Victory: From Blast Furnace to Green Sweep," *Military Review*, December 1992, 76. Unless otherwise noted, the discussion of Operation Blast Furnace and Operation Ghost Zone is drawn from this article.

39. Ibid.

40. Randy J. Kolton, "Combating the Colombian Drug Cartels" *Military Review*, March 1990, 58.

41. John T. Fiskel, "Developing a Drug War Strategy: Lessons from Operation Blast Furnace," *Military Review*, June 1991, 64.

42. Mendel, 76.

43. Ibid., 78.

44. Ibid., 80; also referred to in Levitsky's comments, "Progress in the International War Against Illicit Drugs," 160.

45. Mendel, 80.

46. See graphic in *National Drug Control Strategy: A Nation Responds to Drug Use*, January 1992, 100.

47. Ahart and Stiles, 18.

48. Ibid., 22.

49. *National Drug Control Strategy: A Nation Responds to Drug Use*, January 1992, 104.

50. Ibid.

51. Ahart and Stiles, 4–18. Unless otherwise stated, the discussion of the composite scenario is drawn from this article.

52. Ibid., 4.

53. *National Drug Control Strategy: A Nation Responds to Drug Use*, January 1992, 106.

54. Ibid., 107–8.

55. Ibid.

56. Lippman, A8.

57. Mendel, 81–84.

58. Joulwan, 7.

59. Williams, 13.

60. Office of National Drug Control Policy, *Breaking the Cycle of Drug Abuse: 1993 Interim National Drug Control Strategy* (Washington, D.C.: Executive Office of the President, September 1993), 22.

61. Duncan, 7.

Supporting United Nations and Regional Peacekeeping Efforts

Dr James S. Corum

Peacekeeping and peace enforcement are among the most important issues that will confront the US military in the next two decades. This chapter outlines the problems facing the US military in developing policies and doctrines for peacekeeping and peace enforcement and offers some recommendations.

Supporting and participating in multinational peacekeeping operations have been part of American foreign policy for over 30 years. Since the United States provided air support for the UN's Congo operation in 1960, the US military has been ordered to support more than a dozen peacekeeping operations, ranging in scope from providing a handful of soldiers for a UN observation mission to landing over 30,000 troops in Somalia.[1] Every presidential administration since Eisenhower's has involved the US military in some form of support for peacekeeping.

In the last decade American support for multinational peace operations has increased. In 1982, the US organized the 14-nation multinational observer force to serve as peacekeepers in support of the Egyptian/Israeli peace agreement. Over 1,000 American soldiers continue to serve as part of this very successful peacekeeping mission in the Sinai. From 1982 to 1984, the United States participated in a bloody and unsuccessful peace-enforcement mission in Lebanon along with British, French, and Italian forces. In the late 1980s the US supported the establishment of a UN multinational observer force to assist in the Central American peace process in El Salvador and Nicaragua. The US also provided financial support for peacekeeping operations in regions where the US and US-supported forces were militarily engaged.

In June 1992, with the lessening of cold-war tensions, UN Secretary-General Boutros Boutros-Ghali outlined his vision of an expanded peacekeeping role for the UN. Boutros-Ghali asserted that the UN should go beyond traditional peacekeeping missions to peace-enforcement operations. The peace-enforcement mission would commit troops under a stronger mandate than peacekeeping. Such troops would actively work to restore order in nations.

> Consider the utilization of peace enforcement units in clearly defined circumstances and with their terms of reference specified in advance. . . . They would have to be more heavily armed than peacekeeping forces and would need to undergo extensive preparatory training within their national forces. Deployment and operation of such forces would be under the authorization of the Security Council and would, as in the case of peacekeeping forces, be under the command of the Secretary-General.[2]

In a speech before the UN General Assembly in September 1992, President George Bush endorsed the secretary-general's peace-enforcement proposals. President Bush recommended that special military units be developed and trained by UN member nations for peacekeeping and humanitarian missions and in addition promised increased US support in the form of training, financing, and logistics for UN military operations.[3] The Clinton administration has also expressed support for the increased use of UN forces. One of the first defense decisions of the Clinton administration was to create a regular budget allocation for peacekeeping rather than depend on the previous expedient of special appropriations.

Despite a long and consistent US policy to support peacekeeping operations, the American military has been reluctant to accept the peacekeeping mission or to establish a body of peacekeeping doctrine. The chairman of the Joint Chiefs' 1993 report on the roles, missions, and functions of the armed forces briefly mentioned "humanitarian operations" but contained no reference to peacekeeping.[4] Until the end of the cold war there was little interest in or study of peace-keeping in the US armed forces. The 1993 Joint Chiefs of Staff (JCS) Publication 3-07.3, *Joint Tactics, Techniques, and Procedures (JTTP) for Peacekeeping Operations*, provides a brief description of terminology and a few general guidelines on peacekeeping. Though it is a useful starting point, it still does not resemble a usable or developed doctrine.

The peacekeeping mission is resisted by the military for several reasons. First of all, there is concern that peace operations will absorb too much of the operational funds of a declining military budget. This is a valid concern. The $350 million allocated for peacekeeping operations in the fiscal year (FY) 1993 defense budget was quickly consumed by the Somalia operation, whose cost to the United States quickly ran to several billion dollars. In order to make up the budget shortfall, the Defense Department had to reduce funding for equipment programs.[5] The cost of UN peacekeeping missions has grown from $233 million in 1987 to an estimated $3.5 billion in 1993. The US is assessed 31.74 percent of the UN's peacekeeping costs. This amounts to a $1.11-billion assessment for peacekeeping in addition to the costs of supporting a large US force in Somalia.

Another reason for US military resistance to this mission is the large numbers of troops required for the new peace-enforcement mission and by the expansion of traditional peacekeeping. The US deployed over 30,000 troops to Somalia in late 1992 and early 1993. The possibility of deploying 25,000 American troops as peacekeepers to Yugoslavia was also discussed. Deployments of this size, coupled with the necessary support troops and a further reserve to relieve the deployed troops, amounts to a major commitment of American war-fighting capability to peacekeeping. Deployments such as Somalia are liable to place a great strain upon an ever-shrinking American military.

The peacekeeping mission is resisted also due to a common attitude in the US military: that military forces lose their fighting efficiency if employed on any but the traditional war-fighting mission. A recent article in *Parameters*, the journal of the Army War College, offers one of the best illustrations of this aspect of American military culture.[6] This article postulates a not-too-distant future in which the US military has lost its moral bearings and fighting ability due to its overuse for civilian missions that started in the 1990s. Peacekeeping and humanitarian missions are blamed for diverting the armed forces from training for war: "Training is, quite literally, a zero-sum game. Each moment spent performing a non-traditional mission is one unavailable for orthodox military exercises."[7] Author Charles Dunlap, Jr., argues, "In truth militaries ought to 'prepare for war' and leave the 'peace waging' to those agencies of government whose mission is just that."[8]

Defining Peacekeeping

One of the most serious problems in creating an American policy and doctrine for peacekeeping is simply defining the term. Policymakers today may mean very different things when they use the term *peacekeeping* since there is no common international or legal definition of the word.

I define peacekeeping in accordance with the meaning that it has accrued during 40 years of UN and multinational operations: peacekeeping is a diplomatic method of placing neutral soldiers and observers between two or more parties or nations in conflict, with the intent of monitoring a truce or armistice agreement and assisting the conflicting parties to maintain the truce and eventually to arrive at a permanent, peaceful political settlement. The peacekeeping mission can also be referred to as "trucekeeping," "truce enforcement," and "armistice enforcement."

As a general rule, peacekeeping comes into play when the peace process is already well under way. The three most important traditional principles of peacekeeping are

1. Consent. The warring parties agree to allow peacekeeping forces to enter the conflict zone. Peacekeepers are allowed to operate within a specific mandate that has been agreed to by all the parties in the conflict.
2. Impartiality. The peacekeepers are not to be parties to the conflict or to join the conflict. They are obligated to impartially report violations of the peace to their higher authority—usually, the United Nations.
3. Self-Defense. Peacekeeping forces are authorized to use force only to defend themselves.

Although peacekeeping duties are largely those of diplomacy and observation, neutral military forces have consistently proven to be the best peacekeepers. There are several reasons why military forces are better than civilian diplomats in the peacekeeping role. Military forces are already organized as units, and they can be easily reorganized to meet the task at hand. Military units are quickly deployable. The military has its own logistics and transport capability to access the area and execute its mission. Military units possess tight discipline—a characteristic necessary to operate in a tense environment and still further diplomacy. Soldiers understand military operations and tactics and are the best-qualified people to determine, evaluate, and report compliance or violation of the military terms of an armistice. Lastly, should the peace process break down, military units are capable of defending themselves.

Traditional peacekeeping is a type of practical field diplomacy that holds only a tenuous relationship with the diplomacy of international councils and chanceries. Peacekeeping units deploy between combatant forces as a buffer. Junior officers and noncommissioned officers are commonly required to meet daily with soldiers and junior leaders of the combatant forces in order to defuse tense situations and to allow for the passage of lines and the movement of civilians. Midranking officers negotiate local truces and adapt armistice provisions to local conditions. When violence occurs, the peacekeepers are obligated to impartially and accurately report the events to their military superiors as well as to their international authorities. On this mission, junior officers must exercise discipline and restraint. To be effective, they must additionally possess superior analytical skills and the ability to make rapid, on-the-spot decisions. The peacekeeping and observer missions are among the most difficult missions an individual soldier can execute.

Following the principles of consent, impartiality, and self-defense, peacekeeping has built a remarkable record of success since the first UN military peacekeeping force was deployed to Gaza and the Sinai in 1957. In several cases—notably, in Lebanon—peacekeeping efforts have broken down or been very short-lived. Most of the dozens of peacekeeping operations of the last 40 years, however, have contributed greatly to reducing international tensions and resolving conflicts.

Broadening the Concept

The concept of peacekeeping has recently been broadened and applied to multinational interventions to restore order. Secretary-General Boutros-Ghali refers to such operations as "peacemaking," to be carried out by "peace-enforcement units."[9] Policymakers and the press have generally referred to such operations as "peacekeeping." The US military is now lumping both peacekeeping and peace enforcement under the general term *peace operations*. There is a grave danger for policymakers in confusing peacekeeping and peace-enforcement operations, for the two operations are fundamentally different. Peacekeeping operations are normally conducted within a very clear diplomatic mandate regarding both the mission of the forces and the guidelines that the forces operate under. Peace-enforcement operations are not carried out under the principles of consent and impartiality nor is the authority to use force limited to self-defense.

Some of the differences between peacekeeping and peace enforcement have been demonstrated in the actions and policies of US and international coalition forces operating in Somalia. In Somalia, US and UN forces actively asserted a right to search for and seize weapons held by various political factions. Peacekeeping forces might supervise a negotiated disarmament, but they have no right to carry out offensive operations to seize weapons. The UN forces also claimed the right to operate wherever in Somalia they felt it necessary. Peacekeeping forces are normally limited to specific areas of operations under the truce agreement they support. Another difference between peace enforcement and peacekeeping is the rules of engagement. Peace-enforcement troops may shoot if they feel threatened. Peacekeepers are authorized to shoot only after being fired upon. Finally, peacekeeping forces claim no civil government authority and have very limited authority to arrest or detain civilians. Peace enforcers in Somalia essentially took over the role of civil government, worked to organize a government under their authority, and asserted broad powers of arrest and detainment. Indeed, the UN has not acted to outline any real limits of authority in peace enforcement.

Although the United Nations and the United States have endorsed the peace-enforcement concept by committing forces to Somalia in 1992–93, the concept remains undefined by practice or international agreement. This is in contrast to the concept of peacekeeping, which has acquired a tradition of law and precedent. Defining the concept of peace enforcement and creating a viable military doctrine for carrying out such operations should be a priority for American military policymakers.

Operational Problems of Peacekeeping

Peacekeeping may be a diplomatic/political operation, but it is a true military operation as well. As such, the success of a peacekeeping operation depends upon such military factors as command and control, logistics, intelligence, training, and force structure.

Peacekeeping forces operating under UN control have been plagued for decades with insufficient command, control, and communications assets. The UN has never had a true military staff capable of planning and coordinating all aspects of a military operation. Until 1993 the UN possessed no 24-hour military communications center. The minuscule UN military staff at the UN Headquarters—only a score of officers—did not possess the manpower or funding to maintain a command center. Occasionally, UN force commanders in the field had to contact headquarters during New York working hours, often by commercial telephone.

The lack of an adequate planning staff means that every UN peacekeeping operation is, by nature, an ad hoc operation. The Security Council authorizes an operation and UN officials negotiate the scope and conditions of the operation. Member states are then called upon to provide forces for the operation. While many nations are capable of providing well-trained and disciplined light-infantry units, only a few (mostly Western) nations have adequate numbers of trained logistics troops, medics, communications specialists, transport units, engineer units, and planning staffs to actually support a deployment of forces over a great distance.

Forces committed to UN peacekeeping have had to make do with the units and equipment offered to the United Nations. Consequently, there has been a consistent shortfall in the logistics, support troops, and equipment necessary to carry out even small-scale peacekeeping operations. Shortfalls in logistics support have, on several occasions, crippled the effectiveness of UN operations. The UN mission for the referendum in Western Sahara (MINURSO) was established in September 1991 to verify the cessation of hostilities between Moroccan and Polisario forces. The military peacekeeping force was initially to consist of 1,695 personnel, of whom 550 were to be military observers. Only 350 troops from 26 nations were made available and deployed. The logistics battalion envisioned never arrived, so the small observer group had to improvise its own support system. Consequently, it had too little time and too few personnel to execute the mission.[10] Although the MINURSO mission has not failed, its effectiveness has been greatly limited by the lack of support. In this case, any success has come more by luck and improvisation than by planning.

The recent UN peacekeeping mission to Cambodia, involving 20,000 troops, was deployed without maps of the country since maps were not available through UN channels. Eventually, the military obtained maps via the black market.[11] The UN commander of the Central American peacekeeping mission in the 1980s had no effective logistics support; he had to put observer officers to work organizing a supply system using a fleet of locally obtained banana trucks.[12] Since UN peacekeepers often deploy to parts of the world with little, if any, infrastructure, lack of logistics support has become the primary difficulty in executing operations.

Due to the culture of the United Nations, UN peacekeeping forces are hampered by a lack of intelligence for planning and executing operations. Most of the 183 member nations can be classified as third world nations, and the very term *intelligence* conjures up for them images of nefarious Central Intelligence Agency (CIA) plots to interfere with and overthrow their governments. Whether this is an accurate depiction of intelligence operations or of the CIA is beside the point. Third world diplomats and politicians cannot be seen to support something resembling military intelligence operations. Thus, while the UN itself collects a great deal of information from around the world, its military staff does not have an intelligence section to collate and analyze the information that is available. The result is the deployment of relatively large peacekeeping forces without adequate maps or information about the combatant forces.

The low level of support available to UN peacekeepers also hampers one of the central missions of the peacekeeper: to observe and report. Even the relatively unsophisticated tools of information-gathering equipment common to most Western militaries are unavailable to UN peacekeepers. Much of the UN observation missions consists of observers with binoculars watching a cease-fire line. This is an inefficient use of the limited manpower available.

Basic items for intelligence collection, such as sensor devices, ground radar, and signal intercept equipment, have been used extensively by the US Army in order to enhance the efficiency of the ground forces. With proper equipment a small intelligence team can monitor and record movements over a large area much more effectively than can several observer posts. Add aerial and space surveillance assets to the observation mission and the efficiency of the observer force is multiplied yet again. Nonetheless, due to the cultural bias of many UN officials against intelligence gathering and the limited funds and support available, UN peacekeepers continue to conduct their mission with obsolete and minimally effective means.

In discussing peacekeeping operations, American policy-makers have been concerned with the amount of training necessary to carry out peacekeeping and with whether specific units should be assigned the peacekeeping task and given special training. This concern is perhaps indicative of the American military culture, which sees the peacekeeping mission as a task somehow alien to fighting forces; a task that requires a major re-education effort for the forces involved. Soldiers experienced in peacekeeping do not, however, share this concern over special training. The Canadian Forces, the military with perhaps the most extensive peacekeeping experience, use regular line units for peacekeeping. The Canadians have found that well-trained, deployable combat units need only a short two-week area-indoctrination training course in order to deploy and effectively carry out a peacekeeping operation.

A study by the Canadian Forces concludes that peace-keeping by itself does not necessarily damage the operational effectiveness of a military force.[13] Indeed, according to the

Canadian study, a peacekeeping deployment provides a military unit with opportunities to exercise its military skills.

> There were indications that peacekeeping may be having a positive impact on operational readiness in that it has provided occasions when the Canadian Forces could implement and try many of its standard operating procedures for personal and material deployment.[14]

The study also outlines some favorable training benefits from peacekeeping service.

> Many of the operators interviewed expressed the view that the training, skill exercising, broadening of horizons, exposure to different cultures, exposure to the military approaches of other nations, and the foreign travel all contributed to the professional development of the Canadian Forces' member. Furthermore, the sharing of the experiences and lessons learned upon return to the parent unit or base had a cumulative effect.[15]

Training courses of five weeks' duration for officers involved in peacekeeping and four weeks' duration for enlisted men have been sponsored by the UN since 1969. In the courses, which are offered in Niinisalo, Finland, officers experienced in peacekeeping supervise tactical exercises typical of peacekeeping operations.[16]

In general, training units and officers for peacekeeping duties does not seem to provide any major operational problems nor should deployment of units and officers on peacekeeping duties have a major impact upon the effectiveness of the combat forces as a whole, as long as no more than a small percentage of the total force is deployed for peacekeeping at any one time.

The US Contribution to Peacekeeping

During the cold war, the United States generally remained aloof from direct or significant participation in UN peacekeeping operations. As the world's primary opponent of communism, as embodied by the Soviet Union, the US could scarcely be regarded in the third world as an impartial force. Since peacekeeping operations are approved by the UN Security Council, during the cold war there was an unwritten understanding that the US would refrain from playing a major role in any particular peacekeeping operation as long as Soviet involvement was limited. Had the US desired to play a greater role, or had it even offered its services for peacekeeping, the USSR would have insisted upon an equal role. Increasing Soviet military prestige and overseas involvement, even in a mission so innocuous as peacekeeping, was anathema to US policymakers. As a result, the US and USSR agreed that the small powers and neutral nations would serve as peace-keepers.

With the end of the cold war, there is no longer a logical political reason why the US should remain aloof from peacekeeping. American and Russian forces are now planning joint training and operations. There are even discussions of possible US/Russian peacekeeping operations. Fear of the Soviet Union's expanding its influence in the third world is no longer a policy consideration for the United States. Instead, the US and Russia are now working together to support UN operations in Bosnia.

Given the improved climate of political and military cooperation among the larger powers, the conditions of political support for peacekeeping operations have improved. As more UN peacekeeping operations are likely to take place in the future, determining the appropriate US contribution—and creating a peacekeeping doctrine and policy—are among the most important challenges the US military will face in the near future.

There is much that the US military can do to improve and enhance the operational effectiveness of multinational peacekeeping. America's role in organizing and supporting a 14-nation multinational peacekeeping force in the Sinai demonstrates that the US military can effectively organize and conduct peacekeeping operations. The Sinai operation, part of the Egyptian/Israeli peace accords, was not sponsored by the United Nations. US/USSR rivalry in the UN in the early 1980s caused the Soviets to veto a proposed UN mandate to supervise the Israeli withdrawal from Egypt and the Egyptian/Israeli force-level agreements. Under US direction, a force of several thousand troops from 14 nations was deployed in the Sinai in 1982. This force, which contains over 1,000 American soldiers, has successfully observed the Egyptian/Israeli peace ever since. The peacekeepers have encountered no serious incidents, and Egyptian/Israeli relations have steadily improved.

Considering the factors of the changed political situation, the success of America in peacekeeping in the Sinai, and the operational problems facing UN peacekeepers noted in the previous section, there are several major contributions the US military can make to improve and enhance UN and multinational peacekeeping efforts. The United States can best support peacekeeping by playing to its operational and institutional strengths. The US military has superior and unique capabilities in deployment planning, logistics support, and technology. US support for peacekeeping should center on these strengths. The UN's institutional problem of inadequate staff planning can be partially solved by an infusion of US and NATO personnel experienced in deploying units in multinational operations. This should be coupled with the expenditure of adequate funds to provide a modern, secure, 24-hour communications system for UN peacekeeping operations. This would have to follow major changes in the cultural bias of many UN officials, especially from third world countries, against collecting and analyzing intelligence. When peacekeeping operations are contemplated, UN agencies will have to cooperate fully with the military staff and make economic, geographical, and political information available to the planning staff. If necessary, UN agencies should be required to provide teams of translators and linguists to the military staffs to assist them in basic intelligence analysis. This would prevent recurrences of the problems encountered during the initial US deployment to Somalia in December 1990 when American forces moved into Somali cities without translators or interpreters.

Logistics has been the UN peacekeepers' greatest operational problem for decades. Making available the equivalent of three or four logistics task forces, combined with engineering and medical detachments, could provide effective support for three or four peacekeeping operations. Such a commitment would amount to no more than 1 percent of the total US Army. This type of support could spell the difference between success and failure of a UN operation. The US Air Force has provided airlift assets to numerous UN peacekeeping operations since the Congo in 1960, and it should continue to support such missions.

Modern US technology can also do much to improve the efficiency of UN operations. A commitment of US tactical intelligence teams equipped with sensor devices and ground-surveillance radar can enhance the efficiency of UN troops serving in the observer role. UN peacekeepers should be able to request and receive US Air Force aerial surveillance and reconnaissance support when necessary and appropriate. The US could set up a liaison committee to make satellite-derived photos and intelligence available to UN peacekeepers. Such a liaison committee could ensure that the most sensitive information and technology would be kept within a restricted circle while less-sensitive satellite photos received a greater dissemination to the forces operating in the field.

A small number of staff officers, logisticians, and specialists would do far more to enhance UN peacekeeping operations than a large force of ground troops. In any case, there is no shortage of well-trained, well-disciplined infantry units available for UN operations. Countries such as Kenya, Zimbabwe, and Bangladesh have contributed effective infantry units to UN peacekeeping and are likely to make such troops available for future operations. The third world countries, however, lack the staffs, logisticians, and support troops necessary to support troop deployments. In view of this, US support for peacekeeping is best focused upon the qualitative rather than the quantitative.

The US and Peace Enforcement

Peace enforcement is not a new concept, and it did not originate with the American and UN intervention in Somalia in 1990 and 1991. The United States had participated in two multinational peace-enforcement operations before Somalia: to the Congo in 1960–64 and to Lebanon in 1982–84. Both operations failed.

As defined by the UN secretary-general, the peace-enforcement operations are not carried out with the express consent of the warring parties. Peace enforcement contains a far broader mandate than peacekeeping; a mandate to restore peace and order. The UN and US have authorized a broader use of force in peace enforcement than specified by peacekeeping rules.

The secretary-general has recommended that UN member states make armed forces available to the Security Council to act as "guarantors of international security." This represents a desire by some in the UN leadership to greatly expand international military intervention.

The three peace-enforcement campaigns by the United States—in the Congo, Lebanon, and Somalia—share many common elements. US national interests in those areas were minimal. The US supported the Congo operation out of a desire to keep Soviet influence to a minimum in Africa. The Lebanon and Somalia operations were conducted primarily for humanitarian reasons to help secure a permanent peace in lands torn by war. In all three cases, the UN or multinational mandate to intervene was couched in vague terms: to "assist the Congolese" until they could set up their own security forces; "to provide an interposition force . . . to assist the Government of Lebanon and Lebanon's armed forces in the Beirut area [and to] facilitate the restoration of the Lebanese Government's sovereignty."[17] In Somalia the UN envisioned a long-term mandate in which UN forces would "prevent violence, maintain security and help restore the economy."[18]

In all of these cases, the soldiers on the spot were given vague guidelines as to the amount of force that was authorized. Initially only self-defense was authorized, but in each case the rules of engagement were quickly changed and expanded. American rules of engagement changed at least three times during the first two weeks of the intervention in Somalia. In all three cases, use of force so far as to include bombing, heavy gun employment, and conventional attacks was authorized by the UN and multinational forces.

Any pretense of impartiality, fundamental to the peacekeeping mission, was quickly discarded in the peace-enforcement operations. In the Congo, Lebanon, and Somalia,

UN and multinational forces quickly took sides and began to engage in conventional conflict with one or more of the national factions. In no case was such a situation envisioned by the original peace-enforcement mandate. A further complication originated with the UN charter, which forbids intervention in the internal affairs of another nation. A strong case can be made that both the Congo and Somalia operations are intrinsically in violation of the principles of the United Nations.

Each of the aforementioned peace-enforcement operations resulted in heavy casualties for UN and multinational forces involved.[19] In Lebanon, 241 US marines and 58 French soldiers were killed in one day, 23 October 1983. More than 10 percent of the multinational force in Lebanon became casualties on that day.[20] The US/UN casualties in Somalia exceeded 200 soldiers in the first 10 months of the deployment.

The inability to justify peace-enforcement operations in terms of national interest, the vagueness of the mandate for such operations, and the heavy casualties involved have all served to reduce political and public support for the peace-enforcement mission. One of the fundamental problems has been to speak of peace-enforcement operations in terms of peacekeeping; as noted, however, the two operations are fundamentally different. Neither the UN nor the US government has created a military doctrine for peace enforcement. Establishing a clear policy and doctrine for peace enforcement will remain one of the most important and difficult tasks for the US military in the next decade.

Conclusion and Recommendations

The fiscal year 1993 US defense budget included, for the first time, $350 million for peacekeeping operations. This is at least a first step in recognizing that peacekeeping is part of the overall mission of the US military. Some tentative steps have also been taken to create a military doctrine for peacekeeping. While these are steps in the right direction, it is doubtful that $350 million is anywhere near enough to properly fund US peacekeeping operations.

Traditional multinational peacekeeping operations have proven to be a very useful tool for American foreign policy. It is also cost-effective. The UN peacekeeping force in Cyprus costs $50 million per year, a small price to pay for helping to keep the peace between Greece and Turkey—both NATO allies of the US. The cost of keeping approximately 1,000 US troops in the Sinai is minuscule compared to the costs involved if hostilities broke out again between Egypt and Israel. The world has already seen the Egyptian/Israeli conflict close the Suez Canal, cause a world oil crisis, and generate serious problems for American foreign policy. Peacekeepers have recently helped bring peace and order to Cambodia. Peacekeepers have assisted the United States in ending conflicts in Central America. Considering the benefits of peacekeeping, it would not be unwise to commit a minimum of 1–2 percent of the US defense budget to such operations.

As pointed out earlier, the American military commitment to peacekeeping need not be large in terms of troops committed. Staff specialists, logistics support, and modern equipment will go far to improve the effectiveness of multinational peacekeeping operations.

If the United States makes a firm policy commitment to support international peacekeeping, then certain aspects of the US military policy and culture will need to be changed. A peacekeeping tour should not hurt an officer's career. If peacekeeping is taken seriously, the US military should encourage its best officers to volunteer for the mission. Promotions should be assured for officers who serve several peacekeeping missions. By changing military personnel policies, the US can develop a cadre of officers with extensive knowledge of and experience in peacekeeping.

The peace-enforcement mission is the thorniest problem for the US military. It is a mistake to view such operations within the context of peacekeeping. Peace enforcement is, essentially, military intervention. American policymakers need to decide under what circumstances and for which reasons they will commit US troops in foreign civil wars. The UN has shown itself to be a poor agency for conducting military intervention operations, yet some international response may be required for conflicts such as the Congo and Somalia. One option for dealing with the dilemma of the complete breakdown of order within a country is to support and encourage intervention by regional coalitions. When civil war devastated Liberia in 1989, ECOMOG, a coalition of five West African nations, intervened to restore order. The US has provided diplomatic support and military aid for this intervention. In the case of Somalia, it is possible that forces from the Organization of African Unity or the Arab League might have been a better agency than the UN for intervention. Regional powers have a direct national interest in keeping order in their part of the world. A small, regional organization can create a more specific mandate for the use of force than the large, complex, and bureaucratic apparatus of the United Nations with its 183 member states.

Notes

1. Some of the peacekeeping operations that the US has supported are: UN operations in the Congo 1960–1964 (equipment and airlift); UN security force in West New Guinea 1962–1963 (airlift); United Nations peacekeeping force in Cyprus 1964–1965 (airlift); multinational force and observers in the Sinai 1982–present (troops); UN mission for the referendum in Western Sahara 1990–present (observers); UN operations in Somalia II 1993–1994 (troops); UN protection force in Macedonia 1992–1994 (troops); and UN protection force in Bosnia 1992–present (airlift and air strikes).

2. Secretary-General Boutros Boutros-Ghali, "An Agenda for Peace . . .," Report of the Secretary-General to the 47th Session of the UN General Assembly, 17 June 1992, par. 44.

3. President George Bush, address to the UN General Assembly, 17 June 1992.

4. Gen Colin Powell, chairman of the Joint Chiefs of Staff, *Roles, Missions and Functions of the Armed Forces of the United States* (February 1993), I.4–I.5.

5. Defense Secretary Les Aspin asked Congress to take $750 million out of about two dozen different budget accounts to pay for Operation Restore Hope in Somalia, *Federal Times*, 17 May 1993, 20.

6. See Lt Col Charles Dunlap, Jr., USAF, "The Origins of the American Military Coup of 2012," *Parameters*, no. 28 (Winter 1992–1993): 2–20.

7. Ibid., 11.

8. Ibid., 12.

9. Boutros Boutros-Ghali, "An Agenda for Peace," *UN Chronicle*, September 1992, 3.

10. Lt Col Bill Spracher in *Military Implications of United Nations Peacekeeping Operations*, ed. William Lewis (Washington, D.C.: NDU Press, 1993), 61–65.

11. Maj George Steuber in *Military Implications*, 67–70.

12. Maj Gen J. C. Douglas in *Military Implications*, 54–58.

13. Chief Review Services, Program Evaluation Division, *Final Report on NDHQ Program Evaluation E 2/90 Peacekeeping* (Ottawa: Ministry of National Defence, 30 June 1992), par. 4.31.

14. Ibid., par. 4.38.

15. Ibid., par. 4.34.

16. Keith Greenberg, "The Essential Art of Empathy," *Military History Quarterly* 5, no. 1 (Autumn 1992): 64–69.

17. President Ronald Reagan, White House Statement (Washington, D.C.: 29 September 1982).

18. US Department of State, *Dispatch of April 5, 1993*, 209–10.

19. UN Department of Public Information, *The Blue Helmets*, 2d ed., 1990, 435.

20. Anthony McDermot and Kjell Skjelsbaed, eds., *The Multinational Force in Beirut* (Miami: University of Florida Press, 1991), 276.

Parallel Warfare
Its Nature and Application

John R. Pardo, Jr.

By the morning of January 20 [1991], four days after a U. S. Air Force stealth bomber opened the war with a 2,000-pound laser-guided bomb targeted precisely on the microwave dishes atop Baghdad's International Telecommunications Building, the city was crippled. There was no mainline electricity, no running water, no working telephones.

—Michael Kelly
The New Republic

That is how journalist Michael Kelly relates what he and the other residents of Baghdad experienced during the opening days of Operation Desert Storm. The excerpt from Mr Kelly's article not only describes the far-reaching effects of parallel warfare, but two of its main ingredients—stealth and precision weapons. Despite having been the star of Desert Storm, parallel warfare is not a well-known phenomenon. This chapter will not only define parallel warfare and discuss its history; it will describe the factors that make parallel warfare work, some of the positive and negative aspects of this warfare, and why parallel warfare is important to US armed forces.

Parallel Warfare
What Is It?

Parallel warfare is a *modus operandi*—a way of employing military forces. One working definition of *parallel warfare* is the simultaneous attack of enemy centers of gravity to achieve strategic paralysis. Strategic paralysis or strategic crippling, as it is also known, is the state an enemy is in when he can no longer effectively resist. Along with the idea of simultaneous attacks is the rapidity with which these attacks are unleashed.

An overarching objective of parallel warfare is not only to achieve strategic paralysis but to do so quickly. Parallel warfare is accelerated warfare, often referred to as *hyperwar*. By employing it one can reduce casualties (on both sides), reduce resource requirements, maintain support for one's cause (if time is a factor), and prevent the enemy from recovering or taking countermeasures.

Parallel warfare differs greatly from what most people are familiar with—serial or sequential warfare. Under serial warfare targets are attacked in sequence, one after the other. Electrical engineering provides a good example of the differences between serial and parallel warfare. Figure 1 displays two circuits; the first is a serial circuit in which the current must travel through each "target" before proceeding to the next. Meanwhile, on the parallel circuit, the current travels to each target simultaneously (fig. 1).

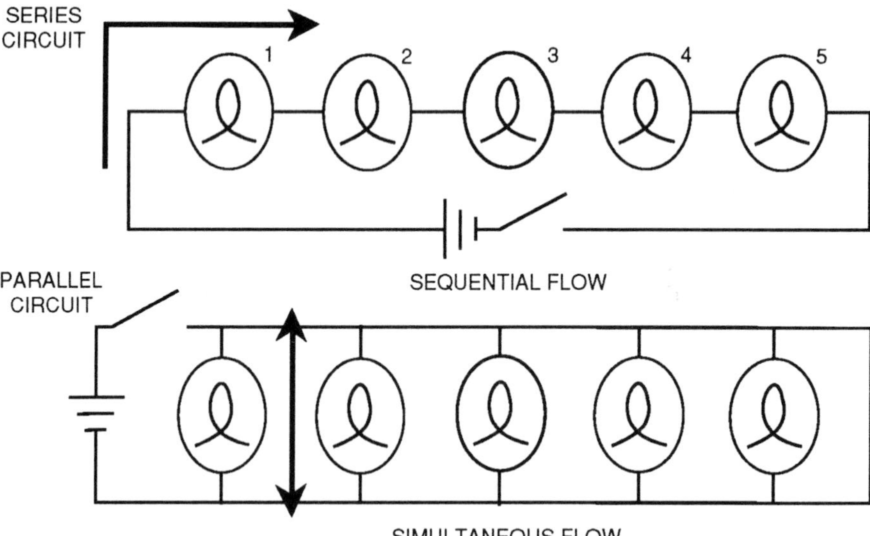

Figure 1. Comparison of series circuit with sequential flow to parallel circuit with simultaneous flow.

Serial warfare has been the primary way of fighting wars throughout history, at least at the strategic level. Obviously, when one looks at single battles, there are numerous instances of the simultaneous employment of forces. The D day landings are a good example. The actual landings on the beaches were near-simultaneous and were coupled with airborne landings, air attacks, naval bombardment, and deception operations. However, the entire Normandy operation was in fact a series of operations with the landings being one part. Additionally, strategic paralysis was not achieved.

Parallel Warfare

The History

Although many of the ideas espoused in parallel warfare such as strategic paralysis, centers of gravity, and decapitation are not new to warfare, the term itself is relatively new. Ever since World War I air-power theorists had championed these ideas in conjunction with the supposed attributes of air power (range, precision, invulnerability, and so on). While men like Giulio Douhet and Gen William ("Billy") Mitchell advocated fleets of bombers attacking vital targets to cripple the enemy's ability to wage war, the practicality of the matter turned out to be something far less.

World War II provides plenty of examples of massive bombing raids against key war-making industries that failed to halt, and in some cases even reduce, the output of military products. While the reasons for these failures are numerous, one of the key factors was a lack of bombing accuracy. As highly touted as the Norden bombsight was, the fact is that high altitude, combined with poor European weather and heavy enemy resistance resulted in poorer-than-expected accuracy. Over half of the bombs dropped by American bombers in Europe during World War II landed more than 3,000 feet from the intended target.[1] The large bomber formations used to enhance survivability sometimes made up for the bombing inaccuracy. Another factor that compounded the accuracy problem was poor battle damage assessment (BDA) capability.

The raids on the ball-bearing factories in Schweinfurt are good examples of these problems. The first raid occurred in August 1943 and resulted in a production drop of 34 percent.

However, due to high American losses and an inability to accurately assess damage, Schweinfurt was not hit for another two months.[2] During those intervening months, the Germans were able to reestablish production rates, and although the follow-up attack in October also did substantial damage and cut production by over 60 percent, the losses incurred by the bomber force (20 percent) were prohibitive and all bombing was halted. As Albert Speer, German minister for production, put it, "As it was, not a tank, plane, or other piece of weaponry failed to be produced because of lack of ball bearings."[3]

This is not to say that the strategic bombing did not have an impact on Germany's conduct of the war. The bombing forced the Germans to redirect resources, disperse industries, and cut consumer production, in order to support war-materiel production. However, the less-than-precise bombing, high-loss rates, poor weather, inconclusive BDA, and changing target priorities (caused initially by the North Atlantic submarine threat and later by D day preparations) all combined to reduce the effectiveness of the campaign.

Strategic bombing did not have the effects envisioned by the original theorists or planners. Much to the relief of the Germans, the previously mentioned factors often resulted in a lack of persistency in attacking so-called vital targets. According to Speer, concentrated attacks on ball-bearing production would have brought armament production to a halt within four months.[4] *The United States Strategic Bombing Surveys* came to the same conclusion regarding several key industries in Germany. The European survey team concluded that continuous attacks against a single industry were crucial for success.[5]

Korea and Vietnam did little to change the nature of "strategic" bombing. Although bombing accuracy improved dramatically, the number of aircraft required to ensure target destruction still prohibited attacking more than one or two target sets (a target set is a target such as an electrical generating plant that has several subtargets or aiming points located within it) at any one time. Towards the end of the Vietnam War, a technological innovation greatly improved bombing accuracy and decreased required sorties per target. That innovation was the laser guided bomb, a subset of a group of bombs referred to as precision guided bombs (PGM).

With these new laser guided bombs, planners and aircrews were able to target and destroy the Paul Doumer Bridge using 32 sorties. That same bridge had previously been attacked by well over 200 sorties without being damaged.[6]

US forces next employed precision weapons against Libya in Operation Eldorado Canyon, hitting several targets in highly populated areas with minimal loss of civilian life. The weapons were used again, in conjunction with the newly revealed stealth fighter, during the invasion of Panama in 1989. The US now had an aircraft, the F-117, that could not only deliver PGMs, but could do so with impunity. Desert Storm planners remembered that lesson.

Using a combination of stealth, precision, and several other important factors, Desert Storm planners unleashed the first true air campaign encompassing the tenants of parallel warfare. Figure 2 shows the difference between a serial air campaign, similar to the strategic bombing of Germany in World War II, and the parallel air campaign seen in the Gulf War (fig. 2). Instead of attacking single-target sets such as ball-bearing factories or aircraft plants, planners could send attacking aircraft and missiles after targets across the spectrum. No target set was immune. Stealth and precision made a big difference, but they were not the only factors.

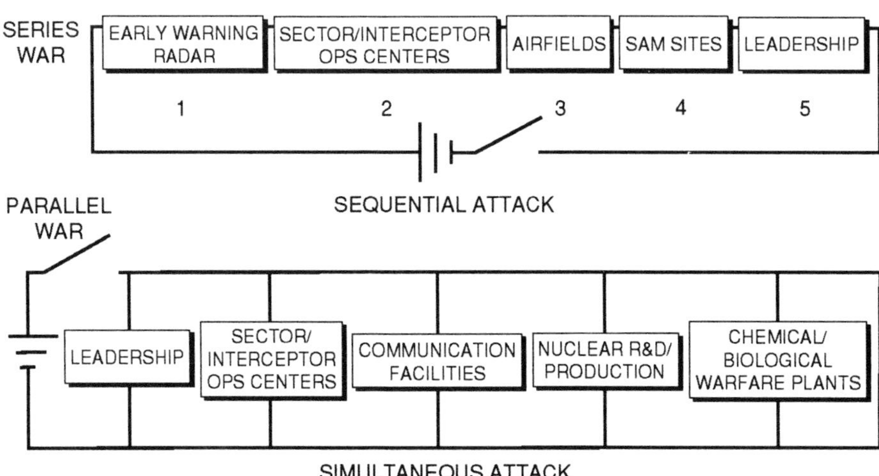

Figure 2. An analogy between types of war and electronic circuits.

Parallel Warfare

Other Factors

Many current air-power advocates believe the Gulf War vindicated the early air-power theorists. As noted air-power historian Richard P. Hallion put it, "Air power execution caught up with air power theory."[7] While this chapter is not included in this book to vindicate the memories of Douhet, Mitchell, and Trenchard, it is included to espouse the benefits of parallel warfare.

Most observers of the Gulf War (military and civilian) saw parallel warfare being employed without realizing what it was. At the time of this writing, there was a plethora of information concerning the air war in the Gulf, to include discussions on PGMs, F-117s, and strategic targets; but the term *parallel warfare* was conspicuously absent. The previously mentioned term *hyperwar* was seen a couple of times as was the term *simultaneity*.

Parallel warfare is what the world saw unleashed against Iraq during the first days of the air campaign. It was an attempt by coalition air forces to achieve strategic paralysis against Iraq. Centers of gravity were identified and then attacked in parallel. Figure 3 illustrates how target sets are serviced during parallel warfare versus serial warfare (fig. 3). Note that in a parallel campaign targets from each set are attacked from the beginning while under serial campaigning, one target set is serviced before the next one is fragged.

A discussion on the Iraqi integrated air defenses (IAD) provides a good example of how this campaign differed from the past. Prior to the Gulf War, IADs were normally among the first targets (if not *the* first) hit in an air campaign. Destroying or degrading enemy IADs allowed friendly aircraft to operate in a less-threatening environment. Using stealth, precision, and electronic-warfare (EW) assets to attack the Iraqi IADs during the opening hours of Desert Storm did exactly the same thing but accounted for only a portion of the initial onslaught. Targets of all types were attacked in conjunction with air defenses.

Whether they called it parallel warfare or not, Americans liked what they saw. The air campaign against Saddam Hussein and

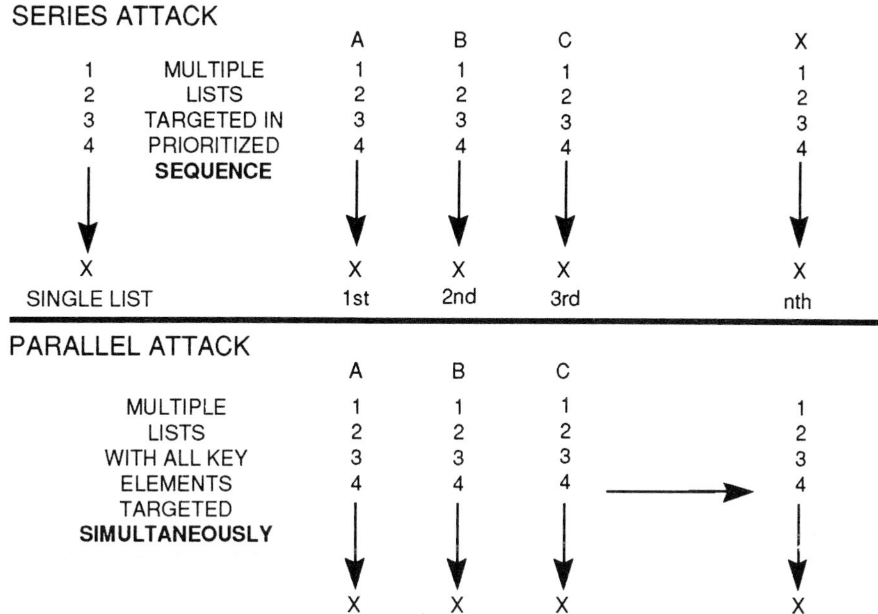

Figure 3. An analogy between types of military attacks and electronic circuits.

his armed forces was rapid, precise, and massive, and it resulted in minimum casualties. Although the air war lasted a total of 39 days (nine longer than planned), it was obvious to the world that a vast number of targets was destroyed and damaged in the first few days of the battle. It was also obvious that great pains were taken to ensure that civilian casualties were kept to a minimum, as was collateral damage to neighboring structures. Additionally, coalition losses were well below even the most optimistic prewar prediction.

As with all of our past wars the most recent war sets the example for our next battle; the Gulf War is no exception. The surgical application of air power with minimum loss of American (and it now appears Iraqi) lives is the new standard. Americans have never been "fond" of battle casualties, but their tolerance for losses has been diminishing since the end of World War II. The most recent example of this intolerance, and its consequence, was the death of 18 Army Rangers in Somalia, the public outcry that followed, and the subsequent decision by the president to remove all troops by 31 March 1994.

Parallel Warfare
What Makes It Work?

Although the underlying ideas behind parallel warfare have existed since the first air-power theorists started theorizing, technology has been the limiting factor in fully employing the concept. From World War I until just recently, bombing accuracy has limited the number of targets that could be attacked simultaneously. Precision weapons have increased that number by a wide margin. The reason for this is simple—probability of kill (PK). As already mentioned, lack of bombing accuracy during World War II resulted in half of the bombs falling over 3,000 feet from the intended target. Even with improved accuracy of 100-foot CEPs (circular error probable—a circle whose center is the intended impact point and whose radius is the distance in which one-half of all bombs will drop) during Korea and Vietnam, target destruction required numerous sorties. Large force packages were sent after each target set in order to ensure a high PK. The Paul Doumer Bridge was a good example. Hundreds of sorties flown over several years failed to do what 32 aircraft accomplished in a few days.

Because the CEPs of current precision weapons are normally in the 10-foot range, hitting the intended aiming point is almost a certainty. If planners know that an aircraft attacking a microwave tower has a 90 percent chance of rendering it unusable, then there is no reason to use more than one aircraft to attack that target (unless the planners need a 99 percent probability of destruction, in which case they would most likely have to send two aircraft). That is still a huge difference from having to send 300 B-17s after the ball-bearing factories at Schweinfurt, or 44 F-105s and F-4s after the steel mills at Thai Nguyen.

Desert Storm provides an excellent example of how precision weapons can "multiply" the attacking force. This particular example compares the abilities of non-PGM-capable aircraft flying out of Turkey with PGM-capable aircraft flying out of Saudi Arabia. While 12 non-PGM-capable F-111Es dropped an impressive total of 168 Mk-82s (500-pound gravity bombs) on two separate targets, a combination of 12 PGM-capable F-117s and F-111Fs was able to attack 26 different targets while dropping just a total of 28 precision bombs.[8] Because precision weapons offer such a high probability of hitting the target, so many more targets can be hit using the same number of aircraft; a critical factor in parallel warfare.

A note of caution before proceeding with this discussion. The previous paragraph describes the capabilities of a like number of precision-capable aircraft with nonprecision-capable aircraft. A benefit of precision-capable aircraft is the reduced requirement for numbers. If 12 aircraft can attack 26 different targets, then six can attack 12 or 13 targets, three can attack six targets, and so on. However, if the number of aircraft is reduced significantly, at some point the benefit vanishes and becomes a liability. The ability to prosecute parallel warfare vanishes with the diminishing numbers.

Precision weapons are a key and necessary element of parallel warfare, but they are not the only element. Another critical component of parallel warfare is stealth. Stealth is the ability of an object to avoid radar detection. The more stealthy something is, the less likely it will be detected by radar. Our stealth aircraft, the F-117, displayed built-in ability to slip through Iraqi air defenses without being detected. In over 1,200 combat sorties flown, most of them in the heavily defended vicinity of Baghdad, not a single F-117 was hit, let alone shot down.[9]

This is not to say that the Air Force's stealth aircraft could have conducted parallel warfare on their own. Even with their ability to attack individual targets with individual aircraft, the F-117s were far too few in number. However, their ability to fly the hostile skies over Iraq with impunity allowed F-117 pilots to strike not only the most heavily defended targets but the command and control portion of the Iraqi air defense system as well. Coupled with the work of nonstealthy EW assets, this reduced losses to coalition air forces while rendering the whole air defense system ineffective. Once that occurred, any coalition aircraft flying at medium or high altitude became "stealthy" at night. F-111Fs with no steathiness at all were able to drop their PGMs in a much more conducive environment thus increasing their effectiveness.

While the combination of precision weapons and stealth aircraft renders parallel warfare a possibility, there are several other factors that ensure its success. Air campaign planning, targeting theory, intelligence, aircraft-mission-capable rates, electronic-warfare assets, and logistics all play a part in the parallel warfare equation.

Loading F-117s with PGMs and launching them at strategic targets does not make parallel warfare. An effective plan is necessary in order to execute the strategy. Objectives need to be determined, intelligence information obtained on potential targets, centers of gravity identified, targeting (deciding what level of damage needs to be inflicted on a target) accomplished, and a master attack plan (MAP) devised. The MAP details how to execute the air campaign.

Campaign objectives should relate (and be subordinate) to the political objective(s). After determining objectives, planners can then look for targets to attack whose destruction/damage will help meet the objectives. Remember, the overarching objective of parallel warfare is strategic paralysis. In any scenario where strategic paralysis is an objective, certain targets such as command and control, electrical power, transportation, and so on, should be attacked. Any number of planning tools, such as Col John Warden's five-ring model, can be used to help identify centers of gravity and potential targets.

Warden's model breaks down a system, whether it be the enemy country, an enemy's military forces, or even an individual enemy soldier, into five separate categories or rings. The innermost ring is the leadership (to include communications) followed in sequential order by the mission essentials (electricity, oil, and so on), infrastructure (such as roads, railroads, and bridges), population, and fielded forces. Warden contends that the most effective and easiest way to attack the enemy is to target the inner-most rings first. In fact, effective employment of air power against the inner rings can render attacks against the enemy forces unnecessary. This is the essence of parallel warfare—hitting selected targets in the inner-most rings to force the enemy to do our will.

After identifying targets, further information about them must be collected to determine aiming points and the desired level of damage (targeting). Aiming points are critical because without effective knowledge of where bombs are going to do the most damage (or at least the desired damage), we are effectively back to square one. For instance, without good intelligence on an aircraft factory, planners would have to virtually blanket the whole facility with weapons in order to stop or slow down production. However, with the proper information those same planners could send one PGM-laden aircraft or a cruise missile after the one critical room in the one critical building and achieve their desired results. While some of this information will come from the intelligence community, a lot of it will come from subject matter experts like electrical engineers, communication specialists, and civil engineers, and still more of it will come from contractors who built the factories or installed the communications systems.

Just as important as determining aiming points is determining the desired level of damage or desired effects. In the past this would often equate to destruction of the target, but as Col Dave Deptula, one of the central planners for the air campaign in Desert Storm, notes targeting theory for parallel warfare has changed the equation.[10] The realization that total target destruction is not always necessary, coupled with an ability to better access target degradation, means that planners are now looking for desired effects versus level of destruction. Effects-driven targeting is another means of reducing weapon systems per target, allowing planners to attack more targets and increasing one's ability to induce strategic paralysis.

For instance, if an objective is to cut off the flow of heavy equipment (tanks, self-propelled artillery, and so on) to the front, and planners know that to destroy a bridge requires four 2,000-pound bombs, but to damage it so that heavy equipment cannot traverse it requires only two 2,000-pound bombs, then the sortie(s) required to deliver those other two bombs can be flown against additional targets. During World War II US planners believed that crippling German ball-bearing production would in turn severely degrade war-materiel production. They determined that production could be cut 43 percent by destroying three of the five ball-bearing factories in Schweinfurt. In order to achieve that level of destruction, 230 B-17s were launched on the August 1943 mission.[11] If planners had known the location of certain critical components of the ball-bearing manufacturing process at Schweinfurt, fewer bombers would have been needed. The other aircraft might have been used to attack ball-bearing plants in other parts of Germany.

Once objectives, centers of gravity, and targets are identified, then planners can construct their MAP. This is the operational level plan—the "big picture." The MAP is the basis from which the daily air tasking orders (ATO) are derived.

The role of intelligence has already been mentioned, but its importance cannot be overemphasized. Good intelligence is critical to the success of parallel warfare. Without it, centers of gravity may not be identified, vital targets missed or inappropriate targets included, and targeting might be a crapshoot that eats up valuable assets and renders parallel warfare impossible. Additionally, effective battle damage assessment is important to overall campaign management. Poor BDA can create unnecessary refragging that again reduces available resources.

While precision weapons and stealth aircraft are obvious by-products of technology, another important aspect of technology's role in parallel warfare is aircraft mission capable (MC) rates (the percentage of aircraft available to fly combat sorties). High MC rates equate to high sortie rates that afford air campaign planners the luxury of hitting more targets. Air Force MC rates during Desert Storm were at an all-time high, exceeding already impressive peacetime rates by more than 5 percent.[12] The Air Force's overall MC rate was an astonishing 92.4 percent.[13] The technology involved in designing, building, and maintaining aircraft like the F-15, F-16, A-10, and F-15E resulted in unprecedented MC rates, which, in turn, resulted in the sortie capacity needed to execute parallel warfare.

Electronic warfare is another important factor in the prosecution of parallel warfare. Although the F-117s slipped through the Iraqi air defense system during the Gulf War, and the air and sea launched cruise missiles flew underneath most of it, all other aircraft were forced to face the threat (albeit in a diminished state) head on. Electronic warfare assets such as the EC-130, EF-111, and EA-6 were crucial to their success and survival. The jamming of command and control nets and ground-based air defense radars, coupled with the employment of lethal-suppression aircraft like the F-4G and F/A-18, and the F-117's bombing of air defense centers and communication nodes allowed the nonstealthy attack aircraft (the vast majority) to complete their missions. This success, as evidenced by the minimal coalition aircraft losses attributed to surface-to-air missiles, was crucial to the air campaign plan. Minimal aircraft losses meant maximum numbers of aircraft available for sortie generation, which meant maximum numbers of targets hit. Until every combat aircraft in the US military is stealthy, EW assets will be critical to the success of parallel warfare.

Logistics is the final key factor important to parallel warfare. Logistics is further divided into three subfactors—parts, air refueling, and weapons. Parts are pretty straightforward and relate to the discussion of MC rates. An important aspect of maintaining high MC rates is parts availability. Skilled maintenance personnel cannot overcome a lack of spare parts. To be able to generate (MC rate) the number of sorties needed to prosecute parallel warfare, an effective supply system is essential.

Another often overlooked aspect of logistics is air refueling. One of the obvious effects of the current drawdown and pullback of US military forces is that in most plausible scenarios we are going to have to deploy a fair distance before we start to employ the majority of our forces. Europe is relatively close compared to many potential hot spots. One of the important lessons of Desert Storm was how critical air refueling assets are—not only to get forces to the area of operations but to sustain them once in place. Except for aircraft based and operating near the Saudi/Kuwaiti border, every combat aircraft that flew required aerial refueling.[14] Without that capability, sortie generation rates again would have suffered. Adequate air refueling assets are critical to parallel warfare.

The final subfactor under logistics is weapons. The importance of PGMs to parallel warfare has already been established. The nice thing about PGMs is that because of their accuracy, you don't need nearly as many total weapons to attack the enemy. A caveat here is that planners need to ensure they have the weapons when they do need them. Precision weapons will not be the suitable choice for all targets, but when they are the suitable choice, they need to be available. Prepositioning and early identification of requirements are important.

This portion of the discussion covered important factors in the parallel warfare equation. Precision, stealth, planning, targeting theory, intelligence, aircraft MC rates, EW, and logistics all play an important part in the prosecution of parallel warfare. Obviously, there are still other factors such as cruise missiles, remotely piloted vehicles (RPV), basing, and command and control, to name a few, that might be important to effectively execute parallel warfare. The point of this section is to highlight some of the more important factors in making parallel warfare work—the ingredients. Different scenarios might make several of these factors moot and introduce entirely new ones, but for the campaign planner, knowing what makes parallel warfare work is critical to success.

Parallel Warfare

The Attributes

Having defined parallel warfare and described its ingredients, it is now important to discuss its attributes. Parallel warfare's prime attribute is its embodiment of the principles of war. Students of military theory should love parallel warfare because it combines so many of the principles of war into one neat package. The objective(s) is identified early in the planning process. Next comes the offensive, proactive, and dictating the pace of operations. Mass is in evidence not by numbers of aircraft or weapons, but by the impressive number of direct hits on targets. Economy of force is obvious in the large number of targets attacked by individual or small number of aircraft. Unity of effort is ensured by the Joint Force Air Component Commander (JFACC). Finally, surprise is a product of not only good planning but the employment of stealth aircraft, cruise missiles, and a combination of the aforementioned principles.

Another attribute of parallel warfare is cost, both in lives and resources. The objective of parallel warfare is to hit the enemy's centers of gravity simultaneously and en masse to strategically paralyze him, creating a situation where he can no longer resist. If successful, then not only will friendly losses be low, but the conflict should be over quickly, further reducing losses on both sides. PGMs will ensure minimum collateral damage, reduced enemy lives lost, and reduced resources required (both in weapons platforms and bombs).

Parallel warfare maximizes the use of advanced technologies. Stealth aircraft, precision weapons, global positioning system (GPS), low-altitude navigation targeting infrared for night (LANTIRN), and cruise missiles are just a few of the many technological gadgets that on their own pose formidable obstacles to an enemy, and when combined with a strategy, overwhelm an enemy.

Because parallel warfare limits damage to an enemy in terms of lives and resources, it can actually make for a better peace; a point often overlooked in past conflicts. During Desert Storm, the goal was not to destroy Iraq but to paralyze it. Upon returning to Baghdad after the war, one journalist noted how little "World War II urban destruction" there was.[15] Peter Arnett reported that Iraqis in most areas of Baghdad ignored the air raid sirens because they knew they were in no danger.[16] Saddam might not have cared that we were very selective in our targeting, but it appears the Iraqi people did and that might be an important factor after Saddam is long gone. The overarching objective of any conflict should be a better peace, and reducing the price paid by the belligerent nation may be important later on.

Public support is a fickle thing, but it is a well-documented fact that Americans do not like protracted wars or heavy losses. The Vietnam War illustrated both of these points well. Parallel warfare offers the national leadership an instrument that, when properly used, can greatly reduce the length of conflict and lives lost. The Gulf War proved that point.

Parallel Warfare

The Problems and Limitations

Just as it has positive attributes, parallel warfare has negative aspects as well. For instance, parallel warfare is highly dependent on stealth and precision, a factor that leaves most nations incapable of pursuing it as a form of warfare (perhaps another positive aspect for the US). Stealth can be a hard sell even in relatively well-off countries like the US. Witness the fight over funding for the B-2, an $825-million bomber whose planned purchase has shrunk from 132 to 20, and is still in jeopardy.[17]

Another problem with parallel warfare is that it requires a certain number of assets to prosecute. Most modern-day countries contain roughly 500 key targets (Iraq was assessed to have just under 400).[18] Four to six aiming points for each target equates to between 2,000 and 3,000 strategic aiming points. In order to hit all of these aiming points in a relatively short time frame, a lot of air-power assets are required. Realizing the limited hard-target kill capabilities of cruise missiles and the limited numbers of stealth aircraft available, it is obvious that quite a few nonstealthy aircraft will be involved in the campaign. This not only limits the number of countries that can employ this strategy, but it means the US must be very smart during the defense drawdown to ensure this capability is maintained. Comparing the numbers from the latest Bottom Up Review with the plan to fight two major regional conflicts near simultaneously might reveal a gap in our capability to fight them using parallel warfare.

One of the key factors of parallel warfare is an effective master attack plan—the road map for success. Two critical attributes of the MAP are a good assessment of enemy capabilities and good intelligence concerning target locations and physical characteristics. Both of these elements require often difficult-to-get-but-necessary information. Assessing the enemy's capabilities is not a job for the layman. Subject-matter experts are critical to the planning cell for both enemy assessment and information on possible targets. Time-sensitive data collected from national, theater, and tactical resources has to be analyzed and assessed for possible use. In the long run, the intelligence community is as important to prosecuting parallel warfare as are air-power assets because without the information it provides, the weapons revert to expensive gravity bombs.

Another related, but probably more contentious problem, is bomb damage assessment. Historically, aircrew reports have exaggerated the effectiveness of combat missions. For instance, during the Commando Hunt bombing campaign in South Vietnam in 1968, crews reported destroying over 20,000 trucks along the Ho Chi Minh highway. At that same time, the CIA estimated that the North Vietnamese Army possessed only 6,000 trucks.[19] Often compounding the exaggerated mission reports is the requirement by intelligence agencies for solid proof of target damage (normally in the form of a reconnaissance photo). The problem now is that even though we have more accurate weapons, intelligence personnel still demand concrete proof. Coupled with the fact that a 2,000-pound bomb through the airshaft of a building or the side of an aircraft shelter doesn't always reveal the extent of internal damage, it is easy to see why the conflict continues. However, this problem needs to be solved. Refragging sufficiently damaged targets is a waste of resources.

The physical environment can be another source of trouble for parallel warfare. Even as "user-friendly" as the environment was for coalition air forces during the Gulf War, the initial air campaign was extended for nine days due to poor weather. Move the conflict to almost anywhere else in the world and the potential problems with not only weather, but terrain, foliage, and various other factors can complicate the parallel warfare equation.

Finally, a major problem with parallel warfare is that it sounds so parochial. There is an obvious air-power smell to it and beyond that a very strong taste of Air Force. The parallel warfare described in this chapter is of the aerial type, but the basic precepts of parallel warfare—simultaneous attacks against key targets to induce strategic paralysis—can be employed by other forces as well. One could make a strong argument that the invasion of Panama (conducted primarily by ground forces) in December 1989 was parallel warfare. At the tactical level, parallel warfare is routine in all mediums. The point being made here is that parallel warfare is a viable means of strategically attacking an enemy and quickly bringing him to the negotiating table.

Against a modern, industrialized, and well-armed opponent, parallel warfare through air power makes sense. On the other hand there are instances, such as guerrilla wars, where parallel warfare may not be an option. Additionally, negating or hindering any of the previously mentioned "how-to-make-it-work" factors could impact the effectiveness, and even the viability of parallel warfare (refer to the next essay for a detailed explanation of how to counter parallel warfare).

Why Is Parallel Warfare Important to US Armed Forces?

There are two very important reasons why parallel warfare is important to US armed forces. First, even though the US public is often accused of having a short memory, it will remember certain aspects of Desert Storm such as the massive air war, precision weapons, low casualties (on both sides), limited collateral damage, stealth, and the relatively short time it took to fight the war. All of these aspects are directly related to parallel warfare. Desert Storm set the standard for the next conflict we may find ourselves in. The armed forces will be expected to do as well and probably better. Therefore, parallel warfare, its attributes and problems, should be studied and restudied to ensure we are prepared to properly employ it during our next conflict.

The second reason why parallel warfare is important to US armed forces is because during the defense drawdown it offers a viable means of reducing force structure and requirements while maintaining capability. Precision weapons allow for fewer aircraft/weapons per target. Stealth aircraft require fewer support aircraft (EW assets, escort aircraft, and so on). Both of these factors reduce the logistics requirements for the entire force while increasing its effectiveness and limiting exposure.

Conclusion

The purpose of this chapter has been fourfold: to define what parallel warfare is; to describe how it is accomplished; to discuss its attributes, problems, and limitations; and to discuss why it is important to US armed forces. Parallel warfare is the simultaneous attack of vital enemy targets to achieve strategic paralysis. An enemy is strategically paralyzed when he can no longer resist our will. Obviously, strategic paralysis can be achieved through means other than parallel warfare (witness Germany at the end of World War II), but the goal is to do it quickly, "cleanly," and with minimum losses.

The how-to of parallel warfare includes stealth, precision weapons, and prodigious planning coupled with effects versus destruction targeting, a massive intelligence effort, high mission-capable rates, effective EW systems, and special logistics capabilities in the areas of air refueling, spare parts, and bomb supply. Not all of these factors will be critical in every scenario, and in some cases, other factors will become important. For the present and near future stealth and PGMs appear to be necessary. An effective plan will always be a necessity. The other factors coupled with such things as cruise missiles, basing, and RPVs are scenario-dependent.

The main attribute of parallel warfare is the way it embraces the principles of war in an attempt to quickly obtain strategic paralysis. If successful, then the conflict should be less costly in both lives and resources on both sides of the battle lines. These factors normally equate to the maintenance of public support, an important factor in modern conflicts. Additionally, by limiting damage to the enemy, there is a better possibility of winning the peace. Finally, parallel warfare maximizes advanced technologies, an achievement which in turn plays an important part in all the other attributes.

Every story has two sides and the parallel-warfare tale is no different. The problems of parallel warfare are directly linked with the capabilities required to execute it. This type warfare is very dependent on stealth and precision weapons. Also, it requires a certain number of nonstealthy assets to ensure success. During the planning phase, there is a critical need for effective assessment of enemy capabilities as well as good intelligence information on target locations and characteristics. Additionally, during the prosecution of the air campaign, there is an essential need for effective BDA. The physical environment can hamper the effectiveness of parallel warfare. Finally, the whole idea of parallel warfare and how it is defined relays a perception of parochialism.

The American public liked what it saw during the Gulf War. It was quick, effective, and relatively low cost with minimum collateral damage. The standard has been set. Parallel warfare will not be the answer to every conflict the US engages in. What is important, especially as our military forces continue to decline in size, is that we understand what parallel warfare is and what it can do. With one-hundredth the bombs dropped in Vietnam and many fewer lives lost, we managed to do in less than two months in Iraq what we totally failed to do in over 11 years in Vietnam.[20] We can't afford to miss that lesson.

Notes

1. Secretary of the Air Force Donald B. Rice, *The Air Force and U.S. National Security: Global Reach—Global Power*, white paper (Washington, D.C.: Department of the Air Force, June 1992), 12.
2. Albert Speer, *Inside the Third Reich* (New York: Macmillan Publishing Company, 1970), 285.
3. Ibid., 286.
4. Ibid., 285.
5. Franklin D'Olier, *The United States Strategic Bombing Survey (European War)*, 30 September 1945, 26.
6. A. J. C. Lavalle, *The Tale of Two Bridges* (Washington, D.C.: Government Printing Office, 1974), 84.
7. Richard P. Hallion, *Storm over Iraq* (Washington, D.C. and London: Smithsonian Institution Press, 1992), 5.
8. *Gulf War Air Power Survey Summary (GWAPSS)*, 29 March 1993, 211.
9. Ibid., 152.
10. David A. Deptula, "Parallel Warfare: What is it?" (Briefing at Air Command and Staff College, Maxwell Air Force Base, Alabama, 6 January 1993), slide 19.
11. Thomas M. Coffey, *Decision over Schweinfurt* (New York: David McKay Company, Inc., 1977), 3.
12. Hallion, 197.
13. Ibid.
14. GWAPSS, 195.
15. Milton Viorst, "Report from Baghdad," *The New Yorker* 67, no. 18, (24 June 1991): 58.
16. Ibid., 199.
17. Susan H. H. Young, "Gallery of USAF Weapons," *Air Force Magazine*, May 1992, 139.
18. Hallion, 143 and 267.
19. Earl H. Tilford, Jr., *Setup: What the Air Force Did in Vietnam and Why* (Maxwell Air Force Base, Ala.: Air University Press, June 1991), 184.
20. James W. Canaan, "Lesson Number One," *Air Force Magazine*, June 1991, 29.

Parallel Warfare
Anticipating the Enemy's Response

Richard M. Kessel

Parallel warfare, the ability to simultaneously attack strategic as well as operational and tactical targets and thus cause a strategic paralysis of the Iraqi forces, was displayed by the US-led coalition in the Gulf War. The US military must anticipate the future enemy's response to parallel warfare to ensure similar success. Expecting the same outcome from parallel warfare in the next military conflict without anticipating updated counters from future adversaries is to track toward defeat. Future adversaries are analyzing the performance of the coalition forces in the Gulf and learning from the failure of the Iraqi forces. This analysis will reveal centers of gravity, or possible weaknesses, that future adversaries can exploit in order to reduce the effectiveness of parallel warfare.

Future threats to parallel warfare can be divided into political, technological, and operational responses. Although the combination of these categories provides a limitless set of options, this study focuses on several of the most likely responses that provide the biggest challenge. Furthermore, counters to parallel warfare can normally be divided into defensive or offensive measures. An understanding of these may provide a clearer view of the enemy's operational strategy.

Political Response

Political alliances and military coalitions formed for political objectives are important to any war effort and can mean the difference between victory and defeat. A coalition formed to resolve a temporary conflict can become a center of gravity susceptible to an enemy's political influence. The importance of coalitions formed to resolve military conflicts is increasing. The end of the cold war brought about new budget priorities for most of the world's industrialized countries, which means decreased military spending. The resulting downsized military forces of the US and her allies means reduced military capabilities; therefore, cooperation among nations will be the key to successful military operations under fiscal restraint. The synergistic effect of combining several countries' monetary and/or military resources, including logistical support and forward basing rights, may be required to conduct parallel warfare in the future. For this reason, the US should expect attempts from any potential adversary to degrade the ability of the US to form military coalitions to meet political objectives.

The concept of undermining alliances, or coalitions by exploiting a vulnerability goes back many years. Sun Tzu talked about dividing the enemy's allies and disrupting his alliances.[1] There are several disadvantages to coalition warfare that our adversaries could exploit. Consensus is difficult to reach, which may mean compromising objectives among the coalition. Different political agendas can change the level of commitment. Additionally, differences in culture and language can be a significant hindrance to coordination and interoperability. For example, the coalition in Desert Storm presented a wide array of military hardware and capabilities; however, not everything was easy to use and coordinate. The coalition command structure, although under the overall command of Gen H. Norman Schwarzkopf, was a complicated structure with Arab forces actually under the command of Saudi general Khalid bin Sultan bin Abdul-Aziz.[2] Missions had to be doled out based on political restrictions because the Egyptians and Syrians would not fight in Iraq. This command structure, along with cultural and religious differences among the coalition, made a promising target for Iraq. Although they were not successful in turning the coalition against the US, the Iraqis tried by attacking Israel with Scud missiles to bring Israel into the war. Had Israel made a counterattack, it is likely that the coalition would have lost the Arab members. This could have been a large loss to the Americans if the forward bases in Saudi Arabia had been unavailable. Also, the forward basing in other Arab countries, as well as the overflight rights that reduced the distance of logistical lines, could have been lost. This would have slowed down the tempo of the coalition operations by adding distance and time to combat sorties, making less sorties possible. This reduces the effectiveness of parallel warfare. The effort to affect adversely a coalition or alliance will normally be a defensive measure—in other words, a political action designed to deny the US some form of military support or increased capability based on support projected from a coalition. The important lesson here is that an alliance or coalition can be the cornerstone of a military strategy and that we can expect these unions to be attacked in the future. But why is an alliance or coalition important to parallel warfare?

A look at Desert Storm will show the impact a coalition can have and will highlight the advantages of military coalitions. In August 1990, Iraqi forces under the command of Saddam Hussein invaded Kuwait and overthrew the government. Almost immediately, US air and ground forces deployed into the region. What would have happened had the US not had the cooperation of many other countries—some like Syria that were not normally allied with the US? The answer is certainly a less efficient effort at parallel warfare. The basing rights in Saudi Arabia may actually have been the most important single asset in reversing Iraq's aggression.

The US received direct support, troops, and ships from 36 countries during the Gulf War. Additionally, the US received basing and overflight rights from numerous countries.[3] The result was that the US-led coalition gained a considerable advantage in basing and supply lines compared to the alternative of basing outside the region. The forward bases in Saudi Arabia and Turkey allowed air operations the luxury of relatively short flights and quick turns. This basing in the region provided the coalition forces the luxury of multiple missions per day by each aircraft. The ability for multiple missions per day translates directly into keeping up a constant pressure, one of the keys to parallel warfare. Also, the logistical lines inside the theater were shorter, reducing the problem of resupply. Furthermore, shorter logistical lines offered a reduced opportunity to the Iraqis to attack these soft targets. Had Iraq succeeded in denying these bases to the coalition forces, and to the US in particular, the result would have been fewer flights per day, which could have prolonged the war. Finally, the biggest advantage of this coalition may turn out to be a forum for increased cooperation in the future. In summary, would the US have been able to conduct the same air campaign had those forces been made to operate from their home bases?

The Vietnam War is a prime example of a belligerent politically achieving military-type objectives by influencing the public opinion and actions of the adversary's people at home and also the opinion of its allies. The US continually held back from a full bombing campaign primarily due to public opinion. Close allies of the US questioned the Vietnam War and were concerned that a large-scale bombing campaign would lead to escalation. This allowed the North Vietnamese to prosecute the war for years without having to endure the full combat air power of the US. The lesson here is that our adversaries will try to affect the opinions of the American people and our allies. Our free society allows for this type of political warfare. The danger of parallel warfare lies in its turning public opinion against overwhelming commitment prior to armed conflict, not after the fact as in Vietnam. Parallel warfare is designed to work best when overwhelming force is used. Even if parallel warfare would not have been effective in Vietnam, the fact remains that public opinion was used to aid the enemy. For this reason, we should expect future adversaries to attempt to affect public opinion negatively so as to reduce our commitment to the use of military force and resources.

The Gulf War had other, far-reaching, political effects. The most profound was on the former Soviet Union, and the current Russia. As early as March 1991, Soviet defense minister Dmitry Yazov stated that the Iraqi air defense system "failed in most cases" and "what happened in Kuwait necessitates a review of our attitude to the country's entire air defense system."[4] This review is important because the Iraqi military forces were almost entirely equipped and trained by the former Soviet Union. The Russian response to parallel warfare is important for several reasons. It's not that the Russians will be our expected threat in the future but more that their response is a calculated military answer to war in the future. Therefore, this response can be expected to be shared by other potential adversaries. The Desert Storm experience has shown the Russians that US technology complements the strategy of parallel warfare for the first time. The offensive strategy of a preemptive strike seems to hold the best option for success in countering parallel warfare, assuming that war is inevitable. According to Professor John Erickson, director of defense studies at Edinburgh University, "The Russians have seen the future and it works. It has caused them to think again. They want to restore overt offensive capability; they argue it can not be caged."[5]

Other countries could adapt this philosophy as well. If the political decision is made to enter into a conflict, then any future adversary will benefit from attacking the US in a preemptive manner. For example, General Schwarzkopf was concerned that the initial influx of aircraft into Saudi Arabia was vulnerable to attack from the air once they were parked on the ramps.[6] Striking these forces while they were marshaling would have been a blow to the conduct of parallel warfare. It's important to note that this kind of attack, once the decision for war is reached, could be as simple as individuals with satchel charges attacking parked aircraft before a combat launch capability is reached. Therefore, the US should expect offensive strikes prior to being ready to conduct offensive warfare.

The last political response to parallel warfare is a result of the strategic effects that advanced conventional munitions had in Desert Storm. The Russians contend that when political events preceding war become irreversible, a preemptive strike that may include weapons of mass destruction may be the only viable defense.[7] The link between advanced conventional munitions and a nuclear response is the strategic effects of the conventional munitions that mirror the effects of nuclear weapons. This link means that the US may have to contend with weapons of mass destruction even when the US plans on using only conventional weapons.

Technological Response

The technological response to parallel warfare will be primarily designed to dilute the US superiority in technology. These can be either low- or high-technology responses. The ability of a country to field a technologically sophisticated military force, one roughly equivalent to the US in capability, will usually dictate the type of response to expect. This capability is usually associated with economically advanced countries with a significant industrial base. Although all that is required is the ability to procure this technology, having the capability to produce it at least ensures that it is available. This is important only in that this economic power will give some advance warning as to how a country will respond to parallel warfare. This must also be tempered with the objectives of any future adversary. Limited objectives will usually mean limited response. This can be very different from a country that is fighting for survival or protecting a vital national interest. First, let us analyze the country that has limited technology at its disposal.

The high technology used for parallel warfare, based on information and command and control systems, is not necessarily good for conducting operations against low-technology forces. This means that the technology used to find hardened aircraft shelters and then destroy those shelters with precision guided munitions is not always adaptable to fighting low-technology systems. For example, North Vietnam fought against a vastly superior US military. However, North Vietnam was able to counter many of the technological advantages the US held by using virtually no advanced technology. People carrying goods on their backs or bicycles instead of trucks can be a suitable alternative if the amount of supplies required is low. Trucks and other motorized vehicles provide a ready target for advanced conventional munitions, but people and mules do not. There will almost certainly be fewer relevant targets for advanced conventional munitions in a low-technology society versus a highly industrialized country.

Communications can be critical in war. However, radio and satellite communications can be affected through electronic warfare. Simple underground telephone lines are easy to use, easy to repair, and may be difficult to render ineffective. Separate communication lines provided for military use, distinct from civilian telephone interchanges, may be effective. Communications by messenger, such as audiotaped instructions, may be expected to counter the electronic warfare spectrum of the US and other advanced nations. Lower technology communications may be slower but are more immune to destruction or interruption.

Deception and camouflage are relatively inexpensive and can be very effective. For example, during Desert Storm, the Iraqis made use of deception to reduce the effectiveness of coalition airstrikes, enhance survivability, destabilize the coalition, and increase uncertainty about their intentions. Overall, Iraq met with some amount of success in their deception program.[8] They deployed decoys, smoke, nets, fake bomb craters, and fake buildings to counter the coalition efforts. Also, they used political disinformation to confuse the coalition. These deception techniques were somewhat successful in complicating the coalition effort, but they were not designed with the modern concept of parallel warfare in mind.[9] The Iraqis were unprepared for the extent, as well as the success, of the military effort of the US-led coalition. The next adversary will realize that deception can play an important role in defeating the technology used in conducting modern parallel warfare.

Finally, mobility can also be used to an advantage against a technologically superior adversary. The Iraqis used mobility to hide their Scud missiles with a good deal of success. The mobility of these Scuds caused political difficulties and tied up a good number of coalition assets that could have been used against other targets. The fact that mobility caused the coalition problems will not be lost on any future adversary. Consideration should be given to the fact that the most effective parallel warfare strategy to combat some low-technology forces may actually be the deployment of a unit of Army Rangers. The use of deception and mobility is primarily a defensive strategy used to deny the effective use of technology associated with parallel warfare.

The US should expect an offensive type of response from a technologically advanced adversary. This type of response will correspond more closely with the traditional force-on-force concept that the US has been trained to fight against. These countries are usually the economically powerful nations that have invested in technology along with significant military capabilities. The successful use of parallel warfare in the Gulf War highlighted several concepts that future adversaries will note.

The ability to effectively attack targets ranging from the tactical to the strategic, including the critical industrial elements of a country, is a leap forward in technological capability. The size of the battlefield has been much expanded from previous wars. The response of a well-prepared adversary will not be the traditional army-versus-army pitched battle of the past due in part to the size of the battlefield. Because the success of the coalition effort in Desert Storm was founded on information, precision munitions, and mobility, it is reasonable to assume that these will be the targets of the future. These capabilities, manifested primarily through air power, will attract the majority of the responses from future adversaries that possess high technology.

The first priority will be to attack forward bases before they can be made operational. As discussed earlier, the destructive capability of air power displayed in Desert Storm should convince all nations that stopping the air power of the US before it can be amassed is a better option than allowing it to become an operational entity. Even destroying the bases before the aircraft are deployed would be a useful strategy. The difference between a technologically advanced country and one that is not advanced may be in the method of attack. The technologically advanced country will have air power, missiles, and even sea power available to launch preemptive attacks. One fallout from this will be more resources committed to defense by the US.

The Russians have analyzed the US concept of operations in Desert Storm and have changed their doctrine accordingly. They now highlight the importance of the reconnaissance-strike system that can be used for intelligence and guiding precision weapons. These will all be coordinated with a command and control system utilizing computer technology. It is the ability to process information from intelligence to targeting decisions to actually coordinating the attacks that will define success in the future. We should plan on these technologically advanced adversaries having the means of delivery and the precision weapons to be effective in the future. This compounds the problem of conducting parallel warfare for the US. Now the US has to be concerned with information on a two-way basis. This means getting information/intelligence about the adversary while keeping intentions and capabilities confidential. The extra resources used to defend against this type of adversary will not be available for offensive actions. Because parallel warfare is an offensive strategy, resources kept from offensive missions will reduce the effectiveness of parallel warfare.

These problems will continue to mount when the technology of any future adversary overcomes two large advantages the US maintains over much of the rest of the world: the ability to operate effectively in any weather and at night, and stealth technology. Both of these attributes played a prominent role in Desert Storm. However, as with any technological edge, it will not last. The immunity displayed by the stealth fighter in the Gulf will be overcome. Additionally, stealth technology will be developed by potential adversaries. Again, this will compound the defensive problem of the US and may actually tend to shift the focus of the next war to the defensive.

The Russians are also investing in futuristic weapons such as directed-energy and nonlethal technology.[10] Coupled with space-based systems for intelligence, command and control, and guidance, these new technologies could again throw the concept of parallel warfare back to a stalemate. This would occur if the defensive side could inflict damage to air power at a rate that would nullify the advantage of night operations combined with stealth technology. These problems would be compounded if these weapons are sold to other states.

The other major advantage that highly developed nations have is mobility on a grand scale. Not just the ability to move a few missiles around but the kind of mobility that could move entire divisions if not armies. The total effect of air power, including cruise missiles, has made the committing of ground forces a secondary requirement. The primary defensive consideration for ground forces will be protection from air attack of all kinds. Mobility will allow a greater freedom of action and also will allow ground forces to be stationed far from the front. The concept of mobility will provide ground forces better protection from attack on a small and large scale. Yet, these forces will be able to react as needed to any situation. This is not to imply that ground forces will be obsolete. They may be the best option for military action, especially against a technologically inferior foe where highly technical precision munitions may not have the type of targets available to be used effectively. The point here is that the technology of air power may make the battle lines of old obsolete, and mobility can keep the ground forces from being a target while still allowing them to function as a combat force.

If one assumes that the adversary will attack the forward bases of the US in order to delay the positioning of air power, it will leave one option open to the US for forward basing: the naval surface and subsurface assets. The world's oceans have the advantage of not requiring formal approval or alliances to use them. Sea-launched cruise missiles can launch well out of range of shore threats and can destroy any number of targets with accuracy. For this reason, technologically advanced adversaries will attempt to engage these naval assets. Countries are developing antiship missiles that will have the range to engage naval assets farther out. Additionally, technology will be developed that will locate and then guide precision munitions to engage surface ships. These will be augmented by submarines. Although the US had virtual immunity on the seas during Desert Storm, this will not last for close-in operations. The US should expect these assets to be attacked because of their important role in conducting parallel warfare. The importance of attacking naval assets increases if remote locations are involved and if forward land bases have been denied.

Operational Responses

Parallel warfare is an operational concept whose technological time has arrived. The anticipated operational response to parallel warfare is also linked to the technology possessed by a future adversary. Operational counters can be predicted based on their purpose of denying the US the opportunity to employ advanced technology effectively, including force multipliers. The low-technology enemy will be more defensive in nature, and the high-technology enemy will be able to take an offensive approach.

The adversary that is outclassed in hardware, the low-technology adversary, will be hard pressed to offer a force-on-force response.

However, this does not imply that nothing can be done. On the contrary, one can look at the successes of both Mao Tse-tung and Ho Chi Minh to see that it is possible to neutralize superior technology. The concept here is to expect a defensive response from the fielded forces of this type of enemy. The operational goals of this force will be based on survival, not offensive action to destroy the fielded forces of the US and other high-tech allies. The US center of gravity most likely to be exploited in this case is the will to fight and sustain casualties against an enemy whose goal is simply to survive. Guerrillas and insurgents, supported with little or no formal infrastructure but with the political will to endure physical hardships, can pose a very real problem. The special forces of the future may well be the answer in this type of warfare.

The operational response from a technologically advanced enemy will offer the greatest insight into the weaknesses of parallel warfare. This response, aimed at our vulnerable centers of gravity, will be linked directly to the technological capability of the enemy. As a result of lessons learned from Desert Storm, the Russians have decided that future conflict will be one of maneuver, not position as in the past.[11] This view is representative of future adversaries with advanced technology. There will likely be no hard and fast fronts where armies battle on the ground. Air power, and air superiority in particular, will be paramount if success is to be achieved. Therefore, there are several force multipliers that will be attacked to defeat the effectiveness of parallel warfare.

One such target could be command and control, highlighted with intelligence, which will have to be denied to a large extent. This will mean devising the capability to deny satellite information, and the communication channels to run the war effort on a minute-to-minute basis. Also, the most effective way to manage the operational side of the air war for the US is to manage from airborne warning and control systems (AWACS) due to the link between the command authority, intelligence, and the warfighters. This link is one primary reason that parallel warfare was effective in the Gulf War. These information and command and control platforms will be targeted from both electronic warfare and conventional attack in an attempt to reduce their effectiveness. The concept here is to negate the capability to direct the operations of a combined force.

Another strategic target that could be attacked is the air refueling force. This force is a definite force multiplier, and it gives a significant boost to the conduct of parallel warfare. The combination of information provided by AWACS and the ability to stay airborne long enough to change targets based on updated information is a cornerstone to success. These systems are strategic in nature and will likely be attacked by any adversary that has the means. They are important enough that developing a means of attacking them in the future is a priority. The air refueling systems, the command and control systems, and the intelligence-gathering systems will be key centers of gravity at the operational level, and we should expect adversaries to target these during future conflicts.

Mobility will be an important capability that high-tech enemies will use operationally against the US—mobility for ground forces to decrease reaction time and air forces to quickly strike and then reposition where needed. The mobility of fielded forces will allow increased offensive action against us while compounding our intelligence and targeting decisions. This will affect the conduct of parallel warfare negatively.

The conventional air forces of a future enemy will emphasize hitting strategic targets, which now will mean information centers and possibly air defense objectives. Ground forces in the field will take on a secondary role because they will no longer be considered the key. The decisive point, our critical center of gravity, will now shift to the computer—in other words, to the ability to process and disseminate information. A combination of electronic warfare and maneuver of forces will therefore be used to deny both information and easy targets to the US. Another way to look at the operational response is to anticipate the use of parallel warfare against us.

Conclusion

The history of successful parallel warfare is short. It involves one campaign (Desert Storm) in which the composition of the adversaries, the capabilities of the US-led coalition, and the geography all contributed to a resounding success. I have shown that there are political, technological, and operational responses we need to anticipate for the future. To expect future success without additional preparation will almost certainly mean failure. There are many counters to parallel warfare. Politically disrupting alliances, technology, and updated operational strategies will have a definite role in the outcome of any future conflict involving the United States.

Perhaps the hardest capability to predict, and potentially the most important asset, is the political coalition formed to solve military problems. These coalitions, which will be the catalyst for successful military operations, may actually become the center of gravity that is vulnerable to a future enemy's action. They combine everything from military hardware to economic might. The smart adversary will plan on affecting adversely our ability to form these alliances before we even see the need. Also, the technology of future adversaries will be a direct indicator of the response we can expect to conducting parallel warfare. One important lesson is that low technology may not translate into easy victory by military means. The low-tech adversary with political savvy and the will to endure hardships may actually be the hardest enemy to take on. The technologically sophisticated enemy will present the force-on-force conflict for which our military normally trains. This will include updated information systems, updated air defense systems, and the ability for preemptive strikes. The operational response in the future will be linked directly to the enemy's technological capability. Survival and avoiding force-on-force engagements may be the operational strategy of low-tech adversaries. The advanced-technology enemy may respond with a combination of weapons and mobility aimed at negating our command and control, intelligence, and refueling capabilities. We should anticipate parallel warfare being used against us.

Anticipating these political, technological, and operational strategies against parallel warfare will provide a significant challenge. Future enemies are learning from Desert Storm and will adapt these lessons learned into countermeasures. Perhaps the biggest key for the US is to maintain our technological edge. The outcome of two roughly equivalent adversaries conducting parallel warfare against each other may well be a defensive war of attrition—a modern version of the trench warfare of World War I. The ability of the US to continue to win decisive and quick military victories will depend on anticipating the enemy's response to parallel warfare.

Notes

1. Sun Tzu, *The Art of War*, trans. Samuel B. Griffith (New York: Oxford University Press, 1963), 69–79.
2. Department of Defense, *Conduct of the Persian Gulf War—Final Report to the Congress* (Washington, D.C.: Government Printing Office, 1992), 24-2.
3. Ibid.
4. James Adams and James Blitz, "Gloom for the Russians in Gulf Weapons Toll," *The Sunday Times*, London, 3 March 1991, 15.
5. Ibid.
6. H. Norman Schwarzkopf with Peter Petre, *General H. Norman Schwarzkopf, the Autobiography: It Doesn't Take A Hero* (New York: Bantam Books, 1992), 351.
7. Mary C. Fitzgerald, *The Impact of the Military-Technical Revolution on Russian Military Affairs*, vol. 2 (Washington, D.C.: Hudson Institute, 1993), 216.
8. Department of Defense, *Conduct of the Persian Gulf War—Interim Report to the Congress* (Washington, D.C.: Government Printing Office, 1991), 24-1.
9. Ibid.
10. Fitzgerald, 31–35.
11. Ibid., 159–65.

Air Theory for the Twenty-first Century

John A. Warden III

War in the twenty-first century will be significantly different for the United States from anything encountered before the Gulf War. American wars will be increasingly precise; imprecision will be too expensive physically and politically to condone. Our political leaders and our citizenry will insist that we hit only what we are shooting at and that we shoot the right thing. Increased use of precision weapons will mean far less dependence on the multitudes of people or machines needed in the past to make up for inaccuracy in weapons. Precision will come to suggest not only that a weapon strike exactly where it is aimed, but also that the weapons be precise in destroying or affecting only what is supposed to be affected. Standoff and indirect-fire precision weapons will become available to many others and will make massing of large numbers in the open suicidal and the safety of deploying sea- or land-based aircraft close to a combat area problematic.

We might hope that more accurate weapons would drive potential enemy leaders to be less enamored of achieving their political objectives with force; if we are very lucky, perhaps the world will move in this direction. Of at least equal likelihood, however, states and other entities will turn to other forms of warfare—such as attacks on enemy strategic centers of gravity. These attacks may be via missiles, space, or unconventional means, but all will recognize that they must achieve their objective before the United States chooses to involve itself. This, in turn, will increase the premium on American ability to move within hours to any point on the globe without reliance on en route bases.

The advent of nonlethal weapons technology will expand our options over the full spectrum of war. These new weapons will find application against communications, artillery, bridges, and internal combustion engines to name but a few potential targets. And of greatest interest, they will accomplish their ends without dependence on big explosions that destroy more property than necessary and that cause unplanned human casualties. Can these weapons replace traditional lethal tools? In theory they can, as long as we accept the idea that war is fought to make the enemy do your will. What we will surely find, however, is that these weapons give us operational concepts and opportunities well beyond what would be possible if we merely substitute them for conventional weapons.

The United States can achieve virtually all military objectives without recourse to weapons of mass destruction. Conversely, other states, unable to afford the hyper-war arsenal now the exclusive property of the United States, will at least experiment with them. The challenge for America is to decide if it wants to negate these weapons without replying or preempting in kind. Accompanying this question is the question of nuclear deterrence in a significantly changed world. Although deterrence will certainly be greatly different from our cold war conception of it, does it lose its utility in all situations? How should US nuclear forces be maintained? This entire matter deserves serious thought, soon.

Information will become a prominent, if not predominant, part of war to the extent that whole wars may well revolve around seizing or manipulating the enemy's datasphere.[1] Furthermore, it may be important in some instances to furnish the enemy with accurate information. This concept will be discussed further in this paper.

The world is currently experiencing what may be the most revolutionary period in all of human existence with major revolutions taking place simultaneously in geopolitics, production, technology, and military affairs. The pace of change is accelerating and shows no sign of letting up. If we are to succeed in protecting our interests in this environment, we must spend more time thinking about war and developing new employment concepts than ever in our past. Attrition warfare belongs to another age, and the days when wars could be won by sheer bravery and perseverance are gone. Victory will go to those who think through the problem and capitalize on every tool available—regardless of its source. Let us begin laying the intellectual framework for future air operations.

All military operations, including air operations, should be consonant with the prevailing political and physical environment. In World War II the United States and her Allies imposed widespread destruction and civilian casualties on Japan and Germany; prior to the Gulf War, a new political climate meant that a proposal to impose similar damage on Iraq would have met overwhelming opposition from American and coalition political leaders. As late as the Vietnam War the general inaccuracy of weapons required large numbers of men to expose themselves to hostile fire in order to launch enough weapons to have some effect on the enemy; now, the new physical reality of accurate weapons means that few men need to be or should be exposed.

Military operations must be conducted so as to give reasonable probability of accomplishing desired political goals at an acceptable price. Indeed, before one can develop or adopt a concept of operations, an understanding of war and political objectives is imperative.

For war to make any sense, it must be conducted for some reason. The reason may not be very good or seem to make much sense, but with remarkably few exceptions, most rulers who have gone to war have done so with the objective of achieving something—perhaps additional territory, a halt to offensive enemy operations, avenging an insult, or forcing a religious conversion. Very few have gone to war to amuse themselves with no concern for the outcome or desire for anything other than the opportunity to have a good donnybrook.

This is not to say, however, that all those who have gone to war have done so with a clear idea of their objective and what it would take to achieve it. Indeed, failure to define ends and means clearly has led to innumerable disasters for attacker and attacked alike. First rule: if you are going to war, know why you are going. Corollary to the first rule: have some understanding of what your enemy wants out of the war and the price each of you is willing to pay. Remember: war is not quintessentially about fighting and killing; rather, it is about getting something that the opponent is not inclined to hand over. Still another way to express this idea is this: war is all about making your enemy do something you want him to do when he doesn't want to do it—and then preventing him from taking an alternative approach which you would also find unacceptable.

There are a variety of ways to make an enemy do what you want him to do. In simple terms, however, there are but three: make it too expensive for the enemy to resist with "expensive" understood in political, economic, and military terms; physically prevent an enemy from doing something by imposing strategic or operational paralysis on him; or destroy him absolutely.

The last of these options is rare in history, difficult to execute, fraught with moral concerns, and normally not very useful because of all the unintended consequences it engenders. We will pass over it in favor of concentrating on the first two.

When we talk about making something so costly for an enemy that he decides to accept our position, we are talking about something very difficult to define or predict precisely. After all, human organizations typically react in an infinite number of ways to similar stimuli. The difficulty of defining or predicting, however, does not suggest that it is a hopeless task. Imprecise, yes; hopeless, no.

We all know from our experience that we regularly make decisions whether or not to do something. We don't go on a trip if it costs more money than we are ready to pay; we don't go mountain climbing if we fear the cost of falling; and we don't drive above the speed limit if the probability of a ticket seems high, and so on. Enemies, whether they be states, criminal organizations, or individuals all do the same thing; they almost always act or don't act based on some kind of cost-benefit ratio. The enemy may not assess a situation the way we do, and we may disagree with the assessment, but assessments are part and parcel of every decision. From an air power standpoint, it is our job to determine what price (negative or positive) it will take to induce an enemy to accept our conditions. To do so, however, we need to understand how our enemies are organized. One might object that understanding how our enemies are organized is an impossible task, especially if we don't know in advance who they are. Fortunately, this is not the case; as we shall see, every life-based system is organized about the same way. Only the details vary.

Whether we are talking about an industrialized state, a drug cartel, or an electric company, every organization follows the same organizational scheme. This is very important to us as military planners because it allows us to develop general concepts not dependent on a specific enemy. Likewise, as we understand how our enemies are organized, we can easily move on to the concept of centers of gravity. Understanding centers of gravity then allows us to make reasonable guesses as to how to create costs which *may* lead the enemy to accept our demands. If the enemy does not respond to imposed costs, then this same understanding of organization and centers of gravity shows us how to impose operational or strategic paralysis on our enemy so he becomes incapable of opposing us. Let's start with the basics of organization (table 1).

Table 1

System Attributes

	Body	State	Drug Cartel	Electric Company
Leader	Brain -eyes -nerves	Government -communication -security	Leader -communication -security	Central Control
Organic Essential	Food/oxygen -conversion via vital organs	Energy (electricity, oil, food), money	Coca source plus conversion	Input (heat, hydro) Output (electricity)
Infrastructure	Vessels, bones, muscles	Roads, airfields, factories	Roads, airways, sea lanes	Transmission lines
Population	Cells	People	Growers, distributors, processors	Workers
Fighting Mechanism	Leukocytes	Military, police, firemen	Street soldiers	Repairmen

As can be seen from the preceding table, a wide variety of systems ranging from an individual to an electric company are organized with remarkable similarity. This organizing scheme is sufficiently widespread to make it an acceptable starting place for working out most military or business problems. It helps us put into effect injunctions from ancient Greek and

Chinese alike to “know thyself” and “thine enemy.” In addition to simplifying the “knowing” process, this organizational scheme gives us an easy way to categorize information, which we must do if we are to make real decisions. For practical purposes, the world contains an infinite amount of information which by definition cannot be totally correlated. Filters of some sort are a necessity; this systems approach provides an easy way to categorize information and to understand the relative importance of any particular bit.

Our primary interest is not in building a theory of organization; rather, it is to derive an understanding of what we might need to impose an intolerable cost or strategic or operational paralysis on an enemy. To grasp the essence of this problem, it helps to rearrange our table in the form of five rings (fig. 1).

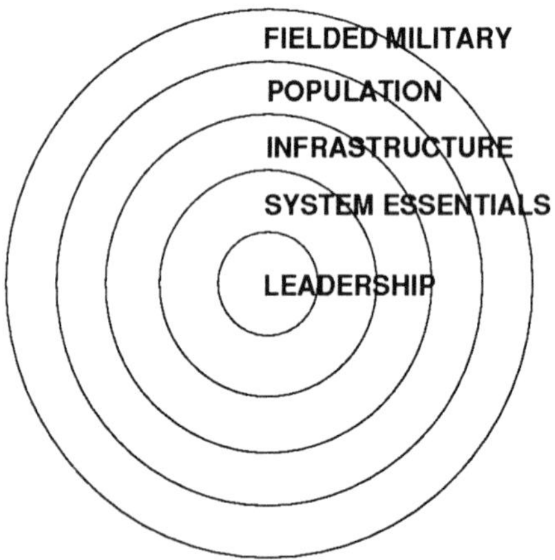

Figure 1. System model.

Rearranging the tabular table into the five rings diagram gives us several key insights. First, it shows us that we are dealing with an interdependent system. That is, each ring has a relationship with all of the others and all play some role. Seeing the enemy as a system gives us enormous advantages over those who see the enemy merely as an army or air force, or worse yet, see the enemy manifested in some quantity of tanks or airplanes or ships or drug pushers without ever understanding what it is that allows these tanks or ships to operate and for what purpose.

Second, it gives us some idea of the relative importance of each entity contained within a given ring. For example, the head of a drug cartel (the leadership ring) has the power to change the cartel considerably whereas the street soldier (in the fielded military forces ring) assigned the job of protecting a pusher in a back alley can have virtually no effect on the cartel as a whole.

Third, it portrays rather graphically an ancient truth about war: our objective is always to convince the enemy to do what we want him to do. The person or entity with the power to agree to change is the leader in the middle. Thus, directly or indirectly all of our energies in war should be focused on changing the mind of the leadership.

Fourth, our rings clearly show that the military is a shield or spear for the whole system, not the essence of the system. Given a choice, even in something so simple as personal combat, we certainly wouldn't make destruction of our enemy's shield our end game. *Contrary to Clausewitz, destruction of the enemy military is not the essence of war; the essence of war is convincing the enemy to accept your position, and fighting his military forces is at best a means to an end and at worst a total waste of time and energy.*

Fifth, and last, the rings give us the concept of working from the inside to the outside as opposed to the converse. Understanding this concept is essential to taking a strategic rather than a tactical approach to winning wars.

In using the rings to develop war ideas, it is imperative to start with the largest identifiable system. That is, if the immediate problem is reversing the effects of an invasion, one would start the analysis with the largest possible look at the system description of the invading country. An example: when the Iraqis invaded Kuwait, Gen Norman Schwarzkopf quickly grasped the idea that his problem was first with Iraq as a state and only secondarily with Iraq's military forces within Kuwait itself. At some point, however, we wanted to understand details about Iraq's army in Kuwait. Not surprisingly, we found that it was organized on the five-ring principle and insofar as our objective with respect to that army was something other than pure destruction, five-ring analysis gave us a good picture of what to strike. Had we so desired, we could have continued our analysis down to the level of an individual soldier because he is organized about the same way as is his country. From a diagraming standpoint, then, we start out with the big picture of the strategic entity.[2]

When we want more information, we pull out subsystems like electrical power under system essentials and show it as a five-ring system. We may have to make several more five-ring models to show successively lower electrical subsystems. We continue the process until we have sufficient understanding and information to act. Note that with this approach, we have little need for the infinite amount of information theoretically available on a strategic entity like a state. Instead, we can identify very quickly what we don't know and concentrate our information search on relevant data.

For the mathematically inclined, it will be clear that we are describing a process of differentiation as opposed to integration. In a complex world, a top-down, differentiation approach is a necessity. Important to note, however, is that virtually all our military training (and business training) starts us at the lowest possible level and asks us to work our way up. Thus, we learn a tactical approach to the world. However, when we want to think not about fighting wars but about winning them, we must take a strategic and operational—or top-down—approach if we are to succeed.

So far, we have not talked explicitly about centers of gravity, but we have derived them by showing how we and our enemies are organized. Centers of gravity are primarily organizational concepts. Which ones are most important become clear when we decide what effect we want to produce on the enemy in order to induce him to accept our position. Which ones to attack become a matter of our capability.

Let us review key concepts discussed to this point. First, the object of war is to induce the enemy to do your bidding. Second, it is the leadership of the enemy that decides to accommodate you. Third, engagement of the enemy military may be a means to an end, but the engagement is never an end in itself and should be avoided under most circumstances. Fourth, every life-form-based system is organized similarly: a leadership function to direct it; a system-essential function to convert energy from one form to another, an infrastructure to tie it all together, a population to make it function, and a defense system to protect it from attack. Fifth, the enemy is a system, not an independent mass of tanks, aircraft, or dope pushers. And sixth, the five rings provide a good method for categorizing information and identifying centers of gravity.

We said earlier that our goal in war would generally be to make the cost—political, economic, and military—to the enemy higher than he was willing to pay or to impose strategic or operational paralysis on him so that he would become incapable of acting. Now, with an understanding of how enemies are organized, we can begin the process of determining how to accomplish either or both with air power tools.

The object of war is to convince the enemy leadership to do what you want it to do. The enemy leadership acts on some cost/risk basis, but we can't know precisely what it might be. We can, however, make some reasonable guesses based on system and organization theory. To do this, put yourself in the center of the five rings as the leader of a strategic entity like a drug cartel or state. You have certain rather basic goals that normally will take precedence over others. First, you want to survive personally (this is not to say you won't die for your system, but you probably see yourself and the system as being closely tied together). To survive personally (in most instances) the system you lead must survive in something reasonably close to its present form.

Let us say that you are the leader of a drug cartel and an enemy threatens you credibly with the following (to which you cannot respond): your bank accounts will be zeroed, your communications with the world outside your mountain retreat will be severed, your cocaine processing facility will be destroyed, and your house will be converted to rubble. To avoid these nasty things, all you have to do is agree to stop selling cocaine in one country. What do you do? If you are remotely rational, you agree immediately. Failure to do so means your system effectively ceases to exist which leaves you personally in a precarious position and unable even to retire in splendor because you can't get at the billions you had socked away in a country with strict privacy in banking laws.

Suppose that only some of these dire events were threatened or deemed likely. In this case, you might choose to negotiate. Perhaps you would agree to sell less cocaine in the target country. Perhaps you would agree to a moratorium on sales. Your enemy might or might not accept these counterproposals; it would depend largely on how much he was willing to spend to create a cost for you. In our ideal world we like to think we don't negotiate with drug dealers or tyrants like Saddam Hussein. In the real world we do so all the time. *Very rarely are we willing to invest the time and effort required to achieve maximal results.*

Our discussion of costs has so far been oriented at a strategic level. Does it also apply at an operational level—the level at which military forces are actually employed? The answer is an absolute yes. Military commanders, with the exception of a few really stupid ones, have always weighed costs as they were planning or conducting an operation. Let's take a hypothetical look at George Patton and the Third Army in World War II.

George Patton was an aggressive commander who believed that speed of advance was key to success. Obviously, then, the Third Army needed to move quickly as a system—not just the tanks, but the whole system that supported them at the front. From the German side if moving fast was good from George Patton's perspective, it was bad from theirs. Now, let us do a quick five-ring analysis of the Third Army from just the cost standpoint. (We will return to it later when we discuss operational paralysis.)

Let us suppose that something catastrophic happened to Third Army's fuel supply in mid-September of 1944. Let us assume that someone tells General Patton at a staff meeting that all fuel deliveries to his Army will cease in two days. His choices are basically two: slow down or stop the movement of his army so that it can assume a reasonable defensive position, or tell everyone to plunge ahead as far as possible until they run out of gas. Since the latter is likely to leave the majority of the army in an untenable and unplanned position and is unlikely to achieve anything final, Patton opts for the former because he has assessed the cost of continuing as too high for the possible results.

Realize also that unbeknownst to the commanding general, every subordinate commander and soldier will start acting on information about an impending fuel shortage as soon as he hears about it. The effect is obvious; by the time the formal order to halt comes down, forward movement would have already ceased and hoarding of remaining fuel supplies would have become widespread. The principle is simple: at all levels, leaders make decisions based on a cost/benefit analysis.

Before moving on to discuss imposition of strategic and operational paralysis, we need to make two more points on the subject of cost. The first is that the enemy leader may not recognize how much attacks on him are costing at the time of attack and in the future. This almost certainly was the case with Saddam Hussein who simply failed to comprehend for several weeks what the strategic air attacks against him were doing to his future. Had he understood, he might have sued for peace the first morning of the war. His lack of understanding flowed from ignorance of the effect of modern air attack[3] and from lack of information. The coalition attack in the first minutes had so disrupted communications at strategic levels that it was very difficult to receive and process damage reports.[4]

A similar event may have taken place in Japan in late 1944 and into 1945. Japanese army leaders persisted in their desire to continue the war even though their homeland was collapsing around them as a result of strategic air and sea attacks. They apparently lacked the in-depth understanding of war and their country to appreciate what was really happening. Like Saddam a half century later, the Japanese were stuck in a paradigm that said that the only important operations in war were the clashes of armies. In the Japanese case part of the problem may have stemmed from the Bushido code of personal bravery that tended to assume that success in war would be a function of agglomerating many tactical successes. The concepts of strategic and operational war were simply not there.

Two lessons flow from these examples: you may have to educate the enemy on the effect your operations are likely to have. You may also have to give him accurate information on the extent of his losses—*and the long- and short-term effects likely to flow from them.*

As we have seen, we cannot depend on the his making the concessions we ask because of a realistic cost/benefit analysis. In the event we cannot educate and inform him properly, we must be ready to consider imposition of strategic and operational paralysis. Fortunately, the effort we put into understanding how enemies are organized and how to impose costs leads us directly into the concepts and mechanisms of paralysis.

The idea of paralysis is quite simple. If the enemy is seen as a system, we need to identify those parts of the system which we can affect in such a way as to prevent the system from doing something we don't want it to do. The best place to start is normally at the center for if we can prevent the system's leadership from gathering, processing, and using information we don't want him to have, we have effectively paralyzed the system at a strategic level.

Let us go back to the drug cartel example we earlier discussed. Suppose that the suppliers and pushers hear nothing from headquarters for some period of time. Their finances begin to dry up, nobody protects them from competitors, and their stocks dwindle quickly. What do they do? They begin to look for other cartels to deal with or for other lines of work. In a short period of time, but not instantly, the paralysis imposed at the strategic level of the cartel destroys the organization's ability to sell the drugs its opposition didn't want it to sell. All while the overwhelming majority of the individuals in the organization are unharmed and not even directly threatened.

The obvious place to induce strategic system paralysis is at the leadership, or brain, level. What happens, however, if the brain cannot be located or attacked? Although the leadership function always provides the most lucrative place to induce paralysis, it is not the only possibility. Suppose that we can't reach the drug lord, but we can reach and destroy one of his system essentials such as his financial net? We are likely to have created a different level of paralysis. The organization may still be able to function, and it will certainly search furiously to repair or replace its financial net. If it doesn't succeed, however, this paralysis in one part of the strategic system is likely to cause much of the rest to atrophy and become ineffective. After all the majority of the organization's suppliers and workers must eat and must pay for services rendered. If they are not getting regular pay, they are going to be forced again to find alternatives outside the organization that can no longer provide them with a system essential.

At a big state level, one can imagine a similar outcome if the state loses a system essential like electricity. Imagine the effect on the United States if all of its electricity stops functioning.

Let us return to our George Patton and Third Army example to look at operational paralysis. Patton depended on speed for success but not unfocused speed. He needed to know where he was going, what his troops were going to encounter, where to send the fuel and ammunition, and where to shift land and air forces as required. Suppose the Germans had succeeded in blinding Patton by depriving him of his ability to gather and disseminate information. Under these conditions, Third Army would have been effectively paralyzed insofar as its ability to conduct rapid offensives simply because offensives on the ground at any speed are extraordinarily complex and require huge amounts of good information.

If the Germans were unable to blind Patton, what else could they have done to induce operational paralysis? Again, going from the center of the rings toward the outside suggests we should look next in the system-essential (or supply) ring for an answer. Most assuredly, Patton's speed depended on fuel for his tanks and trucks—no fuel; no speed. Thus, elimination of fuel, perhaps by interdicting the Red Ball Express, induces the desired form of operational paralysis and converts Third Army into something different. Before its fuel was cut off, Third Army was a fast moving, dangerous threat to the Germans; after the fuel stops, it becomes a slow, slogging beast significantly different in nature and threat.

So far we have discussed effects we might want to produce on the enemy: untenable costs or paralysis at one or more levels. Next, we must look at how we go about doing it. Before proceeding, however, it is useful to note that we have used quite a few pages talking about air theory and have yet to discuss bombs, missiles, or bullets. The reason is simple; well before it makes any sense to talk about mechanics, it is imperative to decide what effect you want to produce on the enemy. Making this decision is the toughest intellectual challenge; once decided, figuring out how to do it is much easier if for no other reason than we practice the necessary tactical events every day whereas we rarely (far too rarely) think about strategic and operational problems. Let us propose a very simple rule for how to go about producing the effect: do it very fast.

It may seem facetious to reduce the "how" to such a simple rule, and, indeed, we will now make it a little more complex by talking about parallel attack. Nevertheless, the essence of success in future war will certainly be to make everything happen you want to happen in a very short period of time—instantly if possible. Why? And what is parallel war?

Parallel war brings so many parts of the enemy system under near-simultaneous attack that the system simply cannot react to defend or to repair itself. It is like the death of a thousand cuts; any individual cut is unlikely to be serious. A hundred, however, start to slow a body considerably, and a thousand are fatal because the body cannot deal with that many assaults on it. Our best example of parallel war to date is the strategic attack on Iraq in the Gulf War. Within a matter of minutes the coalition, attacked over a hundred key targets across Iraq's entire strategic depth. In an instant, important functions in all of Iraq stopped working very well. Phone service fell precipitously, lights went out, air defense centers stopped controlling subordinate units, and key leadership offices and personnel were destroyed. To put Iraq's dilemma in perspective, the coalition struck three times as many targets in Iraq in the first 24 hours as Eighth Air Force hit in Germany in all of 1943!

The bombing offensive against Germany (until the very end) was a serial operation as virtually all military operations have been since the dawn of history. Operations have been serial because communications made concentration of men imperative, the inaccuracy of weapons meant that a great number had to be employed to have an effect, and the difficulty of movement essentially restricted operations to one or two locations. In addition, military operations have mostly been conducted against the enemy's military, not against his entire strategic or operational system. All this meant that war was a matter of action and reaction, of culminating points, of regrouping, of reforming. Essentially, war was an effort by one side to break through a defensive line with serial attacks or it was an attempt to prevent breakthrough.

In any event the majority of the enemy system lay in relative safety through most of a conflict with the fighting and damage confined largely to the front itself. Even when aerial bombardment began to reach strategic depths, the bombardment tended to be serial (again because of inaccurate weapons and the need to concentrate attacking forces so they could penetrate an aerial defensive line). This meant that the enemy could gather his defenders in one or two places and that he could concentrate the entire system's repair assets on the one or two places which may have suffered some damage. Not so in Iraq.

In Iraq, a country about the same size as prewar Germany, so many key facilities suffered so much damage so quickly that it was simply not possible to make strategically meaningful repair. Nor was it possible or very useful to concentrate defenses; successful defense of one target merely meant that one out of over a hundred didn't get hit at that particular time. Like the thousand cuts analogy, it just doesn't matter very much if some of the cuts are deflected. It is important to note that Iraq was a very tough country strategically. Iraq had spent an enormous amount of money and energy on giving itself lots of protection and redundancy and its efforts would have paid off well if it had been attacked serially as it had every right to anticipate it would. In other words, the parallel attack against Iraq was against what may well have been the country best prepared in all the world for attack. If it worked there, it will probably work elsewhere.

Executing parallel attack is a subject for another essay or even a book. Suffice it to say here that those things brought under attack must be carefully selected to achieve the desired effect.

We have now provided the groundwork for a theory of air power to use into the twenty-first century. To summarize: understand the political and technological environment; identify political objectives; determine how you want to induce the enemy to do your will (imposed cost, paralysis, or destruction); use the five-ring systems analysis to get sufficient information on the enemy to make possible identification of appropriate centers of gravity; and attack the right targets in parallel as quickly as possible. To make all this a little more understandable, it is useful to finish by mentioning the Gulf War's key strategic and operational lessons, which look as though they will be useful for the next quarter century or more.

We can identify 10 concepts that summarize the revolution of the Gulf War and that must be taken into account as we develop new force levels and strategy:

1. The importance of strategic attack and the fragility of states at the strategic level of war
2. Fatal consequences of losing strategic air superiority
3. The overwhelming effects of parallel warfare
4. The value of precision weapons
5. The fragility of surface forces at the operational level of war
6. Fatal consequence of losing operational air superiority
7. The redefinition of mass and surprise by stealth and precision
8. The viability of "air occupation"
9. The dominance of air power
10. The importance of information at the strategic and operational levels

Let us look at each of these briefly.

1. The importance of strategic attack and the fragility of states at the strategic level of war: Countries are inverted pyramids that rest precariously on their strategic innards—their leadership, communications, key production, infrastructure, and population. If a country is paralyzed strategically, it is defeated and cannot sustain its fielded forces though they be fully intact.

2. Fatal consequences of losing strategic air superiority: When a state loses its ability to protect itself from air attack, it is at the mercy of its enemy and only the enemy's compassion or exhaustion can save it. The first reason for government is to protect the citizenry and its property. When a state can no longer do so, it has lost its reason for being. When a state loses strategic air superiority and has no reasonable hope of regaining it quickly, it should sue for peace as quickly as possible. From an offensive standpoint, winning strategic air

superiority is the number one priority of the commander; once accomplished, everything else is a just a matter of time.

3. The overwhelming effects of parallel warfare: Strategic organizations, including states, have a small number of vital targets at the strategic level—in the neighborhood of a few hundred with an average of perhaps 10 aimpoints per vital target. These targets tend to be small, very expensive, have few backups, and are hard to repair. If a significant percentage of them are struck in parallel, the damage becomes insuperable. Contrast parallel attack with serial attack where only one or two targets come under attack in a given day (or longer). The enemy can alleviate the effects of serial attack by dispersal over time, increasing the defenses of targets that are likely to be attacked, concentrating his resources to repair damage to single targets, and by conducting counteroffensives. Parallel attack deprives him of the ability to respond effectively and the greater the percentage of targets hit in a single blow, the more nearly impossible is response.

4. The value of precision weapons: Precision weapons allow the economical destruction of virtually all targets—especially strategic and operational targets that are difficult to move or conceal. They change the nature of war from one of probability to one of certainty. Wars for millennia have been probability events in which each side launched huge quantities of projectiles (and men) at one another in the hope that enough of the projectiles (and men) would kill enough of the other side to induce retreat or surrender. Probability warfare was chancy at best. It was unpredictable, full of surprises, hard to quantify, and governed by accident. Precision weapons have changed all that. In the Gulf War, we knew with near certainty that a single weapon would destroy its target. War moved into the predictable.

With precision weapons, even logistics become simple; destruction of the Iraqis at the strategic, operational, and tactical levels required that about 12,000 aimpoints be hit. Thus, no longer is it necessary to move a near-infinite quantity of munitions so that some tiny percentage might hit something important. Since the Iraqi army was the largest fielded since the Chinese in the Korean War and since we know that all countries look about the same at the strategic and operational levels, we can forecast in advance how many precision weapons will be needed to defeat an enemy—assuming of course that we are confident about getting the weapons to their target.

5. The fragility of surface forces at the operational level of war: Supporting significant numbers of surface forces (air, land, or sea) is a tough administrative problem even in peacetime. Success depends upon efficient distribution of information, fuel, food, and ammunition. By necessity, efficient distribution depends on an inverted pyramid of distribution. Supplies of all operational commodities must be accumulated in one or two locations, then parsed out to two or four locations, and so on until they eventually reach the user. The nodes in the system are exceptionally vulnerable to precision attack. As an example, consider what the effect would have been of a single air raid a day—even with nonprecision weapons—on the WWII Red Ball Express or on the buildup behind VII and XVIII Corps in the Gulf War. The Red Ball Express became internally unsustainable, and the VII and XVIII Corps buildups severely strained the resources of the entire US Army—even in the absence of any enemy attacks.

Logistics and administration dominate surface warfare, and neither is easy to defend. In the past these activities took place so far behind the lines that they were reasonably secure. Such is no longer the case—which brings into serious question any form of warfare that requires huge logistics and administrative buildup.

6. Fatal consequence of losing operational air superiority: Functioning at the operational level is difficult even without enemy interference. If the enemy attains operational air superiority (and exploits it)[5] and can roam at will above indispensable operational functions like supply, communications, and movement, success is not possible. As with the loss of strategic air superiority, loss of operational air superiority spells doom and should prompt quick measures to retreat—which is likely to be very costly—or to arrange for surrender terms.

7. The redefinition of mass and surprise by stealth and precision: For the first time in the history of warfare, a single entity can produce its own mass and surprise. It is this single entity that makes parallel warfare possible. Surprise has always been one of the most important factors in war—perhaps even the single most important because it could

make up for large deficiencies in numbers. Surprise was always difficult to achieve because it conflicted with the concepts of mass and concentration. In order to have enough forces available to hurl enough projectiles to win the probability contest, a commander had to assemble and move large numbers. Of course, assembling and moving large forces in secret was quite difficult, even in the days before aerial reconnaissance, so the odds on surprising the enemy were small indeed. Stealth and precision have solved both sides of the problem; by definition, stealth achieves surprise, and precision means that a single weapon accomplishes what thousands were unlikely to accomplish in the past.

8. The viability of "air occupation": Countries conform to the will of their enemies when the penalty for not conforming exceeds the cost of conforming. Cost can be imposed on a state by paralyzing or destroying its strategic and operational base or by actual occupation of enemy territory. In the past, occupation (in the rare instances when it was needed or possible) was accomplished by ground forces—because there was no good substitute. Today, the concept of "air occupation" is a reality and in many cases it will suffice. The Iraqis conformed as much or more with UN demands as the French did with German demands when occupied by millions of Germans. Ground occupation, however, is indicated when the intent is to colonize or otherwise appropriate the enemy's homeland.

9. The dominance of air power: Air power (fixed wing, helicopter, cruise missile, satellite), if not checked, will destroy an enemy's strategic and operational target bases—which are very vulnerable and very difficult to make less vulnerable. It can also destroy most tactical targets if necessary.

10. The importance of information at the strategic and operational levels: In the Gulf War, the coalition deprived Iraq of most of its ability to gather and use information. At the same time, the coalition managed its own information requirements acceptably, even though it was organized in the same way Frederick the Great had organized himself. Clear for the future is the requirement to redesign our organizations so they are built to exploit modern information-handling equipment. This also means flattening organizations, eliminating most middle management, pushing decision making to very low levels, and

forming worldwide neural networks to capitalize on the ability of units in and out of the direct conflict area.

The information lesson from the Gulf was negative; the coalition succeeded in breaking Iraq's ability to process information, but the coalition failed to fill the void by providing Iraqis an alternate source of information.[6] Failure to do so made Saddam's job much easier and greatly reduced the chance of his overthrow. Capturing and exploiting the datasphere may well be the most important effort in many future wars.

Beyond these Gulf War lessons, which have applicability well into the future, it behooves the air planner to think of one other area: what can be done with air power that in the past we knew could only be done with ground or sea power or couldn't be done at all? The question must be addressed for several reasons: air power has the ability to reach a conflict area faster and cheaper than other forms of power; employment of air power typically puts far fewer people at risk than any other form (in the Gulf War, there were rarely more than a few hundred airmen in the air as opposed to the tens of thousands of soldiers and sailors in the direct combat areas); and it may provide the only way for the United States to participate at acceptable political risk (use of air power does not require physical presence on the ground). Let us look at just one example.

Suppose a large city is under the control of roving gangs of soldiers, and it is American policy to restore some degree of order to the city. Normally, we would think that could only be done by putting our own soldiers on the ground. But what if policymakers are unwilling to accept the political and physical risks attendant to doing so? Do we do nothing, or do we look for innovative solutions?

If we define the problem as one of preventing groups of soldiers from wandering around a city, we may be able to solve it from the air. Can we not put a combination of AC-130s and helicopters in the air equipped with searchlights, loudspeakers, rubber bullets, entangling chemical nets, and other paraphernalia? When groups are spotted, they first receive a warning to disperse. If they don't they find themselves under attack by nonlethal, but unpleasant, weapons. If these don't work, lethal force is at hand. It may be very difficult to prevent an individual from skulking around a city or even robbing an occasional bank. Single individuals, however, constitute a relatively small tactical problem as they are unlikely to be able to cause wide-scale disruption as can multiple groups. The latter problem is serious but manageable; the former is a police matter.

By the same token, we know that we will be called on to conduct humanitarian and peacemaking operations. If we think about food delivery as the same as bomb delivery and understand that with food as with bombs our responsibility is to distribute it to the right people, we should be able to do as well with food as we do with bombs. To do so, however, will require putting as much effort into developing precision food-delivery techniques as we put into developing precision bomb or cluster-bomb capabilities. The problem is the same and is theoretically susceptible to an air power solution if we are willing to think outside the lines. And indeed, thinking outside the lines will be a necessity if air power is to prosper and to play a key role in defending American interests well into the next century.

Indeed, there is a new world building around us and the revolutions in politics, business, and war have happened and we must deal with them, not ignore them. Of course, it is human nature to stay with the old ways of doing business even when the external world has made the old ways obsolete or even dangerous. So many examples come so easily to mind: the heavy knights at Agincourt refusing to believe that they were being destroyed by peasants with bows; the French in World War I exulting the doctrine of "cold steel" against the machine gun and barbed wire as the flower of a generation perished; and the steel and auto makers of the United States convinced that their foreign competitors were inept even as their market positions plummeted. Accepting the changes made manifest in the Gulf War will be equally difficult for the United States but by no means impossible, if we all resolve to think.

Notes

1. A term introduced by Don Simmons in *Hyperion* (New York: Bantam Books, 1990).

2. A strategic entity is any self-contained system that has the general ability to set its own goals and the wherewithal to carry them out. A state is normally a strategic entity as is a drug cartel or a guerrilla organization.

3. Saddam made the following statement shortly after his successful invasion of Kuwait. "The United States depends on its Air Force and everyone knows that no one ever won a war from the air." Thus, his preconceived notion (shared by many military officers around the world) made it difficult for him to analyze what was happening to him.

4. As an aside, the planners had recognized that Saddam would not be able to gather information, so they had intended to provide him accurate reports of all attacks by using psychological warfare assets. For a number of reasons, the planners were unable to make this happen; as a result, Saddam lacked information that the coalition really wanted him to have.

5. Some would argue that the Mujahiden in Afghanistan lost operational air superiority and yet still prevailed. The latter is true; the former is not because the Stinger antiaircraft missiles forced the Soviets to operate at an altitude that deprived them of the ability to hit anything. The Soviets simply did not have the precision weaponry and detection capability the United States had in the Gulf War.

6. The coalition provided Iraqi soldiers at the front great quantities of information and did so effectively; the same thing did not happen at the strategic level inside Iraq for a variety of not very good reasons.

Waging Wars with Nonlethal Weapons

Paul G. O'Connor

The object of warfare since its inception has been to exact casualties and impose physical destruction, with the express purpose of driving an opponent to capitulation. Contrary to this assumption, recent developments in technology have demonstrated methods of waging war in a nonlethal and nondestructive way. This chapter addresses the background leading to nonlethal trends in war fighting and discusses technology currently under development that supports nonlethality.

Modern warfare, starting with the American Civil War, marked the addition of wholesale and deliberate destruction of property and infrastructure to the combat arena. This conduct was clearly evident in the Second World War, with casualties and destruction achieving proportions unimaginable in prior conflicts. The culmination of such destructive trends was the relentless conventional and incendiary bombing of German and Japanese cities and ultimately the atomic attacks on Hiroshima and Nagasaki.

During the Vietnam conflict, incessant news coverage and its subsequent delivery into American living rooms effected a clear revulsion for the actual conduct and results of warfare. What began as mostly uncritical media reporting evolved into outright questioning of United States involvement in the war after the 1968 Tet offensive.[1] In contrast to the glamorous recounts of past heroes in the manner of Sergeant Alvin York or Audie Murphy or the heavily propagandized newsreel footage of World War II, television molded attitudes that were manifest by home-front demonstrations and flag burnings, not victory gardens and ration cards. Criticism and debate abounded regarding the legitimate interest of the US in Vietnam. This galvanization of certain sectors of American society reflected the same conviction and commitment that had pledged support for the actions of governments and leaders in the two world wars. Cessation of hostilities and US withdrawal from Vietnam were viewed less importantly as the loss of a war than as a means to halt the violence and death of an unpopular war that had grown so repugnant half a world away.

Body count, death toll, and relentless media coverage have channeled public opinion toward an intolerance for casualties and materiel loss in engagements where US interests are questionable. Conversely, support for the Gulf War was high, even when faced with estimates of thousands of conventional and chemical warfare casualties. In reality, the casualties and aircraft loss rates were minuscule compared with the dire predictions. Additionally, precision weapons allowed for victory without categorical destruction of Baghdad, including strident coalition effort to minimize Iraqi civilian casualties.[2] These results foster a growing faith in technology and the expectation that future wars will have equal or fewer casualties and aircraft loss, with the same concern for lives among the opponent's civilian population.

Even the relatively low number of losses suffered by the United States during the Gulf War may be viewed with incredulity and dismay by an American public accustomed to the spectacular technology now readily available and mostly taken for granted. US citizens rely on technology to meet everyday needs, and they expect the same scientific advances to cement this nation's status and preeminent world position on the battlefield as well. The same engineering brilliance that provides satellite television, cellular telephones, microwave cooking, and instantaneous facsimile transmission should be immediately transferable to achieve victory in the realm of warfare. However, this smug assurance and confidence in technology as liberator and savior leads to misconceptions about the actual nature of warfare, with its accompanying confusion and unpredictability. The American public may now expect wars to be fought quickly and cleanly, with little or no damage to United States armament and equipment and no casualties for American forces.

The logical extension of such reasoning leads to warfare that is both effective in achieving the goals of a nation while at the same time is acceptable to the populace. If a nation can force compliance or acquiescence with minimal risk to both allied and enemy fighting forces and civilian populations, the object of warfare will have been achieved without the usually understood and accepted prerequisites. Heretofore this arguably had been impossible, and generally had not been a recommended method of waging war. Carl von Clausewitz commences his treatise *On War* by asserting precisely the opposite.

> Now, philanthropists may easily imagine there is a skillful method of disarming and overcoming an enemy without causing great bloodshed, and that this is the proper tendency of the Art of War. However plausible this may appear, still it is an error which must be extirpated; for in such dangerous things as War, the errors which proceed from a spirit of benevolence are the worst. As the use of physical power to the utmost extent by no means excludes the cooperation of the intelligence, it follows that he who uses force unsparingly, without reference to the bloodshed involved, must obtain a superiority if his adversary uses less vigor in its application. . . . This is the way in which the matter must be viewed, and it is to no purpose, it is even against one's own interest, to turn away from the consideration of the real nature of the affair because the horror of its elements excites repugnance.[3]

The question of why people and nations go to war has been argued for centuries and no resolution appears imminent. Therefore, as the debate proceeds and the bellicose tendencies of nations appear unmitigated, a secondary question remains: How can a nation wage conflict so as to impose its will on another, without putting its warriors in harm's way? Further, can this be accomplished without killing civilians and with only minor damage to the enemy's infrastructure?

One need only take a cursory look at the Marshall Plan in postwar Europe and the infusion of money into postwar Japan to see that the cost of rebuilding a country after a war can be as staggering as the conduct of the war itself. The Marshall Plan, designed to resuscitate a virtually bankrupt Europe while simultaneously averting an American postwar depression hinged on European recovery, required a $13-billion loan program from the United States.[4] Currently, fiscal constraints in a country saddled with debt will not permit the expense of rebuilding a country where previous attempts at annihilation have been pursued. This is unacceptable and probably financially impossible; therefore, it appears plausible that a path be taken to reduce or eliminate destruction and death at the outset. This direction is desirable for fiscal reasons, if not as a moral imperative.

The Gulf War brought to the fore weapons that had been developed during the preceding decades of the cold war, marked by significant technological advances. This bolstered theories of Western–cold-war technological superiority. A portion of these weapons are known as "smart weapons"—for example, those that can target a particular building, or even a floor of that building, obviating the need for destruction of an entire city block to achieve the objective. This is perhaps what the American public has become used to and will expect in future conflicts. Pilots and ground forces should not be placed at undue risk when the same objective can be achieved with cruise missiles and other standoff smart weapons. Can this reasoning be carried to the point where a nation can achieve its objectives with little or no casualties on either side?

Nonlethality is not a new concept, only one that is now receiving more attention for the aforementioned reasons, sparked primarily by interest in the advanced weapons of the Gulf War. This trend has possibilities and applications in urban settings and low-intensity conflicts as well as war on a larger scale. The application of nonlethal weapons in a total war scenario, either as stand-alone weapons or those used in conjunction with more conventional weapons, requires further development.

There has been a history of incorporating nonlethal aspects of warfare with lethal weapons—those that kill people and additionally damage equipment and infrastructure. Examples of nonlethal integration with conventional warfare range from basic infiltration and human intelligence to the advanced technologies of signal interception, signal exploitation, electronic countermeasures, and electronic-surveillance measures. Recent examination, however, focuses on stand-alone nonlethal weapons and methods of actual incapacitation rather than just adjuncts to conventional warfare.

Janet Morris of the US Global Strategy Council advances the requirement for the development of nonlethal weapons:

> Nonlethality's allure is simple: between the moment when diplomacy fails and conventional military force is considered, the United States needs more options to either sending in a totally lethal force or accepting the status quo. Technology now offers such options, and they are life-conserving, environmentally friendly, and fiscally responsible.[5]

Among the technologically advanced nonlethal weapons that Morris identifies are laser radars or low-energy laser rifles that can blind optical sensors and targeting devices and temporarily blind human operators. Very low-frequency infrasound generators could be employed to temporarily incapacitate human beings. Further, Morris discusses generators of nonnuclear electromagnetic pulses, possibly transported by truck, aircraft, or satellite, to paralyze electronic systems and chemical agents designed to embrittle metal, destroy optics, and disable engines and equipment.

Whether or not these technologies will make a difference in the warfare arena is as of yet untested on a large scale. Morris suggests that the success of nonlethal weapons will depend on the circumstances. Scenarios can be envisioned where the introduction of nonlethal technologies will alter the mission of the deployed forces from actually destroying the enemy and his equipment to simply capturing such equipment. This would aid in the subsequent reverse engineering and development of countermeasures for the equipment fielded by an enemy force. Urban raids are arguably another circumstance in which the application of a nonlethal capability would add substantial flexibility to the range of available options.[6]

This is especially important when considering the changing nature of the role of the military. No longer is the military called on solely to perform actual war fighting. Now the roles extend to counternarcotics operations, peacekeeping and peacemaking forces, and humanitarian assistance. Having an array of weapons with varying degrees of lethality would be of great benefit to those with unclear and indistinct assignments in burgeoning spheres of military responsibility.

In the realm of urban warfare, often associated with police departments but increasingly coming under the possible purview of military forces, nonlethal aspects have been investigated and attempted with limited success. Methods of imposing order in an urban environment include the use of water pressure, rubber bullets, and chemical sprays, although these are not without problems. Water pressure is not always effective and presents problems in getting hoses where required. Rubber bullets have proven to be lethal at short range, and chemical agents may affect different people in various ways, posing some risk to the deployer as well as to unintended victims. Other immobilizing agents are the "Taser," which is a handgun-type device that fires two dartlike electrodes connected to the Taser by small wires and delivers an immobilizing shock. The stun gun is a handheld gun operating on the same principle but only at arm's length, thereby limiting its range and effectiveness. Tasers have limitations through heavy clothing and near water. Criteria for the ideal urban nonlethal weapon should include a structure that is similar to a gun, effective but not deadly and with varying degrees of power settings.[7] Although these may seem more applicable to police and law enforcement agencies, the possibilities extend to a military forced to do noncombatant evacuation operations (NEO) and other forms of extractions and engagements in cities where the possibility of unintended collateral civilian damage is great and where there is a risk of a subsequent outcry from the casualty-intolerant developed nations.

Strictly military-oriented weapons are also currently being developed by US scientists and engineers. These "disabling technologies" as nonlethality is also known, could disable enemy soldiers with such weapons as lasers or acoustics as described above and render their weapons and support systems inoperative with methods such as electromagnetic pulse (EMP) generation. Particularly susceptible are the heavily technologically dependent areas of command, control, communications, computers, and intelligence (C^4I).

The question of how far the military should go in developing nonlethal technologies must be addressed, as well as the issue of whether or not the four services should coordinate their efforts along the lines of the Strategic Defense Initiative Office (SDIO). This would establish funding priority and facilitate training and acquisition. Currently most nonlethal development is primarily the work of the Army, with a lesser amount conducted by the Air Force. The Army's Armament Research, Development and Engineering Center (ARDEC) at Picatinny Arsenal in New Jersey directs a program called low collateral damage munitions (LCDM). According to an ARDEC statement, the research is focused on technologies leading to weapons that can "effectively disable, dazzle or incapacitate aircraft, missiles, armored vehicles, personnel and other equipment while minimizing collateral damage."[8]

Army officials are presently testing laser rifles that incapacitate enemy soldiers without necessarily inflicting harmful long-term health effects. These laser rifles are an outgrowth of an older Army research program that sought a means of blinding electronic and optical sensors used by an adversary's helicopters, tanks, missiles, and artillery for target detection and tracking. Whether the antipersonnel variant uses the familiar low-power laser for sighting and guidance or employs the advance technology such as a pulsed chemical laser or acoustic bullet is not known. It is also unclear whether the effectiveness of these devices can be fine-tuned from a disabling to a lethal degree.[9]

Lasers were employed in the battle arena in Vietnam and are used presently in the munitions-guidance and range-finding roles. The laser pulses are not lethal, yet they are strong enough to inflict permanent damage to a person's eyesight. Since the laser beam spreads out over distance, the closer to the laser, the more damaging they become to one's vision. The effects are exacerbated for those using binoculars or other similar optical devices. Problems must be considered on the battlefield as well as in the training environment.

Some of the problems with actually fielding laser weapons and their potential capabilities are described as follows:

> While the high powered lasers needed to destroy distant targets remain impractical, principally because they would be bulky and the atmosphere would distort their beams, lasers of much lower power are capable of destroying or disabling the sensors used to collect information and direct weapons. Sensors are vulnerable because they respond to light—and lasers can accurately deliver concentrated low-power light from a long range. Even if the lasers are not powerful enough to cause physical damage, they can make a sensor ineffective in the same way that bright headlights can overwhelm a driver's night vision without harming the eyes.[10]

Targeting the eyes of opposing personnel specifically has been denied by both the former Soviet Union and the United States, while speculation abounds. There has been some evidence that the British employed a shipboard device in the Falkland Islands that caused three Argentine planes to crash. The system may be designed to cause only temporary loss of vision or serious eye injury. Either way the same desired result is achieved, whereas the pilot must abandon his attack.[11]

A device known as a pulsed chemical laser is also being investigated by the US Army. This apparatus may be capable of producing energy from a pulsed laser that would project hot, high-pressure plasma in the air in front of a target. There is speculation that these pulsed lasers may be able to vary their effect on personnel and materiel.[12]

In the area of acoustic weapons, *Aviation Week & Space Technology* (*AW&ST*) reported that technology under development includes an acoustic generator capable of breaking windows, incapacitating humans, and potentially damaging internal organs at short ranges. Such a weapon would force the intended recipient to either flee to escape injury or risk incapacitation by remaining in the vicinity. This type of device would be relatively large in size and require substantial amounts of fuel; however, it would be well suited for guarding installations. Plans are also being considered for smaller versions of the device that could disrupt the enemy for short periods of time. For example, they could be used as point defenses or dropped into critical areas such as airfields.[13]

A development at the Los Alamos National Laboratory is the "optical-flash" 40-mm artillery shell, designed to temporarily blind personnel or sensor systems.[14] Both the acoustic weapon and the optical-flash weapon are supported by policymakers recognizing the need for a flexible array of weaponry, lethal as well as nonlethal, particularly when considering the peacekeeping duties the military is now increasingly tasked to perform. Having a range of options will contribute to their capabilities as peacekeepers as well as war fighters.

Microbes that can turn aviation fuel in storage tanks to a useless jelly and chemical sprays on roads and runways to damage rubber tires are also projects currently being investigated. *AW&ST* further suggests that ceramic shards fired into the air could damage but not destroy aircraft engines or degrade stealth technology enough to make radar detection possible.[15] Further, *AW&ST* contends that one nonlethal weapon was used in the Gulf War to minimize US casualties and reduce long-term damage to Iraqi public utilities:

> Carbon-fiber filled warheads, fitted to ship-launched Tomahawk cruise missiles, dropped thousands of small reels of wire on the outdoor transmission grids of Iraqi powerplants. The resulting electrical

> shorting and overloads temporarily put the powerplants out of action, thus blinding centralized, computer-controlled air defenses and leaving radar and surface-to-air missile sites to be destroyed piecemeal. However, many of the Iraqi powerplants were soon back in operation, thus softening the impact of the war on civilians.[16]

This capability to disrupt power generation in a nonlethal manner was also inadvertently demonstrated in 1985 when chaff dropped by a US Navy aircraft drifted in from a Pacific combat range over San Diego, California. The small metallic strips caused shorts in the city's electrical grid, resulting in lost electrical power for 60,000 residents.[17]

Air launched cruise missiles (ALCM) are currently being retrofitted for use in a conventional role and possibly a nonlethal role. Some older variants, the AGM-86 for example, are being modified to carry a nonnuclear, electromagnetic-pulse (EMP) generator. As these missiles are removed from their obsolete nuclear-attack role, they are being made more stealthy in addition to their other modifications. Such a deliverable weapon could have overwhelming effects on the modern battlefield. *AW&ST* reports that "an EMP missile, flying at low altitude into an area with key enemy command and control sites, can explode, thus producing a momentary burst of microwaves powerful enough to disable all but special, radiation hardened electronic devices."[18]

To produce a nonnuclear EMP burst, a magnetic field is created in a coil. It is then "squeezed" by the detonation of conventional explosives. The pulse of microwave energy that is produced is capable of being carried thousands of feet, along the way disrupting or damaging electronic components. EMP can damage solid-state ignition on vehicles, detonators, communications, radar, and aircraft electronics. In the broad view, the disabling of vital systems with an EMP weapon could disrupt electrical production and distribution as well as other vital resources without actually damaging the production facilities on a long-term basis.[19] Another aspect of the nonnuclear EMP weapon is the development of hardening for US systems that should continue coincidentally with EMP generator development.

The US Army is also developing EMP weapons for the purpose of disabling aircraft and vehicles. These weapons are focused on attacking the aircraft "fly-by-wire" system of electronic sensors and computers that operate the flight controls. If the computer chips are destroyed while the aircraft is airborne, the result would be uncontrolled flight. If employed while the aircraft are still on the ground, it would remove their ability to become airborne. The same technology could be employed against tanks, disrupting their communication and navigation equipment and possibly inducing engine failure, again targeting the electronic ignition. The Army is conducting research on delivery systems for a variety of weapons of various calibers including small arms, artillery, rockets, and air defenses.[20] The implications of such weapons, should they prove to be feasible and effective, would be enormous. Multiple aircraft groups could be disabled on the ground, and tanks and artillery pieces would be rendered inoperative, all without the use of conventional lethal weapons.

The specific weapon systems described above are merely a sample of the technology under development in this expanding field. The realm of nonlethal weapons is one with multiple applications and possibilities in the disparate tasks assigned to military forces.

Clearly the United States is not the only country pursuing developments in the nonlethal arena. The possibility that US and allied forces could face many of these same weapons on the battlefield of the future must be considered when planning their employment and devising countermeasures. There is evidence to suggest that Russia is engaged in the development of one such weapon. *Jane's Defence Weekly* reports the discovery of high-powered "microwave weapons capable of paralyzing almost all modern Western defence systems."[21]

Another consideration involving nonlethal weapons is their applicability to international law in respect to both military use and civilian proximity to such usage. The relatively recent evolution of these devices dictates that they be examined and made subject to international law. Laser weapons in particular are undergoing scrutiny because of their potential indiscriminate application and the possible permanent damage they may cause to the eye.[22]

The opposing viewpoint to the supposed quantum leaps and possible applications of technology in warfare must be addressed. The military must recognize exaggerations and separate them from real capabilities. Regardless of public opinion and political or budgetary pressure, the military must employ the fielded weapons to the utmost advantage. Criticism has been raised regarding the supposed phenomenal success of the array of weapons in the Gulf War—for instance, Patriot missiles. The distinction must be made according to actual verifiable results of the high-tech weapons, not solely on media hype and unsubstantiated claims, however attractive they may be. John Condry of Cornell University opines

> The public still believes that the Patriot was the most effective weapon of the Gulf War for two reasons: primacy and the power of visual images. People saw the Patriots go into the sky, like a Nintendo game, blowing up the Scuds, they thought. Words to the contrary came later and failed to change those impressions. It is a psychological principle that primacy is critical to forming impressions, and the compelling nature of visual information is hard to deny, especially if it fits in with what we want to believe.[23]

This is not to say that the Patriots were ineffective; only that the reliance on technology, while attractive, may not be the panacea some purport.

However attractive developments in warfare technology may be, there is still the staggering reality that war fighting is chaotic and unpredictable. The success of technology in the Gulf War leads to the possible conclusion that this technology will lead to even greater precision weapons and, consequently, achievement of objectives with less casualties and destruction. Nonlethal weapons rightly fit this thought progression. The challenge remains that nonlethal weapons be integrated into existing arsenals and weapon systems to be used perhaps at the interim stage in a crisis when diplomacy has failed, yet full hostilities are unwarranted. In the era of increasingly complex roles for the armed forces, with lines blurred between peacekeeping, noncombatant operations, low-intensity conflict, and actual war fighting, it is imperative that all options be thoroughly explored.

Notes

1. Walter LaFeber, *The American Age* (New York: W.W. Norton and Co., 1989), 584–85.

2. Richard P. Hallion, *Storm over Iraq* (Washington, D.C.: Smithsonian Institute Press, 1992), 196–200. Hallion discusses the precision air attack and its effect on civilians and the media and public perception.

3. Carl von Clausewitz, *On War*, ed. Anatol Rapoport (London: Penguin Group, 1968), 102.

4. LaFeber, 455–56.

5. Janet Morris, "Enter Nonlethal Weaponry," *IEEE Spectrum* 28, no. 9 (1991): 58.

6. Ibid.

7. Abraham N. Tennenbaum and Angela M. Moore, "Non-Lethal Weapons: Alternatives to Deadly Force," *The Futurist* 27, no. 5 (1993): 20–23.

8. Mark Tapscott and Kay Atwal, "New Weapons That Win without Killing on DOD's Horizon," *Defense Electronics* 25, no. 2 (1993): 42–43. Tapscott and Atwal address nonlethal weapon development considerations as well as current programs.

9. Ibid., 42.

10. Jeff Hecht, "Lasers Designed to Blind," *New Scientist* 135, no. 1833 (1992): 27–28.

11. Ibid., 28.

12. Bill Harris, "Less-Than-Lethal Munitions to Give Army Greater Flexibility," *Ordnance*, May 1993, 23.

13. "Nonlethal Weapons Give Peacekeepers Flexibility," *Aviation Week & Space Technology* 137, no. 23 (7 December 1992): 50.

14. Ibid.

15. Ibid., 51.

16. David A. Fulghum, "US Weighs Use of Nonlethal Weapons in Serbia If U.N. Decides to Fight," *Aviation Week & Space Technology* 137, no. 7 (17 August 1992): 62.

17. "Nonlethal Weapons Give Peacekeepers Flexibility," 51.

18. David A. Fulghum, "ALCMs Given Nonlethal Role," *Aviation Week & Space Technology* 138, no. 8 (22 February 1993): 20.

19. Ibid., 20–21.

20. "Army Prepares for Non-Lethal Combat," *Aviation Week & Space Technology* 138, no. 21 (24 May 1993): 62.

21. Nick Cook, "Russia Leads in Pulse Weapons," *Jane's Defence Weekly* 18, no. 15 (1992): 5.

22. Bengt Anderberg, Ove E. Bring, and Myron L. Wolbarsht, "Blinding Laser Weapons and International Humanitarian Law," *Journal Of Peace Research* 29, no. 3 (1992): 287–97. A discussion of new weapons technology, particularly antipersonnel laser weapons, and the implications for international law and international lawmaking.

23. John Condry, "TV: Live from the Battlefield," *IEEE Spectrum* 28, no. 9 (1991): 48.

Economic Warfare
Targeting Financial Systems As Centers of Gravity

Dr H. David Arnold

The purpose of warfare is to cause a change in the behavior of an opponent. The mechanism of warfare throughout time has ranged from rocks to spears to muskets to armored divisions to chemical weapons to airborne platforms. Warfare has also taken the form of economic sanctions, blockades, and the freezing of the assets of foreign governments held in another nation-state. There is a next step—an intensity of economic warfare over artillery or tank warfare, an aggressiveness in economic warfare without large losses of human resources. This next step is a continuing movement from low-intensity to no-intensity conflict. This is not to imply that destructive activity against financial centers of gravity is not intense—just that the intensity is targeted against nontraditional military targets. Carl von Clausewitz said that warfare is the pursuit of political aims by other means. This can well be applied to economic warfare as much as "classic" warfare.

This chapter is a partial reprint and synopsis of the Hukill, Kennedy, Cameron (HKC) document published in 1993 at the US Air Force's Air Command and Staff College,[1] a work that should become a critical piece in strategic national security planning. The hypothesis states that financial systems can be critical centers of gravity in effecting a change in an opposing nation-state's actions or stature. The HKC document explored (1) an empirical process to identify nation-states whose national power might be influenced through attacks on their financial centers and (2) the financial elements of that nation's financial system that have the greatest effect on its national power. The latter elements can then be expunged as necessary to effect an intended change.

Interdependence of national economies is widely documented in the literature. The late 1970s produced rapidly expanding and generally nondiscriminatory trade, large-scale and rapid movement of funds from one financial center to another, and the rapid growth of multinational enterprises. Advances in transportation and communications technology have accelerated the interdependence. This economic interdependence has made national and international financial institutions critical to the smooth operation of nation-state economies.

Financial institutions such as banks, stock exchanges, trading houses, and commodity exchanges are important for the real factors of economic power—production, natural resources, and so forth—of nation-states to operate at a maximum. Disrupting these economies by attacking the financial institutions could reduce the overall economic power of a nation-state and influence a change. Of course, the aforementioned economic interdependencies may have a negative effect on one's own economic elements. This downside risk is a consideration in the decision equation.

Disrupting an adversary's economy will affect the ability of its infrastructure system to support its military forces and to provide the nation with organic essentials (energy, food, minerals, and other commodities whether they are natural resources or imported) and infrastructure (highways, ports, and railroads). Such disruptions could weaken the political base of the leader and make him or her more responsive to external influence.

Methodology

The HKC research identified those financial elements of the nation-state that have the greatest effect on national power. The analysis reviewed five financial elements to examine their effect on a nation's gross domestic product (GDP): banks, stock markets, foreign debt, value of exports, and value of imports. In any industrialized and internationalized economy, banks are a critical path that is necessary in the transfer and exchange of goods and services. Similarly, stock exchanges for capitalist economies provide the necessary capitalization conduit for investment and growth in production and services. National debt provides the leverage for growth in contemporary economies and helps to smooth out crests and valleys in business cycles. (Such leverage in an economically weak nation-state may be a weakness or potential weakness.) Trade is an important sector of any modern economy because it reflects specialization of resources. Trade's "subsets," the relative value of imports and exports, are key contributors to economic power and hence national power.

Gross domestic product is the most comprehensive measure of a nation's total output of goods and services. It is a convenient and widely accepted indicator of national power.[2] In the HKC analysis, changes in GDP for 99 countries were correlated with changes in indicators for the five financial elements. For banks, the study used total assets (a reflection, of course, of only assets listed on financial statements without regard to their form or location, if appropriate); for stock markets, total capitalization; for foreign debt, the total amount held outside the country; and for trade, the total value of imports and exports.

HKC introduced a linear regression relationship between the various financial elements and GDP for each of the sample countries:

$$GDP = \alpha + \beta_B B + \beta_S S + \beta_D D + \beta_E E^2 + \beta_I I^2$$

In this equation, GDP is predicted by the sum of the products of the value of the financial indicator (banks, stocks, foreign debt, imports, and exports) and the regression coefficients for each financial element (β_n), plus the error component for the equation (α). Note that the data indicates an exponential relationship between GDP and both exports and imports. There are two important points. First, a quantitative relationship can be established among the variables—quantification being a cornerstone in any impact analysis. Second, the financial indicators are only derivative elements of real economic factors. For example, the stock market reflects certain underlying economic strengths and/or weaknesses, and so on.

Regression analysis was used to compute R^2—the coefficient of determination that describes the proportion of the variation in Y determined, explained, or accounted for by variation in X—for the above equation. This gave a measure of how much change in the GDP was explained by changes in the five financial elements. In short, if those financial elements that most directly affect a country's GDP can be ranked in quantified terms, an order of targeting can be established. This is the first attempt, to the author's knowledge, to place economic targets in a framework of a quantifiable measure of merit to gauge the results of action, or potential action, against a nation-state's economy. The possibilities of such targeting represent a breakthrough in the strategy of influencing nations.

Blockades, sanctions, and similar economic forces have long been included in history as part of an arsenal of one country's abilities against another nation-state. However, the normal attitude has been to "put economic pressure on them and see what happens." The HKC methodology provides some definitive quantification to the evaluation. In addition to being a major breakthrough in strategic planning, the methodology will prove to be a tool for justifying critics who support actions identified as "economic warfare."

Analysis

The statistical analysis confirmed the hypothesis that GDP varies directly with the value of financial elements within the country. While this hypothesis confirmation is nothing obvious, the analysis does suggest quantitatively that disrupting financial elements will have a negative effect on GDP and hence perhaps on economic power. The author is not prepared to concrete the notion that a leap from GDP to economic power, then to national power, is natural or omniapplicable, regardless of the Kennedy and Olson books that directly link changes in GDP as an indicator of changes in national power.[3] Indeed, the Peoples Republic of China has a relatively high GDP. However, there are few that would argue that it *is* a significant economic power. It may be one day, but not today. All that is being suggested is that the leap may be credible in some cases. In others cases, maybe a similar or closely resembling leap can be quantified.

Furthermore, the analysis suggested a threshold level of GDP that warrants attention. Attacking the financial elements of banking, stock exchanges, and foreign debt of countries whose GDP falls below this level would be ineffective since changes in the financial elements have little correlation to changes in GDP. The quantifiable identification of such a threshold is a significant event—witness Bosnia and Somalia. Sanctions against either have been ineffective. The GDP of both is basically zero. An established and acceptable model defining a "waste-of-time" threshold would have saved a lot of energy expended against those two countries by the United States and the United Nations.

Shortcomings of the Analysis

Several weaknesses of the initial model are noteworthy. First, there is no indication of a time-lag effect. A correlation might be strong between banks and a country's GDP, but how long until the country feels the effect is reserved for future research. Furthermore, the strength of the correlation tells us nothing about the vulnerability of the financial element to be attacked. Even though the element may be an important center of gravity, it could be well protected or widely distributed, making it invulnerable to attack. Finally, the data represents a cross section of all countries. The regression is a test of variation from country to country and does not correlate changes in GDP with the five financial elements over time. While this preliminary study suggests some interesting relationships, additional time-series data of individual countries would improve the model and allow for more detailed analysis.

The model does not replace the need for detailed country analysis because it does not account for specific peculiarities of a single country. Two specific characteristics require independent comment. They are (1) dependency on a few or a single export (a "monoeconomic culture" [MEC]), and (2) heavy economic sponsorship by another country.

Monoeconomic cultures are scattered throughout the world but are most notable in developing countries. Many African countries are still dependent on one commodity, and the major energy exporters tend to rely excessively on only oil or natural gas. Latin American countries whose economies are more developed than many poorer areas of the world are also often overly reliant on individual commodities. If the economy of one of these MECs is integrally tied to a single commodity, then the financial center that controls it would be a suitable target.

The writer notes that the GDP of an MEC is irrelevant as an indicator of evaluation for targeting success against such a country. The very nature of a nation-state being a MEC lends itself to economic vulnerability. The export(s) itself or themselves would be the critical center of gravity for that MEC country. GDP doesn't have a role.

For example, Cuba is an MEC dependent on sugar. Sugar is critical to the Cuban economy for several reasons. First, sugar made up two-thirds of export revenues in 1991, accounting for 21 percent of Cuba's gross national produce (GNP), and prior to 1991 was the key element in a subsidized trade agreement for oil with the former Soviet Union. Cuba received oil at very low prices in return for selling sugar at above-market prices. In fact, the Cubans would buy more of the cheap oil than they needed and sell the rest at the higher market price. It was through this process that they received the majority of their hard currency. The impact of the flow of sugar on the Cuban economy was demonstrated in reality. In 1991 Soviet subsidies dropped from $4 billion in 1990 to $1 billion because of a lower price paid for Cuban sugar and a sharp decline in Soviet exports to Cuba. These actions have crippled the Cuban economy. Cuba, having put all its eggs in one basket, is in trouble. It has lost its largest trading partner and can no longer acquire large amounts of cheap oil. This has caused an energy and hard-currency shortage, which means it has no money to pay market price for items such as oil, food, industrial raw materials, and spare parts. The reduction of this sugar trade dropped the aggregate output of the economy by one-fifth in 1991.

Cuban leaders are trying to diversify the economy, but as of this writing, Cuba is still dependent on sugar. If the export of sugar could be restricted even further, then the Cuban economy would grind to a halt. Cuba needs oil for its energy-intensive industrial sector, which accounts for 45 percent of total energy use. It produces only 6.5 percent of its requirement and imports the rest. Imported oil is traded for sugar with the former Soviet Union on a much smaller scale than prior to 1991. A shortage of oil hurts industrial production, which accounted for 45 percent of GDP in 1989 and causes lower sugar production by reducing mechanized harvesting and fertilizer production. A death spiral is established: no sugar means no oil, which means lower industrial and sugar production, which means less oil, and so on.

The second characteristic warranting further comment is economic sponsorship. Economic sponsorship occurs when a developed country heavily subsidizes another country—whether a developed one (Israel) or an underdeveloped one (Haiti)—through foreign aid. There are two critical points to consider when somehow ranking the sponsored country's aid by a "significance" factor. First, is economic aid commodity or cash, or both? (Yes, cash is a commodity!) Second, what is the GDP threshold of the sponsored country? This measurement is determined without the external aid included. Would the loss of the aid cause the sponsored economy to collapse? Will the loss cause the sponsored country to divert resources from internal capital development to something else? Unlike in the MEC scenario, a country's GDP is a critical factor. This situation is not as prevalent since the end of the cold war/bipolar world order but was important in two previous limited wars and may have future implications.

A good example of this phenomenon is Vietnam. Looking at the statistical data, the GNP of North Vietnam increased during the height of the US bombing of the North from 1968 to 1972. This fact defies logic until one realizes that the real financial centers affecting the leadership of North Vietnam lay outside of the country. The leadership of North Vietnam could have been affected by attacking the financial centers in the Soviet Union and China. However, expanding the target set beyond the focus country may not be acceptable based upon political objectives, but such targets must be considered analyzing centers of gravity.

Lethal Attacks on Financial Institutions

Financial institutions of just the developing countries can represent a single critical node. This makes them susceptible to direct attacks. A well-placed bomb in either a financial institution itself or a communication center used to carry out transactions has the potential to severely cripple such a country's economy. If a country's financial institutions are suitable to attack, how can this attack best be achieved?

A few examples show the potentially disrupting impact on a critical node financial institution. While the examples deal with the United States—and its very sophisticated financial system (with very few critical nodes)—we can deduce the potentially negative impact that an attack would have on a critical node financial institution.

On 26 February 1993 a terrorist bomb was detonated in the parking garage of New York's World Trade Center. A rented van, packed with explosives, was casually driven into the underground parking garage. The car bomb was detonated and extensive damage was done to one of the towers of the World Trade Center. The building next to the Trade Center houses New York's five big commodity exchanges that deal predominately in oil, gold, coffee, cocoa, and sugar. While the commodity exchanges were not damaged by the blast, electrical power and air conditioning were cut to aid in fire-fighting efforts. This resulted in 25 percent of the exchanges' transactions going unprocessed on the day of the blast and a late start on opening the following Monday. The terrorist attack did not totally disrupt the financial system of the United States. However, the attack was not without impact. The chairman of the New York Mercantile Exchange stated that "a full day's closure of the exchange would have cost the oil trading community $25 million and an extended shutdown would have been devastating".[4]

A direct attack on the commodity exchanges would have been catastrophic. Hohn Damgar, the president of the Futures Industry Association, said that "the exchanges had decided previously that having backup trading facilities at another location would be cost prohibitive."[5]

However, after the blast, a secondary off-site location was sought. In addition, the computers that store the data for New York's automatic teller machines (ATM) were damaged in the blast. The machines were unusable for approximately three weeks. This damage, while being predominately an irritant, attests to the extremes of the results of a direct attack. As a side note, the owners of the World Trade Center, the Port Authority of New York and New Jersey, estimated that the cost of the damage will exceed $1 billion.

The disruptive nature of direct attacks on advanced financial institutions has been well exploited for many years by terrorist organizations. The Irish Republican Army has made numerous devastating attacks against London's financial district. These attacks, while causing civilian casualties and structural damage to buildings, has only caused short-term disruption of financial activities. Catastrophic destruction of the country's economy has been avoided for a number of reasons. The London financial community has anticipated these attacks and has prepared elaborate contingency plans for backup facilities and communications. In addition, the financial institutions themselves may not be the appropriate center of gravity for the optimum disruption of the financial system.

Contingency disaster plans are becoming the norm for almost all commercial financial institutions. For years US financial institutions felt isolated from the threat of terrorist activities. However, during the Persian Gulf War, Saddam Hussein sent a clear message that international terrorism would be one of his weapons as retaliation for US action in the Gulf. US financial institutions were forced to develop security procedures and contingency operations. Part of the contingency plans was to simply curtail operations at overseas locations and recall employees back to the United States. This practice basically enforced the terrorist threats by cutting US profits at overseas sites and removing US presence. While the terrorist threat never materialized, the contingency plans were adopted and are here to stay. The recent World Trade Center bombing drove home the necessity of the plans. While bombing an individual bank or financial center could prove to be nothing more than an irritant in a well-advanced economic nation-state, there are nation-states where critical nodes are worthy targets.

As financial institutions become more dependent upon communications for fund transfers and transactions, the communication centers themselves become the center of gravity, not the financial institutions. Paperwork transactions are becoming a thing of the past with most financial transactions occurring electronically. In the US there are approximately 10 clearing houses that handle all electronic fund transfers and financial transactions for all the large US banks. When a bank draft is submitted for payment at an overseas location, it is actually sent to one of the clearing houses instead of going to the parent bank for payment, and the draft is debited electronically. This benefits the banks in a number of ways. First, the operation is simplified so the draft actually clears the system faster, and second, the bank doesn't have to pay for the overhead to manage the fund-transfer operation. The clearing house is paid a fee to manage the operation. Disrupting the activities at the clearing houses would virtually shut down operations at the banks that the clearing house services. From a targeteer's perspective, it should be infinitely easier to disable a few clearing houses than to target multiple financial institutions, and this has the potential to be much more disruptive.

As mentioned above, the communication process in financial transactions may also be a critical node. If the electronic transfers are handled over regular telephone lines, as is the case in the US, these lines themselves become valuable targets for a number of reasons. Destroying a country's communications makes the country's leadership blind, striking right at the heart of the leadership center of gravity. It also eliminates the country's capabilities to communicate with the financial centers, stopping fund transfers and all other transactions, basically impeding the country's ability to function. Communication nodes are a valuable target because one can affect many facets of a country's operations. Of course, highly advanced countries will have multiple communication networks that may render this aspect not a critical node.

In short, targeting a single financial institution may have a short-term effect of disrupting a portion of a country's finances. It may also have a tactical effect as a terrorist function. However, it will probably not have a long-term strategic effect. To achieve strategic effect, one must disrupt a country's capabilities to conduct financial transactions. This could be achieved through disruption of the financial institutions' clearing houses, but even more important, disruption of the communication process would achieve a longer-term, and a more devastating, effect.

Nonlethal Attacks on Financial Institutions

Lethal attack on facilities containing banks and stock and commodity exchanges is an indiscriminate way of affecting national wealth and vitality. Such attacks risk collateral damage to unintended targets, and, by their very nature, cannot be covert. Nonlethal attack can be more deliberate and discriminate. In some forms they can also be more deniable and secret.

Nonlethal attack falls into two general categories, conventional and unconventional. Conventional methods include embargo, asset seizure and forfeiture, and other macroeconomic interventions. Such conventional, nonlethal methods are an indirect way to attack financial institutions, but such actions can have a significant direct effect on national wealth and vitality. Unconventional, nonlethal attack involves efforts to disrupt communications and financial transfer systems, computer databases, and similar elements of the financial trade by electronic means at specific nodes.

Nonlethal Conventional Methods

Nonlethal conventional attack can be very effective against countries at certain levels of development. By targeting financial institutions for attack, one can have a significant effect on countries with a large gross domestic product. As suggested above, disrupting trade, particularly for countries with high GDP and for MECs, can have significant effects on these countries' economic system. For example, in July 1941 the United States attempted to disrupt Japan's war aims by freezing Japanese assets in the United States and enforcing an embargo against shipments of aviation fuel. The embargo was soon expanded to include all types of petroleum products. The financial freeze and termination of oil shipments left Japan with a choice of watching its oil reserves drain away, withdrawing from China to appease the United States, or expanding its ambitions in the East Indies to achieve strategic autonomy in petroleum. Japan chose an aggressive path. Other examples include the freezing of Iranian assets after the seizure of the US embassy in Tehran in 1978 and the freezing of assets and the embargo against Iraq after the 1990 invasion of Kuwait.

Debt, particularly foreign debt, can be a lucrative target of nonlethal attack at many levels of GDP. An attack on debt instruments can exacerbate national economic problems. For example, many net-debtor countries finance accumulated budget deficit—their national debt—through bonds issued by their national treasury. The United States is such a debtor country. Because Japan is a major purchaser of US Treasury issues that finance the US national debt,[6] Japanese investment decisions can play a significant role in our economy. If the Bank of Tokyo should decide not to buy their full share of US Treasury bills, Wall Street would respond with catastrophic sell-offs. The Federal Reserve Bank and Treasury Department would have to stimulate investor interest in short-term notes and would respond by drastically raising interest rates to curb the money supply or risk spiraling inflation. Either way the gradual US economic growth since 1989 would be over, and we would ultimately face an extended period of high unemployment, high inflation, or both.

In fact, Yusuke Kashiwagi, chairman of Japan's Bank of Tokyo, Ltd., speaking to the Japan Society in New York in January 1990, noted that Japanese intervention may have been responsible for the October 1987 crash of the US stock market. He said, "It was very clear that the termination of Japanese investment in US Treasuries was a trigger for the (stock market) crash."[7]

He warned that narrow spreads between interest rates on Japanese and US Treasury issues "might trigger another kind of difficult situation in the US" as Japanese investors chose treasury instruments in their own country over investment in the US market.

Just as the US is vulnerable to Japanese pressure, similarly many third world countries are vulnerable to financial intervention by the United States. Much of the debt in Latin America, for example, is controlled by US banks. In a crisis, such leverage could be used to force concessions or to topple a regime.

Nonlethal Unconventional Methods

According to the US Congress' Office of Technology Assessment (OTA), the most serious problem related to international banking is the increased payment risk on telecommunications networks used for electronic funds transfer. In shared networks, whether operated by central banks or consortia of banks, the failure of one or more participants to settle end-of-day deficits resulting from "daylight overdrafts" could result in unacceptable demands on central banks as lenders of last resort or in a cascade of settlement failures that would precipitate national or even international crisis. While the OTA study focuses on accidental disruptions of electronic transfer communications, the impact of a deliberate shutdown of funds-transfer systems would be equally disastrous. Because of the interrelated nature of such electronic data-interchange systems, care must be exercised to minimize collateral damage to the data of friendly financial systems.[8]

OTA notes that until recently, state-owned postal, telephone, and telegraph (PTT) services operated the public telecommunications networks in European countries, although some of these have recently been privatized. These public networks afford universal access to highly standardized services at regulated rates or tariffs. Private networks offer dedicated access to select and usually tailored services at rates set by contract with the users. US banks overseas primarily serve large corporations rather than individuals, offering "wholesale" services such as cash management, financial market data, and currency trading. Banks have two needs for international communications:

- As intracorporate business support: voice, voice mail, fax, e-mail, and data transmission; and
- As a means to create and deliver financial products and services: electronic transfer of funds, cross-border electronic letters of credit, customer account information and cash-management financial information.

Manufacturers Hanover Trust, which merged with Chemical Bank in January 1992, was fairly typical. This bank's "Global Wholesale Bank" used international telecommunications primarily for internal bank business, while its operating services group (Geoserve) delivered electronic banking products and services to corporate customers around the world. Geoserve customers using the network could access the bank's computers to check their account balances and to initiate funds transfers and letters of credit.

In the 1980s, many large US commercial and investment banks or security houses set up their own private telecommunications networks made up of facilities leased from the PTTs. These leased facilities included cable circuits and satellite capacity, interconnected to the public network, with some network and terminal equipment owned by the financial institution. The bank exercises full financial and managerial responsibility over network operations. While only very large financial institutions have elaborate international private data networks, many financial institutions have a few point-to-point leased circuits to tie their dispersed locations to larger operating centers.

The existence of these independent telecommunications systems presents some questions for the campaign planner. If only the financial system is targeted, these private networks allow selective destruction of financial nodes while leaving public data networks for nonfinancial operations intact. However, in a generalized attack to create strategic paralysis of the country, these private data networks could provide redundant capability to the state telecommunications systems and should be included in the strategic target set. Interestingly, as the OTA reports note, many US banks control these private networks and could provide details on the arrangement of telecommunication facilities in targeted countries.

The OTA reports that financial institutions in the industrialized countries are shifting back to reliance on the public switched network. The comparative cost of public and private networks are changing in Europe and North America, which have well-developed and integrated public telecommunications systems. Technology is allowing these public networks to provide better control and reliability and to offer value-added services. As private networks become less effective as product differentiators, costs and reliability become the primary selection criteria. New technologies are making private networks cheaper, but the same technologies are allowing public switched networks to offer customized "virtual network" services. In addition, the migration of financial institutions back to public networks may also be greatly encouraged because there is a growing need for financial institutions to be linked electronically with customer computers. The scope of internetworking among corporations is growing, and banks may have to participate in electronic payments and electronic data interchange in order to retain their traditional customer relationships and avoid being bypassed. Private networks cannot always provide direct access to customers as can public networks.

The appearance of private data networks parallels technological changes that have widely distributed the processing of information. As public telecommunication systems evolve from oligarchic networks of large centralized switching facilities to distributed or geodesic networks, they will become increasingly difficult to target by conventional, lethal means. Distributed networks are inherently survivable. In fact, they may reverse the effect of the military technological revolution (MTR) by denying the capability provided by advanced conventional/ precision guided munitions. Before this MTR, the inaccuracy of bombing technology required bombardment of wide areas to ensure the destruction of specific enemy centers. Now, when targeting science permits the selective destruction of a particular room in an individual building, the target of such attack can be distributed across a wide area and become invulnerable. The best way to attack such systems may be to enter the microcosm of high-technology electronics ourselves, using software viruses and other malevolent technologies to prosecute the attack electronically.

Banks and other institutions are increasingly worried about the problem of electronic intrusion. The National Academy of Sciences noted in 1991 that the trends in computer use in business and industry suggest that whatever trust was justified in the past cannot be justified in the future.

Networking and embedded data systems are proliferating, and computers have become such an integral part of business in developed countries that computer risks cannot be separated from general-business risks. The ability to use and abuse computer systems is becoming widespread. In addition, the international system is unstable, raising questions about the potential for transnational attacks at a time when international corporate, financial, research, and other computer networks are growing.

There is an excellent basis for these fears. Celebrated cases of intrusions into government and private computers have been recorded in the press and in fiction. The 1983 movie *Wargames* recounted the fictional story of a teenage computer hacker who used the family telephone to break into a classified government computer and nearly start global thermonuclear war. William Gibson's 1984 novel *Neuromancer* introduced the term *cyberspace* to describe a globe-circling, interconnected telephone network where "console cowboys" steal data and commit other mischief for hire. In real life 1986, members of a West German computer club, using commercial telephone connections, broke into computers associated with the Lawrence Livermore Laboratory and took what they believed were critical files on the Strategic Defense Initiative. The group had made contact with East German and Russian agents and planned to sell the documents, but they were thwarted by US and West German authorities.[9]

Access to the source code of the computer system—the basic instruction set that turns a computer from lumps of silicon into a working machine—is a necessary prerequisite for the skilled virus maker. Most of the viruses infecting personal computers in the US and Western Europe come from Bulgaria where computer hackers—sponsored by the state—reverse engineered Western computers and software to build their own computer industry. In the late 1980s, while Bulgarian factories built poorly manufactured clones of Apple and IBM products, Bulgarian students and computer scientists began copying Western programs, cracking any copy protection schemes that stood in their way, and became more skilled at programming their way around any problem. They learned the hidden routines and trap doors of the IBM and Apple operating systems, assimilating all of the skills necessary to become first-class virus writers.[10]

Such viruses could clearly have military utility. A persistent rumor circulated during the 1991 Gulf War that coalition forces had infected Iraqi air defense computers with a virus that would impair their ability to react to allied air strikes. As the story went, the virus was programmed into a French-made computer printer used by Iraq. While no confirmation was ever forthcoming from military sources, the possibilities of such weapons are intriguing.

Financial systems, with their reliance on computers and electronic data networks are particularly susceptible to such attack. Since many of the private financial networks operating around the world are controlled by Western banks, it may be possible to get access to system codes to enable the development of sophisticated and subtle programs.

Conclusion

The development of a quantitative relationship between national power and financial elements (GDP, banks, stocks, foreign debt, exports, and imports) is the initial step in a long-term process of exploring and exploiting economic warfare to a level not before deemed significant. This embryo study provides a simplified tool to identify nation-states that may be vulnerable to influence via attacks against financial centers of gravity. Using a country's current financial data, the military specialist can use the model to determine if an enemy country is ripe for attack against its financial centers of gravity.

Future research should include an analysis of time-series data to further validate the model developed. Time-series data on a per-country basis would substantiate the regression model and indicate whether the relationships hold over time. In addition, the methodology could be used to analyze data over time for each country to determine which of the financial elements is most closely related to GDP and national power. Furthermore, time-series data would provide an empirical basis for an analysis of a country's specific vulnerabilities.

Future studies need also to look more closely at the details of those nation-states that are economically sponsored. Finally, an extension of the HKC regression analysis evaluating per capita GDP would prove most informative.

Notes

1. Majors Jeffery B. Hukill, John J. Kennedy, and Arthur B. Cameron III, USAF, *Targeting Financial Systems as Centers of Gravity: "Low Intensity" to "No Intensity" Conflict*, May 1993.

2. See, for example, Paul Kennedy, *The Rise and Fall of the Great Powers* (New York: Vintage Books, 1989); and Mancur Olson, *The Rise and Decline of Nations* (New Haven, Conn.: Yale University Press, 1982). Olson and Kennedy both use changes in GDP to indicate changes in national power. Kennedy's best-seller defines national power as the rate of growth in GDP and gross national product.

3. Guy Halverson, "Financial Markets Deal with Explosion Aftermath," *The Christian Science Monitor*, 1 March 1993, C1-3.

4. Jeanne Iida, "Wall Street to Build an Emergency Site," *The American Banker* 157, no. 15 (23 January 1992): 3.

5. According to Drexel Burnham Lambert, 14 percent of US government bonds were held by foreign investors as recently as January 1990. Japan has been the biggest source of that liquidity. In the late 1980s, Japanese and other foreign investors at times purchased as much as 40 percent of the US Treasury notes and bonds sold at government auctions.

6. Values for exports and imports are based on regression of GDP against the squared volumes of exports and imports.

7. Constance Mitchell and Michael R. Sesit, "Foreign Buyers Could Pull Back on Treasurys," *The Wall Street Journal*, 22 January 1990, C1, C19.

8. US Congress, Office of Technology Assessment, *U.S. Banks and International Telecommunications* (Washington, D.C.: US Government Printing Office, 1993).

9. Clifford Stole, *The Cuckoo's Egg: Inside the World of Computer Espionage* (New York: Double, 1989).

10. Paul Mungo and Bryan Clough, *Approaching Zero* (New York: Random House, 1992).

Changing Status of Nuclear Forces

Thomas J. Stark

In the January 1993 *National Security Strategy of the United States*, President George Bush wrote just before leaving office that America "stands at a crossroads in history."[1] Bush wrote of a world that had changed dramatically during the past five years. Democracies and free market institutions and values have flourished. "Our former nemesis, the Soviet Union, . . . is gone." The threat of a thermonuclear war has been "radically" reduced. The dangerous nuclear arms race between the US and the former Soviet Union is over. "The Communist ideology . . . is today, in most of the world, discredited, despised, and discarded." The president asserted that "our collective victory in the Cold War fundamentally changed the strategic environment." Moreover, the US and coalition victory in Iraq has also shaped the international environment as the Gulf War demonstrated the regional volatility of the new world. These events and subsequent changes are a clear indication that the US has moved into a new historic period.

These changes and events have had a tremendous impact on US nuclear policy. A dynamic arms control process has produced initiatives calling for deep reductions in strategic nuclear forces. America is rethinking its overall nuclear requirements. With US nuclear weapons being removed from Europe and South Korea, the concept of extended nuclear deterrence, known as flexible response, is evolving. However, the proliferation of nuclear and ballistic-missile technology, as well as other weapons of mass destruction, continues at an alarming pace and is one of the greatest future threats to US national security. In this new historic period, America also stands at a crossroads with its nuclear policy and strategic forces. In this new era of great opportunities and great dangers, America must decide on a new nuclear strategy and an appropriate strategic force structure.

Former secretary of defense Les Aspin described the new historic period. "There is a terrible irony associated with this new world. We face a greatly reduced chance of seeing many nuclear detonations, but perhaps an increased chance of seeing one nuclear detonation."[2] Secretary Aspin pointed out three propositions that can help us deal with the new nuclear age. The first is that the traditional concept of deterrence, the policy for handling nuclear superpowers, may no longer work. In the past, nuclear deterrence was based on rational actors operating on a similar logic with each side putting at risk something the other side holds dear. Can we be sure that this concept of deterrence will work in the future? The second proposition is that the US has undergone a "complete reversal" in its interest regarding nuclear weapons. During the cold war, the US depended on nuclear weapons to offset numerical inferiority of conventional forces. But with the disintegration of the Soviet Union, the US finds itself as the world's biggest and the most capable conventional power and no longer in need of a nuclear equalizer. The final proposition is that the US needs "a new set of answers" for the new nuclear threat. Aspin warned that this will not be easy.

> No single policy, like deterrence, will meet our needs, nor will the US be able to "go it alone," as we did under Cold War deterrence. Most interestingly, the US can no longer count on the old left-right wing political divisions in American politics to guide solutions. Solutions will have to be borrowed, such as missile defenses and the Comprehensive Test Ban Treaty, from both the right and the left. The distinguishing characteristic of policies today is whether they are suited for the new world. Whether a policy is favored by the right or the left no longer tells you where it fits in the real world. And the pertinent axis is not right-left, it's a new-old, because it really is a new world.[3]

Overview

The purpose of this analysis is twofold: first it examines the evolving US nuclear policy and strategic force structure; and then it addresses the issue of nuclear proliferation in the new strategic environment. In looking at US nuclear policy, it describes how the military is attempting to reshape its nuclear forces and strategy. Then, the following questions will be addressed. What is the new US regional defense strategy, and what role does strategic deterrence play in it? What weapons make up the strategic force, and how are they being reduced? Is there a need to modernize the strategic force? And finally, how is the US strategic deterrence force organized? In looking at nuclear proliferation, this analysis describes the new strategic environment. And it answers the following questions. Why do states seek nuclear weapons? What role does Russia and the Commonwealth of Independent States (CIS) play in nuclear proliferation, and why is Ukraine determined to keep its nuclear weapons? Does Russia's new military doctrine have significant nuclear implications? What role does North Korea play in nuclear proliferation? Lastly, this examination describes the new American response to global nuclear proliferation.

US Nuclear Policy Under Review

In September 1992 the Air Staff at the Pentagon issued a white paper entitled *Nuclear Sufficiency in the 1990s and Beyond: The New Strategic Equation*. The paper assessed the general direction of change in US nuclear policies. It also proposed new criteria for judging the adequacy of US nuclear forces. Trends were identified that permit the US to consider deep reductions in existing nuclear arsenals. One trend is "a decline in the perceived utility of US nuclear weapons."[4] Factors that contribute to this perception include the following:

> Many emerging threats to US national security may not be deterred by nuclear weapons; and new non-nuclear weapons technologies (including precision guided conventional munitions and ballistic-missile defenses) have given, or will give, the US the capability to accomplish most strategic war-time missions without the use of nuclear weapons.[5]

The paper asserted that the disintegration of the Soviet Union and the "revolution in conventional weapons technology potentially renders obsolete"[6] many of the traditional strategic planning assumptions. In the absence of a Soviet threat, there is no longer a need to have large numbers of nuclear weapons on alert poised for immediate launch. With the threat of large-scale nuclear war reduced, crisis-warning time has increased. If the

US can use advanced conventional weapons to deter or control escalation and to retaliate decisively in battle, nuclear weapons may not be needed.

In rethinking nuclear sufficiency, the paper stated several hypotheses for consideration. They are:

> First, distinctions between tactical and strategic nuclear weapons are disappearing.
>
> Second, the term "strategic" may, in the future, refer to a broad range of forces, including ballistic-missile defenses and certain advanced conventional weapons.
>
> Third, nuclear sufficiency can no longer be calculated in isolation from the potential contributions of other strategic weapons.
>
> Fourth, as future strategic forces assume roles beyond mere deterrence [one example is *extended defense* instead of extended deterrence], or as nuclear weapons become less relevant to desired security outcomes, measures of ability to limit damage, rather than inflict damage, may be more relevant yardsticks of sufficiency in the future.
>
> Fifth, there is an enduring lexicon of strategic sufficiency that will probably be retained [a secure nuclear reserve] even as their traditional definitions are revised or modified.[7]

The Air Staff white paper concluded that the *new strategic equation* "calls for a strategy of Damage Limitation at the strategic level, to replace Second Strike Counterforce, and a policy of Decisive Force (the application of overwhelming conventional power) to replace Flexible Response at the theater level."[8] The required strategic force structure to implement the new strategic equation would include advanced conventional weapons, ballistic-missile defenses, and a small secure nuclear reserve.

Secretary Aspin authorized the first comprehensive review of the nation's nuclear doctrine since the end of the cold war. R. Jeffrey Smith wrote in an October 1993 *Washington Post* article:

> The review is meant to take a fresh look at the number, type and targets of all such arms remaining in the US arsenal, with the aim of producing "a new national policy" that will eventually be submitted to President Clinton for his approval.[9]

Smith cited the anomaly that exists with the current US nuclear weapons policy. The number of nuclear warheads has been reduced dramatically in recent years. But US targeting and employment policy based on a massive Soviet threat has remained unchanged since 1981.

The purpose of the Department of Defense review is to design the long-term structure of the US nuclear arsenal. Questions asked concern the basic purpose of nuclear weapons, the rationale for keeping them, how many weapons in the US arsenal should be kept on alert, and whether the weapons should be targeted in advance. In a related January 1994 *Los Angeles Times* article, it was reported that the US is preparing a plan to aim its nuclear missiles away from targets in the CIS and point them at desolate spots in the open seas.[10] Russia and Ukraine are preparing similar plans. It is a "symbolic" move that will slow the now immediate response time for launching nuclear weapons and could reduce the dangers of accidental launchings. Another related policy review conducted by the staff of the National Security Council will decide on the total level of nuclear weapons that the US should seek in a future round of arms control negotiations.

Two of the most controversial policy questions are as follows:

> Whether Washington should adopt a policy of "no first use" by pledging it will not employ nuclear arms first in a conventional conflict.
>
> And whether US military doctrine should include planning for potential nuclear strikes in response to attacks against US forces by chemical or biological weapons.[11]

Some analysts argue that if the US adopted a no-first-use doctrine, it might discourage nonnuclear nations from attempting to acquire nuclear arms. Moreover, the superior Soviet conventional threat, which initially led to the US option of using nuclear weapons first, is gone. Other military analysts believe that nuclear arms can be used as a new sort of "equalizer" to deter chemical and biological attacks.

New Regional Defense Strategy

The disintegration of the Soviet Union ended the traditional cold-war threat of global conflict. But the world remains a dangerous place. R. James Woolsey, Director of Central Intelligence (DCI), sees "a more lethal version of the world than existed before 1914."[12] Woolsey cites "virulent" nationalism, international uncertainty, and the "risk of cross-border spillovers" as key concerns. Multiple threats to US security remain, typified by Saddam Hussein's attempt to dominate Kuwait and the strategic oil reserves of the Persian Gulf. "Today's challenges are more complex, ambiguous, and diffuse than ever before. They are political, economic, and military; unilateral and multilateral; short- and long-term."[13] Consequently, the focus of the new national security strategy is on meeting the regional threats, opportunities, and challenges that the US is more likely to face in the future. According to the secretary of defense's 1993 *Annual Report to the President and the Congress*, the most fundamental goal of the new regional defense strategy is to deter or defeat attack from whatever source, against the US, its citizens and forces, and to honor our historic and treaty commitments.[14] The new regional defense strategy contains four critical elements to guide defense planning and military force structure: strategic deterrence and defense, forward presence, crisis response, and reconstitution. These fundamental elements will remain valid for the foreseeable future. This analysis focuses on the first element, strategic deterrence and defense.

Strategic Deterrence and Defense

The 1993 *National Security Strategy of the United States* clearly defines strategic deterrence and defense.

> Deterring nuclear attack remains our top priority. We must still possess modern strategic nuclear forces and a reliable warning system. We must develop a system for global protection against limited ballistic-missile attack. We must maintain responsive, highly trained, technologically sophisticated, and broadly capable conventional and unconventional forces. We must maintain and improve space systems integral to strategic and tactical operations worldwide.[15]

The defense secretary's *Annual Report to the President and the Congress* is the primary source for outlining strategic deterrence and defense. It states that US strategic forces must remain survivable and flexible to deter against strategic nuclear attack. "At the same time, US nuclear targeting policy and plans have changed and will continue to change in response to developments in the former Soviet Union." It asserts that the US welcomes "opportunities to reduce the numbers of strategic nuclear weapons and increase the stability of the strategic balance by eliminating the most destabilizing types of weapons." The combination of the July 1991 Strategic Arms Reduction Treaty (START), former President George Bush's September 1991 and January 1992 nuclear initiatives, and the January 1993 START II treaty will reduce the size of US nuclear forces to about one-quarter of the 1990 level by the year 2003. START II limits the US and Russia to 3,500 warheads each. The elimination of all multiple warhead intercontinental ballistic missiles (ICBM), called for by START II, will greatly enhance nuclear stability. "The remaining strategic forces will continue to support America's global role and international commitments," including maintaining the nuclear umbrella for NATO, Japan, and South Korea. The US "must continue to prepare to deal with threats of limited attack." The threats come from countries which seek to acquire nuclear, chemical, and biological weapons and the means to deliver them and from accidental or unauthorized missile launch from unstable nuclear states. To counter the threats, the US must deploy ballistic-missile defenses (BMD) to protect the US and shield its allies and its forward-deployed forces. The element of strategic deterrence and defense requires the US "to maintain a balanced deterrent force with both tactical and strategic capabilities." The secretary's report concluded by noting that the US must develop "a proper mix of offensive and active defense capabilities to deter or defeat the threat posed by weapons of mass destruction."[16]

US Strategic Forces

The strategic force structure implements the deterrence and defense element of the regional defense strategy. The strategic force structure is one of the four force packages of the base force, a total force structure designed to meet the requirements of future regional security challenges. The other three force packages include Atlantic, Pacific, and contingency forces. The base force must be credible, but it must take into account the realities of reduced defense budgets and the domestic imperative. US strategic deterrent and defense forces primarily counter nuclear threats. Joint Publication (Pub) 3-11, *Joint Doctrine For Nuclear, Biological, and Chemical (NBC) Defense,* states that the fundamental purpose of US strategic nuclear forces is to deter aggression that threatens the basic security interests of the US and its allies.[17] Strategic forces include a triad of nuclear offensive forces; strategic command, control, communications, and intelligence (C^3I) systems; and ballistic-missile defenses. Each component plays a unique role in deterring and defending against nuclear attacks. Since the scope of the present examination is limited to nuclear forces, it will not provide discussion of strategic defenses.

Modernization of US Strategic Forces

While the START and START II treaties will dramatically reduce US nuclear offensive forces, "residual" nuclear forces must provide "an effective and robust deterrent to nuclear attack."[18] This will require continued maintenance, a reliable command, control, communications, and intelligence network, and most importantly, appropriate modernization. According to Gen George Butler, USAF, commander in chief, US Strategic Command, "Critical modernization decisions loom that have vital implications for future force levels."[19] The currently planned modernization efforts were summarized by former secretary of defense Dick Cheney in his annual report before he left office.

> Efforts to extend the service life of the existing Minuteman III ICBM force, along with the previously authorized introduction of the B-2 stealth bomber in the mid-1990s and completion of the 18-ship Ohio-class ballistic-missile submarine force in 1997, are the extent of modernization efforts currently planned.[20]

US Nuclear Offensive Forces

US nuclear offensive forces are made up of three elements: long-range bombers, land-based ICBMs, and sea-based ballistic missiles. These elements are known as the three legs of the strategic triad. In testimony to the House Armed Services Committee in February 1991, former secretary of the

Air Force Donald Rice and Air Force Chief of Staff Merrill McPeak stated the rationale for the continued validity of the strategic triad.

> The triad concept remains fundamental. Each leg of the triad possesses unique and complementary characteristics which synergistically provide a retaliatory capability that no adversary could hope to successfully overcome.[21]

The triad concept served the US well in the cold war. It provided a secure second-strike capability to counter a surprise Soviet nuclear attack. It also provided redundancy sufficient to offset system failures or possible technological breakthroughs that could render one leg of the triad ineffective. Today, in a world of great uncertainty, the triad remains essential to deter potential adversaries not to launch an attack against the US or its allies.

US Strategic Command (USSTRATCOM) has made recommendations for a post–START-II strategic force structure that are currently under review by the secretary of defense. These recommendations, if accepted, will preserve the strategic triad. According to General Butler, the recommended force structure, based on the triad, "will provide a sound conceptual basis from which to pursue further reductions, . . . or to achieve a more robust posture, should political outcomes in the former Soviet Union so dictate."[22] General Butler cautions against force structure decisions based purely on fiscal factors. Survivability and planning flexibility are characteristics of the triad that must be maintained.

> The crucial point here is to avoid eroding the deterrent value of the strategic forces by budget-driven decisions that ignore vital planning considerations or depreciate the carefully conceived rationale that underpinned our objectives in the START negotiations.[23]

Long-Range Bomber Force

The US long-range bomber force is made up of B-52, B-1B, and B-2 aircraft. All three bombers are capable of delivering either conventional or nuclear weapons to any point on the earth's surface. Bombers provide stability and flexibility to the triad. According to Secretary Rice and General McPeak:

> In the nuclear arena, the bomber enhances the stability of the nuclear balance. Its high survivability promises any aggressor that an attack

> will be met with devastating retaliation, while its relatively slow speed compared to ballistic missiles means that the bomber does not pose a first strike threat. Because it can be generated, dispersed, launched under positive control and then recalled and redirected, the bomber also provides our nation's leaders with a highly flexible means of sending a variety of unmistakable messages to an adversary—messages that can help defuse and stabilize crises.[24]

In the nuclear role, the bombers can deliver a combination of standoff weapons and gravity bombs. The START II treaty will result in far fewer nuclear bomber warheads than allowed by the START treaty. START II permits each party to exempt up to 100 heavy bombers from its warhead limits by reorienting them to a conventional role. The B-1Bs will be reoriented to a conventional role. The planned post–START-II US nuclear long-range bomber force will consist of 20 B-2s equipped with gravity bombs and 95 B-52Hs equipped with standoff air launched cruise missiles (ALCM) and advanced cruise missiles. B-52Gs and the short-range attack missiles (SRAM) are being retired at an accelerated rate. "These changes will result in a smaller, but highly potent, and modernized nuclear bomber force."[25]

In the dynamic strategic environment, the bomber force is becoming increasingly available for conventional missions. B-52s, operating out of various worldwide locations, effectively applied combat power in Operation Desert Storm. According to General Butler, the B-52s demonstrated "the value of long-range heavy bombers in major regional conflicts." The B-1B, an aircraft with untapped potential, will form the core of future US conventional bomber capability. General Butler cautions, "Realizing [the B-1Bs] potential calls for better organic maintenance capability, enhanced weapon system survivability and an expanded scope of conventional weapons carriage."[26] The B-52H and B-2 are also scheduled for conventional upgrades.

Land-Based Intercontinental Ballistic Missiles

Land-based intercontinental ballistic missiles will be significantly reduced by the end of the century. Unique characteristics of the ICBM force include promptness, reliability, accuracy, and low operating cost. Five hundred silo-based Minuteman III missiles, downloaded from three to one warhead each, will be the only deployed US ICBM under the START II treaty. Planned upgrades and modifications to the 50 silo-based Peacekeeper missiles, the nation's most modern missile force, have been canceled in light of its anticipated retirement under START II. Age and survivability are two key problems with this leg of the strategic triad. President Bush's unilateral initiatives included cancellation of both the small ICBM and the Peacekeeper Rail Garrison, the two proposed solutions to the survivability problem. According to the secretary of defense's 1993 *Annual Report to the President and the Congress*, the US must now "focus on ensuring that the service life of the Minuteman III can be extended to the year 2010 and beyond." Specific areas of concern are the missile's "aging components in the guidance computer and associated electrical systems and refurbishment of the second- and third-stage rocket motors."[27] The aging ICBM fleet is an immediate problem that demands near-term solutions.

Sea-Based Ballistic Missiles

Nuclear-powered ballistic-missile submarines (SSBN) are playing a greater role in providing strategic deterrence. The ability to remain virtually undetected at sea for long periods of time makes the SSBN force "the most survivable and enduring" leg of the strategic triad. Under the START II treaty, the US will deploy eight Trident I SSBNs, each capable of being armed with 24 C-4 missiles, and 10 Trident II SSBNs, each capable of being armed with 24 D-5 missiles. The D-5 missile, "with its increased accuracy, range, and payload, gives the force the capability to hold at risk essentially the entire range of potential strategic targets now and in the foreseeable future." START II also calls for submarine missiles to be downloaded from eight to four warheads each. Modernization of the C-4 missile is a current key issue. According to General Butler, options include backfitting the eight Trident I's with the newer D-5 missile or extending the service life for the C-4.[28]

Command, Control, Communications, and Intelligence (C^3I) Systems

In 1992, President Bush's secretary of defense Dick Cheney wrote, "As US forces shrink and increasingly relocate from overseas locations, and as alert levels are lowered and the ballistic-missile threat proliferates, the ability to detect and assess attacks against the United States becomes even more critical."[29] Warning sensors, command centers, and communications systems make up the strategic C^3I systems. The Defense Support Program (DSP) space sensors provide timely, accurate, and unambiguous attack information. Intelligence provides critical warning and assessment of attack. Command centers are a vital part of decision making and effective control of strategic forces. Communications systems provide connectivity between warning sensors, command centers, and combat forces.

Modernization efforts center around improving satellite warning capabilities. The follow-on early warning system, a new system, will offer "worldwide coverage, enhanced detection capability, greater survivability, and faster reporting." This system will provide warning and assessment of both long- and short-range ballistic-missile attacks. If the US decides to deploy national ballistic-missile defenses, the current command and control infrastructure at the Cheyenne Mountain complex and other locations must be modified to handle the new capabilities. Finally, new Milstar communications satellites will provide strategic forces with "two-way, low-data-rate communications links that are highly resistant to jamming and nuclear effects."[30]

US Strategic Command

USSTRATCOM is the unified combatant command that commands and controls the nation's nuclear forces. It is organized to deter a major military attack on the US and its allies, and should deterrence fail, employ forces. Based on the recommendation of the Joint Chiefs of Staff (JCS) and secretary of defense, USSTRATCOM was established on 1 June 1992, thus merging Navy and Air Force strategic nuclear forces. The commander in chief of the United States Strategic Command (USCINCSTRAT) will be the military's advocate for strategic nuclear forces, nuclear force structure, and modernization issues. USCINCSTRAT assignments will rotate between the Navy and Air Force. Specific duties include establishing force requirements, conducting integrated strategic operational planning, and participating in establishing strategic nuclear deterrent and targeting policies. As outlined in the *Implementation Plan for Integration of US Strategic Command*, USCINCSTRAT responsibilities include:

> Supporting the national security objective of strategic deterrence.
>
> Employing assigned forces, as directed.
>
> Providing support to other combatant commanders, as directed.
>
> Conducting appropriate worldwide strategic reconnaissance.
>
> Ensuring command, control, communications, and intelligence (C^3I) for strategic force employment.[31]

USSTRATCOM is assigned forces from service component commands to include long-range bombers, strategic reconnaissance aircraft, and battle management assets from Air Combat Command, intercontinental ballistic missiles from AF Space Command, and ballistic-missile submarines and command and control aircraft from US Atlantic and US Pacific fleets.

Gen George Butler, the first USCINCSTRAT, has stated that "the shift to unified command of strategic forces went smoothly. . . ." The reorganization has already "reaped fiscal, operational and planning dividends." General Butler uses the term *strategic disengagement* to describe the prolonged period that the US has entered into with the former Soviet Union.

> Given the sheer size of their respective nuclear arsenals, the length of arms control implementation schemes and the turbulent politics in Russia and the other republics holding nuclear weapons, the path ahead offers much to hope for but also leaves much to be seen. Nuclear policymaking must be informed by a rigorous assessment of the complex interaction among force posture, arms control entitlements and constraints, funding requirements and targeting directives.[32]

In its first 18 months of existence, USSTRATCOM has completed "landmark" analysis on alternative force structures; consolidated command, control, and communications airborne assets; and activated the Joint Intelligence Center to assess the growing threat of global proliferation of weapons of mass destruction. Moreover, it is working with other regional unified commands to explore the transfer of planning responsibilities for employment of nuclear weapons in theater conflicts.

Proliferation of Nuclear Arms

In the 1993 edition of *Games Nations Play*, Professor John Spanier wrote that the immediate future will witness a "new strategic environment" for the nation-state system, characterized by the proliferation of nuclear arms.[33] Today, there are five declared nuclear powers: the US, Russia and the Commonwealth of Independent States, China, France, and Great Britain. There are also four probable nuclear states: India, Pakistan, Israel, and South Africa. In March 1993, President F. W. de Klerk declared that South Africa was abandoning its nuclear weapons program. Probable nuclear states are perceived as dangerous because of their undeclared intentions and capability to quickly assemble and/or employ nuclear weapons. Several other third world states may acquire nuclear weapons in the future: North Korea, South Korea, Indonesia, Taiwan, Argentina, Brazil, Chile, Iran, Iraq, Egypt, Libya, Algeria, and Syria.[34]

New Strategic Environment

The new strategic environment is influenced by several key factors. One factor is the collapse of the Soviet Union. It is now replaced by the CIS. According to Spanier, "About 80 percent of the Soviet strategic nuclear weapons were in Russia; the others were in Ukraine, Belarus, and Kazakhstan."[35] The Soviet disintegration will be studied in greater detail in the case study to follow.

Another factor is the breakdown of the bipolar East-West security structure. States once protected by the US and Soviet Union are now seeking their own nuclear arsenals. In *Disorder*

Restored, Professor John Mearsheimer wrote that bipolarity will be replaced by multipolarity. As the bipolar barriers to proliferation come down, great regional powers will emerge. They include Germany, France, Britain, and perhaps Italy in Europe, and China, India, Japan, and possibly Pakistan in Asia. Russia will be a great power in both Europe and Asia. The US will certainly remain a great power capable of influencing events worldwide. Mearsheimer described the falling proliferation barriers:

> First, none of the great powers in the new multipolar world is likely to have the preponderance of military power necessary to extend its nuclear shield far and wide, like the Americans and Soviets did in the Cold War. Second, great powers will face credibility problems if they attempt to extend nuclear deterrence. Alliance patterns are typically much more fluid in multipolarity than in bipolarity, where rigid alliance structures are the rule. . . . Consequently, "fair weather" friends are more commonplace in a multipolar than a bipolar system, a situation that will work to reduce the credibility of nuclear commitments proffered by great powers. Third, future great powers will not have as much bargaining leverage vis-á-vis Third World states as the superpowers did in the Cold War.[36]

Like Spanier, Mearsheimer concluded that the most probable scenario in the new strategic environment is further nuclear proliferation.

Mearsheimer warned that nuclear proliferation is particularly dangerous for the third world. Powerful incentives may exist for intensely hostile nuclear states to strike nonnuclear powers. Furthermore, "Third World states are not likely to build survivable retaliatory forces, the sine qua non of nuclear stability." Finally, will all third world leaders "fully appreciate the destructiveness of nuclear weapons," and can the third world guarantee the required security and safeguards for nuclear weapons?[37]

Another factor influencing the new strategic environment is the diffusion of nuclear technology. According to Spanier, "496 civilian nuclear reactors are in operation or under construction in 32 nations to produce energy to meet legitimate economic and industrial needs."[38] Also, greater advances in technology have been made that make it easier for third world states to build the bomb. This does not mean that these states will automatically produce nuclear weapons, but if a political decision were made to develop the bomb, the reactors and the needed technical skills are in place.

A discomforting proliferation trend in the new strategic environment is that several nuclear weapons programs have escaped detection from the international nonproliferation mechanisms. The Nonproliferation Treaty (NPT), International Atomic Energy Agency (IAEA), London Nuclear Suppliers Group, and intelligence gathering failed to detect or stop the nuclear program in Iraq. In the early days of the NPT, the sure sign of a nuclear weapons program was an easily detectable nuclear test. Today, the situation is much more complex. In his article, *A Proliferation Primer*, David Albright reported, "The cases of Pakistan and South Africa show that it is not necessary to conduct a full-scale nuclear test to be a nuclear-armed power."[39] Despite the tremendous cost, security, and national sacrifice required for a nuclear weapons program, these states covet nuclear arsenals.

Why Do States Seek Nuclear Weapons?

Spanier provided three reasons why states seek this "dangerous and expensive" power: national security considerations, status and prestige, and domestic politics.[40] In terms of national security, nuclear weapons may give states an increased ability to deter or threaten other states. Despite the US pledge for protection of Western Europe from the Soviets, Britain and France felt the need to acquire nuclear capabilities. China acquired nuclear weapons after Sino-Soviet relations soured in the 1960s. India's 1974 detonation of the bomb undoubtedly was a response to China's acquisition. And Pakistan soon followed with a nuclear program to counter India. Spanier cited Israel and Taiwan as good examples of states trying to enhance their security by acquiring nuclear arsenals. Israel, "often isolated politically and pressured by friends to settle conflicts," has acquired a sizable nuclear arsenal.[41] Taiwan's interest in the bomb was stimulated in the late 1970s when the US officially recognized China and dropped its security treaty with the Nationalists. And if North Korea gains nuclear status, can South Korea or Japan be far behind?

Nuclear weapons are seen by many states as symbols of prestige and strength. A third world state may see nuclear weapons and the acquisition of a credible delivery system as symbolic acts to establish itself as a major regional power and increase its international status. While the Israeli nuclear arsenal is reason enough for an Arab bomb, Iran, "potentially the strongest Gulf Power, and Algeria may be seeking the bomb" to realize their potential power.[42]

States also seek nuclear arms because of domestic politics. Spanier asserted that "such considerations may reinforce the other two reasons." A nation with economic, social, and morale problems may, if it is technically capable, seek the bomb "to boost morale, restore national confidence, divert attention from domestic problems, and, of course, mobilize popular support for the government."[43] And a government may have economic incentives to develop nuclear technologies in order to generate export sales.

The Case of Russia and the CIS

The disintegration of the Soviet Union created four nuclear states: Russia, Ukraine, Belarus, and Kazakhstan. *The Bulletin of the Atomic Scientists* estimated the former Soviet nuclear stockpile at 33,000 warheads, with 15,000 deployed and 18,000 awaiting disassembly.[44] Immediately after the Soviet collapse, Russia offered to take possession of all strategic weapons located in the other three republics. After the CIS was established, the leaders of the nuclear states decided in December 1991 that a decision to use nuclear weapons would be "made by the president of the Russian Federation" in agreement with the heads of the other three republics and in consultation with the heads of the other member states of the Commonwealth.[45] And under the terms of side letters to the Lisbon Protocol, signed in May 1992, Kazakhstan, Belarus, and Ukraine became parties to the START treaty and agreed to accede to the NPT as nonnuclear weapons states in the shortest possible time. Russia would be the only nuclear power in the CIS. START II is only between the US and Russia since the other three parties to START are obligated by that treaty to eliminate all of the strategic nuclear weapons on their respective territories.

The Ukrainian Factor

There are dangers that threaten to unravel this disarmament process. One danger is the new republics' "strong sense of nationalism, especially Ukraine's."[46] When the Soviet Union collapsed in late 1991, Ukraine instantly became the world's third largest nuclear power. At stake are 130 six-warhead SS-19 strategic missiles and 46 10-warhead SS-24 strategic missiles and an estimated several hundred nuclear-tipped cruise missiles carried on heavy bombers.[47] In all, Ukraine had about 1,700 ex-Soviet warheads on its soil.[48] There is strong nationalistic sentiment in the Ukrainian Parliament where mistrust of Russia's intentions has grown. Since its independence, Ukraine has sparred with Russia over stewardship of nuclear weapons, control of the strategic Black Sea fleet, and the port of Sevastopol—a navy base on Ukrainian soil.[49]

Ukraine's nuclear politics have caused controversy. Some members of the parliament say that Ukraine should keep all or some of its nuclear weapons. Perhaps the lawmakers feel that nuclear weapons add to Ukraine's national prestige and independence; a perception that represents another danger in the disarmament process. Ukrainian president Leonid Kravchuk has called his nation's nuclear weapons "material wealth" and has said that Ukraine would "demand material compensation" before relinquishing them.[50] And it is the US, and to a lesser extent Russia, that will pay the material compensation. A military cooperation agreement was signed between the US and Ukraine in July 1993 in which America promised $175 million in aid.[51] In return, Ukraine has begun deactivating and dismantling a portion of its 130 SS-19 missiles. In January 1994 the US, Russia, and Ukraine signed an agreement to eliminate all of Ukraine's nuclear arms over the next seven years in exchange for US and Russian aid and promises for security. Pavel Polityuk of the Associated Press reported in a *Washington Times* article that in addition to the $175 million for nuclear weapons dismantling, now authorized by Congress, the US has promised $155 million in direct economic aid to Ukraine.[52] Moreover, the US will purchase the extracted uranium from the Ukrainian warheads at a price tag of $1 billion. And Russia has agreed to sell oil and natural gas to Ukraine at cheap prices.

Both the US and Russia have promised not to launch a nuclear attack at Ukraine. But this latest agreement must still be ratified by the Ukrainian Parliament. Polityuk concluded that many of Ukraine's lawmakers are "likely to oppose giving up" the nation's nuclear arsenal. Will Ukraine honor its pledge to get rid of the weapons? Is Ukraine merely stalling as it seeks additional economic aid? Does Ukraine have the right to keep its missiles to ensure its national security? And, if Ukraine decides to keep its weapons, can it deter the Russians? These are tough questions with no clear answers. Clearly, a nuclear Ukraine could upset the NPT regime and START II.

In November 1993 Ukrainian Parliament agreed, in principle, to ratify START, but it attached conditions to stretch out the process of giving up its warheads.[53] The Ukrainian government reports that it desires to join the NPT and supports all the provisions, but its actions seem determined to buy time in an attempt to gain additional financial incentives. Ukraine may try to join the NPT with the "special status of a transition country" with nuclear weapons.[54] Ultimately, Ukraine will do what is best for Ukraine. In his article, *US Anxiously Eyes Ukraine Atomic Arsenal*, Peter Grier of *The Christian Science Monitor* wrote, "In exchange for renouncing its nuclear weapons, Ukraine's parliament wants extensive security guarantees from the West."[55] Ukrainians view it as matter of national survival. US efforts must center around "playing honest broker" between Moscow and Kiev, persuading Ukraine to join the NPT and dismantle its nuclear arsenal, and obtaining the strongest possible security guarantees for Ukraine.[56] Ukraine's role in the new international environment must be acknowledged. The January 1994 agreement between Washington, Moscow, and Kiev represents a step in the right direction.

Russia (CIS) Strategic Nuclear Forces

At the end of 1992, Russian (CIS) strategic nuclear forces were approximately the same size as the Soviet forces were in 1991.[57] The mobile single warhead SS-25 ICBM is the only weapon system in production, and it continues to be fielded. The START II treaty will facilitate the Russians' reducing to a level of relative parity the 3,000 to 3,500 warhead range that each side is permitted. If ratification and implementation of the START treaty stays on track, SS-18 missile silos in Kazakhstan and SS-19 missile silos in Ukraine will be destroyed.

A notable feature of the START II treaty is that all SS-18 missiles must be destroyed. The SS-18 missile is the world's largest and most powerful ICBM. Since it is silo-based, the missile is not survivable. Thus, it is considered a destabilizing weapon. The retirement of this heavy ICBM has begun. Additionally, all land-based multiple warhead ICBMs must be downloaded to single warheads.

In March 1993 *The Bulletin of the Atomic Scientists* reported that between 1990 and 1994 Russia will have reduced its nuclear-powered ballistic-submarine fleet from 62 to 27 SSBNs.[58] In January 1992 former director of Central Intelligence Robert Gates told the Senate, "We see for the first time in decades the total absence of any SSBN under construction."[59] Work continues on a new SLBM to replace the SS-N-20 on Typhoon-class submarines.

The Bulletin of the Atomic Scientists also stated that the Russian bomber force is "practically immobile, and reportedly at low rates of readiness."[60] The Russian bomber force is made up of 75 Tu-95 Bear and 25 Tu-160 Blackjack bombers equipped with short-range attack missiles, air-launched cruise missiles, and gravity bombs. Most of Russia's newest bombers, the Blackjacks, are not operational.

Russia's New Military Doctrine and Nuclear Implications

In November 1993 Russia published a new, more assertive military doctrine that "sanctions the use of troops beyond Russia's borders to protect national interests and their use at home to quash civil conflicts or terrorism."[61] The new doctrine was adopted by President Boris Yeltsin immediately after troops loyal to him put down a hard-line revolt in October. The timing of the new doctrine seems to indicate a strengthening of the Russian military's political position.

Natalie Gross, a researcher at the US Army Institute, wrote in *Jane's Intelligence Review* that the threats to Russia's national security interests include the West, the third world, and the fragile CIS. The Russians "view with apprehension an impressive array of military capabilities amassed by Western powers." Western rapid deployment and mobilization forces pose a potential danger to Russian security. New global and regional powers, such as Germany, Japan, Iran, and Turkey are watched with anxiety. Dangers, such as political concessions against national interests, which the "leverage of Western economic aid may create," are key concerns. Political instability, nuclear proliferation, and terrorism are also identified as threats. According to Gross:

> Closer to home, the military establishment has defined the rules for what it would consider a legitimate use of military force in the successor states or inside the Russian federation. From a military viewpoint, the use of force could be authorized when the civil rights of Russian citizens or of persons maintaining a Russian identity have been violated. The Russian army will view as a serious breach of its security arrangement a direct projection of military power by other countries into neighboring states or any force deployment close to Russia's borders.[62]

The distinct local aspects of the doctrine will certainly raise eyebrows in the CIS republics. The message is clear. The suppression of the rights and freedoms of the millions of dispersed Russians is viewed as a military threat to Russia itself.[63] Will an overhauled Russian army be settling bloody conflicts in the former Soviet Union on Moscow's terms?

The new military doctrine has a significant impact on Russian nuclear policy. The most noticeable feature of the new doctrine is the reversal of the promise not to use nuclear weapons first. This is a reversal of former Soviet president Gorbachev's vision of a nuclear-free world. (The US has also not pledged a no-first-use policy.) The new doctrine promises that nuclear weapons will not be used against nonnuclear states that have signed the nuclear NPT, unless they are operating in alliance with nuclear states.[64] The new doctrine views nuclear arms, the most capable part of Russia's military, as the basis of the nation's future defense. This could be another signal of a "rightward shift of Russia's foreign and military policy."

Russia's new military doctrine views nuclear war as an extension of large-scale conventional war. Strikes by conventional precision guided munitions (PGM) at elements of Russia's nuclear forces such as early warning centers, command and control facilities, chemical and biological weapon storage depots, and nuclear energy and research facilities represent a threshold beyond which nuclear escalation remains a real possibility.[65] This doctrine has significant implication for US combatant commanders and campaign planners. We may be seeing a reversal of role between the former superpowers with Russia now depending on the nuclear equalizer to counter America's superiority in conventional capability.

Other Russian (CIS) Nuclear Concerns

Another potential danger that follows the disintegration of the Soviet Union and reduction of its arms industry is that thousands of unemployed nuclear scientists and technicians might try to sell their knowledge to the highest third world bidder.

> There were an estimated 900,000 military and civilian personnel in the nuclear weapons community. Of these, about 2,000 have a knowledge of nuclear weapons design and 3,000–5,000 have worked in uranium enrichment and plutonium production.[66]

Spanier cited an alarming example of a group that is selling "peaceful nuclear explosives" for such commercial applications as the incineration of toxic wastes and breeder reactors. Another example is Iran's secret nuclear program. It has been reported that Iran has assembled several nuclear bombs with the help of nuclear experts from Kazakhstan. There are other reports of nuclear scientists and technicians from the former Soviet Union earning high salaries in India, Iraq, Brazil, and Pakistan. This type of activity has serious implications for nuclear proliferation.

The security of tactical nuclear weapons is another major challenge. Rodman Griffin, writing for *CQ Researcher*, stated that there are about 15,000 tactical nuclear weapons in the former Soviet arsenal.[67] These weapons are stored at some 200 depots. This presents a tremendous security risk. The sale of a "small nuke" to a criminal or terrorist organization or a rogue nation is a dangerous potential threat.

The sale and control of nuclear materials is another major concern as well. In two documented incidents in 1991, small amounts of plutonium were seized in Europe. Both seizures involved plutonium produced in the former Soviet Union and headed to the Middle East.[68] James Woolsey, new CIA director, attempted to minimize the alarm during testimony before the Senate in February 1993:

> So far, we have detected no transfers of weapon-grade material in significant quantities. We have no credible reporting that nuclear weapons have left CIS territory, and we do not believe that nuclear weapons design information has been sold or transferred to foreign states.[69]

President Clinton has announced that as part of his nonproliferation and export control policy, the US will purchase highly enriched uranium from dismantled nuclear weapons and civil nuclear programs from the former Soviet Union.

The Case of North Korea's Nuclear Program

North Korea is one of the last totalitarian regimes of the cold war. This society has been isolated from outside influences for four decades. By 1984 the US had learned of North Korea's small reactor at Yongbyon. A secret plutonium reprocessing plant soon followed. North Korea signed the NPT in 1985, but it has refused full IAEA safeguard inspections. The US and South Korea have taken action to apply pressure on the North. In 1991 all US nuclear weapons were removed from South Korea and inspection procedures were granted to the North. South Korea also pledged to remain nonnuclear.

During IAEA inspections in 1992, the agency discovered that North Korea had separated plutonium at the Yongbyon reactor. By early 1993 the IAEA announced that it could not account for the North's total amount of separated plutonium. Under mounting international pressure, North Korea threatened to withdraw from the NPT. In December 1993 the IAEA stated that the agency can no longer verify that the North's nuclear activities remain peaceful. David Kyd, a spokesman for the IAEA, said that since the agency cannot perform its duties in North Korea, the UN Security Council is free to take up the issue at any time.[70]

Since then, the US policy towards the North has been a series of threats and concessions. President Clinton has offered economic incentives and cancellation of the annual Team Spirit military exercise with South Korea in exchange for the North's assurances to forego development of nuclear arms and fulfill its NPT obligations. A US push in cooperation with China, South Korea, and Japan for United Nations economic sanctions is the next likely step. The North has responded that US-led sanctions will be seen as an act of war. Mr Woolsey told the Cable News Network (CNN) in a television interview that the possibility of a North Korean attack could not be excluded.[71] He also added that US intelligence believes that the North Koreans have enough plutonium for one or two bombs.

With tensions mounting, some analysts call for an end to the nuclear hype in North Korea. These analysts argue that there is no reliable proof that the North has the technical means to build, deploy, and employ a nuclear device. Furthermore, they assert that all parties benefit from a reduction in Korean tensions. Edward Olsen, a writer for *The Christian Science Monitor*, stated, "The punitive American economic card is as risky for the US as the North Korean nuclear card is dangerous to Pyongyang."[72] What is needed is more "diplomatic sophistication" than either side normally displays. Why is the administration determined to prevent the North from developing an atomic weapon?

Fear of nuclear proliferation in Asia is the primary concern. North Korea's secret program has spurred talk in South Korea and Japan about acquiring a matching nuclear deterrent. In a related matter, the US announced in December 1993 that it will assist Japan in deploying a missile defense system for protection against possible North Korean ballistic-missile attacks. Responses from other Asian states could be asymmetrical, creating complicated diplomatic and security concerns. Another concern is for the integrity of the nonproliferation mechanisms, particularly the NPT and the IAEA. North Korea's snubbing of the control mechanisms is seen by the international community as grievous and unacceptable behavior. There is a limit to how much Washington will be able to tolerate. Moreover, North Korea has a history of supplying arms to the world's hot spots. There is a growing concern that "North Korea might become a conduit for technologies related to chemical, biological, and even nuclear weapons."[73] Finally, the administration would like to see an immediate end to this threat because time is on the side of North Korea's nuclear program. As each month passes, North Korea certainly gets closer to perfecting the bomb. In his 1993 *Security Dialogue* article on North Korea, Ronald Lehman concluded, "The North Korean nuclear program poses a fundamental challenge to the nonproliferation objectives of the world community in the post–Cold War era."[74]

America's Response to Nuclear Proliferation

On 27 September 1993, in an address to the UN General Assembly, President Clinton announced a new proliferation and export control policy. He outlined three principles that will guide US nonproliferation policy:

> Our national security requires us to accord higher priority to nonproliferation, and to make it an integral element of our relations with other countries.
>
> To strengthen US economic growth, democratization abroad, and international stability, we actively seek expanded trade and technological exchange with nations, including former adversaries, that abide by global proliferation norms.
>
> We need to build a new consensus—embracing the executive and legislative branches, industry and public, and friends abroad—to promote effective nonproliferation efforts and integrate our nonproliferation and economic goals.[75]

One key element to the policy includes a comprehensive approach to control the growing accumulation of fissile material. Another key element concerns nuclear proliferation. "The US will make every effort to secure the indefinite extension of the NPT." The US will ensure that adequate IAEA resources are in place to implement nuclear inspections. And the US will work to improve the IAEA's ability to detect secret nuclear activities. Regional nonproliferation initiatives are another critical part of the policy. The US will "make special efforts to address the proliferation threat in regions of tension . . . including efforts to address the underlying motivations for weapons acquisition, and to promote confidence-building steps."[76] Proliferation will also get a higher profile in military planning and doctrine.

In December 1993 new military efforts to counter weapons proliferation were announced by the Pentagon. Efforts include better intelligence gathering and development of nonnuclear "penetrating munitions" capable of destroying deep underground weapons facilities, theater missile defenses to protect against hostile launches, better defenses against biological weapons, and new sensors to locate mobile missile launchers.[77] A critical aspect of the new military approach is in identifying strategies and weapons for coping militarily with proliferation threats after diplomacy fails. The president tasked regional combatant commanders to "develop detailed plans for thwarting proliferation threats in their area." This new approach appears to be an admission that the US and its allies "could not win the war against global nuclear proliferation."[78] The US plan is to increase reliance on technology to defend against the development and use of nuclear and other mass destruction weapons.

Conclusion

America has entered a new period of challenge and opportunity. US nuclear policy is evolving and traditional concepts and assumptions are being challenged. Although START and START II represent an excellent opportunity for deep strategic force reductions, there is no guarantee that they will be implemented. Economic, social, and political chaos in the former Soviet Union presents a real danger to the START process. The full implication of the new Russian military doctrine, with its emphasis on the nuclear deterrent, is yet to be seen. The Soviet disintegration has also complicated the nuclear proliferation problem.

It is imperative that the US demonstrate leadership in dealing with the changing status of nuclear weapons. The US must take strong steps to preserve the START process and the NPT regime. Resources are needed to strengthen the effectiveness of the IAEA. Other nuclear states could be involved in the arms control process. A comprehensive test-ban treaty is another step that can reduce the threat of nuclear weapons. Even if deep reductions continue below the START II levels, the need for a secure, small, but modern US nuclear reserve force seems appropriate.

Concerning nuclear proliferation, President Clinton's new proliferation and export control policy appears sound. It remains to be seen if Congress will provide the money needed to ensure effectiveness of the policy's comprehensive initiatives. New military efforts to counter proliferation will enable the US to defend against the manufacture and use of weapons of mass destruction. Because nuclear proliferation poses a great threat to international peace and security, America must develop the military strategy and capability and more importantly possess the will to deal with the new world threat.

Notes

1. The White House, *National Security Strategy of the United States, January 1993* (Washington, D.C.: Government Printing Office, 1993), i.
2. Les Aspin, editorial, *Star Tribune*, 29 July 1992.
3. Ibid.
4. Air Staff, "Nuclear Sufficiency in the 1990s and Beyond: The New Strategic Equation," White Paper (Washington, D.C.: Headquarters, USAF, 2 September 1992), ii–vi.
5. Ibid.
6. Ibid.
7. Ibid.
8. Ibid.
9. R. Jeffrey Smith, "Nuclear Arms Doctrine to be Reviewed," *Washington Post*, 19 October 1993, 17.
10. Art Pine, "US Missiles to Be Re-Aimed at Distant Seas," *Los Angeles Times*, 13 January 94, 1.
11. Smith, 17.
12. John Prados, "Woolsey and the CIA," *The Bulletin of the Atomic Scientists*, July–August 1993, 34.
13. The White House, 1.
14. Department of Defense, *Annual Report to the President and the Congress, January 93* (Washington, D.C.: Government Printing Office, 1993), 3.
15. The White House, 14.
16. Department of Defense, 4.
17. Joint Publication 3-11, initial draft, *Joint Doctrine for Nuclear, Biological and Chemical (NBC) Defense*, September 1992, 11–12.
18. Department of Defense, 67.
19. Gen George Lee Butler, "Refocusing the Nation's Nuclear Arsenal," *Defense 93*, no. 314 (1993): 53.
20. Department of Defense, 69.

21. Donald B. Rice and Merrill A. McPeak, "FY92 Air Force Posture Statement," presented to the House of Representatives Armed Service's Committee, 26 February 1991, in *Air Force Update*, Secretary of the Air Force, Office of Public Affairs, 26 February 1991, 4.
22. Butler, 51–54.
23. Ibid.
24. Rice and McPeak, 5.
25. Department of Defense, 70–71.
26. Butler, 53.
27. Department of Defense, 69–70.
28. Butler, 53
29. Department of Defense, 71.
30. Ibid.
31. Secretary of Defense, *Implementation Plan for Integration of US Strategic Command, 1992* (Washington, D.C.: 1992), 1.
32. Butler, 51–54.
33. John Spanier, *Games Nations Play*, 8th ed. (Washington, D.C.: Congressional Quarterly, Inc., 1993), 594.
34. Joint Pub 3-11, initial draft, A-1.
35. Spanier, 594.
36. John J. Mearsheimer, "Disorder Restored," in *Rethinking American Security*, ed. Graham Allison and Gregory F. Treverton (New York: W. W. Norton & Company, 1992), 227–35.
37. Ibid.
38. Spanier, 598.
39. David Albright, "A Proliferation Primer," *The Bulletin of the Atomic Scientists*, June 1993, 15.
40. Spanier, 595–98.
41. Ibid.
42. Ibid.
43. Ibid.
44. "Nuclear Notebook," *The Bulletin of the Atomic Scientists*, May 1993, 48.
45. "Commonwealth Agrees on Unified Nuclear Command," *Arms Control Today*, January–February 1992, 39.
46. Spanier, 599.
47. "Ukraine's Lawmakers Claim Nuclear Arsenal," *Baltimore Sun*, 3 July 1992, 4.
48. Peter Grier, "US Anxiously Eyes Ukraine Atomic Arsenal," *The Christian Science Monitor*, 2 December 1993, 3.
49. Jane Perlez, "Ukraine May Ask Special Status in Atomic Pact," *New York Times*, 26 July 1993, 8.
50. "Ukraine Calls Arms 'Material Wealth'," *Washington Post*, 1 December 1993, 21.
51. "Taking Ukraine Seriously," *Sacramento Bee*, 1 August 1993, F-4.
52. Pavel Polityuk, "Ukrainians Upset At Missile Deal," *Washington Times*, 18 January 1994, 15.
53. "Ukraine Calls Arms 'Material Wealth'," 21.
54. Perlez, 8.
55. Grier, 3.

56. "Taking Ukraine Seriously," F-4.

57. "Nuclear Notebook," *The Bulletin of the Atomic Scientists*, March 1993, 49.

58. Ibid.

59. Ibid.

60. Ibid.

61. Fred Hiatt, "Russia Shifts Doctrine on Military Use," *Washington Post*, 4 November 1993, 1.

62. Natalie Gross, "Reflections on Russia's New Military Doctrine," *Jane's Intelligence Review*, August 1992, 339–40.

63. James Sheir, "Russia's New Threat to Neighbors," *Wall Street Journal*, 17 December 1993, 14.

64. Hiatt, 1.

65. Gross, 340.

66. Spanier, 600.

67. Rodman D. Griffin, "Nuclear Proliferation," *CQ Researcher* 2, no. 21 (5 June 1992): 40.

68. From statements of Roman Dolce, an assistant prosecutor in Rome, Italy, in Dunbar Lockwood, "US Seeks to Avert Ex-Soviet Nuclear-Expert 'Brain Drain'," *Arms Control Today*, January–February 1992, 40.

69. Quoted in Dunbar Lockwood, "CIA Shed Light on Nuclear Control in CIS," *Arms Control Today*, March 1993, 21.

70. John J. Fialka, "North Korea's Nuclear Moves Go Unwatched," *Wall Street Journal*, 3 December 1993, 5-E.

71. Bill Gertz, "US Intelligence: North Korea Could Have Nukes," *Washington Times*, 2 December 1993, 3.

72. Edward A. Olsen, "Navigating North Korea's Nuclear 'Straits'," *The Christian Science Monitor*, 29 November 1993, 23.

73. Ronald F. Lehman II, "A North Korea Nuclear-Weapons Program, International Implications," *Security Dialogue* 3, no. 24 (1993): 269.

74. Ibid.

75. Message, 280345Z Sep 93, Secretary of State to all diplomatic and consular posts, 28 September 1993.

76. Ibid.

77. John Lancaster, "Aspin Pledges New Military Efforts to Counter Weapons Proliferation," *Washington Post*, 8 December 1993, 7.

78. Steven Robinson, "America's Set to Hunt Down the World's 'Loose Nukes'," *London Daily Telegraph*, 8 December 1993, 14.

Developing Space Assets

Victor Janushkowsky

Before the nineteenth century, the size and structure of a nation's land forces determined the potency of its military instrument of power. During the nineteenth century, sea powers were dominant. In the twentieth century, air power asserted itself and began to dictate supremacy. In the coming twenty-first century, according to Air Force Chief of Staff Gen Merrill A. McPeak, control of space assets will be the primary measure of a nation's power.[1]

Much of the past writing on space needs reflects the bipolar United States–Union of Soviet Socialist Republics (USSR) world, and how to counter the significant nuclear missile, bomber, and submarine forces of the former Soviet Union. This essay reorients to a multipolar world and shows space in a snapshot. It first gives a short history of space and shows recent examples and lessons learned from the use of space assets in an actual conflict—the Gulf War with Iraq. It then forecasts the future needs of space, including new technology applications as the new world unfolds while the year 2000 approaches.

The old world was relatively predictable; if the Soviets became aggressive, the US countered with a flexible response that was programmed to get the word to US forces using a system that ranged from early warning and indications satellites and space sensors to the Satellite Communications System (SATCOM) and Military Strategic and Tactical Relay Satellite (MILSTAR). Now the former states of the Soviet Union, including those client countries such as Cuba that depended on the Soviets for their care and feeding, are on their own without support and, needless to say, without space support. The newly independent countries of the former Soviet Union, to keep up with the rest of the world, will want to secure their own space assets. The US, on the other hand, must now react to regional crises between these states, not knowing where the next one will erupt.

Fundamentally, the US needs to improve upon the capabilities of existing highly valued, force-enhancing satellite systems and should apply new space systems utilizing new technologies helping the nation open up and retain access to and the use of space. Such capabilities will give the US instantaneous presence anywhere in the world by providing situational awareness as well as the command and control needed to deal with current and future unpredictable crises.

Basic Assumptions and Definitions

Space assets are employed across strategic, operational, and tactical levels of warfare. There are three basic elements in a space operation: the orbiting vehicle, the link to the earth, and the ground station. A weakness in any one of these is a weakness in the system, which is connected with the air and surface mediums to provide information and communication connectivity.

Space is a unique medium. Scientists and specialists live there only for relatively short periods of time. Yet vehicles operating from space allow a line-of-sight view of very large portions of earth and therefore can provide connectivity between two places on earth that cannot see the other. A constellation of satellites can scan simultaneously and cover the entire earth. This aspect of space makes it a logical and suitable location to watch and listen to all the world's activities.

Space vehicles can sustain altitude for long periods without fuel expenditure because of the lack of gravity. The average life expectancy of earlier (1970s vintage) satellites is from three to five years, although many have lasted much longer, especially with space maintenance and replacements of limited life components. The latest Defense Satellite Communication Satellite (DSCS) III has a nominal life expectancy of 10 years.[2]

More countries will exploit space in the future. Currently, approximately 21 countries use space, either independently or by purchasing rights, commercially. A growing demand for space infrastructure is evident since more of the world's nations are able to make use of space because of their political, military, and, most important, economical growth.

Notably, vehicles in space (at lower orbit) are highly vulnerable to interception by a hostile nation. However, there is no specified, identified threat to satellite vehicles at the time of this writing.[3] This is an area to be watched, especially by the nation's intelligence agencies. Also, it will soon become possible to reduce vulnerability by more fully utilizing a maneuver capability in deep space or by deploying active defensive measures—that is, to actively defend satellites with weapons on board to guard against attacks.

The current national and military space organization is being changed so it can respond to the changes in the military structure and the world order. Air Force Space Command (AFSPACECOM), the first service space command, was established in 1983. US Space Command was established in 1985 as a unified war-fighting command, combining the strength of all three services, although the Air Force provides over 90 percent of the personnel to the command, performs nearly all launches, controls the main satellite systems on orbit, and pays most of the space budget.[4] President George Bush established the National Space Council in 1989 to oversee space policy-making and activity.[5] However, it was disbanded early in 1993.[6] Interestingly, AFSPACECOM took on an offensive mission in its space arsenal when it assumed responsibility for the US intercontinental ballistic missile (ICBM) forces in 1992. This was viewed by some as essentially a first step toward putting weapons in space and moving from a totally "benign" to a "threatening" mission since this was the first time an offensive "space" military capability was assigned to the space command.[7]

Although they have integrated space operations in the joint arena, the three services have retained separate responsibilities for significant portions of the space missions. The Air Force provides ballistic missile warning, protection from and negation of enemy space systems, satellite operations through ground command and control, and space lift. The Army commands and manages DSCS satellites and operations centers, the Strategic Defense System (SDS), and antisatellites (ASATS) in event of future deployment. The Navy provides ultrahigh frequency (UHF) communications through operations of its Fleet Satellite Communications System (FLTSATCOM) and provides a backup to Cheyenne Mountain's Space Surveillance Center and alternate Space Defense Operations Center (besides upgrading the UHF communication system).[8]

Numerous other organizations are involved, including commercial enterprises, consortiums, the National Reconnaissance Office (NRO), the Ballistic Missile Defense Organization (BMDO—the old Strategic Defense Initiative Organization, SDIO), the Advanced Research Projects Agency (ARPA), service and national laboratories, Joint/AF Space Applications and Warfare Center, National Aeronautics and Space Administration (NASA), and the Space and Missile Systems Center. Integration of all these and other entities providing space planning will ensure that space assets are created and deployed so they can respond to the challenges that confront the US.

History of Space

Human use of space has a history of just over 50 years, when Germany's short-range ballistic missiles transited space in the early 1940s. Since then the Soviets and the Americans have been the dominant players in the arena. Other countries, including Canada, France, and India, have joined in space activities.

Incredibly, the first man was put into space in 1961, only 33 years ago. Other nations have dabbled in space activity since that time, but the greatest number of space launches and controllable satellites continue to be those of the United States, European Space Agency, Russia, and other consortiums. Russia has assumed the Soviet role of leadership in space, even though their internal transitional problems may not allow extravagant ventures into space. Most agree that the Russian space activity and capability will remain robust.[9]

The US space shuttle program is now back on track after the *Challenger* disaster. The recent repair of the embarrassing faulty lens in the Hubbell Space Telescope showed the ability of the shuttle to recover an ineffective satellite and fix it in space with only 35 hours of space work. Space assets of most importance to the military, however, are the capabilities of space that serve as the "force enhancers" discussed below.

Communication

Their line-of-sight position allows space satellites to serve as a communication link or relay. Two types are voice and data. Voice satellites are primarily SATCOM, which are dual use civilian and military, and Military Satellite Communications (MILSATCOM), which provide voice communications for tactical forces through UHF. Data is sent via the 1970s technology DSCS, which processes data at very high speeds. MILSTAR is the modern technology data communication system designed for reliable strategic nuclear force communication, although it is slow and has a low capability.

Navigation

The Global Positioning System (GPS) is the newest navigational tool. It provides 24-hour, real-time pinpoint accuracy using 24 evenly spaced satellites that cover the entire land mass of the earth. GPS uses an atomic clock and a triangulation of three GPS satellites to notify a user of his exact coordinates within feet. Two modes are available, one for military use and one for civil navigation. The best attribute of GPS, besides accuracy, is its small size (some versions are as small as a pack of cigarettes, enabling the field soldier to use it as well).[10]

Indications and Warning

This most important capability notifies command authorities of imminent attack by a hostile country using missiles, rockets, airplanes, or other airborne or spaceborne vehicle. It has the technology to assess the attack, to forecast when and where attacks are likely, and to assist the command authority in preparing a proper response. The Defense Satellite Program (DSP) has been the primary missile warning asset. Using infrared monitors, DSP watches the earth for any heat-producing events and is quite capable of detecting the launch of an intercontinental or shorter-range ballistic missile.

Weather

Basic use of space capability can be easily observed by viewing television weather reports. The Defense Meteorological Support Program (DMSP) has had three satellites in orbit for some time. This capability is being supported by additional "environmental-monitoring" capabilities such as land satellites (LANDSAT) and other such multispectral imagery (MSI) satellites. Weather satellites play an important role in mission planning, since armed forces can be greatly affected in varying weather phenomenon.

Reconnaissance and Surveillance

Space photographs, signals, and other earth emissions can increase situational awareness and understanding while providing targeting information, bomb damage assessment, and enemy military data to the theater commanders.

Lessons Learned in the Gulf War

Operation Desert Storm was a showcase of space assets, demonstrating the capabilities of all the various force enhancers, and proving US reliance and ability to handle high technology. The conflict also showed some limitations and deficiencies, primarily that space is generally useless without ground terminals in the hands of those who need them. It was a testing ground as well. Prototype MILSTAR terminals were deployed and used very successfully as a national command authority (NCA)—United States Central Command (USCENTCOM) communications link. One key lesson that needs to be highlighted is the fact that no fight was required for control of space. The adversary in this case had no space assets or offensive space capability, while the coalition had control in space. In the future, this may not be the case. In order for the US to be better prepared for the next major conflict, six lessons from Operations Desert Shield/Desert Storm are discussed below.

Good Warning but Poor Defense against Ballistic Missiles

Within minutes, space satellites evaluated and warned Central Command (CENTCOM) forces of Scud launches. This warning of attack had some value since those in targeted areas were able to don chemical defensive gear and retreat to protective shelters. However, on the defensive side, the Scud missiles were relatively successful in inflicting terror. The Patriot missile system only intercepted 60 percent of the missiles, and those it did destroy in the terminal phase of the missiles' flight scattered remnants over the intended target area, inflicting some collateral damage and casualties. If these Scuds had carried weapons of mass destruction (nuclear, chemical, biological, or some other future technology capable of destroying large groups at one time), further casualties would have rained down upon the coalition or its allies even if the missiles had been shot down in the terminal phase.[11] What is badly needed is the capability to negate the threat of a missile before it enters the atmosphere of friendly territory.

Shortage and Vulnerability of Communication Channels

The demand for quick, long-haul communications put stress on the available satellites. The sheer numbers of personnel deployed to the Gulf stressed the system. Twenty-five percent of the Air Force, 50 percent of the Army, and 66 percent of the Marine Corps were deployed to fight Iraq. Ninety percent of all communications to, from, and within the Gulf moved through space. Half of the long-haul communications used commercial satellites because the military system had a heavy drain on it. A DSCS satellite on orbit had to be moved into a needed location by giving it commands and modifying its software from Falcon Air Force Station (AFS), Colorado. Remotely, they turned the motor on and ordered the satellite to move into a required orbit. After the satellite moved into proper orbit, it provided vital communication with the American embassy in

Kuwait until the evacuation. A more capable enemy could have exploited these communications using beaconing, jamming, intercepting, and monitoring.

"Information Dominance" Importance Recognized

Secretary of the Air Force Sheila Widnall said, "In the future, meeting our political and military objectives will increasingly hinge on what's being called 'information dominance,' with space playing an expanded role."[12]

Iraq relied heavily on Cable News Network (CNN) for their view of the events unfolding. The coalition utilized this use of satellites by propagating information of an impending marine amphibious attack from the beaches of the Persian Gulf. While the enemy was fortifying for such an assault, Gen H. Norman Schwarzkopf was engineering the "Hail Mary" envelopment maneuver from the western flank to surprise and overwhelm the enemy. We could see; Hussein could not. The recognition of the importance of information dominance applies to intelligence as well. The greatest source of information is intelligence, and most of the usable intelligence today comes from space assets in the form of photographs, signals, communication intercepts, and other valued pieces of information. Situational awareness was exploited in the Gulf War at the expense of the Iraqi military.

No Single Organization Responsible to Coordinate Space Support

Operational planning for the use of space assets was not well developed when Iraq invaded Kuwait.[13] Assets were deployed ad hoc instead of in a concerted, preplanned manner. In several instances during the war, CENTCOM's staff had to call the continental United States (CONUS) to resolve problems and create work-arounds and fixes to communication problems. There was no space staff deployed to the theater of operations to assist in this matter. Since the war, US Space Command has begun planning in accordance with the Joint Chiefs of Staff's mechanism to have in place plans for deployment of certain space assets and will deploy to a theater of operations to assist the commander on space matters.[14]

Weather Was Critical to Operations and Bomb Damage Assessment

Weather in the Gulf was the worst in 16 years. This was crucial, especially in the desert, where many coastal fogs and sandstorms could reduce visibility to zero and rain could turn sands into bogs. This could have been a problem, but sensors from space were able to perform three-dimensional analysis of the environment using multispectral imaging and DMSP satellites. At worst the weather delayed bomb damage reports because of the inability to take pictures of buildings through clouds. DMSP allowed analysis of sandstorms and was instrumental in planning attack packages through brief breaks in the cloud cover. There was a shortage of DMSP ground terminals to fielded forces and ships; field units could never get enough information, especially when waiting and planning for battle.

LANDSAT and the French SPOT (Satellite Probatoire d'Observation de la Terre) multispectral imagery satellites were successful, as they were able to ascertain Iraqi command and control, troop movements, and natural underground hazards such as mud. MSI was able to show depth of water and heat on the ground from enemy movement. It assisted in updating badly needed maps often 10 to 30 years old, which helped locate modern airfields, roads, trails, and water. The US MSI resolution was roughly 30 meters, whereas the French SPOT satellites were 10 meters and the Soviet Meteor Proida system had a resolution down to five meters. Merged with national imagery, MSI produced detailed, unclassified maps.[15]

F-111 pilots used MSI in preparing for their missions to bomb Iraqi oil well heads that were pumping oil into the Persian Gulf. After the mission was successfully completed, the pilots commented that it seemed as if they had flown the mission before they ever climbed into the cockpit.

Navigation Equipment Critical to Fighting Forces

GPS provided highly precise, all-weather, and three-dimensional position, velocity, and timing data to the military. Unfortunately, when Iraq invaded Kuwait, only five percent of USAF aircraft had GPS installed. Since 1982, the Navy has had GPS on virtually all its ships. It was eventually used more extensively than planned because of the perceived utility of this technology in the barren desert environment. Unfortunately, insufficient military versions were available, requiring thousands of civilian versions of the GPS receivers that did not have "selective availability" (SA), an option reserved for military use that increases accuracy and performance. GPS success in Desert Shield/Desert Storm was evident in many ways: first, it has taken the accuracy of determining position from miles down to feet. GPS led an F-16 and a search-and-rescue (SAR) helicopter to find a downed American F-16 pilot behind enemy territory. Second, it increased the lethality of standoff munitions like the Navy's sea launch attack missile (SLAM) and the Tomahawk cruise missile and increased the accuracy of air assets. Air Force helicopters led the first wave of Army attack helicopters into Iraq because the Army's helicopters did not have GPS receivers installed. Third, GPS has revolutionized logistics. It is much easier today to locate a position on earth, therefore easier to get the meal trucks, supplies, ammunition, fresh troops, and the like to that position. Finally, it is very popular with the troops, so they will use it! It is a passive device, that is, it doesn't give off any signal but just reads the signal from the satellite; therefore, it does not make the troops vulnerable to interception. Their portable nature made these devices so popular that fielded units "passed the hat" in order to buy more hand-held units to be used in the Gulf. Some parents bought units for their sons and daughters deployed in the war, just as a personal item, knowing it might help them.

While listed as the final lesson learned from the war, the importance of GPS to the coalition's victory cannot be underestimated. Furthermore, the availability of at least the civilian version of GPS to future enemies of freedom will complicate America's plans for decisive, quick, low-casualty crisis resolution.[16] Since Space Command has the ability to distort GPS signals to keep wartime enemies from taking advantage of them, its control of GPS satellites into the future will be essential.[17]

Future Space Requirements

What is our future in space? Since the base force, bottom-up review, and downsizing analysis began after the end of the cold war with the former Soviet Union, several space programs were changed, added, canceled, and/or postponed, and some canceled programs have been given new life. Rather than identify what specific space assets are still alive, which are dying, and which are dead, this paper focuses on what the author believes the country's direction in space ought to be. It will consider the budget environment the military will work with and current general thought. Some assumptions and forecasting can be made based on what we know today. Below are eight general prognostications of what should, and probably will, happen in space in the interest of national security.

Better Support to Conventional Forces

The number one priority of the current commander of US Space Command is "putting space into the fox hole, cockpit, or combat information center in real time."[18] Following are several ways to do this.

First, the Defense Department must create more handheld space link miniaturized information-processing equipment that incorporates MSI, navigation aids, and any other real-time information needed by the holder of such a device. Information dissemination in-theater could be improved and made much tighter.

Second, navigation aids must continue to be improved using GPS and other pinpoint accuracy tools for cargo drops and SAR missions.

Third, robotics must be more appropriate in future conflict to avoid direct human-to-human confrontation and the risk of excessive casualties. Satellites are essentially robots that do not require manned presence. Therefore, interfaces with air- and land-based robots will be required in future conflicts.

Fourth, continued search for devices that will disable weapons of mass destruction (nuclear, biological, chemical) will be desired and accepted by the world community. Most agree that a theater ballistic-missile threat persists in many areas of the world. At the time of this writing, 20 nations either control or seek short-term, medium-range ballistic missiles. A defense against this from space may be a logical development. The free world needs a ballistic-missile defense that is supportable, reactive, able to destroy short- and medium-range missiles in the near term and long-range missiles in the long term. It must be able to intercept missiles in the boost phase (those six or so minutes from launch until entry into the upper atmosphere) in order to prevent collateral damage currently suffered in terminal-phase defensive-missile systems such as Patriot. The replacement for the DSP early warning satellites, the follow-on early warning system (FEWS), and the Brilliant Eyes satellite will improve the tracking and intercept of ballistic missiles if funding for the programs is continued.

Continued Search for Better Technology

The military technology revolution continues unabated, with better and brighter ideas still to come. Acquiring the best technology will continue as a national objective, albeit in a more budgetary-critical perspective. Identified below are four basic technological improvements that will change the way space assets are employed.

First, those sensors currently deployed in space will be improved so the information processed will be sharper, clearer, more resolute, easier to hear, and easier to identify. These improvements will gradually change the nature of the data collected.

Second, better computers will result in better artificial intelligence (AI). This will help the military by allowing fast, accurate threat forecasting using reliable automation.

Third, there will probably be less reliance on kinetic kill weapons and more use of directed-energy weapons (DEW). Laser weapons are faster and more accurate and cause less collateral damage. Inevitably, space devices will incorporate such means to protect itself and possibly to be used in an offensive role.

Fourth, "virtual reality" aids will come closer to reality. Computers are merely scratching the surface of virtual reality, where visual aids recreate key maps and other realistic representation for the use of targeting, navigation, and other such uses for armed forces to be more effective. Information from space will be an important component since much information comes from space and offers a view or angle different from any other sea, land, or air perspective.

Deployment of a Trans-Atmospheric Vehicle

The current record holder as the world's fastest airplane is the SR-71, which was clocked at about Mach 3 (2,100+ mph). The National Aerospace Plane (NASP) would be capable of Mach 15 to 25, enabling it to achieve a temporary orbit in space and return to earth in record time. The NASP makes possible a flight from New York to Japan in about two hours. The military implications of such a vehicle that can transport troops and special operations personnel around the globe are that it will reduce response time to minutes and add another flexible response to a localized conflict. In fact, many predict dual use for this new transportation technology in the twenty-first century.[19] Economic wars with the budding nations of the Far East may demand such a quick transport to get goods to market before the competitors do so.

On a related note, advanced engines may be developed and incorporated in this vehicle. There are unlimited possibilities, including research into engines or nuclear-powered aerospace engines, and even the famous antimatter engines enabling "warp drive."[20] The military technological revolution (MTR) will continue to produce such paradigm-shifting ideas of space transportation, and the nations that incorporate the good ideas are the ones that will retain the high ground, militarily and economically.

Manned Space Presence

Space is a rough environment, without breathable air and with a temperature of approximately 200 degrees below zero. However, inevitably there will be an international space station, incorporating the US Freedom Space Station, Russia's Mir space station, and the contributions of a consortium of other countries.

Unilaterally, the US continues to explore long-term manned presence. The areas in space known as the "Lagrangian Points" are one reason for this. These points are located between the earth and the moon, and between the earth and the sun. From there an adversary could access any satellite in geosynchronous orbit, thereby potentially blocking both communications and a field of view of earth.[21] The US must continue to explore manned and unmanned presence in space to ensure continued access in this environment. These two "high grounds" of space make friendly control of the points a necessity.

Standardized, Multipurpose, Dual-Use Launch Infrastructure

Currently, each launch of a satellite into orbit is like building a Rolls-Royce automobile—one at a time. Each satellite is married to a unique Titan, Delta, or Atlas rocket booster that was specially designed to fit only that satellite. Each launch is a custom event, costing an average of $85.5 million (the space shuttle averages $650 million). The average time on a launch pad for a rocket is 47 days, with launch crew members numbering from 100 to more than a thousand. It has been reported that Gen Charles A. Horner, commander in chief, Air Force Space Command, wants to standardize procedures and enforce discipline in the design of future satellites, much like foreign space organizations are doing, in order to add operational robustness and forgiving margins, thus in some cases reducing the costs in half. Furthermore, even Congress has asked for rugged, cheap, reliable "trucks," not complicated, fragile, high-strung "race cars."[22]

The secretary of the Air Force stated, "Any future launch program will have to be dual-use—meeting the needs of government and commercial users."[23] The Air Force budget, the largest of the services, runs about $6 billion per year. While almost all other mission areas are reducing budgets, the space mission is growing. The nation will need fast-launch capability to put up satellites as needed for crises. This may mean a US military launch capability, but interestingly, the Senate told the Department of Defense in 1993 to consider using foreign launch capabilities to launch national security payloads.[24] For example, Russia's need for hard currency and her strong capability for putting satellites in orbit may be tapped. During fall 1993, Vice President Al Gore signed numerous agreements in this area with President Boris Yeltsin, and although most are civil ventures, there is a possibility of using their infrastructure for quickly and efficiently launching satellites for communication, navigation, or other uses, as the needs arise.

Commercial, nonstate consortiums are another source for launch assistance. Rather than developing unique US launch capability, the climate exists to contract out the launches, security permitting.

More International Agreements/Cooperation

The move from the bipolar to the multipolar world has expanded the importance of the world community in space matters. Following are several specific areas in which the world of nations will come together cooperatively for common goals.

First, there will be more lending of support to civil authorities in areas of instability. This may mean sharing of information gathered from space assets.

Second, arms control agreements will be expanded to include much more intrusive monitoring, much of it from space, to enhance the concept of "transparency," whereby countries demonstrate openly that they have only peaceful, defensive intentions, and nations monitor world activities using remote earth-sensing devices. Agreements such as Open Skies, permitting overflight of aircraft over a nation's airspace, will need to be made so space assets can communicate and pass information through.

Third, the rising number of countries getting involved in space may require an international body like the International Civil Aviation Organization (ICAO) as a form of space "traffic control" to prevent mishaps, especially where there is manned activity in space. Satellites in orbit travel about 25,000 feet per second, which is about 17,000 mph. Out of the 190 or so countries of the world, 25 to 40 will have their own payloads by the end of the twentieth century. In orbit today are approximately 2,154 payloads, and the number of launches is increasing.[25] This, combined with the rising volume of space debris from satellites, may require more international activity in combined monitoring. This complex task requires the highest technology.

Fourth, the proliferation of ballistic missiles throughout the world may require the community of nations to share ballistic missile warning information, be it information about terrorist movements, weapon sales, or possibly intelligence to be shared with another nation. Sharing of intelligence is not a new concept, as we have shared secrets even with Russians in 1991, 1992, and 1993 concerning the Persian Gulf crisis, and other regional concerns. The rising world concern about threats from weapons of mass destruction may eventually allow some form of interceptor from space to knock out missiles during the boost phase of flight.

Fifth, some countries may buy or sell space-originated information. In Desert Storm, Saddam Hussein attempted to purchase space-based information, but through diplomatic efforts of the coalition, he was denied. Maps, photographs, communication information, and other information from space are viewed by many as invaluable.

Need for Space Surge Capability

Related to the last area above is the need to surge in a time of crisis. As seen during the Gulf War, the need for expanded communication channels rose in direct proportion to the number of personnel deployed to the area. Some regions of the world will require more satellite coverage to meet the demand. Civil and commercial space industries should be signed up to provide this surge, much like the Civil Reserve Airlift Fleet (CRAF), to assist the nation's security in its time of need. Costs would be reduced since a large-standing space force would not be required if suitable guarantees are available elsewhere.

Weapons in Space

Other than ballistic missiles traversing space, apparently no country has deployed any form of weapons in space . . . yet. The Outer Space Treaty forbids weapons of mass destruction in space, and perhaps current "customary law" forbids any type of deployed system.[26] However, an arms race in space may require the nation to quickly develop the capability to protect itself and retain access to space and its assets. Carl Sagan and other scientists have expressed interest in military assistance in using a space-based device to defend the earth from an asteroid collision, much like the collision that is assumed to be the cause of the demise of dinosaurs. A huge deflector, using directed energy or a nuclear explosion, would be used to deflect an asteroid.[27] Besides the asteroid-deflector idea, the two other potential weapons in space are offensive-(ASAT) and defensive-satellite (DSAT) weapons. The US decision on satellite weapons was recently kicked down the road, but could return quickly. Whether to station such a system in space may be answered by the capability to deploy such a system on the ground. Testing is being continued at White Sands Missile Range on a triservice high-energy laser.

The offensive satellite weapon can be one of two types: destructive and nondestructive. The nondestructive type could be used to temporarily disable an enemy's satellite but not destroy it using jamming, interference, or interception of its signal. The destructive type would use kinetic or collision destruction or more modern directed-energy weapons to permanently disable the satellite. One such proposed system is the Broad Area Destructive Antisatellite System, or "BADASS." The DSAT has a better chance of gaining world acceptance.

Conclusion

Air and space capability will dominate future wars. The US must now concern itself with many areas of the globe versus just one adversary, the former Soviet Union. However, the proliferation of weapons will give a growing number of nations an opportunity to increase their national power and lead them to eventually attempt to exploit space as well as the more traditional mediums of land and sea. Since the world's economy is spreading, more countries will be able to better exploit space and develop, buy, rent, and steal space assets for their own use.

Customary international law may be difficult to overcome in developing needed space assets of the future, but there will be a host of bad actors in the world with the means and capability to do so, thereby wreaking havoc on US interests and objectives. US space agencies and organizations must look for opportunities to develop the right assets at the right time and have them available to deploy rapidly in crisis situations.

The current space force enhancers will need continual refinement and modernization to keep up with the military technological revolution and its advantages. New missions of space, space transportation, and defensive satellites, for example, will require incorporation into the new Air Force and joint doctrine (Air Force Manual 2-25 and Joint Publication 3-14, respectively) currently being developed.

The main lesson from the Gulf War is that space has its place on the winning side, with much room for improvement. The winning coalition forces showed how important it is to use assets from not only the US but its many allies to respond to crises. This applies to the space environment as well. The US, with its stated, demonstrated, and proven support of freedom throughout the new world, must provide the leadership in the realm of space that others will follow down the peaceful course. The US must also be able to quickly observe any hostile intentions in space and aggressively control, eliminate, or convince the hostile nation to desist in its actions.

The organization of space forces is an important consideration for our nation's leaders. Should all services be responsible for a piece of the pie, or is one service better suited to provide the country the assets it needs? Perhaps a separate service, a "space force," should be designated the fourth military arm. Gen Colin Powell has said, "If there is one thing I learned in the past two years, space is a new frontier of warfare. Land, sea, air, and space."[28] Parochialism runs rampant in the military and often runs contrary to the best interests of the nation as a whole. Identifying an optimal service of responsibility is beyond the scope of this chapter, but the idea of how best to organize space assets is one that needs exploring and reexploring. Control of the "high ground" will remain possible only with continual advancement in space activity.

Notes

1. Quoted in John T. Correll, "Slipping in Space," *Air Force Magazine* 76 (October 1993): 2.

2. Jeffrey Rowe, "US Space Command: Managing Critical Military Assets in Space and on the Ground," *Defense Electronics* 24 (March 1992): 41.

3. Alan D. Campen, "Gulf War's Silent Warriors Bind US Units Via Space," *Signal Magazine* 46 (August 1991): 81.

4. John T. Correll, "Fogbound in Space," *Air Force Magazine* 77 (January 1994): 22.

5. National Space Council, *Final Report to the President on the U.S. Space Program* (Washington, D.C.: US Government Printing Office, January 1993), 91.

6. The National Space Council's function was transferred into the vice president's Office of Science and Technology Policy.

7. Susan Koch, assistant director for strategic programs, US Arms Control and Disarmament Agency, interview with author, February 1992.

8. Rowe, 35.

9. Gen Charles Horner, "Space Seen as Challenge: Military's Final Frontier," *Defense Issues* 8, no. 34 (1993): 1–10.

10. Bruce D. Nordwall, "Imagination Only Limit to Military, Commercial Applications for GPS," *Aviation Week & Space Technology* 135 (14 October 1991): 60.

11. "Scud Success," *New York Times*, 21 November 1993, 13.

12. Sheila Widnall, secretary of the Air Force, address to the Women in Aerospace Convention, El Segundo, Calif., 26 August 1993.

13. James W. Canaan, "A Watershed in Space," *Air Force Magazine* 74 (August 1991): 32.

14. Lt Gen Thad A. Wolfe, interview with author, 16 November 1992.

15. Canaan, 36.

16. Nordwall, 60.

17. Correll, "Fogbound in Space," 28.

18. Horner, 34.

19. "Patriot Missiles Less Successful Than Reported," *Los Angeles Times* (Washington edition), 22 November 1993, B-7.

20. Interim report of the Spacecast 2020 study group to Lt Gen Jay Kelley, commander, Air University, Maxwell AFB, Ala., 20 November 1993.

21. Wiley J. Larson and James R. Wertz, eds., *Space Mission Analysis and Design*, 2d ed. (Torrance, Calif.: Microcosm, Inc.; Boston: Kluwer Academic Publishers, 1991), 185.

22. Correll, "Fogbound in Space," 25.

23. Widnall, 2.

24. Correll, "Fogbound in Space," 22.

25. Ibid., 24. Figures are taken from TRW's *Space Log*.

26. The Treaty on the Principles Governing the Activities of States in the Exploration of and Use of Outer Space, Including the Moon and Other Celestial Bodies (also called the Outer Space Treaty) entered into force on 10 October 1967.

27. Carl Sagan, speaking with the Spacecast 2020 study group, Air War College, Maxwell AFB, Ala., via telelink from Cornell University, Ithaca, N.Y., 1 November 1993.

28. Quoted in "Air and Space Doctrine: Enduring Attributes and Emerging Opportunities," USAF Air and Space Symposium, Maxwell AFB, Ala., May 1993.

Conflict Termination
Every War Must End

Mario A. Garza

Warfare has been a fascinating phenomenon in man's history and the primary instrument of social change. Empires and single states have risen or fallen based on how they fared on the battlefield. However, it is usually not the outcome of battles but the way the conflict is terminated that has a long-term impact on the future of the warring parties.

There is no lack of literature on the study of waging war and why wars were fought. However, historians and military strategists have not devoted much literature to the complex and elusive concept of conflict termination. Fred Ikle, who wrote one of the most thought-provoking books on the subject, stated:

> This imbalance in the understanding of past wars affects how political leaders and military planners will approach questions of war and peace in the future. Regarding the beginning of wars, they can call on historic data, rich concepts, and extensive prior planning: how to deter aggression, how diplomacy might avert the outbreak of war, how to mobilize forces, and how to design the initial military campaigns. Much less is known about how to bring a war, once started, to a satisfactory end.[1]

Conflict termination may mean different things to different nations. When Americans go to war, we want to roll up our sleeves, rush into battle, crush the enemy, dust ourselves off, and proceed with life as before. We tend to view war as an interruption of the normal state of peace. As Russell Wiegley seems to suggest in *The American Way of War: A History of United States Military Strategy and Policy*, Americans want an unambiguous start, a short war, and total victory.[2] Unfortunately, our earnest desire for a "better state of peace" frequently confronts the reality of unanticipated political and social change. This has led to numerous incongruencies between the national aims and the military means to achieve those aims. Some examples include the post–World War II

Communist occupation in Eastern Europe, political and military failures during the Vietnam War, and continued hostilities and military intervention after Operation Desert Storm. That our wars haven't ended neatly is frustrating, yet we have often eagerly embraced minimally satisfying "settlements" to conflicts during the last 40 years.

Conflict termination conjures up thoughts of peace, tranquillity, and the restoration of the peaceful conditions prevalent in the preconflict period. This, however, oversimplifies the complex nature of conflict termination. This chapter presents some basic concepts on the nature of conflict termination and the cessation of hostilities. It examines the issues involved in the conflict termination process. Finally, it covers what the campaign planner must consider when planning a military campaign in terms of conflict termination and the post-hostility activities.

Nature of Conflict Termination

The objective of the conflict termination phase is to restore the peace found prior to the conflict. Conflict termination involves more than merely ending hostilities. If this were the only criterion, then the nation's leaders could simply decide to stop fighting. Fred Ikle, in his seminal work on war termination, *Every War Must End*, states that military officers often fail to perceive that it is the outcome of the war, not the outcome of the campaigns within it, that determines how well our campaigns serve the nation's interests.[3] An example from history illustrates this point very well. Three months before the attack on Pearl Harbor, the emperor of Japan asked the army chief of staff, Sugiyama, how long it would take the army to finish the war against the United States. Sugiyama answered that the Japanese military would terminate operations in the Pacific in three months. The emperor, knowing this could not possibly be done in only three months, pointed out that Sugiyama had previously told him the Manchurian campaign would be over in one month. The campaign had then been going on for over four years. Ikle observes:

> Since Japan became involved in a war with the United States neither gradually nor inadvertently, but by a considered and clear-cut decision, one would expect the Japanese military to have had some ideas about how they would reach a successful conclusion in the gigantic undertaking that they proposed.[4]

The Pearl Harbor attack was one of the most successful military operations in history. However, the attack did little to serve Japan's interests in the war. For Japan the outcome of the war was certainly not successful. Nations often devote great resources and effort developing great militaries (means) and spend little effort relating the means to their national aims and objectives (ends).

Another example is Germany's reaction after defeating France in 1940 and driving the British forces from the Continent. Field Marshal Erich von Manstein states that "Hitler and O.K.W. found themselves wondering 'What next?' . . . It was quite obvious that prior to—or even during—the offensive in France, Germany's supreme command had no kind of 'war plan' to determine what measure should be taken once the victories it hoped for had been won."[5]

One might question whether the Japanese and German examples were the military's failure or the politicians' failure. The answer is both. The national political leaders determine the "ends"—the national strategic objectives and, to some extent, the "means"—the resources used to achieve the specified ends. Obviously, decisions at this level are always political decisions. However, to terminate the conflict on favorable terms, one must first consider the nature of the conflict and one's national objectives. A state would not risk its survival or commit all its resources for limited political objective. Carl von Clausewitz wrote:

> War plans cover every aspect of a war, and weave them all into a single operation that must have a single, ultimate objective in which all particular aims are reconciled. No one starts a war—or rather, no one in his senses ought to do so—without first being clear in his mind what he intends to achieve by that war and how he intends to conduct it. The former is its political purpose; the latter its operational objective. This is the governing principle that will set its course, prescribe the scale of means and effort that is required, and makes its influence felt throughout down to the smallest operational detail.[6]

Next, a state must have a strategy to achieve its national strategic objectives. This is often "where the strategic process breaks down because the national strategic objectives are obscure. . . . Indeed, while national policy goals often are reasonably well articulated, rarely are these translated into strategic political-military objectives expressed as end-states and attainable supporting objectives."[7] Next, the military leaders must develop strategic and operational strategies that link the national strategic objectives and military operational objectives. Basil H. Liddell Hart, in his book *Strategy*, stated:

> Strategy depends for success, first and most, on a sound calculation and coordination of the ends and means. The end must be proportioned to the total means, and the means used in gaining each intermediate end which contributes to the ultimate must be proportioned to the value and the needs of the intermediate end—whether it be to gain an objective or to fulfill a contributory purpose.[8]

Furthermore, the military leaders must translate these "ends" into executable military objectives and allocate the resources to achieve the overall ends—the national strategic objectives.

Conflict termination, then, should be viewed as the bridge over which armed conflict crosses into more peaceful forms of interaction. Consequently, conflict termination is the study of how to connect military means and military ends to the larger political objectives of a conflict. For the campaign planner, the issue is, How does the operational commander translate the political or military objectives of a conflict into campaign termination conditions to be achieved as the product of a campaign?

Conflict Termination Process

Conflict termination is a process in which each warring party interacts with other belligerents to achieve its policy objectives within the limits of acceptable costs. Gay M. Hammerman describes the beginning of the war-termination process as that "point at which an informed, objective outside observer could predict the outcome of the war."[9] By this he means that war termination is the point at which one side seems clearly destined to achieve its national strategic objectives at the expense of its adversary. The objective of the conflict termination phase is to restore the peace found before the conflict.

Conflict is a fact of international relations. Conflict at an international level occurs when there is a disagreement of ideas or national interests. For our purposes, we will use Bruce Clarke's definition: conflict is that "portion of a dispute where the use of military power is contemplated or actually employed. Such disputes will go through a series of phases. Within each phase there are forces at work that will cause the dispute to either move toward termination or toward hostilities."[10]

The first phase of the conflict is the dispute. This occurs when two groups' objectives are not compatible concerning some issue. For example, two states may disagree about the control over resources each side views as nonsharable. At this point, the dispute is not "normally perceived in military terms by either party."[11] To solve the dispute, states will employ economic, political, or diplomatic means, not military means. When a dispute arises, the United States has historically emphasized the political and economic solutions. For example, the United States offered great economic incentives to Egypt and Israel as part of the Camp David Accords. Many times, the United States has a tendency to offer economic incentives or to deny the potential adversary economic benefits as an inducement to act in the desired manner.

When political and economic instruments of power are ineffective in producing the desired results, the next step is to either change our objectives or transition to the second phase—the prehostility phase. In this phase either of the parties to the dispute introduces the military option. This may include a show of force, movement of military units, increased levels of readiness, partial mobilization, and so on. Clarke states that the introduction of a military option does not mean that hostilities have begun, only that the possibility exists that they may begin sometime in the future.

Clarke states that "as objectives become more firmly held and the possibility of compromise lessens, the conflict may transition to the third phase—the commencement of hostilities."[12]

During the hostilities phase, armed conflict occurs with the aim of achieving military objectives. Thus, if objectives still do not change, the probability of continued hostilities increases and settlement decreases. If both sides change their objectives, the dispute will move toward settlement.

Next, once hostilities are terminated, the conflict moves to the fourth phase, posthostilities. Clarke observes that during the "post-hostility phase the conflict may well continue, but the fighting is, at least temporarily, suspended. . . . If the quarrel cannot move toward some form of nonviolent resolution, it can return to the hostility phase. However, once the use, or consideration, of military means ceases, the conflict ends."[13]

In the fifth stage, the dispute stage, the state discards the military option, but there are still issues in dispute. The warring states have ended the conflict but not the dispute.

The sixth and final phase is the settlement. Historically, warring states rarely settle their conflicts. Clarke also states that "frequently the dispute cycles back to the beginning of the process. Often the seeds of the next conflict are sown in the present one."[14] This is especially true if there is no clear vision of the desired end state. Within each phase "there are forces at work that will cause the dispute to either move toward termination or toward hostilities."[15] Herein lies the challenge campaign planners must deal with in conflict termination.

Types of Conflict Termination

There are several ways conflicts can be ended, according to William O. Staudenmaier. The first is that states can terminate conflicts by armistices, truces, and cease-fires. Surrenders are usually preceded by a cease-fire or an armistice. The second major way that conflicts end is a formal peace treaty. However, due to the time required to negotiate them, formal peace treaties are less likely to be the vehicle for ending conflicts. The Camp David Accords are a recent example of such a peace treaty that attempts to manage the Arab-Israeli dispute. The third major way of ending a conflict is the "joint political agreement." This type of agreement between the warring parties usually stipulates how they will end the conflict and maintain peace. One example of such a political agreement is the "Agreement on Ending the War and Restoring Peace in Vietnam" that provided for a cease-fire throughout Vietnam, withdrawal of US troops, release of prisoners of war, restoration of the demarcation line between North and South Vietnam, and the creation of an international body to supervise the truce. The fourth major way of terminating a conflict is capitulation. The final form of conflict termination is the unilaterally withdrawal of a belligerent from active participation in the conflict. Somalia's withdrawal from Ethiopia in 1978 in the wars for the Ogaden region and China's withdrawal from Vietnam's border regions are examples of this form of termination. Obviously, the nature of the national objectives in the conflict and the nature of the dispute will determine the method of conflict termination. It is also possible that terminating a conflict may involve a combination of methods.[16]

Environmental Factors

To get a better idea of what is necessary and possible, one must understand the environment of the conflict. The nature of the environment is a direct result of, and is defined by, several factors. The first factor is domestic politics, including public support for the objectives being sought. The influence of domestic politics affects the conflict objectives (ends) and public opinion. Recall the turmoil in the United States during the Vietnam War and how internal politics affected the way the nation prosecuted the war. Michael Handel wrote:

> Most of the historical accounts of the process of war termination refer in great detail to the inner struggles between those who want to continue the war and those who advocate its conclusion. Among the forces that participate in this process, we can cite the government and its leaders, the opposition parties, the military elite and the rank-and-file armed forces, and public opinion.[17]

A second factor is the degree of third-party involvement in the conflict. An example is the influence of international organizations such as the United Nations. Furthermore, in earlier times, before the universal impact of mass media, nations were less constrained by world opinion. Aggressive states could prepare and complete their offensive actions before organized multinational opposition could be formed. For example, Japan's aggression against Manchuria in 1931 went unnoticed by most of the world, including the League of Nations, because communications from such a distant area were slow and not very accurate. Today, partly due to the influence of the mass media and instant worldwide communications, no nation is an island unto itself.

A third major environmental factor—whether the war is fought unilaterally or by a coalition—has a tremendous influence on the postcombat phase. The old adage, the enemy of my enemy is my friend, is a truism that binds together unlikely bedfellows when common national interests are threatened. When the common enemy is defeated, however, the reasons for cooperation and harmony among members of the coalition become less important. According to Stuart Albert and Edward Lucke:

> In the immediate post-war period it is likely that in certain areas harmony will prevail, while in others the situation will be one of dissension. The mixture of discord and cooperation will fall somewhere along a functional continuum. It is as possible for an alliance to continue in name with little real content as it is to imagine an end to formal ties followed by extensive cooperation.[18]

The wartime alliance against Germany in World War I is a good example. After the war, England and the United States wanted to rebuild Germany and reestablish their prewar commercial and financial relationships. They reasoned that this would be the best way to bring Germany back into the community of nations. France, however, in view of its security concerns and the ill will created by the 1870 German-imposed peace conditions, wanted a harsh retributive and militarized peace.[19] The result was a treaty that sowed the seeds for World War II.

A fourth major environmental factor is the conflict objectives, which will affect how states terminate the conflict. A conflict objective should clearly state what the peace should look like immediately after the conflict. Clausewitz told us that war is an extension of politics by the use of arms. He points out that all of our efforts should focus on creating the conditions that will allow the state to achieve its political objectives. If we keep in mind Liddell Hart's warning to look beyond the battlefield with the purpose of creating a "better state of peace," it will require a strategic vision of the desired end state. The desired end state is what we envision the postconflict environment to look like—politically, socially, and militarily.

At the political level, a state is victorious when it accomplishes its political objectives. One should also bear in mind Liddell Hart's views on victory:

> If you concentrate exclusively on victory, with no thought for the after effect, you may be too exhausted to profit by the peace, while it is almost certain that the peace will be a bad one, containing the germs of another war. This is a lesson supported by abundant experience. The risks become greater still in any war that is waged by a coalition, or in such a case a too complete victory inevitably complicates the problem of making a just and wise peace settlement. Where there is no longer the counterbalance of an opposing force to control the appetites of the victors, there is no check on the conflict of views and interests between the parties to the alliance. The divergence is then apt to become so acute as to turn the comradeship of common danger into the hostility of mutual dissatisfaction—so that the ally of one war becomes the enemy in the next.[20]

Again, the key is to be able to clearly define the political conditions of the envisioned end state. Next, the military leaders must translate the political conditions into a set of national military objectives. As Clarke states, "This is not as easy as it sounds. One must be able to envision what is necessary to do to cause the opponent to change his political and resultant military objectives."[21] Thus, one must overcome the adversary's will to resist. If the military leaders know the environment, the opponent, and the objectives in the conflict, their strategists will have a more realistic chance to overcome the enemy's will to resist.

The best test of a successful conflict-termination plan is whether the "vanquished" party embraces the outcome. Unless total annihilation of the enemy is achieved, as in Rome's last war with Carthage, conflict termination must consider the needs of the defeated, both domestically and internationally. H. A. Calahan writes, "War is pressed by the victor, but peace is made by the vanquished. Therefore, to determine the causes of peace, it is always necessary to take the vanquished's point of view."[22] Failure to structure the postconflict peace with the vanquished's needs in mind is the first step towards starting the next war.

Implications for Conflict Termination

If its interests are directly threatened, the United States is willing to use military force in pursuit of its objectives. "A strong US military posture, backed by domestic, political, and popular support as well as resolve to protect US interests, conveys the firmness of US commitments to allies and friends, thereby enhancing deterrence and increasing the incentives for adversaries to seriously negotiate toward favorable outcomes."[23] The challenge for the campaign planner is to define the military conditions and relate those conditions to the national objectives, based on the nature of the conflict scenario. Consequently, as James Reed points out:

> The process of explicitly and clearly defining terminal conditions is an important one, since it requires careful dialogue between civilian (strategic) and military (operational) leadership that may, in turn, offer some greater assurance that the defined end state is both politically acceptable and militarily attainable.[24]

For the campaign planner, conflict termination is a phase of military operations that must be considered early in the campaign-planning process. Furthermore, campaign planners must plan the conflict-termination issues in full coordination with war fighting. As John Fishel points out, the state's political and military leaders need to define the political and military objectives in clearly defined end-state terms with supporting objectives that are both military and civil-military in nature.[25] One must ask, What do we want the situation to look like after the conflict phase? What is the nature of the settlement that we seek? If the campaign planner does not know the answers to these questions, he or she must ask!

As Michael Rampy points out, "Effective conflict termination requires a continuous discussion and decision process between [sic] political decision makers, military strategists and the theater commander."[26] The national political leaders will ultimately decide when and, many times, how to terminate a conflict. However, these decision makers rely on senior military leaders for advice on terminating the conflict. The theater commander translates the political objectives into the operational design to coerce the adversary and induce conflict termination. He is in the best position to assess what is possible in the theater of operations and whether his forces can achieve the desired end state.

The campaign planners must identify a distinct conflict termination phase in their plan. They must not wait until after hostilities cease to begin thinking about termination issues and posthostility activities. Fred Ikle warned that military planners should not take the first steps toward war without considering the last steps. Consequently, every aspect of the campaign plan such as target selection, rules of engagement, forces employed, and psychological operations should be designed and evaluated according to contributions made or the effect upon the clearly defined end state to be achieved.[27] Furthermore, the campaign planner must, according to Reed, "define the operational conditions to be produced during the terminal phase of the campaign in explicit, unambiguous terms. The absence of definition or detail in operational objectives may produce unintended consequences in the course of a campaign."[28] This should prompt increased communication between the civilian and military leadership, ensuring congruence between operational objectives and the larger policy aims of a campaign.

Rampy also states that once military forces engage in conflict, the political leaders must provide direction for the "operational design" without interfering with military operations. Conversely, the military leaders must maintain a broad-minded view of strategic and operational design:

> Many roads lead to success, and . . . they do not all involve the opponent's outright defeat. They range from the destruction of the enemy's forces, the conquest of his territory, to a temporary occupation or invasion, to projects with an immediate political purpose. . . . Any one of these may be used to overcome the enemy's will: the choice depends on circumstances . . . bear in mind how a wide range of political interests can lead to war, or think for a moment of the gulf that separates a war of annihilation, a struggle for political

> existence, from a war reluctantly declared in consequence of political pressure or of an alliance that no longer seems to reflect the state's true interests. Between these two extremes lie numerous gradations.[29]

The military is only one element in conflict termination. It must cooperate with other government agencies to deal with the political, economic, and informational issues arising in a posthostility situation.

Postconflict Activities

The cessation of hostilities is not the last step in conflict termination. The last step is the effective implementation of postconflict activities. As mentioned above, warring states have rarely achieved the sixth phase of conflict termination—settlement. Many times the underlying causes of the dispute remain. Postconflict activities occur in this type of environment. Military postconflict activities may include humanitarian assistance, nation assistance, civil affairs, and possibly peace operations. "The objective of these activities is to restore order and tranquillity to a previously hostile environment."[30] These postconflict activities try to meet the needs of the noncombatants.

Critical to the success is the unity of effort by three main groups of players. The first group of players are the government agencies such as the State Department, Central Intelligence Agency (CIA), Agency for International Development (AID), US Information Agency (USIA), Justice Department, Commerce Department, and others. The second group of players includes allies, coalition partners, United Nations, intergovernmental organizations (IGO), and nongovernmental organizations (NGO). Unity of effort among these groups of players is essential for successful planning and execution of civil-military operations. Interagency coordination is an absolute must. As always, the fundamental question that should be asked is, What do we want the situation to look like after the conflict when order is restored? The answer to this will dictate the level of involvement and planning required for conducting postconflict activities.

To be successful in conflict termination, the military must provide a secure and stable environment for the conduct of postconflict activities. As Rampy points out:

> Therefore, post-conflict activities will most likely begin with a predominance of military control and influence and progressively move toward civilian dominance as hostilities wane. Conflict termination must be an element of operational design to prevent an uncontrollable situation during post-conflict activities. While the political decision makers have the official responsibility for conducting post-conflict activities, the military's organizational ability in applying resources rapidly in a crisis means that they will have the most de facto lead in most post-conflict activities until a smooth transition can be made to civilian control.[31]

This was certainly the case in the post–Desert Storm activities, especially with Operation Provide Comfort. According to Fishel,

> President George Bush's rhetoric calling for the overthrow of Saddam Hussein gave the Kurds of northern Iraq just the impetus they required to rebel. But when Iraqi forces assumed an offensive posture and the United States led coalition took no action to stop Saddam, the rebellion fell apart. Jubilation turned to panic as hundreds of thousands of Kurds abandoned their homes and sought refuge over the borders of neighboring Turkey and Iran.[32]

The Kurdish refugees in Turkey fled above the snow line on the grounds that the Iraqi forces would not follow them. Thousands would die each day due to disease, malnutrition, and exposure. After media reports of the Kurdish refugee situation attracted the world's attention, President Bush directed US forces to begin humanitarian assistance operations to help the Kurds. Besides the military organizations, the USAID, State Department, IGO, NGO, and other agencies got involved. The military had to stop the dying and "stabilize the situation." According to Fishel, "providing security for the refugees was a major part of the story of Operation Provide Comfort."[33] Thus, Operation Provide Comfort represents one of the postconflict operations that the United States has embarked upon in the recent past. Postconflict activities are an essential part of conflict termination.

Conclusion

Conflict termination involves more than merely ending the hostilities. It involves the transition from war to peace. The goal after any conflict should be a better state of peace. For us, conflict termination is the study of how to connect military means and military ends to the larger political objectives of a conflict.

To avoid Ikle's criticism, military officers should recognize that it's the outcome of the war, not the outcome of their operational campaigns, that determines how well the campaigns serve the nation's interests. The military must translate the initial political and military objectives of a conflict into conflict-termination conditions that will achieve the desired end state of the campaign.

This is the challenge for the campaign planners, who must identify a conflict-termination phase early in the campaign-planning process. Every aspect of the campaign plan should contribute to achieving the desired end state. By taking the elements of conflict termination into account, campaign planners will contribute to the successful termination of future conflicts. In the future these planners will realize that the effective conflict-termination plans will contribute to outcomes that serve the nation's interests.

Notes

1. Fred C. Ikle, *Every War Must End*, rev. ed. (New York: Columbia University Press, 1991), vii.

2. Russell Wiegley, *American Way of War: A History of United States Military Strategy and Policy* (Bloomington, Ind.: Indiana University Press, 1973), passim.

3. Ikle, 2.

4. Ibid., 3.

5. Erich von Manstein, *Lost Victories*, ed. and trans. Anthony G. Powell (Novato, Calif.: Presidio Press, 1982), 152–53.

6. Carl von Clausewitz, *On War*, ed. and trans. Michael Howard and Peter Paret (Princeton, N.J.: Princeton University Press, 1976).

7. John T. Fishel, *Liberation, Occupation, and Rescue: War Termination and Desert Storm* (Carlisle Barracks, Pa.: Strategic Studies Institute, 1992), 2.

8. Basil H. Liddell Hart, *Strategy*, 2d ed. (New York: Meridian, 1967), 322–23.

9. Gay M. Hammerman, *Conventional Attrition and Battle Termination Criteria: A Study of War Termination* (Loring, Va.: Defense Nuclear Agency Report no. DNA-TR-81-224, August 1982), 11.

10. Bruce B. G. Clarke, "Conflict Termination: A Rational Model," in *Terrorism* (Bristol, Pa.: Taylor & Francis, 1993), 28.

11. Ibid.

12. Ibid.

13. Ibid.

14. Ibid.

15. Ibid.

16. Ibid., 31.

17. Michael Handel, "War Termination—A Critical Survey" in *Termination of Wars: Processes, Procedures and Aftermaths*, ed. Nissan Oren (Jerusalem: Hebrew University Press, 1982), 75.

18. Stuart Albert and Edward Lucke, *On the Endings of Wars* (New York: Kennikat Press Corp., 1980), 75.

19. Ibid., 86.

20. Hart, 366.

21. Clarke, 34.

22. H. A. Calahan, *What Makes a War End?* (New York: Vanguard Press, 1944), 18.

23. Joint Publication 3-07, *Joint Doctrine for Military Operations Other Than War*, final draft (Washington, D.C.: Defense Printing Service, 1993), B-2.

24. James W. Reed, "Should Deterrence Fail: War Termination in Campaign Planning," *Parameters*, Summer 1993, 14.

25. Fishel, 69.

26. Michael R. Rampy, "The Endgame: Conflict Termination and Post-Conflict Activities," *Military Review*, October 1992, 50.

27. Reed, 49.

28. Ibid.

29. Clausewitz, 94.

30. Rampy, 53.

31. Ibid., 54.

32. Fishel, 51.

33. Ibid., 56.

Contributors

Lt Col Anthony D. Alley is a USAF command pilot with tours in RF-4C and T-37 aircraft. He currently serves as the Chief, Curriculum Development Division, Associate Programs, Air Command and Staff College. He holds a MEd from the University of Oklahoma and is a graduate of the Royal Air Force Staff College Advanced Staff Course.

Dr H. David Arnold is a professor of defense economics at the Air Force Air Command and Staff College. His current academic concentration lies in the economy of the Russian Federation and the aligned political stability.

Dr James S. Corum holds graduate degrees from Brown and Oxford universities and a PhD in history from Queen's University, Canada. Dr Corum is professor of comparative military studies at the USAF School of Advanced Military Studies at Maxwell Air Force Base, Alabama, where he teaches courses in air power history and low-intensity conflict.

Lt Col Bradley S. Davis is currently on the faculty of Air Command and Staff College. He holds a BA in history from UCLA and an MS in organizational behavior and human resource management from Chapman University and has completed Squadron Officer School, Marine Corps Command and Staff College, and Air War College. Most recently, he worked at Headquarters, USAF, with responsibility for the policy and implementation of arms control treaties for the Air Force.

Maj Rali M. Dobberstein, Air Command and Staff College, received her MA degree in sociology in 1983 from Arizona State University. She is an intelligence operations officer specializing in imagery interpretation.

Maj Martin L. Fracker is a member of the faculty at the Air Command and Staff College. He holds a degree in cognitive-experimental psychology, 1987, from the University of Illinois at Urbana-Champaign. Previous assignments are Sheppard Technical Training Center, Air Force Occupational Measurement Center, and Harry G. Armstrong Aerospace Medical Research Laboratory.

Lt Col Mario A. Garza is the course director for campaign termination studies at the Air Command and Staff College and a former assistant professor of military studies at the US Air Force Academy. He was a B-52 radar navigator instructor and is a graduate of Squadron Officer School and Air Command and Staff College.

Dr Paul Hacker is a foreign service officer detailed for the 1993–94 academic year as a visiting instructor to the Air Command and Staff College, Maxwell AFB. He has served 20 years in the US Foreign Service and specializes in East European affairs. His last assignment was as first charge d'affaires at the US Embassy in Slovakia.

Maj Victor Janushkowsky is a student at the Air Command and Staff College. He began his career in the Minuteman missile program. He was assigned to the National Security Agency, Fort Meade, Maryland; US Arms Control and Disarmament Agency (State Dept); Headquarters USAF; and Secretary of the Air Force/ International Affairs, the Pentagon, as Russia/Eurasia country director. He holds a BS from California State University, Sacramento, an MBA from the Air Force Institute of Technology Minuteman Education Program, and is working on a masters degree in political science at Auburn University.

Maj Richard M. Kessel is a 1978 graduate of Embry-Riddle Aeronautical University and was awarded an MBA from Golden Gate University in 1988. He is a senior pilot and has logged over 3,000 hours in F-15s, AT-38Bs, and helicopters. His assignments prior to the Air Command and Staff College include stints at Eglin AFB, Florida; Holloman AFB, New Mexico; Minot AFB, North Dakota; Elmendorf AFB, Alaska; and a staff tour in MPC at Randolph AFB, Texas.

Maj Joseph W. Kroeschel is a student at the Air Command and Staff College. He received a BA in management from Texas Lutheran College and a MS in management from the Naval Postgraduate School. Major Kroeschel is a 1981 Officer Training School grad-uate and has worked as a personnel officer at base level, the Air Staff, and Air Force Manpower and Personnel Center.

Dr Karl P. Magyar is professor of national security affairs at the Air Command and Staff College. He studied in Mexico and Germany, and obtained a BA in philosophy from Michigan State University, and a PhD in political science from Johns Hopkins University. He has held academic posts in the US, Japan, and South Africa; served in the US government in Washington, D.C., and Africa; and served as Economic Development Adviser to an African government.

Lt Col Maris McCrabb is assigned as a department chairman at the USAF Air Command and Staff College. He is a command pilot with over 3,000 hours in F-4 and F-16 aircraft. He has MS degrees in business management and public administration. He has completed Squadron Officer School, Air Command and Staff College, and Air War College.

Lt Col Albert U. Mitchum, Jr., is a member of the staff at Air Command and Staff College. He served as International Officer Liaison, chief of the Nuclear Warfare Branch of resident school curriculum, and finally as Dean of Associate Programs at Air Command and Staff College. He received his doctorate in public administration from the University of Alabama in 1994. He is attending the Argentine War College for the academic year of 1994.

Lt Comdr Paul G. O'Connor is an Air Command and Staff College student, class of 1994. Lt Comdr O'Connor is a Naval Flight Officer, having flown the E-2C Hawkeye early warning aircraft. He is a 1981 graduate of Siena College, N.Y., and received a masters degree in political science from Auburn University of Montgomery in 1994.

Maj John R. Pardo, Jr., received a bachelor of science degree in military history from the USAF Academy in 1979 and a master of science degree in international relations from Troy State University in 1990. He is a senior pilot with over 1,500 hours in the F-4 and F-16. He is a graduate of Air Command and Staff College where he is currently on staff.

Maj Thomas J. Stark is a senior pilot with over 1,000 hours of instructor experience in the KC-135 and KC-10 aircraft. He holds a bachelor of science degree in international affairs from the USAF Academy and a master of business administration degree in Aviation from Embry-Riddle Aeronautical University. Currently, Major Stark is the chief, War and Conflict Branch, for the Air Command and Staff College nonresident program.

Col John A. Warden III is commandant, Air Command and Staff College. He is the author of the *Air Campaign,* was a major Gulf War planner, and has been a wing commander and special assistant to the vice president of the United States.

Dr Lewis B. Ware is course director for the war, conflict and military objectives block of instruction at the Air Command and Staff College and former chief of the Political-Military Affairs Division at the College of Aerospace Doctrine, Research, and Education, Air University. He is a Middle East specialist with research interests in Islamism and Arab North Africa.

Maj Steven W. Zander (BS in government, University of Maryland, 1985; BS/MA architecture, University of Wisconsin-Milwaukee, 1975/1980) was an Air Command and Staff College student in 1994. After attending Officer Training School in 1979 he has had tours in civil engineering, including bed-down of the air launched cruise missile at Griffiss AFB, N.Y.; working air base survivability issues at Headquarters USAFE, Ramstein AB, Germany; beddown of the ground launched cruise missile at Florenes AB, Belgium; working rail garrison basing at Norton AFB, California; and served as executive officer to the civil engineer, Headquarters USAFE, Washington, D.C.